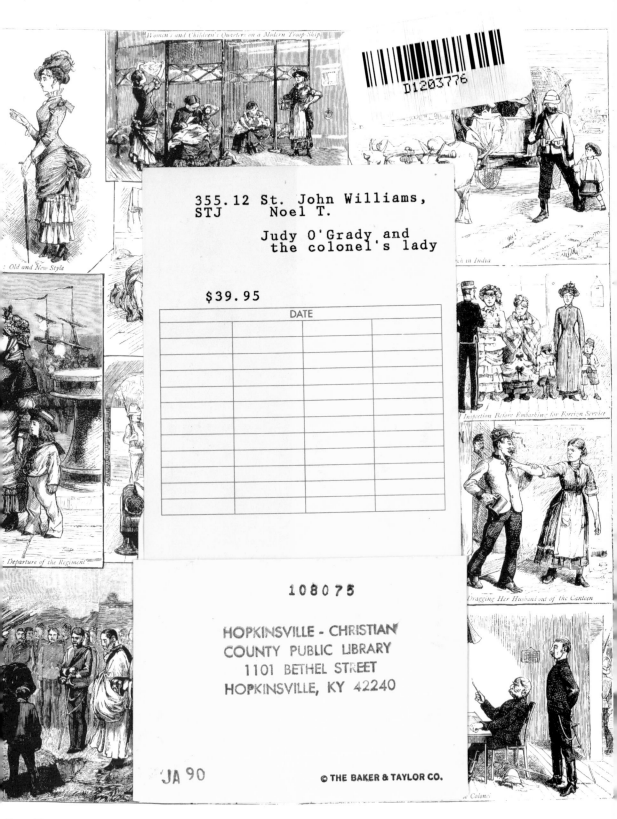

D—PAST AND PRESENT

Judy O'Grady
and the Colonel's Lady

*The Army Wife and
Camp Follower Since 1660*

Other Brassey's Titles of Related Interest

BAYNES
Soldiers of Scotland

DIETZ
Garrison: Ten British Military Towns

JOLLY
Military Man, Family Man: Crown Property?

LIDDLE
Gallipoli 1915: Pens, Pencils & Cameras at War

LIDDLE
Home Fires & Foreign Fields: British Social
and Military Experience in the First World War

PERKINS
A Fortunate Soldier

SWEETMAN
Sword & Mace: Twentieth Century Civil-Military Relations in Britain

The author and his wife are presented to Her Majesty The Queen.
Eltham Palace, July 1970. (*The Kentish Times*)

Judy O'Grady and the Colonel's Lady

The Army Wife and Camp Follower Since 1660

Colonel Noel T. St. John Williams B.A.

(*late The Sherwood Foresters and Royal Army Educational Corps*)

BRASSEY'S DEFENCE PUBLISHERS

(a member of the Maxwell Pergamon Publishing Corporation plc)

LONDON · OXFORD · WASHINGTON · NEW YORK
BEIJING · FRANKFURT · SÃO PAULO · SYDNEY · TOKYO · TORONTO

U.K. (Editorial)	Brassey's Defence Publishers Ltd., 24 Gray's Inn Road, London WC1X 8HR
(Orders)	Brassey's Defence Publishers Ltd., Headington Hill Hall, Oxford OX3 0BW, England
U.S.A. (Editorial)	Pergamon-Brassey's International Defense Publishers, Inc., 8000 Westpark Drive, Fourth Floor, McLean, Virginia 22102, U.S.A.
(Orders)	Pergamon Press, Inc., Maxwell House, Fairview Park, Elmsford, New York 10523, U.S.A.
PEOPLE'S REPUBLIC OF CHINA	Pergamon Press, Room 4037, Qianmen Hotel, Beijing, People's Republic of China
FEDERAL REPUBLIC OF GERMANY	Pergamon Press GmbH, Hammerweg 6, D-6242 Kronberg, Federal Republic of Germany
BRAZIL	Pergamon Editora Ltda, Rua Eça de Queiros, 346, CEP 04011, Paraiso, São Paulo, Brazil
AUSTRALIA	Pergamon-Brassey's Defence Publishers Pty Ltd., P.O. Box 544, Potts Point, N.S.W. 2011, Australia
JAPAN	Pergamon Press, 5th Floor, Matsuoka Central Building, 1–7–1 Nishishinjuku, Shinjuku-ku, Tokyo 160, Japan
CANADA	Pergamon Press Canada Ltd., Suite No. 271, 253 College Street, Toronto, Ontario, Canada M5T 1R5

First edition 1988

Library of Congress Cataloging in Publication Data

St. John Williams, Noel T.
Judy O'Grady and the colonel's lady: the army wife and camp follower since 1660/Noel T. St. John Williams.
p. cm.
Includes index.
1. Army wives—Great Britain—History. 2. Camp followers—Great Britain—History. 3. Women and the military—Great Britain—History. 4. Women and war—Great Britain—History. 5 Great Britain. Army—Military life. I. Title.
UB405.G7S73 1988 355.1'2'0941—dc19 88-4320

British Library Cataloguing in Publication Date

Williams, Noel T. St. John
Judy O'Grady and the colonel's lady: the army wife and camp follower since 1660.
1. Great Britain. Army. Officers' & soldiers' wives. Social life, 1660–1988
I. Tilte
355.1'0941

ISBN 0–08–035826–8

Printed in Great Britain by A. Wheaton & Co. Ltd., Exeter

For my wife Christina,
and children, Noel and Jacqueline,
who also followed the drum

Acknowledgements

The author and publishers thank the following individuals and institutions for their help and for permission to reproduce copyright material in this book:

Mr C. A. Potts and the staff of the Ministry of Defence Library; Mr Angus Madders and staff of the Chester Public Library; Mr T. W. Finch and staff of the Doncaster Library Service; Major J. Kenny MBE of the Queen's Lancashire Regiment, Warrington RHQ; the Librarians of the National Army Museum, the RAMC College, the Imperial War Museum and the staff of the India Office Library and Records; Lieutenant Colonel R. W. Nye and the Museum of the R.A.Ch.D.; the Directors of NAAFI and SSAFA. The King's Own Royal Border Regiment [Colonel L. I. Cowper: *The King's Own Story*]; *The Times; Soldier Magazine;* Mrs C. Day-Lewis [Jill Balcon] [Antony Brett-James: *Life in Wellington's Army* (Allen & Unwin)]; The Society for Army Historical Research; The Controller, HMSO [Army Welfare Enquiry Committee (Spencer Report), Colonel N. T. St. John Williams (*Tommy Atkins' Children*), unpublished Crown copyright material in the India Office Records]; Unwin Hyman Ltd [Douglas Botting: *In The Ruins of The Reich* – Allen & Unwin]; George Bell: *Soldier's Glory* (Bell); David Higham Associates [Christopher Hibbert: *The Great Indian Mutiny 1857* – Allen Lane]; Pat M. Barr [*The Memsahibs* – Secker & Warburg]; J. M. Dent & Sons Ltd [J. K. Stanford: *Ladies in the Sun*]; William Collins & Sons Publishers Ltd and Watson Little Ltd [Licensing Agents]: Major General James Lunt: *Scarlet Lancer* – Hart Davis]; R. E. Scouller [*The Armies of the Queen* – Oxford]; Grafton Books [Brigadier Gordon Blight: *The History of the Royal Berkshire Regiment 1920–1947* – Staples Press]; Theon Wilkinson [*Two Monsoons*, 2nd Edition – Duckworth 1987]; Associated Book Publishers Ltd [Dennis Kinkaid: *British Social Life in India* (1608–1937)]; William Heinemann Ltd [Jane Vansittart: *From Minnie, With Love* – Peter Davies Ltd]. John E. Costello: *Love, Sex and War 1939–45* [Collins 1985]: Marquess of Anglesey [*Sergeant Pearman's Memoirs* – Jonathan Cape Ltd].

For the pictures used, thanks are recorded to: The Ministry of Defence (DPR): *Kentish Times; Illustrated London News* Picture Library; Victoria and Albert Museum Picture Library; The Black Watch [Royal Highland Regiment]; SSAFA; Associated Book Publishers Ltd [Lieutenant Colonel Frank Wilson's illustrations in Kinkaid]; HQ, NAAFI; Trustees of the British Museum; National Army Museum, London; The British Library [India Office Library and Records]; The National Portrait Gallery; Christies [Louise de Keroualle]; Public Information BFG [BAOR]; The Keeper, Department of Photographs, Imperial War Museum. The Psywar Society: The Federation of Army Wives.

Wherever possible the source of references and quotations have been acknowledged in the Notes. For any omission I apologise and will correct in any future editions.

Finally my thanks are due to my publishers, especially Angela Clark and Bryan Watkins for their unfailing assistance throughout; Mrs Pat Latham for typing services; and to Bob Clough-Parker, my Literary Agent, for help and support.

Chester   NOEL T. ST. JOHN WILLIAMS
March 1988

Contents

Contents

Introduction

For Rudyard Kipling, the Colonel's lady and Judy O'Grady were 'sisters under their skins'. They shared the same emotions and sexual appetites and both were capable of the same care and affection for husband, lover and children. It was in their exteriors that they differed, conditioned by social distinctions of birth and breeding, by wealth and education. There was a wide gulf between the upper and lower classes of 17th and 18th century Britain but a wider gap between the officer and private soldier of Charles II or Queen Victoria's army — and few private soldiers ever rose to commissioned rank. The same social gulf separated the officer's 'lady' from the soldier's 'woman' — and again only a few women of beauty and ability were able to bridge the gap of social acceptability in a regiment. My story begins with these differences, codified in the Army's regulations and provisions for its married women: but as the story develops, we see that the choice of a mate in today's army, whether by officer or other rank, mirrors the social changes that have taken place during this century, although even now those Army wives who survive best have to conform to the traditions and expectations of their husband's regiment or corps.

Women have always been regarded as a hindrance to the profession of arms. Venus could grace the soldier's bed, but she distracted the youthful Mars from learning his trade and was a distinct liability to him on active service. There was a formal ban on marriage by serving Roman legionaries, until the beginning of the third century, although their illegal unions, concubines and illegitimate children were tolerated outside the fortress area. In 1650, when the regiment known as the Coldstream Guards was quartered in Scotland, a stern edict not only forbade all weddings with native lasses but ordered that all soldiers caught in amorous dalliance with them were to be whipped. In Ireland, William III permitted his soldiers to marry local girls, except Roman Catholics, but made no provision for their support or accommodation. Queen Victoria's army actively discouraged matrimony and recognised only a limited number of wives 'of use to the regiment, of good character and with the commanding officer's permission'. Camp followers have been a feature of all armies of every age and all commanders have had to cope with the size of the baggage train. Since the British Army discouraged marriage, it is hardly surprising that it regarded prostitutes as a necessary evil; they were certainly cheaper and caused less trouble! The arrival of the 'memsahibs' in India in the 18th century changed the social pattern of military life there but, even today, whenever cuts in military expenditure are debated, the cost of accompanied tours is queried.

This book traces the story of the British Army's women and their changing fortunes from the days of Marlborough and Wellington, through the social changes of Victorian England and two World Wars to the Battle of the Falklands and Northern Ireland. It is a story of courage and endurance, of deprivation and neglect, as we follow the Army's changing attitudes to marriage and provision for the married state against the background of the country's revolutionary changes in family life and

JO—A•

welfare over the last 300 years. Drawing upon Army orders and regulations, the reports of official committees, official publications, contemporary reports and journals, and documented biographies, I have tried to give an authentic picture of army wives in many lands where they have followed the drum. Wherever possible, I have used the words of serving soldiers. Of special value, but scarcer, are the accounts left by army wives themselves.

There is no such being as a typical army wife — for the army is a large organisation and our story ranges the globe in peace and war over many years. Nevertheless, there are some qualities they hold in common, of which pride in their regiment and army traditions is not the least. Oman described the army women of the Peninsular War as "an extraordinary community — as hard as nails, expert plunderers, furious partisans of the supreme excellence of their own battalion, much given to fighting".[1] He added that they were much married — 'widows twice and even thrice over — for when a married man was shot and his wife was a capable and desirable person, she would receive half a dozen proposals before her husband was 48 hours in his grave'. Faced with the alternatives of destitution for herself and her children or a long and hazardous journey home to her parents, who might have disowned her when she 'ran away with a soldier', 'most of the widows stayed with the battalion, with a new spouse and a new name'. In 1842, the wife of a distinguished Indian soldier, Honoria Lawrence wrote 'a woman when she marries a soldier ought to recollect that his profession entails on her definite and often very arduous duty ... she has to bear as best she may the privations peculiar to her lot.'[2]

More recently an army wife, Veronica Bamfield,[3] brought these qualities up to date — 'We are a tough lot. We have had to be. For more than 300 years we have travelled the world with our men, often at a moment's notice. We loved and courted, married and bore children in all parts of the globe. Our ghosts must surely haunt married quarters up and down the British Isles, in Gibraltar, Malta, Bermuda, Germany and the Curragh. We kept house in bungalows in India, Malaya, Hong Kong, Shanghai and the West Indies and in the dwellings of South Africa, North America and Canada. We endured capture, wounding, imprisonment, kidnapping, shipwreck, rape and murder.'[3] Many survived — a few to tell their tale. Today's wives are more independent, conscious of their 'rights', averse to patronage and regimental 'handouts', seeking careers of their own and a second income to support their families and to purchase their home.

'Soldiers' wives are a special breed', said an army padre recently. 'They have to be — to put up with soldiers.'[4]

Such are the women of my story. My aim in writing this book is to give them a recognised place in military history, to reveal them to a wider public and if the modern army wife recognises something of herself in the officer's lady and the Judy O'Grady's of the past, my purpose will have been achieved.

List of Illustrations

Front Cover (Left) Summoned for Active Service. *(The Graphic 11 June 1879).*
(Right) Colonel and Mrs Dalbiac. *(National Army Museum).*

Endpapers Tommy Atkins Married. Past and Present. *(The Graphic 12 January 1884).*

Frontispiece The author and his wife are presented to Her Majesty The Queen. Eltham Palace 1970. *(The Kentish Times).*

Chapter 1

Husbands in the Days of Charles II and Marlborough

TANGIER

The British soldier traces his ancestry back to the Standing Army of Charles II: he can also claim military kinship for his wife and children with Charles's bride, Catherine of Braganza, whose dowry included Tangier and the island of Bombay. Tangier offered a good harbour and base for naval operations in the Western Mediterranean and to defend the town against the Moors, the King appointed Henry Mordaunt, Earl of Peterborough, to be its Governor and the Captain General of his expeditionary force, which arrived there on 29 January 1662. The original garrison consisted of The Tangier Regiment [later named after Catherine, the Queen's Royal Regiment] and The Tangier Horse [The Royal Dragoons] and *a number of wives and children*. Thus began the British Army's proud record of over 300 years of continuous service to the Crown, at home and overseas, and of dealing with the problems of its women and camp followers. And if the soldier himself has been the principal character on the stage of military history, at least it may be said that his wife and children have always appeared in the chorus line!

We know much about the military life of the garrison[1] but only a little about the wives and children. Tangier's original inhabitants, the Portuguese, soon grew tired of their new masters and were evacuated, 'leaving the town without a civilian population, except for the wives and children of the military'.[2] The King ordered a survey of 'the state of the Citty and Garrison of Tanger'[3] on 30 December 1676, including the wives, servants, slaves and children [See Appendix A]. The total inhabitants numbered 2225, of whom 50 were Army Officers, 1231 other ranks and 302 Army women and children. Social distinctions were strongly marked. The Governor and his family, with the principal officers of the garrison, formed the small upper circle of about 20 families, followed by the municipal dignataries, the minister, the doctors and the schoolmaster, together with the more important merchants and the military officers below the rank of Major. Below these again were the soldiers

1

and their families, the mole-workers, the shopkeepers etc. The attractive climate and the short two-week journey from Falmouth made Tangier a place for the Court and its noble ladies to visit. There were balls and banquets, pretty walks and gardens and a popular resort called White Hall 'where the ladies, the officers and the better sort of people do refresh and divert themselves with wine and fruits and a very pretty Bowling Base'.[4] There was a hospital which served the Queen's Regiment and also a school[5], in which the King 'thought fit to employ in April 1675 Richard Reynolds, Master of Arts and Fellow of Sidney Sussex College, in our service as Schoolmaster in our Towne of Tanger'.[6]

But conditions were hard, especially for the soldiers for whom there was little amusement or recreation, except sitting on the sea-shore playing cards or dice or drinking in the taverns, many of which were kept by soldiers' widows. Discipline was strict, court-martials frequent and punishments severe. A number of soldiers married local women, 'even though they have wifes and husbands livinge in other places'.[7] Death was everywhere with sieges, sorties and snipers' bullets, whilst everyone straying outside the boundary walls risked slavery for life, if captured by the Moors. In 1680, when the depleted garrison was faced with a full-scale Moorish offensive, it was reinforced with a composite battalion of Grenadier and Coldstream Guards and with regiments of the 1st and 4th of Foot [The Royal Scots and The 2nd Tangier Regiment respectively]. To the dangers of battle were added dirt, bad food, hard drinking and 'flux and scurvy' to kill off the soldiers and their families and to ruin the health of the survivors. 'The goods of such as die in the Army or Garrison, or be slain in the Service, if they make any will by word or writing, shall be disposed of according to their Will; if they make no Will, then they shall go to the wife or next kindred.'[7]

For Charles, Tangier proved an expensive wedding present, costly to maintain and difficult to defend, and in 1683 he decided to evacuate the garrison after 21 years of occupation. Samuel Pepys, to whom he gave the responsibility for carrying out his orders as Secretary of the Navy, wrote in his diary:

> 'In the whole place, nothing but vice of all sorts, swearing, drinking, cursing and whoring, the women as bad as the men.'[8]

He recorded in detail how Colonel Kirke, at that time the Governor, and his officers publicly boasted of their conquests and how they defamed every woman who would yield to their invitations. The Portuguese monks also complained that 'he had forbidden them to marry soldiers (to local women) without his permission, which he refused, thus encouraging immorality.'[8]

One of the chief concerns of the last Governor, Lord Dartmouth, was the evacuation of the sick soldiers 'and the many famelyes and their effects to be brought off.'[9] The hospital ship 'Unity' sailed for home on 18 October 1683 with 114 invalid soldiers and 104 women and children under the care of John

Eccles 'usher and writing master of the school and gunner'[10], who had served the school for seven and a half years at a salary of £30 per annum. The families were 'quartered at Falmouth on an allowance of 3d a day to each soldier's wife, until the arrival of the battalion'[9]. The 'Unity' was followed by the hospital ship 'Welcome', a hired merchant vessel, specially adapted for the purpose, with a Dr Lawrence and three women [wives?] aboard to nurse the sick.

The main force of 2830 officers and men and 361 wives and children, finally completed the evacuation of Tangier during February and March 1684.[10] The 2nd Tangier Regiment, for example, left on 13 and 14 February, with some 600 men and 30 wives and children, including those of Captain Collier and 3 subalterns.[11]

Thus from its earliest days the Standing Army had to make special arrangements for its wives and children. In an overseas garrison, on active service, some soldiers' wives were accepted and some facilities provided for them and their children [school, return family passage and financial help on landing], although it would not be for another 100 years [1792] that the Army would officially recognise a limited number of soldiers' wives who married 'with leave', in return for help with the barrack chores and the washing of the soldiers' linen.

It was, however, necessary to try to control the numbers of married women who attached themselves to the regiments and an Order was issued in 1685 that 'no soldier was to marry without the consent of his captain'.[12] What is certain is that many women, married or not, would follow husband or lover round the country and overseas to survive as best they could. Collectively, they would be known as the 'Army Women'. For the Officer's 'lady' there would be no such limitations: they lived and travelled at the Officer's own expense, but he, too, would be discouraged from early marriage.

MARLBOROUGH'S HUSBANDS

Who were the husbands or companions of the women who followed the armies of Queen Anne and the Royal Georges? If the husband was an officer, he would almost certainly have come from the aristocratic upper classes, from the wealthy landed gentry or the peerage; he would probably have been a younger son, cut off from the family wealth and title by the primogeniture principle of inheritance by the eldest son. Charles II's small army had only 613 officer vacancies and competition for them would have been high, since his army offered a genuine alternative to a career in the navy, the law or the church. To avoid becoming a family liability and sometimes to restore its fortunes, a younger son would have to marry well, usually within his own class, or seek a sinecure, (such as an army commission) — or both — permitting him to follow the customary pursuits of a gentleman. Since it was no longer possible for an officer to live on his pay, as in Cromwell's army, and because almost all commissions had to be purchased, he needed private means, without which he would have to seek his fortune by serving overseas, as the impoverished John Churchill, the future Duke of Marlborough, was forced to do in Tangier and on the Continent.

For the ordinary soldier, marriage was discouraged. 'A typical Restoration soldier would be unmarried, without a permanent home, carrying all he possessed on his back and serving for life'.[13] A married man was not recruited and was discharged if he later married, as the Regulations of Charles II in 1663 make clear:

> 'No muster-master shall knowingly muster a private soldier in any troop or company that is married. Nevertheless, if any soldier desires leave to marry, it shall not be denied to him, but at the same time to be discharged, and paid to the day of his discharge, and another unmarried to be entertained in his place at the same time'.[14]

Almost without exception, the foot soldier was recruited from the lower social order, most likely from the rural areas, with a large number from Scotland and Ireland. Some would be volunteers, who craved excitement and adventure, loot and rape; some would be discontented agricultural workers, vagrants, unemployed apprentices and paupers, for whom the army offered a haven from debt and crime. The Guards and the Cavalry, however, would recruit a superior type of soldier, including younger sons of the poorer gentry, who hoped that their experience in the ranks would fit them for a commission in the course of time.

But Army life was tough and uncertain and pay was poor, as indeed it was for many in civilian life. At worst, the army offered employment, food, clothing and free quarters. Enlisting, moreover provided an opportunity for a husband to escape from the responsibilities of a wife and family by a false attestation. Since the Army was constantly on the move, the soldier would pick up his 'woman' from wherever he happened to be stationed, at home or abroad. Some soldiers would marry their women: most would co-habit or seek temporary liaisons. Some women would be the usual camp followers of all armies down the ages.

An authentic picture of contemporary recruiting methods and of recruits is given by George Farquhar in 1706 in his play 'The Recruiting Officer'. His scheming recruiting Sergeant Kite announces to the crowd, assembled by beat of drum in the market-place at Shrewsbury:

> 'If any gentleman, soldiers or others, have a mind to serve Her Majesty, (Queen Anne), and pull down the French King; if any 'prentices have severe masters, any children have undutiful parents; if any servants have little wages, or any husband too much wife, let them repair to the noble Sergeant Kite, at the sign of the Raven in the good town of Shrewsbury, and they shall receive present relief and entertainment.'

To the gullible potential recruit, Sergeant Kite offered visions of a new life:

> 'Our 'prentice Tom may now refuse,
> To wipe his scoundrel master's shoes,
> For now he's free to sing and play,
> Over the hills and far away —
> To Flanders, Portugal or Spain.'
> 'We shall lead more happy lives,
> By getting rid of Brats and Wives,
> That scold and bawl both night and day,
> Over the hills and far away.'

George Farquhar was in an ideal position to know recruits and recruiting methods, since he had been an actor and then a second lieutenant in the Earl of Amery's 4th Foot[15] and a Recruiting Officer himself. Born in Londonderry, the son of a poor clergyman, he married an officer's widow in 1703, believing her to be a rich heiress. Disappointed, he was forced to sell his commission to pay his debts.

Once enlisted, normally for life, the soldier needed pay and accommodation. The Foot soldier received eightpence per day, of which sixpence went to the Company Captain for his subsistence (food and drink etc) and twopence was retained by the regiment, from which to deduct 'off-reckonings' for clothing, laundry and other necessaries. At the end of the week, the soldier might finish up with a few pence for himself (and his family, if he had one). He would not receive any pay increase until 1797, when his pay and allowances were consolidated at one shilling per diem. Since barracks were practically non-existent, the soldier was usually billeted in an inn or ale-house, the Captain giving fourpence of the soldier's sixpence subsistence money to the inn-keeper for accommodation (usually in the attics or outhouses). This small sum was to pay for food, small beer and candles, which frequently left the host out of pocket and resentful for having the soldier thrust upon him. The soldier, whose idea of Paradise in all ages was 'to eat, drink, sleep and make love and have nothing to pay' would take his revenge 'by making free with the inn-keeper's property, victuals and wife, against the threat of knocking his teeth down his throat, if he objected'.[16]

A popular view of the foot soldier in 1703 was 'a man coaxed from a trade, whereby he might live comfortably, to bear arms for his King and Country, whereby he can hope for nothing but to live starvingly. His lodging is near Heaven (i.e. the attic of an inn) and his soul as near Hell, as a profligate life can sink him. He is generally beloved by whores and lice, because both sorts of vermin are admirers of a scarlet coat. Adept at begging and thieving, he is always boasting of his deeds in battle. If he spends 20 years in war, he might become a sergeant and, if he survives three score, he may get a hospital. The best end he can expect is to die in a bed of honour and the greatest living marks of his bravery are crippled limbs'.[17]

One soldier, who fought many campaigns, found shelter as a pensioner and survived to a ripe old age, was William Hiseland, whose portrait hangs in a place of honour in the Great Hall at The Royal Hospital, Chelsea. Born in 1620, he died in 1732, aged 112. He fought under King William in Ireland, under Marlborough in Flanders and was admitted as a Pensioner in 1714. On his tombstone in the Chelsea cemetery is written:

> 'When above 100 years' old, he took unto Him a Wife'.

What he did with her is not known — but he could not have lived with her inside the Hospital, since women were not, and still are not, permitted as inmates.

A mid 18th century recruiting advertisement of Colonel (later General) John Burgoyne, who surrendered to the American forces at Saratoga, gives a very different picture of the life of a soldier:

> 'NOW THEN! Think of all the advantages that will be yours by joining in with His Majesty's 16th Light Dragoons (popularly known as Burgoyne's Light Horse) . . . you are everywhere respected . . . you are admired by the fair, which together with the chance of getting switched to a buxom widow, or brushing with a rich heiress, renders the situation truly envious and desirable. Young men out of employment or uncomfortable . . . Nick in instantly and ENLIST'.

'Gentleman John' Burgoyne, who raised the 16th Lancers during the Seven Years War, (and whom we shall meet later (Chapter 4) did, in fact, marry an heiress — Lady Charlotte Stanley, daughter of the Earl of Derby (who at first opposed the marriage) — with whom he eloped as a young Cornet in 1743. Her inheritance paid for his subsequent military advancement. Throughout his life he was to remain loyal, if not always faithful, to her. He was reluctant to leave her behind, when he was appointed to North America in 1775 — 'To separate for a length of time, perhaps forever, from the tenderest, the faithfullest, the most amiable companion and friend that ever a man was blessed with.'[18] In fact, he was never to see her again.

When his wife died in 1776, Burgoyne (who survived his wife for another 24 years) took as his mistress Susan Caulfield, a popular opera singer, by whom he had four children between 1782–1788. Their eldest son, John Fox Burgoyne, gained an international reputation as a military engineer and became a Field Marshal, serving with Sir John Moore at Corunna, Wellington in the Peninsula and Lord Raglan in the Crimea.

Authentic accounts of life among the British rank and file during the first half of the 18th century are rare, especially from the pens of soldiers themselves. One who did write a diary was Corporal William Todd, a Yorkshireman from Holderness, who died in 1763 when only 38. He was a man of some education, although only a labourer, for in Ireland in 1754 he acted as a regimental schoolmaster and taught some of the local children and townspeople. He enlisted in the 30th Foot in 1749 and later served with the 12th Foot (The Suffolk Regiment). He described how his regiment, helped by the local constabulary at Reading in 1757, obtained large numbers of conscripts. Every Saturday, the market day, the constables brought them in.

'There we have an officer and a sergeant and a corporal and 12 men waiting at the Town's Hall, where a bench of Justices of the Peace sits. Any man that is brought by the constables, if our officer approves of him, he asks him to enlist. If he agrees, the officer gives him a guinea and a crown. If he won't enlist, the corporal takes him to the gaol and puts him in the 'black hole', until he changes his mind'.[19]

This was perfectly legal, he claimed and 'any unemployed young fellow or has a girl with child or has any loose character' would be certain of being brought in by the constables. Corporal Todd also gives us a glimpse of the soldiers' women on the continent during the Seven Years' War, at the conclusion of which the four British Divisions[20] left Munster on 25 January 1763 and marched through Nijmegen and Breda to their port of embarkation at Wilhelmstadt. The 16500 men were accompanied by their women, numbering 1666, many of whom had followed the drum for the past five years. Some of these were German women. Corporal Todd, writing at Gesecke on 24 April 1761, said 'Several of our men gets married here, as the Younkers thinks it a great honour to marry with an English soldier, their wages being so very small here'. Their place in the military world had never been clearly defined and they had been the subject of ribald remarks.

'It is safe to assume, however, that they ministered to the creature comforts of their men and that, when after a battle or at the end of a march, they came up with the quarter-masters, they vied with each other in being the first to provide not only for their husbands but also the men of his section or platoon with their billy-cans of hot food and such other simple amenities as may now be provided by more organised bodies. They may, in short, have been an almost indispensable part of the quarter-master's staff'.[21]

Different accounts are given of the quality and character of these early soldiers — Blackader, one of Marlborough's best officers, for instance, called them 'lewd, dissipated creatures, the dregs and scum of mankind'.[22]

But under good leadership they became well-disciplined and successful armies —

'These soldiers, all sorts and conditions of men, from patriots to fortune hunters and vagabonds; ill-fed when they were fed at all; massacred in sea transports; mangled, when wounded, by surgeons more akin to carpenters than doctors; on the march, shoeless and ragged, cut off from their nearest and dearest, as if dead; poorly paid, when paid at all; if disabled or discharged, thrown on to the streets without thanks or money. Yet when properly led and their loyalty tested their courage was unequalled and their skill at arms without parallel'.[23]

Appendix A to Chapter 1
'Survey of the State of the Citty and Garrison of Tanger, covering the Inhabitants, Wives, Servants, Slaves, Children, Strangers, Priests and wight [people] of all sex', by Order of Charles II, 30 December 1976

(a) *The Army*

ARMY WIVES	Servants		Children		NCO's Soldiers and Troopers	Officers Commissioned and Staff	The Sum of All	Whereof		
	Male	Female	Male	Female				Men	Women	Children
129	2	7	98	75	1,231	50	1,592	1,283	136	173

(b) *In the City and Army*

House-holders (157) Labourers (56) Foreigners (44) Servants/ slaves (29)	Wives— Citizens 62 Molemen 26	Widows and Single Women	Children		Churchmen and Priests	City & Mole	The Whole Army in Men, Women and Children	All the People in the City, Mole and Army Are
			Male	Female				
286	88	70	86	83	20	633	1,592	2,225
			169					

John Bland, Comptroller of His Majesties Revenues.

Source: Lieutenant Colonel John Davis: History of the Second Queen's Royal Regiment 1887.

Chapter 2

Unhappy She Who Takes a Soldier

Much has been written about the soldier and his campaigns over the years but few contemporary records are available of the soldier's wife and her circumstances during the 17th and 18th centuries. As we have seen, the Army preferred the single soldier and offered him, through its recruiters, an escape from 'too much wife and squalling children'.[1] Marriage was incompatible with military efficiency and wives and children hindered the Army's mobility. The Army could not legally prevent a soldier from marrying, but he could be prevented from enlisting or preference could be given to the single man. During the enlistments of 1689, for instance, 'married men were especially objected to as soldiers'[2] and during the general reduction of the Army, which followed the Peace of Ryswick (1697), 'The married men were discharged, whether they liked it or not, while the unmarried soldiers were compelled to remain'.[2] Increasingly, the Army set out to discourage marriage, as well as to control the number of married men in its regiments, by requiring the soldier to seek his ɪCompany Commander's permission to his marriage and then only to a woman of good character.

An Order of the Coldstream Guards (dated 3 November 1671) stated:

> 'No soldier to marry without the consent of his Captain, upon pain of being cashiered, and losing the pay that might be due'.[3]

On 1 June 1685 this Order was extended to the whole Army and remained the Army's policy for the next 200 years.

Not only was the Army against the marriage of a soldier but so were most parents, who regarded with horror the idea of their daughters marrying a 'Red-coat' or even of consorting with them. 'The most honest man in England had but to don the red-coat to be dubbed a lewd profilgate wretch', wrote Fortescue.[4] The soldier's reputation for arrogance, drinking, indiscipline and licentious behaviour was notorious and to have soldiers billeted in their village, let alone in their house, was a matter of grave concern, if not to the girls themselves, at least to their parents.

9

'Women adore a martial man', wrote William Wycherley[5] in 1676 and certainly literature is full of stories of parents trying to protect their daughters — and of daughters scheming to circumvent them. One favourite trick was for a girl to disguise herself as a soldier, in order to follow her husband or lover. This practice had been so prevalent in the Royalist Army of King Charles I that in July 1643 he issued an Order to be published at the head of every regiment — 'Let no woman presume to Counterfeit Her Sex by wearing man's apparel under pain of the Severest punishment which Law and our displeasure shall inflict'.[6] And real life can be stranger than fiction. St. Nicholas Churchyard, Brighton has a tombstone inscribed:

> 'In memory of Phoebe Hessel, born Stepney 1713. Served for many years as a private soldier in the 5th Regiment of Foot in different parts of Europe. In the year 1745 she fought under the Command of the Duke of Cumberland at the Battle of Fontenoy, where she received a bayonet wound in her arm. Her long life, which commenced in the time of Queen Anne extended to the Reign of George IV, by whose munificence she received comfort and support in her latter years.
> Died at Brighton, where she had long resided, 12 December, 1821. Aged 108 years'.[7]

Following her soldier lover (or lovers, since she was married 5 times), Phoebe is reported to have served without detection in Gibraltar and to have fought bravely in America at the Battle of Bunker Hill.

> 'A misdemeanour at length put an end to her martial career. She was brought to the halberts to be whipped and, having her neck and shoulders bare, her sex was discovered. Her answer was 'Strike and be damned'. The careers of Christian Ross and Hannah Snell also show that a woman might serve in the army for years and be more than once wounded in action, before she was revealed a woman',[8] wrote a Saddler sergeant of the 13th Light Dragoons.

When Christian Welch (born Davies; on the death of her husband she married her 'protector' Captain Ross) enlisted in 1693 in The Scots Greys to follow her husband on the Duke of Marlborough's campaigns, she took advantage of the slip-shod attestation procedure:

> 'Having ordered my affairs, I cut off my hair, and dressed me in a suit of my husband's, having had the precaution to quilt the waistcoat to preserve my breasts from hurt, which were not large enough to betray my sex, and putting on my wig and hat . . . . . I went to the Sign of the Golden Last, where Ensign Herbert Lawrence was beating up for recruits . . . . . I was called a clever, brisk young fellow, given a guinea enlisting money, and a crown to drink the King's health and ordered to be enrolled forthwith'.[9]

Like many another army wife, 'Mother' Ross became a sutler,[10] selling provisions to the soldiers and their families and exchanging their loot for cash or drink. She ended her days as an out-patient of Chelsea Hospital, where her third husband was an in-pensioner, and was buried there in 1739.

Mary Anne Talbot (1778–1808) was the youngest of the 16 illegitimate children of the 1st Earl Talbot. Her guardian, Captain Essex Bowen, of the 82nd Foot seduced her and, when he was posted overseas in 1792, made her dress in uniform and sail to the West Indies with him under the name of John Taylor. She came back to Europe with him, disguised as a drummer boy and was wounded in Flanders. When Bowen was killed at Valenciennes in July 1793 she deserted but received a pension of 20 pounds a year from Queen Charlotte 'on account of her wounds.'[11]

On 18 March 1690 The King's Own Regiment (4th Foot) was ordered to march from Bideford to embark for Belfast. The wives of the Regiment accompanied them; the officers' ladies riding, while the soldiers' wives and those of a few of the 'Inferior Officers' walked with the baggage under the control of the regimental marshal. The women were expected to stay at the rear of the column with the regimental baggage but were difficult to control and were frequently put under the command of one of their number, who was responsible for keeping them together.

> 'The women were of great assistance to the regiment, for they bought and prepared the food for the Company, brought in fuel for the fire, washed the linen, and generally tended the men. Especially were they useful in camp, for then they were permitted to go miles from the regiment in search of victuals and of other necessaries'[12].

On the other hand, Marlborough gave orders to his Provost Marshal 'to chase away all loose women from the camps'.[13] In 1702 the King's Regiment embarked at Plymouth, 12 companies strong, for an attack on the coast of Spain on the outbreak of the War of the Spanish Succession. '3 women were allowed to embark with each Company.'[14] 'The booty, after one-tenth had been taken for the relief of the sick and maimed, was divided between the regiments concerned, each according to his rank'[15]. The property of the dead soldiers was sold and the proceeds given to their widows.

This practice of recognising a limited number of soldiers' wives to accompany the regiment overseas to help with the soldiers' domestic chores, even on active service, is confirmed in other regimental records and Order Books dating from this time. For example, the Lord Lieutenant of Ireland wrote to the Secretary of State in 1703 explaining why additional space in the transports taking the first British troops for service in Portugal was needed.' That which adds (to the numbers) is the necessary allowance for 4 women to a company, which is the least that has been permitted and cannot be avoided'.[16]

Such practical reasons for officially recognising the value of a few wives of soldiers did not change the Army's attitude to marriage in general; but the Duke of Newcastle, when Secretary of State in 1754, at least thought these reasons sound —, 'the soldiers would be disgruntled, if the women did not accompany them to do the cooking, washing, sewing and to serve other purposes for which women naturally go with the Army.'[17]

A War Office letter dated 16th October 1758 authorised 10 women per Company to embark with the six regiments of Foot (The Buffs, 4th, 61st., 63rd., 64th., and 65th.) under General Peregrine Hopson for the West Indies.[18]. 'Within a year, 800 officers and men had found their graves in Guadeloupe' records the official History of the Manchester Regiment (63rd

Foot), while many others were invalided home. The deaths among women and children are not recorded but they must have been considerable.

That the Army did oppose the married state for its soldiers is clear from these Regimental Records and Order Books of the second half of the 18th. Century. Thus the Order Book of the Queen's Bays for 1792:

> 'Marriage is to be discouraged as much as possible'.
>
> 'A bad soldier's wife must be got rid of as soon as possible'.
>
> 'No man who presumes to marry an improper woman, or to marry at all against the consent of the Commanding Officer of his troop, is to be allowed separate lodgings or to be out of quarters'.
>
> 'Three women per troop' is the matrimonial limit, and then only 'if the wives are industrious'.
>
> 'The Regiment has already more women than could possibly be allowed to embark for foreign service'.[19]
>
> 'Officers must explain to the men the many miseries that women are exposed to, and by every sort of persuasion, they must prevent their marriage, if possible'. (*Regulations for the Cavalry 1795*)

The regulations for Foot soldiers were the same as those for the Cavalry, as the Standing Orders for a Scottish Regiment of the same date show, and gave other reasons for a celibate life:–

> 'Soldiers ought to be particularly careful not to contract rash or improper marriages, which tend to encumber them for life, to break their spirit and damp every hope of promotion'.[20]

The policy is clear — marriage is to be discouraged by persuasion and by emphasising the problems: official permission must be obtained and the wife must be of good character and industrious. Penalties will be applied to offenders by withholding accommodation, sleeping out passes and promotion. Privileges will be given to the few soldiers' wives officially recognised.

Furthermore, the soldier's pay was not designed to support a wife: a soldier trying to feed a wife and children only injured his own health, as Sir John Pringle pointed out in 1744.

> 'The greatest impediments to messing are the wives and children, who must often be maintained on the pay of the men. In such circumstances, it is not improper food but the want of it that may endanger a soldier's health'.[21]

Another problem for the married soldier was accommodation. In 1720, a few new barracks were being constructed. They were, for the most part, three storeys high, with four small towers for their defence. On each floor was a barrack room about 17 feet by 18 feet, containing five double beds. In this room 10 men lived and ate and slept: no women or children were allowed to enter on any account. Barracks were inspected daily by a subaltern and no soldier was permitted to be absent, except on a ticket of leave. Before dark, every man had to be in his quarters, whether married or single. It was the same on active service. In 1744, the Duke of Cumberland's son, who commanded the King's Army in the Jacobite rebellion, ordered that:

'The huts which married men were accustomed to build near the camp were forbidden, every man being made to sleep with his company, while the women were given tents in the rear. Only authorised women were allowed room in these tents; those who could give no account of themselves to be turned out of the Line, with positive orders not to return on pain of being severely punished'.[22]

One of the officers, who served under the Duke of Cumberland, was the future General Wolfe, killed at Quebec. In 1749, he was the commanding officer of the 20th Foot, stationed in Glasgow. Born in 1729, he had already served as an Ensign with the 12th Foot in Flanders, with George II at Dettingen and with the Duke of Cumberland at Fontenoy and Culloden but was destined to live for only 32 years. His Regimental Orders on marriage dated 1749 make very interesting reading!

'Any soldier that presumes to marry clandestinely wanting credible witnesses, and shall neglect the publick ceremonies of the church, or shall not consult his Officer before his marriage that the woman's character may be enquired into — every such offender shall be punished with vigour'.[23]

In 1751 Colonel Wolfe was stationed at Banff. Again, his Orders were clear.

'The Officers are desired to discourage Matrimony amongst the men as much as possible. The Service suffers by the multitude of Women already in the Regiment'.[24]

Despite these Orders, the marriage registers of Banff about this time record the attractions the 'redcoats' had for the women of the town and more than half a dozen soldiers found brides there in 1751. For example:

'20 July 1751 Robert Willers, private soldier in the Regiment of Foot commanded by the Rt Hon Lord Viscount Bury and in Lieutenant Colonel James Wolfe's company, and Elizabeth Stephen, born in the parish of Fordon, in Mearns, and last from Montrose'.[25]

Inverness November 1751. Another stern warning!

'The Lieutenant Colonel is informed that several soldiers have been married in this town in a clandestine and illegal manner. This practice is contrary to all Order and Discipline and deserves an exemplary Punishment as well from the Civil Magistrates as from the Military. The first Soldier who shall disobey the repeated orders that have been given upon the Subject and shall presume to Marry in this Infamous manner and without his Officer's knowledge must expect to be proceeded against with the utmost Rigour. The Lieutenant Colonel further Recommends to the Soldiers not to Marry at all; the long March and Embarkation that will soon follow must convince them that many Women in the Regiment are very inconvenient, especially as some of them are not so industrious nor so useful to their Husbands as a Soldier's Wife ought to be'.[25]

On 6 September 1753, Wolfe left Scotland for Carlisle and Dover Castle.

'The Soldiers are to acquaint their wives that if any of them are found Pilfering or stealing in their Quarters or upon the march, or are known to receive anything that is stolen, they will be immediately imprisoned and punished by the Civil Power'.[26]

Wolfe was equally concerned that his young officers should not spoil their careers by a rash marriage. They were expected to learn the social graces, to brighten the local assemblies and dinner tables but not to take on the responsibilities of early matrimony. While at Dover, there was a complaint from the local dignataries that his officers were neglecting their social duties, especially in not giving and attending balls. Wolfe replied:

'Some of our finest performers are at present disabled. Notwithstanding this, I always encourage our young officers to frequent balls and assemblies. It softens their manners and makes them civil; and commonly I go along with them to see how they conduct themselves. I am only afraid that they shall fall in love and marry. Whenever I perceive the symptoms, or somebody else makes the discovery, we fall upon the dilinquent without mercy, until he grows out of conceit with his new passion. By this method we have broke many an amorous alliance and dissolved many ties of eternal love and affection'.[27]

There are frequent references in these Order Books to complaints from civilians and municipal authorities about the behaviour of soldiers and

'of the great number of women and children they carry with them'.[28]

The disciplinary Board of Officers at the Commander-in-Chief's Headquarters at the Horse Guards looked into these complaints and recommended that 'commanding officers take care that all women not legally married be chased away'. William Agar, Chaplain to the 20th Foot estimated in 1756 that each Battalion had at least 200 women, some 300.

'Ours had but 150 at the Camp near Blandford. It might be heartily wished that all, unless proved lawfully married, had been sent away for the better support of the honest and industrious'.[28]

In garrisons at home and overseas where military law prevailed, the camp followers came under army discipline and could be convicted summarily or by court martial under the Articles of War and the Mutiny Acts, the first of which was passed in 1689. (It was renewed annually for 167 years from 1712 to 1879, when a permanent Army Disciplinary Act was passed). The range of punishments varied according to the severity of the offence or the whim of a commanding officer.

'One very common punishment for trifling offences committed by petit sutlers, jews, brawling women and such-like persons', according to Walton,[29] 'was the whirligig. This was a kind of circular wooden cage which turned on a pivot: and when set in motion, whirled round with such an amazing velocity, that the delinquent became extremely sick, and commonly emptied his or her body through every aperture' — much to the amusement of the spectators!

A woman was tried at a Court-Martial in Ireland in 1691 and sentenced to death 'for inciting to desertion while in the field;' and death was the penalty from 1662 for a soldier 'to force a woman to abuse her' (whether she belong to the enemy or not). Corporal Todd, for example, described the execution of a soldier for rape near Cherbourg, during The Seven Years War, though his victim interceded for him and offered to marry him.

In Tangier on 25 June 1664 a woman found guilty of incitement to mutiny was sentenced by a Court-Martial 'to be gagged and receive on her bare back 50 lashes, 10 at five different spots and to be sent out of the garrison by the first ship, being whipped also from the prison to the water side'.

On 26 January 1669, another Court ordered: 'a petticoat to be hung around a soldier's neck while riding the wooden horse for beating and ill-treating his wife'.[30]

The Orders of the Duke of Cumberland in 1755 prohibited a soldier's wife from selling 'Gin or any other Spiritous liquors' to the troops on pain of severe punishment; while in Scotland in 1746 he awarded '200 lashes with a Cat of Nine Tails' to a number of 'disorderly women' and drummed them out of camp — a punishment which could leave them destitute. In 1745, during the War of the Austrian Succession, a soldier's woman was 'convicted of petty larceny' and, as General Pulteney described to the Duke of Cumberland,

'her tail was immediately turned up before the door of the house, where the robbery was committed, and the Drummer of the Regiment tickled her with 100 very good lashes, since which time the ladies have behaved like angels. The sex is not the worse for correction'.

However harsh such punishments may seem, they must be judged in the context of the violence, disorders and brutal punishments prevalent in 18th Century England and with the hangings at Tyburn, the transportations to the colonies of men, women and children for petty theft, the methods of the press-gangs, the bull-baiting and the brutal, brawling scenes in tavern, brothel and work-place. The treatment of women in the overcrowded and filthy prisons and in the houses of correction (bridewells) was often cruel and punishments severe. The Liverpool Bridewell in 1766 placed women in heavy chains, tortured them on the ducking stool and flogged them weekly at the whipping post for petty thefts. There was no separation of the sexes and many historians speak of the drunkenness, debauchery, sickness and misery in prisons, where women condemned to death could plead 'with child' to stop their execution, until they were delivered. If they were not pregnant, there were always plenty of men in prison ready to assist them. As late as 1820, men were still being drawn on hurdles to their place of execution, then hanged and decapitated in public spectacles. The flogging of women was permitted in England until 1817 (and of soldiers until 1881) and fashionable society would go to the Bridewell Prison to watch the women being whipped before the Court of Governors.

One must have regard, also, to the low status of women generally during the 18th Century and of the lower classes in particular. In a male dominated society, married women were legally subjugated. Her husband had supreme rights over her person, her children and her property. He could lock her up, treat her like a dog, and if she ran away, he could apply for, and usually obtain, the restoration of his conjugal rights. Every husband had the right of reasonable domestic chastisement of his wife, 'an ancient privilege still claimed and exerted by the lower rank of people', according to the legal expert Sir

William Blackstone in 1793.[31] Judge Butler declared in a judgement of 1782 that 'it was perfectly legal for a man to beat his wife, as long as he used a stick no thicker than his thumb'.

For a wife of the lower classes to obtain redress for an assault on her person or to end an unhappy marriage was usually beyond her means, even if possible in law, and other alternatives were found — separation by mutual agreement, desertion, bigamy or wife sales. Wife sales were frequent during the 18th century — 'a practice among common people of ending a marriage when a husband and wife find themselves heartily tired of each other', as one writer noted in 1777:

> 'Thinking that his wife is his goods and chattels, he puts a halter about her neck and thereby leads her to the next market place; and there puts her up to auction to be sold, as though she was a brood-mare, or a milch-cow, to the highest bidder'.[32]

In 1805 a drummer of the King's Own Regiment, a mulatto, went to the market place in Hythe and for sixpence bought the wife of one of the Irish labourers employed on building the Shorncliffe canal. 'She was not more than twenty years and of a likely figure', records the Regimental History.[33]

A notice in *The Times* for 22 July 1797 stated 'By some mistake or omission in the report of the Smithfield market we have not learned the average price for Wives for the last week'. It noted, however, that the increasing value of 'the fair sex' was supported by the fact that 'the price of Wives has risen in that market from half a guinea to three guineas and a half'.

'Feminine degradation could scarcely go much further than to be bought and sold like a slave', concludes Eric Hopkins in his Social History of the English Working Classes.[34]

Coming from such a background, the women who followed the Army and who marched with their men on campaign were tough and resourceful and prepared to share their dangers and deprivations. Such were the women of the King's Own, who followed the Duke of Cumberland in his campaign against Bonnie Prince Charlie, as he strove to subdue the clans at Culloden (1746). They had to wade across rivers 'still chill from the wintry snows, reaching above their waists, carrying their clothes upon their heads to keep them dry'.[33] The women were not allowed, however, to take part in the battle, for the Duke ordered that they 'remain with the bat horses, between the general officer's luggage and the wheel baggage of the rest of the army'.[33] Any woman found forward of the wagons was whipped by the drummers at sunset. The Duke, like every commander before and since, was concerned with the women and their baggage cluttering up the fighting troops.

> 'The Wallets (Knapsacks) of the Dragoons are to be inspected narrowly, whenever they March to hinder them from carrying their wives' things and spoiling their Horses'.[35]

Life was the same for the women who followed the English regiments in Europe during the Seven Years War. The History of the Northumberland Fusiliers (5th Foot) notes in 1760:

'It is not surprising that the English regiments lost a quarter of their strength during these long and hard campaigns: but worse than the men's sufferings were the hardships endured by the soldiers' wives. Six women were allowed to each company and these drew their rations and shared their husband's bivouac. The unfortunate women who followed 'unauthorised' depended on the generosity of the soldiers for their subsistence'.[36]

Keeping these women in order was difficult and a writer described one attempt in 1786.

'Women who follow an army may be ordered (if they can be ordered) in three ranks, or rather classes, one below another: the first shall be those that are ladies, and are the wives of the general and other principal commanders, who for the most part are carried in coaches. The second class is those who ride on horseback, and they must ride in no other place than where the baggage of the regiment to which they belong marcheth, but they are very often extravagant, gadding here and there and therefore in some place are put in companies, and have one to oversee them, called in Germany Hureweibles, 'rulers or marshals of the whores'. The third class is those who walk on foot and are the wives of inferior officers and soldiers; they must walk beside the baggage of the several regiments to which they belong and over them the regiment marshals have inspection'.[37]

In 1795 the post of barrackmaster-general was created and during the Napoleonic Wars large numbers of barracks were built at strategic towns and ports to meet the threat of a French invasion. The custom grew up of permitting the soldier and his 'officially recognised' woman to occupy a corner of a barrack room, where, screened from the unmarried soldiers by a blanket or a piece of canvas, they carried out their married life; or, if they were under canvas, to occupy space in a tent shared with the men at the authorised ratio of 1 woman to each tent. Here, exposed to the twin evils of the barrack room profanity and drunkenness, their children grew up, sleeping on the floor or in a bed vacated by a soldier, absent or on duty. This custom was sanctioned in the first Barrack Regulations ever issued (1817) —

'the Barrackmaster may permit (when it does not interfere with or restrict the soldiers' accommodation), as an occasional indulgence and as tending to promote cleanliness and the convenience of the soldier, 4 married women per Troop or Company of 60 men (or 6 per 100 men) to be resident within the Barracks. Such women to be displaced for any mischief or damage'.[38]

The 'greater cleanliness and convenience of the soldier' meant to do his washing and to prepare the food for the soldiers in her 'barrack', for which the woman received the small sum of sixpence and a half ration of food for herself and a quarter ration for each child of the marriage. Primitive washhouses, fitted with boilers, were provided and outdoor drying posts but often washing was dried and ironed in the barrack rooms, much to the inconvenience of the men.

NEW REGULATIONS FOR FAMILY TRAVEL AND ALLOWANCES 1800

On 29 October 1800 HRH. The Duke of York issued the following Order:

'Except on occasions when circumstances may render it necessary for troops to embark entirely without women, *His Royal Highness permits women, being the lawful wives of Soldiers, to embark in the proportion of 6 to 100 men, (Non-commissioned Officers included),* but in order to obviate the distress to which the families of Soldiers are liable to be exposed, *the women exceeding the above number, being the lawful wives of NCO's or Soldiers, shall,* if natives of England (or Wales), on their husbands embarking for foreign service, *receive for themselves* one guinea each, *and for each child born in lawful wedlock,* under 10 years of age, the sum of 5 shillings *to enable them to return home.* (N.B. Natives of Scotland or Ireland shall receive the same allowance, and, should they require it, be provided with a passage by sea, to the nearest port of the country to which they belong)'.[39]

Directions were issued to Paymasters,[40] explaining how these allowances were to be given to the lawful wives of soldiers not permitted to embark with their husbands. A Commanding Officer had to supply an alphabetical list to his Regimental Paymaster of 'the women whose intended residence is in England or Wales, Ireland or Scotland respectively, specifying the allowances paid to each' and whether a sea passage was provided.[40] These allowances were provided at public expense, including for those arriving in Scotland or Ireland by sea, 'a further sum of ten shillings for herself and three shillings for each of her children'.

Another Regulation[41] to Paymasters stated 'No stoppage of pay is required for rations supplied to the wives, widows and children of soldiers'. This applied to service overseas and to the 'authorised wives' only.

In April 1800, the married soldier was given another privilege —

'In future no man is to be allowed to sleep out of his quarters, except such as have families, who are, together with their wives, of good character and who (if not married previous to enlistment) have married with the consent of their Commanding Officers'[42] — limited the following year to 'Ten men for every Hundred'.

Clearly the Army was having problems with the number of men marrying *without* the permission of their Commanding Officers and with the number of men wishing to sleep out of barracks. These orders also show the Army's use of this privilege as a disciplinary measure against women and soldiers of bad character. An Order of 1807 goes even further and adds other criteria for the selection of wives to go with the regiments overseas:

'They should be carefully selected, as being of good character and having the inclination and ability to render themselves useful; it is very desirable that those who have children should be left at home'.[43]

Private James Anton, whom we shall meet later during the Peninsular War, was a private soldier who was fortunate enough to have his wife selected to accompany him overseas — and one of the few private soldiers (he later became an NCO) to give his views on married life:

'It is generally the case in selecting women to follow the Army to a foreign station, that choice is made of those without children, as they are considered more capable of performing the services that may be required of them than those encumbered with a family. This, though just as regards our wants, is not so with respect to many a well-deserving woman, who is thus cast on the public or left to her own exertions, which too often fail her in the endeavour to support herself and children, while the childless woman is selected to profit from that circumstance'.[44]

It is interesting to see how good regiments interpreted these regulations for the benefit of their soldiers and their wives. The 95th Rifle Corps, stationed at Shorncliffe in 1801, a year after its formation, published the following:

RULES FOR THE SOLDIERS' WIVES[45]

The marriage of soldiers being a matter of benefit to a regiment, of comfort to themselves, or of misery to both exactly in proportion as it is under good or bad regulations, this article has been much considered.

Authorised Number of Wives

'The number of women allowed by Government to embark on service are six for every hundred men, inclusive of all Non-Commissioned Officers' wives. This number is ample and indeed more than sufficient for a light corps, as every officer and soldier who have ever seen service must admit. It should never be exceeded on any pretext whatever, because the doing so is humanity of the falsest kind. Women who have more than two children can also never be of the number to embark, except in extraordinary cases, because that is a still greater act of inhumanity.
The Rifle Corps shall be a home of comfort to those who are entitled to feel its benefits, but shall not be a source, as is too often the case, of multiplying misery and prostitution among those who should be under every good soldier's peculiar care and protection.

Character and Employment

All women of immoral or drunken character, or who refuse to work for the men, are warned that they will not be permitted to remain ever to disgrace the Corps; but their friends will be written to or they must be received into some poor house or situation where they can earn their bread. To help the married women all regimental needlework and washing is to be done by them. The Colonel requests that the officers will never give their linen to wash out of the regiment, and also that they will distribute it nearly equally among the sergeants' wives.
The washing of all soldiers linen to be distributed in equal proportion among the other women of the companies. The number of shirts and socks which are washed for each soldier per week is two of each and at least two turnovers. For this the laundress is paid 5d by the pay sergeant. The Quartermaster will never give any needlework out of the regiment which can be done in it, and officers are requested to do the same; the women are also recommended to look for needlework in the neighbourhood of wherever the regiment may be, and the officers to give them any aid in their power to procure the same.

Welfare

Whenever a soldier's wife requires pecuniary aid for illness, her husband will apply to the surgeon, who will represent it to the Commanding Officer, when such assistance as the Charity Fund can afford will be given her.'

Selection of the women allowed to accompany their regiment overseas was decided by ballot. Donaldson of the 94th Scots Brigade described the tragic result for one wife unsuccessful in his regiment's ballot for the 6 places allocated:

'The next day the regiment sailed and Sandy's wife trudged the weary six miles to the sea, and made a last agonised attempt to go with him — all in vain. She never made it. Distraught with grief, the poor widower went on, unable to bury his wife and newborn child before the transport sailed. His comrades hardly heard him speak again, and he never returned from the Peninsula'.[46]

For the women left behind, whether married or single, 'recognised' or not, the future was usually very bleak. Whilst the regiment was in Britain, they could follow their men from station to station. Even when they lacked official recognition and failed to qualify for pay or rations, they could eke out a living on the few coppers and scraps of food their men could pass over to them or which they could earn by casual work on the way. Charles James, in the Military Companion of 1803, wrote:

> 'It is notorious that, during a march, these unfortunate women were at the mercy of every inn keeper in the Kingdom. Obliged to every waggoner for occasional conveyance on the roads in the worst of weather; and when they arrived in camp or barracks, they and their husbands were left to provide for themselves without the least regard to common decency or good order'.

Some regiments tried to help them from regimental funds or by the generosity of their officers — providing money, clothing, travel and maternity aid. But such charity varied greatly between regiments and was usually limited to those wives and children 'on the strength', for fear of encouraging more marriages and adding to their soldiers' burdens. For example, just before the first expeditionary force sailed for Portugal in 1793, the officers arranged a Ball at Cork for the distressed soldiers' wives and realised £50. When the 18th Light Dragoons sailed for Lisbon in 1808 and had to leave 91 wives behind, the Regiment made them and their children allowances from their funds to help them return home.[47]

Often, the deserted family was unknown to the regiment. If a married soldier wished to get away from 'too much wife', he could enlist far away from home and give his status as single. Once enlisted, the mobility of army life and foreign service made him virtually untouchable: furthermore, he could desert other women and children in the same way. Elizabeth Newton, for example, begged for relief from the parish of St. Margaret's in Leicester after her husband 'had gone for a soldier, leaving her with six small children and in extreme want'.[48]

THE POOR LAW UNTIL 1834

The only alternative was recourse to the Poor Law, still largely the legislation of Queen Elizabeth I, which formed the basis for the relief of the poor until 1834.[48] Each parish was responsible for its own poor relief, established by place of birth or length of residence, a wife and child under 16 taking the husband's or father's parish and paid out of a rate levied on each household and administered by parish overseers of the poor, under the general supervision of the local Justices of the Peace. The able-bodied, unemployed pauper was given out-door relief; the sick and aged were relieved in almshouses; the children were apprenticed, the boys to sea-service or the more laborious trades and to husbandry; the girls usually to domestic service; and the sturdy beggars or vagrants were punished in a house of correction (or enlisted in the Army). But as Scouller[49] states:

'An age which had scant regard for its soldiers, serving or discharged, could hardly be expected to be particularly solicitous about their dependants'.

For the orphans and widows of other ranks, little help was available from the War Office, from the regiment, or from voluntary funds, although, as we have seen, some aid was sometimes provided. For them, the workhouse was the only alternative and they were grim and forbidding places during the 18th century, whose inmates were invariably the old, the young, the infirm. Furthermore, the hardships bore especially hard on the women, since the social conditions of the day produced a high proportion of widows, deserted wives and unmarried mothers, whilst most of the occupations open to them were overstocked, ill-paid and irregular. For the Army woman, constantly on the move following her man, work was almost impossible, and, if she had children, work or financial aid provided outside the workhouse, even if she were able-bodied, was almost impossible for her to accept. If she were sick or burdened with young children, she had to be 'institutionalised', with the attendant stigma of pauperism.

In 1800 the War Office took a review of the families of the Brigade of Guards and estimated that the 9300 men had 5550 women and children between them with a further 1450 widows and orphans.[50] It estimated that over half these women and children frequently claimed relief from the Parish and charitable institutions; but such relief was barely sufficient. 'Some additional aid is necessary, not only for subsistence but also for educating the children and instilling into their minds the principles of morality and religion: at present they are reared up in the grossest ignorance and vice, the females become prostitutes at an early period of life and the males herd with the Thieves and Pickpockets, who affect society with their depredations'.[51]

BOUNTIES

Little, if any, charitable provision was available for the soldier himself when his fighting days were over while his widow would have to wait another 100 years for her pension. In 1680 England was thronged with wounded and sick soldiers from Tangier, the West Indies and the Low Countries and Kilmainham Hospital for aged and infirm Irish soldiers was founded in Dublin, the first charitable institution for the Army. Two years later (opened 1683) Charles II founded Chelsea Hospital on the lines of Louis XIV's Les Invalides for 'the relief of indigent officers and maimed and decayed soldiers'. Tradition ascribes to Nell Gwyn, the honour of having originated the plan, a tradition the old Pensioners used to maintain in their first toast after dinner. It is more likely that the land on which the Hospital stands was given to her by Charles II and exchanged later for a fine house in Pall Mall (the original site of the Army and Navy Club), adjoining the King's St. James's Palace.[52] From

March 1684 a day's pay was deducted annually from all ranks to meet the Hospital's expenses and a year's pay was given to any man who lost an eye or limb in His Majesty's Service, with lesser sums for less serious injuries.

Bounties for the widows of soldiers killed in battle are recorded as early as 1651,[53] in the Army of the Commonwealth, and afforded them some sort of compensation for the loss of their means of support. To obtain the weekly grant of about three shillings for herself and two children, a widow had to plead destitution. After the Restoration, the 'King's Bounty' was given to the nearest relative of the slain soldier.[54] For instance, 'To Mary Heathley, whose husband blew up Whitby Fort at Tanger and lost his life there, £60' (16 Feb: 1679/80). Royal Warrants of 1 January 1685 and 1 May 1689 authorised the 'Bounty' to be provided

> 'for the widow of any person slain in fight who may claim 11 months pay for herself and one third of that sum additional for each orphan unmarried at the time of the father's death. If there was no widow, and the mother of the slain was over 50 years of age, a widow and in indigent circumstances, she might claim the bounty as widow'.

One notable exception in the provision 'for the support of NCOs, their widows and orphans' was 'The Benefit Society of Non-Commissioned Officers of his Majesty's Coldstream Regiment of Foot Guards', which was in existence earlier than 1 February 1797, since on that date the fund was enrolled at the Quarter Sessions. A sergeant's subscription was fourpence, a corporal's two-pence per week: the benefits were pensions for life, varying according to length of service, and a sum of money to the family on decease in the regiment. In November 1824 the pension system was abolished, because 'the pensions granted were found to be too great for the stoppages'.[55]

SCHOOLS FOR THE CHILDREN

One benefit the Army provided for the soldier's family was a school for his children. We have seen that Charles II sent a schoolmaster to Tangier, where he would probably have taught the children part-time, his main responsibility being the education of the soldiers, since that was the regular practice by 1800.[56]

Thus the Regulations of the Rifle Corps state[57]:

> 'A school will be established in the Rifle Corps for the instruction of those who wish to fit themselves for the situation of NCO's, who are expected to be master of reading, writing and the four first rules of arithmetic. For one hour when the school is not likely to be occupied by the men of the regiment, the Sergeant schoolmaster is to give instruction to the children'.

Children paid 2d a week, the school being open every day, except Sunday, and had to be visited daily by the senior Orderly Officer. The soldiers' wives were required to send their children to school regularly, punctually, clean and tidily dressed. They were called to account, if they did not.

Once begun, regimental schools flourished, without State aid or recognition, supported, as Lord Palmerston said in Parliament in 1812 'by the zeal, intelligence and liberality of the officers, and by private contributions'.[58] Meanwhile, two military schools were founded, which were to become well-known for the education of army children.

On 18 April 1769, a petition was addressed to George III by philanthropic people in Ireland,

> 'appalled by the great numbers of Boys and Girls of soldiers serving in Ireland, and of Irish soldiers overseas, left destitute without either Publick or private Aid for their Sustenance, who had raised a Fund by public Subscription to support the Establishment of a Hospital in Order to preserve such objects from Poppery, Beggary and Idleness and to train them up so as to become usefull, Industrious Protestant Subjects'.[59]

The Petition was granted and The Royal Hibernian School was established in Dublin for 90 boys and 50 girls, the first British boarding school maintained by public funds. The King gave the site, the Irish Parliament gave a substantial grant and the public and regiments found the rest.

On 19 June 1801 the Duke of York, second son of George III, laid the foundation stone of the sister school — The Royal Military Asylum, Chelsea (now the Duke of York's Royal Military School Dover). The school was built on a site in Chelsea, purchased from a naval Captain, named George[60] and the original building still stands in the Duke of York's Headquarters in King's Road; George Street has been renamed Sloane Gardens. The school opened in 1803 with 150 boys and 50 girls but by 1809/10 the number had risen to 1140. They were clothed and fed to the age of 14, when most of the boys enlisted in the Army and the remainder apprenticed to trades: the girls mostly found situations as domestic servants or in the factories. The School was largely self-supporting, a proportion of the boys learning cobbling or tailoring in the workshops from Army Sergeant craftsmen (pensioners from the Royal Hospital Chelsea nearby) and some of the girls working under the seamstress or in the laundry.

On 1 January 1812 the Duke of York issued an Order establishing regimental Schools and sergeant schoolmasters at public expense and providing schoolrooms, winter fuel and money for stationery and books. All Generals and Commanding Officers were to take the regimental schools under their special protection. Regimental chaplains, as part of their duties, were 'to inspect and diligently supervise the schools and the conduct of the sergeant schoolmasters'.

> 'The aim is to give the Soldiers the Comfort of being assured, that the Education and Welfare of their Children are objects of their Sovereign's paternal Solicitude; and to raise from their Offspring a succession of Loyal Subjects, brave soldiers, and good Christians'.

In 1812 Parliament authorised the expenditure of £20,000 to cover the cost of the schools for soldiers' children. It was, as Palmerston said, a small beginning but the English educational system had to wait another 20 years before Parliament approved a financial grant for its own elementary schools!

The Duke of York, who, as described above, gave his name to the school and established the regimental schools for army children at public expense, was, according to Fortescue 'the best Commander in Chief the Army ever had'. Appointed in 1795, he commanded the British Army until 1827, except for a break during 1809–11, caused by the scandal over his mistress Mary Anne Clarke and 'the talk of female influence over the sale of commissions and officer promotions'. Married at 16 and early deserted by her husband, Mrs Clarke was forced to use the two assets she possessed — considerable physical charms and a complete lack of moral scruple — to support herself and her two children. She found that it was easier to get into the beds of the aristocracy than to get money from their pockets and, not surprisingly, she used her favoured position with her royal lover to put forward her own nominees for commissions at less than the official rates, (£400 for an ensign; £550 for a lieutenant; £1500 for a Captain and £2600 for a Majority). Called to account before the Bar of the House of Commons[61], the Army Commander and Mrs Clarke gave the lampoonists a field day:

> When we retire to bed,
> Enchain'd in love's embraces,
> A list is at the head,
> Of numsculls wanting places.

Despite his weaknesses for 'wine, women and song', the Duke's fatherly interest in the welfare of the rank and file and their families provided 'an admirable example of the influence for the Army's good of a Royal Commander-in-Chief.'[62]

Chapter 3

Aristocratic Ladies and Officers' Dependants

When Charles II entered London in May 1660 at the head of his Life Guards and five regiments of Foot to the peals of bells and the cheers of his people, his two most pressing problems were money and the future of his army. He solved the first 'in the simplest fashion, by marrying an heiress, Catherine, the 23 year old daughter of the King of Portugal, who brought him half a million in money, Bombay and Tangier and rich trading rights in the Orient and the Mediterranean'.[1]

Command of his army, he gave to General George Monck, archetype of the professional Royalist officer and later one of Cromwell's ablest generals, whom he created Duke of Albemarle. Monck owed some of his advancement to his wife Anne, formerly his mistress, whilst he had been imprisoned in the Tower for two years, after his capture at the Battle of Nantwich. Through a previous marriage to a servant in Prince Charles's household, she had used her influence in promoting her King's and her husband's causes and demonstrated the petticoat influence in military affairs, which was to be a feature, not only of Charles's court, but also of many of his Royal successors.[2]

Parliament was worried about the dangers of a Standing Army in peace-time and believed the evil could be averted by 'drawing the officers from that social class, the members of which are more likely to lose than to gain by Military Aggression. Therefore, as a rule, while the rank and file of the Army have been recruited from the lower stations of society, the command of these men has been entrusted to the higher class and never — save at the time of the Commonwealth — to any other'.[3] Places had to be found, too, in the commissioned ranks to reward the royalist supporters of the early Stuarts and of William of Orange (William III). John Russell, son of the Earl of Bedford, was given command of the 1st Foot Guards and Aubrey de Vere, the Earl of Oxford, became Colonel of the Royal Horse Guards (The Blues). Another was Robert Sidney, third son of the Earl of Leicester and friend of Charles in exile, who was given the colonelcy of the Holland Regiment (The Buffs). Command of the 2nd Foot (The Queen's Regiment) was given to Henry Mordaunt, 2nd Earl of Peterborough, who was later appointed Captain-General of Tangier, while Charles Churchill, brother of the Duke of Marlborough, and the 2nd Earl of Chesterfield became Colonel of the Buffs in their turn. James II, who added six regiments of cavalry and the 7th to 15th Regiments of the Line to the Standing Army during his brief reign, gave command to the Earls of Plymouth, Arran, Shrewsbury, Bath and Somerset, to Lord Lumley and to the Dukes of Beaufort and Norfolk amongst other noblemen.

Nearly all the Army officers were drawn from the landed and aristocratic classes, or from the minor gentry, who had the same status in England as the lesser nobles on the continent. Military service to the King had been the origin of the nobility and it was in their best interests as a class to support the monarchy and the constitution, from which their titles and privileges stemmed. The monarch was his own Commander-in-Chief and the fount of all high civil and military appointments: all commissions (except Engineer and Ordinance commissions and a few promotions from the ranks) were awarded by the Sovereign, even though purchased by the officers themselves, as investments for their future, since the State issued no military pensions.

During the 18th Century the number of officers, some 2000 in 1715, would double and the social mix would broaden. In 1769 32 out of 102 regimental colonels were peers (or sons of peers) and more than half had peerage connections. One in every four regimental officers would come from the nobility and landed gentry, whose birth and wealth would open up the highest ranks in the Army. Half of the officers would originate from the junior branches of good families, the lesser gentry, now engaged in trade or in the professions, gentlemen often without birth or much money, but able to obtain their commissions and promotions with the help of the great. The others, apart from a few older subalterns promoted from the ranks, would come from a wide spectrum of the other two groups — gentlemen of birth and education but without lands or wealth, whose sons would create a tradition of army families and — like the Churchills, Howards and Campbells seek a career — and some their fortunes — in military service.

Whatever the rights and wrongs of the purchase system, whereby an officer bought his first commission and then each step in his promotion up to and including colonelcies, or place in a more fashionable regiment, it brought into the Army, as Wellington said:

> 'men of fortune and character, men who have some connection with the interests and fortunes of the country, besides the commissions which they hold from His Majesty. It is this circumstance, which exempts the British army from the character of being a 'mercenary army' . . . Three fourths of the whole number receive but little for their service besides the honour of serving the King'.[3]

For most, this meant that an officer had to have wealth to purchase his ensign's commission (at least £400 in a regiment of Foot and more in a fashionable regiment) and another £200 or more for his uniform and equipment. His army pay[4] would be quite insufficient to meet his monthly expenses in the Mess, to maintain the living standards set in the Regiment by the Colonel and his brother officers and to follow the life style of a 'gentleman'

— to hunt, shoot, drink and entertain, to attend the Balls, concerts and fashionable events of London and County society. These pursuits and the natural inclinations of a wealthy and leisured class would involve the young officer in frequent absences from duty and lead to an unwillingness to stay with his regiment, when it was employed on distasteful service, especially in such an unhealthy and unpopular station as the West Indies.[5]

Marriage in such circumstances would not be practicable for most officers and out of the question for those without independent means, at least until they had reached the rank of Major. Sons were expected to make a suitable match and, since the family title and possessions were inherited by the eldest son, the younger sons, especially of an impoverished family, had to marry into money, often to be found in the richly-dowried daughters of city merchants and business men.

Charles II wrote to his sister, Minette, in France in 1664: 'I find the passion Love is very much out of fashion in this country, and that a handsome face without money has but few gallants, upon the score of marriage'.[6] The upper classes were expected to marry within their own class; marriage was a duty, not a romantic passion, and often a commercial transaction between two families. Sir William Temple, who married his sweetheart, Dorothy Osborne, in 1655, despite strong family opposition and who now lies buried beside her in Westminster Abbey, wrote: 'Our marriages are made, just like other common bargains and sales, by the mere consideration of interest or gain, without any love or esteem, or birth or of beauty itself'.[7] A proverb of the day put it more colloquially — 'Who marrieth for love without money hath good nights and sorry days'. If a woman defied the conventions of her class, she faced disinheritance and the loss of her dowry and the risk of being treated, as Sir Edward Coke, Speaker of the House of Commons and Attorney General, treated his daughter, Frances, when she refused to marry the hideous John Villiers and thus link her family with the wealthy and influential Buckinghams — 'He tied her to the bedposts and whipped her, till she consented to the match'. . .

The career of the noble but impoverished John Churchill, the future Duke of Marlborough, illustrated these conventions. At the age of seventeen, in 1667, and a page in the service of Charles's brother, James, Duke of York (the future James II), he was gazetted an ensign in the King's Regiment of Foot Guards (Grenadiers). Scandalmongers of the period said he owed his commission to the fact that his eldest sister, Arabella, was the Duke of York's mistress: if true, comments his biographer, Correlli Barnett, 'then it is fortunate for England and Europe that the Duke of York found her person so agreeable'.[8] 'But', recorded the Count de Grammont at the time 'all agreed that a man who was the favourite of the King's mistress and brother to the Duke of York's favourite was in a fair way of preferment and could not fail to make his fortune'.[9] In 1671, as a poor but very handsome young officer, lately returned from voluntary service with the English garrison in Tangier, Churchill attracted no small share of notice from the beauties of the court of Charles II and even awakened a passion in one of the royal mistresses herself, Barbara Villiers. Courtin, the French Ambassador, writing to his master Louis XIV in 1676, observed that 'Churchill had a reputation in London in the debauched Court circles in which he mixed, for trading on his fine figure and handsome face'. That sort of vice was frequent at the French court, where pretty fellows of high birth and light purses received money, jewels, and sometimes estates, from women of wealth and quality'.[10] Barbara, now at 29 the Duchess of Cleveland, made her handsome young lover a present of £5,000, which he invested as an annuity, and which laid the foundation of the Churchill family fortunes. When Charles discovered them in bed together, he said 'I forgive you, for you do it to get your bread'[11], and to remove a dangerous rival in her unsteady affections, gave him a company in the Foot Guards and sent him off to Flanders to campaign under the Duke of Monmouth. On his return to London, his brilliant military reputation and his personal qualities made him the idol of beauty and fashion and he plunged into the vortex of courtly dissipation. But the libertine in him died in 1675, when he first set eyes on the 15-year old Sarah Jennings, one of the many pretty maids of honour, with whom the Duchess of York surrounded herself.

Sarah came from modest country-gentry stock and, like Churchill, found that the Court offered the only source of advancement for the poor and gentleborn, whether able- or beautiful-bodied. Bringing down these 15 year old virgins from respectable families was the fashionable sport of the Court,[12] but Sarah considered herself above falling to a lecher and certainly not to Barbara Castlemaine's lover, however handsome and gallant a soldier he might be. Like her sister Frances '*La belle Jenyns*', who preferred marriage to Captain Sir George Hamilton of the King's Guards (a grandson of the Duke of Abercorn) to becoming the Duke of York's mistress, Sarah, too, wanted marriage — not to be just another 'great belly' at Court. For their part, Churchill's parents wanted him to make a successful match with the rich but plain heiress, Catherine Sedley, who replaced Arabella as the Duke of York's mistress, and establish the family fortune. But he wanted his Sarah.

Because of the opposition of his family, they married in secret in 1678 ('the only time Marlborough was ever forced to surrender', commented his famous descendant Sir Winston Churchill[13] 'and then only to a chit of 17'.) They started their married life with little money but with bright hopes for the future. It was a love-match, which was to last for the rest of their days, despite the frequent partings associated with army life, he campaigning abroad, she on duty with the Duchess of York. They now lie side by side in the Chapel at Blenheim Castle.

It was Sarah who largely built up the Churchill family fortune. In an age when most women, however high in rank, were but domestic and social appendages to their husbands, Sarah shrewdly invested in land and property to gain family, social and political power, obtaining 'the broad acres' needed for rank and status. Her friend, Queen Anne, made her husband a Duke in 1702 and their daughters married into the ranks of the highest and wealthiest in the land — the Blandfords and Godolphins, the Spencers and Montagus. Her granddaughter was the first Lady Diana Spencer, ancestor of the present Princess of Wales. For children, too, were a form of investment for upper class families. Titles could be traded for marriage settlements and inter-marriage gain money, power, privilege and high places. The Duke of Monmouth, Charles II's illegitimate son by Lucy Walters, was married at 14 to the extremely rich 12 year old heiress of the House of Buccleuch and later purchased command of the Life Guards for £10,000. General Sir Alan Cameron married a 13 year old schoolgirl and heiress and thereby advanced his own military career. In 1793 he founded the Cameron Highlanders (79th Foot) on the inheritance.[14] Breeding was a wifely duty; pleasure and wantonness could be left to whores and mistresses. Royalty set the pace, both in mistresses and children — for George II had nine children, as did his eldest son: George III had fifteen.

The beauties of Charles II's court, whether wife or mistress, founded a number of army families, some of which continue to this day. Arabella Churchill's eldest son (by the Duke of York) became the famous Marshal de Berwick, one of the greatest soldiers of the 18th Century, while her daughter, Lady Henrietta, married the first Earl Waldegrave, whose son followed in the footsteps of her uncle the Duke of Marlborough. Arabella married Colonel Charles Godfrey. Frances Jennings, after her first husband Captain George Hamilton had been killed in battle, married Richard Talbot, Earl of Tyrconnel, who commanded James II's forces in Ireland. Three daughters married Viscounts and a son commanded the 5th Foot. The wealthy heiress, Lady Elizabeth Percy, Countess of Ogle, married at 15 the 6th Duke of Somerset, Colonel of the 3rd Hussars, and her son, the Earl of Hertford, distinguished himself in the Marlborough Wars as Colonel of the 15th Foot and of the 2nd Troop of Horse Guards.[14]

The loveliest was Barbara Villiers (1641–1709), whose rich auburn hair, dark blue eyes and voluptuous figure so enchanted all contemporaries and especially Samuel Pepys. Her beauty and sensuality attracted the King and she became his acknowledged mistress. Their three sons, Charles, Henry and George Fitzroy (*fils du roi*) were created Dukes of Southampton, Grafton and Northumberland respectively, while their daughters married the Earls of Sussex and Lichfield. She was herself nobly born, the daughter of an officer and peer, Colonel-General, Viscount Grandison, who was killed at the head of his regiment at the siege of Bristol in 1643.[14] At 15, she became the mistress of the 2nd Earl of Chesterfield (Colonel of the 3rd Foot) who gave her a taste for high living. At 18 her mother married her off to another Royalist, a law student of the Inner Temple and heir to a considerable fortune, Roger Palmer, who was created Earl of Castlemaine in 1661 by Charles to ensure Barbara's social respectability.

Ten years later, Charles created her Duchess of Cleveland[15] and lavished money and honours upon her to compensate for her demotion from the royal bed. As we have noted, she left her five children by Charles with fine titles and good prospects. Rich heiresses were found as child brides for the three sons and Henry was appointed Colonel of the Grenadier Guards (1681) and George of the Horse Guards (1685). Barbara was related to the Villiers (Buckinghams) whose blood is in our present Queen Elizabeth and in a number of aristocratic families, producing no less than 13 Prime Ministers and a long tradition of officer service to the Crown.

In 1705, after 40 years of a marriage, which had been a mere mockery, she became a widow: but within four months, at the age of 64, she became an army wife — or so she believed! Her choice was Robert Fielding, a Major General of the Earl of Denbigh's family, claiming descent from the Counts of Habsburg.[16] Having married two heiresses in succession, he was now a widower and looking for a third.

As soon as he had married her, he moved in with his bride and began to fleece her. He would have left her with nothing had not her grandson, the young Duke of Grafton, discovered that Fielding had married another woman two weeks earlier, mistaking this recent inmate of Bridewell for the rich widow she pretended to be. Fielding was arrested and committed to Newgate.

So his marriage to the Duchess was brief and stormy: it was declared null and void. Although he received a pardon from Queen Anne, he ended his days in the Fleet prison for debt.

A line of distinguished and high ranking military officers resulted from Charles's liaison with his next mistress, the 20 year old French Maid of Honour Louise de Kéroualle. Her aristocratic but impoverished condition left her little choice — either 'to yield unreservedly to the King or to retire to a French convent'. She capitulated[17] and in due course having pleasured the King received her reward when, after a shorter period of probation than Barbara Villiers, Charles created her Duchess of Portsmouth and spent vast sums of money on her. Their son, Charles Lennox,[18] became the first Duke of Richmond. He married Anne, the daughter of Lord Brudenell, son and heir of the Earl of Cardigan. William III took him as his ADC and he served with distinction in Flanders.[18]

His son, the 2nd Duke of Richmond, was Colonel of the Royal Horse Guards (1750), fought at Dettingen and against the Jacobites, became a General and Member of Parliament for Chichester. At the age of 18 he was married (1719) to the 13 year old Sarah, heir of Marlborough's favourite General, the 1st Earl of Cadogan in order, it is said, to cancel a gambling debt between the two families. The marriage was not consummated, as she returned to school and he set off on his travels. Three years later he returned to London, 'where at a theatre he admired an unknown lady, the reigning toast of society. He discovered she was his wife, the beautiful Lady March'. Their marriage proved a very happy one and she bore him 12 children. Their eldest son (3rd Duke) became a Field Marshal and also Colonel of 'The Blues', and distinguished himself at the Battle of Minden. He married a descendant of Robert Bruce. We shall meet the 4th and 5th Dukes later at the Battle of Waterloo.

'I can't bear when women of quality marry one don't know whom!' said George II to the widowed Lady Pembroke, who had just married Captain Bernard North-Ludlow of no birth or fortune.

For an aristocratic girl to marry a poor army officer, even though nobly born, could bring social and family disapproval — as Lady Sarah Lennox, fourth daughter of the 3rd Duke of Richmond found. She married at the age of 17 the famous racing baronet Sir Charles Bunbury, many years her senior, who was more interested in breeding horses than children. (He was the owner of the first Derby winner, Diomed). She left her husband and lived for 12 years with her cousin Lord William Gordon, without reproach by her father, the Duke of Richmond, even though she was divorced from her husband in 1776. But then she committed the social blunder of marrying in 1781, the Hon George Napier (1751–1804) (the sixth of the ten sons of the 6th Lord Napier), who served throughout the American War of Independence.

George Napier had lost his first wife Elizabeth, daughter of an Army Captain, and his children to yellow fever in America and was himself put on board ship seemingly dying but he recovered. His only crimes were that he was poor and honest. Lady Sarah had an income of £500 a year, and Colonel Napier's army pay was slightly less. He became Quarter-Master General in Ireland in 1794 and Controller of Army Accounts in 1799 and could have made a fortune as others had done before him. The result of his honesty and comparative poverty was that both he and his wife were despised as poor relations. As some recompense, perhaps, they had five sons and three daughters, among the former being the distinguished soldiers General Charles James Napier (Conqueror of Scinde), General George Thomas Napier (Governor of the Cape of Good Hope), General William Francis (Historian of the Peninsular War) and Henry Edward Napier, Captain, Royal Navy and historian. Sarah died in 1826 aged 88 and was said to be last surviving great granddaughter of Charles II.[18]

General Charles adored his mother and only married after her death. Like many nineteenth century officers, he believed marriage hindered a military career, preferring mistresses instead, by whom he had a number of illegitimate children. When he did marry at the age of 44, he married two widows in succession, both almost old enough to have been his mother.

A matrimonial story of another kind concerned James Wolfe, the hero of

Quebec, whose ancestors emigrated from Glamorganshire to Ireland in the 15th century, in company with other impoverished and adventurous English gentry, many of whose sons served in the army. His father, one of Marlborough's officers in the 3rd Foot Guards, married, when over 40 and with the rank of Lieutenant Colonel, a young beauty of 24, of the landed gentry but with no money. He settled in Westerham, Kent, where his son James was born in 1727, to be near the Court and favour. He was thus nicely placed to obtain for his son a commission at an early age and to watch over James's ambition to succeed in his chosen army career. James had a contempt, however, for the soldier of fashion and of the court and attained the rank of Lieutenant Colonel, largely by force of character and personal merit, at the early age of 22.

Love always came a poor second to his army career. In 1752 he wrote:

> 'There is a great probability that I shall never marry. I shall hardly engage in an affair of that nature purely for money. Unless some gentle nymph persuade me to marriage, I had much rather listen to the drum and trumpet than any softer sound whatever'.[19]

But like many another of his generation, he saw nothing immoral in seeking a good match and his mother cast around to find an heiress for him. Her choice fell on a Miss Hoskins of Croydon, plain but with a dowry of £30,000, but to Wolfe's relief someone else carried her off. He preferred a Miss Elizabeth Lawson, niece of his Brigade Commander in Scotland, General Sir John Mordaunt, beautiful but considered a woman of inadequate fortune by his mother.

Wolfe's forebodings, that he might never marry, proved correct. In the last few months of his life he became engaged, just before he sailed for America in 1759, to a Miss Katherine Lowther, sister of Sir James Lowther, Earl Lonsdale. She was Mrs Wolfe's neighbour at Bath and one of the most fashionable women of the day. While he was at sea, his earlier love, Miss Lawson, died unmarried despite many suitors. Miss Lowther soon after Wolfe's death married Admiral the Duke of Bolton.[20]

Although marriage outside one's class was frowned upon by the aristocracy, beauty created its own rules. 'A pretty girl, a good dancer, and showy rider', wrote Captain Gronow, 'will have more partners and invitations than Lady Drystick, with her ancient pedigree and aristocratic airs'.[21] This was especially true when it concerned 'actresses' who first appeared professionally after the Restoration. It quickly became fashionable for men about town, including the military, to take an actress as a mistress — and even as a wife!

Such horizontal elevations had royal precedents. Among Charles II's actress friends were Moll Davis, the illegitimate daughter of a Colonel of the well-known Howard family and Nell Gwynne whose father, an impoverished Captain in the Royalist Army, married beneath him and died in a debtor's prison in Oxford. Nell's wit and nubile beauty first caught the eye of the actor manager Charles Hart and then of the philandering Lord Buckhurst, who 'particularly admired her fine bosom and shapely thighs'[22], before she became the King's mistress at the age of 17.

Charles created their elder son Duke of St Albans and appointed him Colonel of Princess Anne of Denmark's Regiment of Horse (8th Horse). In 1694 he married Lady Diana de Vere, a noted beauty of high lineage and the sole heiress of the Earl of Oxford, Colonel of the 'Blues', who married the beautiful Court courtesan Diana Kirke. A granddaughter of the marriage linked the family to that of the Duke of Marlborough. Moll Davis became the mother of Mary Tudor, who at 14 was married to the future Earl of Derwentwater, while Peg Hughes became the mistress of the King's cousin, Prince Rupert, and their daughter Ruperta married General Emanuel Howe, whose illustrious military descendants included Brigadier Lord George Howe (killed leading the attack on Fort Ticonderoga (1758), Admiral Richard Howe (who relieved Gibraltar) and General Sir William Howe (Commander-in-Chief in America).

Actresses, claimed the straight-laced Evelyn in his Diary (1666), were 'foul and indecent women, which inflaming several young noblemen and gallants, became their whores and to some their wives'. The word 'actress' soon became synonymous with 'courtesan' and 'kept woman', as girls, poor and of humble birth, saw in the bawdy roles of Restoration comedy an opportunity to display their charms and catch a rich admirer. 'It was hard for a pretty woman to keep herself honest in a Theatre, as 'tis for an apothecary to keep his Treacle from the Flies in the hot weather; for every Libertine in the audience will be buzzing about her Honey-pot', wrote a contemporary.[23] Such liaisons were not confined to the Restoration, for, down to the present day, actresses have fascinated the aristocracy and the Brigade of Guards from Mistress Gwynne to the Gaiety Girls, from Mrs Dorothea Jordan, who bore William IV ten children, to the Countess of Derby (Eliza Farren in 1797).

The first professional English actress to win a peer was Anastasia Robinson who married (1722) the 60 year old General Charles Mordaunt, 3rd Earl of Peterborough, while Lavinia Fenton ('pretty Polly Peacham') became the stage's first Duchess (1751), when she married the 3rd Duke of Bolton, Colonel of the Horse Guards. The beautiful Louisa Brunton married General Uffington, 1st Earl of Craven (1807), while the 4th Earl of Harrington, a Major General (late Coldstream Guards) and one time leader of the 'bucks' in Regency society, met his match in Maria Foote, who became his Countess in 1831. Far from being 'foul and indecent', such actresses (37 between 1722 and 1935) have brought youthful vivacity and charm to many a connubial bed and produced many generations of officers who have served with distinction in the armed forces of the Crown.[24]

Early marriage for the young officers, especially of the Guards and Household Cavalry, was discouraged by their profession, whatever their natural inclinations. 'Few Guards or Household Cavalry officers deigned to marry, while serving their Regiments', comments Russell Braddon,[25] 'perhaps because the Season offered pickings too easy, and procureurs provided bed-mates too diverse for marriage to be attractive'. It was pardonable for a young officer to fall in love with a beauty of a lower station, but not to marry her. The sowing of wild oats before settling down to the responsibilities of a husband, moreover, was fashionable in the upper class 18th Century society, and initiation by mature married women was more advisable than with ladies of the town, shop girls or maidservants, who could be troublesome over family settlements. For those officers stationed in or around London the attractions of the Capital and of the Season were compelling, especially if they had the wealth to indulge their tastes or could obtain the necessary credit from their bankers. According to *The Times*, for example, the officers of the 10th Hussars whose Colonel in Chief was The Prince of Wales (George IV) 'associate with no one but their own corps. Most of them keep their own blood horses and their girls.'[26]

Lord William Alvanley, who had purchased a commission in the Coldstream Guards in 1804 at the age of fifteen, and who, with his friend Cornet 'Beau' Brummell of the 10th Hussars, was one of the dandies of Regency society, received from his Banker's Agent, the following account, dated 7 December 1808, asking for early settlement, before he left for Spain.[25]

(Lloyd's Bank, London, have given special permission for this account to be used.)

6 Months' Account (Messrs Lloyd's Bank Ltd) Cox's & King's Branch.

	£	s.
Lady	5	0
Ditto a country girl	2	2
The same	2	2
One night Mrs. Dubois (grande blonde)	5	5
Few days after at daytime	2	2
11th. June Modest girl	3	3
26th. June Sunday morning	2	2
27th. June by particular appointment	5	5
1st. July An American Lady	10	10
Lately one night with Eliza Farquhar	3	3
30th. November	2	2
1st. December	3	3
4th. December	3	3
11th. December. All night Miss N from the Boarding School, Chelsea	5	5

Signed Derville (Agent)

It was the same in the fashionable Cavalry regiments. Edward Ball Hughes, for example, was blessed with a wealthy uncle, Admiral Hughes, who not only purchased for him a cornetcy in the 7th Queen's Own Hussars in 1817 but also gave him a handsome allowance and, a little later, an inheritance of £40,000 a year. With his fortune and his remarkable good looks, this 18 year old subaltern was 'courted, followed and admired by everyone who had daughters to dispose of. He was devoted to female society; no dinner, ball, picnic or party was complete, unless the popular millionaire formed one of the social circle. Having been jilted by his Colonel's daughter, Lady Jane Paget, Ball fell under the spell of a 15 year old Spanish danseuse, Senorita Mercandotti, said by some to be the protegée, by others the natural daughter of Lord Fife', records the regimental history.[27]

She gained a huge reputation on the stages of Madrid, Paris and London and was the target of many eligible young bachelors. When she finally fell to the 'Golden Ball', a wag commented:

'The fair damsel is gone; and no wonder at all
That, bred to the dance, she is gone to a Ball'.

One fruitful meeting place during the 18th Century for officers and County ladies to pursue their social life of Balls, concerts and entertainment, was the Assembly Room to be found in every county town. Here fashionable society enjoyed the opportunities for 'gallantry and play'. A contemporary wrote:

'By means of these Assemblies, matches are struck up and the Officers of the Army had pretty good Success, where Ladies are at their own disposal'.[28]

The social historian, Laurence Stone[28], summarised upper-class marriages thus — 'During the 17th Century, the squirarchy married within the county and all strata of society drew their brides from a limited social and geographical range. During the 18th Century the development of a national marriage market through the London and Bath seasons greatly widened for them (as it did for the aristocracy in the 17th Century) the pool of potentially satisfactory spouses with the necessary financial and social qualifications.'[28]

WIDOWS AND CHILDREN

The treatment of officers' dependants was at first a regimental responsibility. Orphans were commissioned into the regiment in the father's vacancy, a practice often abused, so that orders had to be issued to ensure that regiments ordered overseas were not rendered unserviceable by carrying a large number of 'officers' who were safe abed in their swaddling clothes in England.[29] An Order of 1705 did, however, recognise the children of officers, who had been slain or suffered extremely in the service. There were never to be more than two such in any regiment and when the regiment went overseas these two were to be cross-posted with officers in regiments remaining at home, so that the regiment could go overseas with a full establishment of officers.

Marlborough expanded this regimental provision for orphans into a theatre scheme for the succour of widows, by which all officers voluntarily subscribed 'for the support of their widows, whose husbands were actually killed or died of their wounds'. The 'Queen's Bounty' provided for yearly payments of £50 to the widow of a colonel and £40, £30, £26, £20 and £16 for the widows of a lieutenant colonel, major, captain, lieutenant and of an ensign respectively. The widow had to swear an oath before a Justice of the Peace that she had no pension or allowance from the Crown and no reasonable maintenance left by her husband. The bounty was to cease on remarriage or death. 99 officers' 'relics' drew pensions in 1697, for example.

By a Royal Warrant of 25 June 1806 the pension of officers' widows was increased to £80, £60, £40, £26 and £20, for the widows of colonels, lieutenant colonels, captains, ensigns and chaplains respectively, because of the 'increased cost of living and to a level more appropriate to their husband's former appointment in the Army'.

THE BATTLE OF WATERLOO

The position of Widows' Pensions at the time of the Battle of Waterloo was summarised in Major Charles James's Military Dictionary of 1816 —

> 'The widows of all commissioned officers belonging to the British service are entitled to receive a certain annual allowance, according to the several ranks of their husbands. Instructions to this end are signed by the King and lodged with the Paymasters General. The widows of warrant officers are not included in the regulations, but sometimes the King has granted a pension of £15 a year to the widow of a quarter-master of dragoons, who is a warrant officer, when His Majesty has thought such a widow a proper object of his bounty'.

As for the widows and orphans of soldiers killed at Waterloo, a grateful Government and public collected some £350,000 and invested it to provide annuities for them.

If an officer died in the service the money he paid for his commission was lost to his family but these regulations were modified in March 1856 to sanction 'the repayment to an officer's widow, children, or other relations, of the regulation price paid for his commissions, provided the officer has been killed in action or has died of wounds received in the face of the enemy, within 6 months after being wounded'.[30]

Chapter 4

Following the Drum Overseas

During the 18th Century Britain's overseas possessions increased and troops garrisoned the Channel Islands, the Mediterranean islands of Gibraltar and Minorca and the Colonial Plantations in America, Canada and the West Indies. There were campaigns to be fought on the continents of Europe, America and India. Wherever the troops were stationed, fought and died, the soldiers' wives or 'army women' went with them, sharing their dangers and privations. Conditions varied with climate and terrain, but service in nearly all of them was unpopular with officers, the men and their wives. In North America they felt alien and unwelcome; in the West Indies, so appalling was the mortality rate from fever and other health hazards that to be posted to any island in the Caribbean was tantamount to a death sentence. Indeed, convicted murderers were released from prison, if they would agree to serve in the West Indies. In 1795, the 15th Foot (East Yorkshire Regiment) was ordered to Dominica to help to quell a Negro Insurrection and took 102 women with them. When the regiment returned a few years later only seven wives came home.[1] Yet women and children survived, tough and resourceful, sometimes a nuisance but often courageous in the face of danger.

UNDER SIEGE IN GIBRALTAR

Because of its dominating position at the entrance to the Mediterranean, Gibraltar has been settled and fought for by Romans, Moors, the Spanish and the British. Between 1704 and 1783, the Rock survived 14 sieges, as the Spaniards tried to recapture it, the last being the most notable. Army wives and children took part in them all, except the first, when the Spanish Governor surrendered Gibraltar to the British in 1704.

The first officially recognised wives arrived in 1710 with the relieving regiments and shivered with them in the bleak winters. They were hungry and stricken with disease from exposure and poor food. Off duty, the soldiers and their wives had little to do to alleviate the constant boredom but drinking. Drunkenness became so prevalent that floggings featured daily on the morning parade:

'Here is nothing to do nor any news . . . but the harmless diversions of drinking, dancing, revelling, whoring, gaming and other innocent debaucheries to pass the time: Sodom and Gomorrah were not half so wicked and profane as this worthy city and garrison of Gibraltar', wrote a soldier in his diary for 2nd January 1728.[2]

All camp followers came under the Articles of War 1722 for discipline and could be 'tried in Gibraltar, Minorca or in any Place beyond the Seas, where there is no form of our Civil Judicature in Force'. They could be flogged for drunkenness and plunder. For example, Mrs Drake, belonging to the Artillery, Mrs Mitchal and Mrs Clarke 'were flogged thro' the camp for buying and receiving stolen goods from the Plunderers; one of them was an honest Midwife who will be of great loss to the Garrison, if she is sent out as order'd, for we marry and breed faster than ever known in peaceable times'.

Their punishment was to be stripped to the waist and to receive one dozen lashes on their bare backs with the cat-of-nine-tails by the hands of the Common Hangman, 'having at the same time a label apprising their crime, pinned to their respective breasts'.[3]

The degrading whirligig, reserved 'for unruly and lewd women', was a punishment often used during the sieges as an amusement and diversion to raise the morale of the weary soldiers.

Entries in the Garrison Order Book

13 March 1727. After being confined to the black hole or dungeon for the space of a night, the next day a poor lady by name of Chidley was conducted to a whirligig. It contains room enough for one person. It is fixed between two swivels, so is turned round till it makes the person a little giddy and landsick. This office was performed by two of the private gentlemen of the garrison for the space of an hour in the market place, being well attended. All this was to oblige her for the too frequent bestowing of her favours.[4]

17 March 1727. Mrs Malone committed to the whirligig for 2 hours. It gave great pleasure to the spectators.

2 December 1727. Yesterday, a private soldier desired leave to marry a woman of the town, but instead of receiving an answer in the affirmative, was sent to cool his courage in the black hole for the night and this morning for breakfast received one hundred lashes for presuming to marry a lady of no good reputation.

Next day the soldier, despite his bleeding back, again asked his commanding officer 'to marry the lady for whom he had the honour to suffer'. The Commanding Officer, 'in consideration of his sufferings and undaunted gallantry', relented and the nuptials were celebrated 'with great splendour that afternoon' (much to the disappointment of her other lovers).

January 1728 a gentlewoman of the Foot Guards was pinioned in the market place, with her neck and hands fastened by chains. The time of suffering is 3 hours.

7 February 1728. Came in a ship from Ireland laden with women, from whence come great numbers of these necessary evils.

The troops felt forgotten and neglected, especially when they were left for long periods of service on the Rock. The 6th and 13th Regiments of Foot almost mutinied over their length of tours of duty there — the 13th Foot for instance, served in Gibraltar for 28 years continuously from 1710 to 1738. In November 1760, soldiers again watched other units going home, leaving them behind, together with some of the unit wives, who had not obtained the obligatory health certificates from the regimental surgeons, declaring 'upon honour they are neither pox'd or clapp'd, as none will be received on board, without such certificate'.[5]

During the intervals of peace, the officers lived well in their messes, giving weekly dances, visiting and receiving hospitality from the neighbouring Spanish towns and manor houses. Colonel Thomas James,[6] who served in the garrison 1749–55, described the women he had known around Gibraltar:

> 'For a complete woman, let her be English to the neck, French to the waist, and Dutch below: and for hands and feet, let them be Spanish.
> Let the French women grace the dance, the Dutch women the kitchen, the Italian the window, the English the board and the Spanish lady the bed.
> This may be: but no nation can boast of having their women so complete in general as the English'.

In 1777, the civilian population was 3,200 and the military garrison 4,000 men, 500 women and 1,000 children, many of whom were 'unrecognised' by the Army and lived on what their husbands could provide from their pay and rations.

The Great Siege of Gibraltar lasted from 1779 to 1783, during which the Rock endured a continual blockade by the French and Spanish fleets and soldiers, reducing the survivors to near starvation. The Rock stood firm. The honour of firing the first shot was given to the wife of Lieutenant Skinner, who had only been married a month.

Mrs Miriam Green, wife of Lieutenant Colonel (later General Sir) William Green, Chief Engineer, who was largely responsible for strengthening Gibraltar's defences, kept a diary of the Siege.[7] She was the eldest daughter of a Colonel of the Engineers and her son commanded the 1st Royals. The house (Mount Pleasant) which the Greens built in Gibraltar is now the official residence of the Senior Naval Officer. She described the shortage of food and 'great complaints for want of fresh provisions': the onslaughts of small-pox which 'carried off during the first 6 months of 1780 more than 500, including 50 soldiers, while their poor families are greatly thinned'. Occasionally, boats got through to revictual and reinforce the garrison and to evacuate 'the useless mouths' of women and children.

Admiral Rodney, for instance, landed 1,000 73rd Highlanders in January 1780 and removed the women and children without 12 months' reserve of food. But amid the suffering 'Mrs Rogers married this evening (27 February 1781) to Lieutenant Wilks of Artillery'.

She described the severe bombardment of 1781 which forced her to join other garrison families in temporary huts in the South of the Rock. Catherine Upton,[8] wife of an Ensign, wrote 'That night, my husband and I lay among 100 soldiers, screened by a curtain. The 'silken sons of ease' in England know not what the Army have endured in Gibraltar'. Samual Ancell (58th Foot) recorded. 'A husband is called upon for duty: on his return his wife is no more and his beloved children are now reduced to lifeless lumps of clay'.[9]

During July 1781 Mrs Green sailed for home, a sick woman, worn out by the privations of the Siege. With her went 140 women and children, handed over by the Spaniards, who had captured them aboard vessels which had left the Rock three months earlier. Mrs Green died in England in 1782 from a chill, originally contracted in the dark and damp bomb-proofs of Gibraltar.

In October 1782 Admiral Richard Howe's fleet carried out the third and final relief of Gibraltar and hostilities ceased in 1783.

In 1802 the 54th Foot returned to duty in Gibraltar, 'with fond memories of their former drinking and whoring on the Rock' but to their dismay they found a new regime under a new Commander, the 35 year old Duke of Kent, son of George III. Strict discipline was maintained by severe floggings. So harsh were his methods that the Garrison mutinied and the Duke was recalled. For 27 years the Duke lived with his French mistress, Madame de Saint Laurent (whom he lodged in a farmhouse beyond San Roque during his service in Gibraltar), until the need for an heir to the throne, forced him to put his mistress into a Paris convent. At the age of 51 he fathered the child who was to become Queen Victoria.

Garrison Standing Orders, published by him in 1803, contained instructions for the married families. 'Commanding Officers are ordered to ensure the inspection, by frequent visits, of the Huts and Sheds occupied by the Married People, to see that they are kept decent and clean and to confine anybody in a state of intoxication'. 'Any NCO's or soldier's wife who shall at any time presume to charge for her washing more than the price established by the Board of Regimental Colonels is to be confined in the Provost (Guard Room) on bread and water, until an opportunity offers of turning her out of the Garrison'.[10]

But conditions for the unrecognised women were desperate. 'When a regiment comes here it brings with it, of course, no more than the regulated number, or six women to every hundred men. But it has scarce taken up its quarters, when every potato ship brings shoals of deluded women, who have taken the earliest opportunity of following their lords'.[11] These women received no accommodation or rations and were forced to live on their husband's pay 'and a private soldier has little to spare for pin-money'.

An officer's wife saw their position as pitiful, without a helping hand 'a prey for every low vice'. Many were forced into some form of prostitution or more often into the protection of one man, in order to survive.

During the Peninsular War, Gibraltar became the Navy's refuge, storehouse and dockyard. It helped to defeat the Spanish Grand Fleet at Cape Saint Vincent and Napoleon off Trafalgar. It received Nelson's body, before it was taken back to England on the 'Victory', when the ship docked there for repairs. His dead lie buried on the Rock, amid the graves of army soldiers and their families.

NEW SOUTH WALES

New South Wales and Van Diemen's Land (renamed Tasmania in 1855) were used as convict settlements from 1788 to 1839, during which 122,600 men and 24,900 women were transported there. From 1810, guards for the convicts were provided by Line regiments, two being stationed in New South Wales and one in Brisbane, Queensland, each with its small groups of officers' ladies and authorised wives and children. The Records of the 57th Foot (West Middlesex Regiment), for example, show that between October 1824 and November 1825, 73 women and 101 children accompanied the 563 Other Ranks to guard the convicts on Norfolk and Melville Islands, at Moreton Bay and in Van Diemen's Land.[12]

The first convoy of 700 convicts, including 188 females, was escorted by 400 troops and officials: the second by the specially formed New South Wales Corps. 'Every man on board took a wife from among the convicts, they nothing loath'.[12] Later convoys brought selected female convicts 'of marriageable age', as part of the Government's policy to colonise Australia. When the ships docked, the upper deck became 'a slave market — the female convicts washed and dressed for the occasion'. Military officers had the first choice, then the NCOs and private soldiers, followed by ex-convict settlers, 'such liaisons being free of legal ties'. The 'rejected' were sent up-river to the Female Factory at Parramatta to make convict uniforms. It became the colony's main marriage market (a second was built at Hobart in 1827), where settlers came to select a 'Factory lass' for a mate, from among women, brutalised by their circumstances, without any rights 'save to be fed'.[12]

There was a prison, housing both male and female convicts, in Sidney —

> 'Sometimes in the morning the shrieks of convicts being flogged in the prison yard could be heard above the ordinary tumult of city life, but as evening drew in all these sights and sounds miraculously ceased', recorded the Official History.[13] 'No signs of the penal community were visible: the regimental band played after evening parade in the barrack yard; the citizens gathered round to listen and nothing could be seen but gaiety and prosperity'.

So much did the military like Australia that the Colonel of the 4th Foot sold his commission and settled down with his family to civilian life and six of the officers married during the Regiment's eight years' duty there. Here, too, Major A. C. Innes of the 3rd Foot (East Kent Regiment), which escorted batches of convicts from Deptford to New South Wales in 1822, married the daughter of the Colonial Secretary (Macleay), settled and made a fortune cattle- and horse-rearing around Port Macquarie, where some of the Buffs' 96 Peninsular War veterans were discharged in 1826; 'some of whom have large families and wish to remain here'.[14]

NORTH AMERICA

The 18th Century saw the colonial struggle between France and England culminate in English supremacy during the Seven Years War (1756–1763), thanks largely to the victories of Clive in India and Wolfe in Canada. North America was the principal theatre for Pitt, England's Prime Minister, with Quebec the key to the capture of Canada. Quebec was the centre of a system of forts, built by the French to block the westward expansion of the British settlers. In 1665, it was a small trading post, which Louis XIV determined to transform into a French province. First, the population had to be increased, which was achieved by 'the importation of assorted consignments of nubile but dowerless wenches willing to marry anyone in a position to provide them with a home. Bridegrooms singled out their Brides, just as a Butcher does a Ewe from amongst a Flock of Sheep', wrote one of the garrison. 'There was as much variety of size and shape and colour, and change of Diet as could satisfy the most whimsical appetite'.[15] Such business transactions doubled the population of 3,000 in three years.

Pitt sent a large force of 24,000 men, supported by some 20,000 American Provincial troops, to North America and a large contingent of army women went too. These numbers were greatly increased as young soldiers took wives in the colonies and by the customary addition of camp followers, especially where the troops were stationed in one place for any length of time. 'The majority of the soldiers' women in America were legally married and most of the rest enjoyed fairly stable common-law relations', concluded a recent American researcher.[16] Whether they were protected from female blandishments by the following old colonial statute (still unrepealed in 1889) is not stated —

> 'All women whatever age, profession or rank, whether maids or widows, who shall, after this Act, impose upon, seduce or betray into matrimony any of His Majesty's subjects, by virtue of scents, cosmetics, washes, paints, artificial teeth, false hair or high-heeled shoes shall incur the penalty now in force against witchcraft and like misdemeanours'.[17]

MARRIAGE

What is certain is that the Army in America carried out a similar marriage policy to that at home. Marriage was to be discouraged: there must be official permission: the women's characters must be investigated and only those who were useful were to be encouraged. For example — General Wolfe, as he had done at home when commanding his regiment, threatened severe punishment for any soldier in his army who married without consulting his superiors, in order that 'the Woman's Character may be enquired into'. He reminded his officers 'to disencourage Matrimoney amongst the men as much as possible: the Service Suffers by the Multitude of Women already in the Regiment'.[18]

It is difficult to determine the number of women authorised to accompany their units, numbers varying according to commander and circumstances. General Edward Braddock's Orderly Books[19] show that in May 1755 he authorised six women per company in each of the two Regiments and the Independent Companies, four women in each company of Carpenter's

Virginia and Maryland Rangers, five women in the troops of Light Horse and in 'the detachment of seamen' (Marines) and five in the Artillery detachments — 'and only provisions of that number will be supplied'. [Rations were free, half of the soldier's to each woman and a quarter for each child]. The women of each Regiment were to march with the Provost and 'none upon any account are to appear with the men under arms'. In June he ordered that 'no more than two women per Company to be allowed to march from the Camp: a list of names of the women allowed to stay with the troops to be given to the Brigade Major and any woman that is found in the camp and whose name is not on that list will, for the first time be severely punished and for the second suffer Death'.

In another Order, Braddock noted that a greater number of women had been 'brought over' than allowed by the Government for washing 'with a view that the Hospital might be served'. These women were 'to serve for sixpence per day and their Provisions'.

The Regimental Orders of the 42nd Foot, dated 15 May 1759, stated 'The Commanding Officers of Companies to give in the women's names they intend should receive the allowance for provisions this campaign and are to recommend the first that came with the Regiment from Europe, if they are willing to be nurses to the General Hospital when required. They are not to exceed four per Company, according to General Orders'.[20] The King victuals the women, in order to render them useful to the men, General Murray reminded his commanders.

The women, as Camp Followers, were subject to Military Law:

'The Articles of War to be read tomorrow morning, at which time the servants, women and followers of the army are to attend with the respective corps and companies that they belong to'.[21]

250 lashes without a Court-Martial was the punishment for any Sutler caught giving 'any liquor to the Indians' and any soldier or woman caught outside the boundaries of the Camp without a regimental pass was 'to be tyed up and given 50 lashes'. Death was the penalty for 'any sutler or woman stealing, purloining or wasting army provisions'.[21]

Louisburg 1747: Private Daniel Buckley — tried by court-martial for the murder of Sergeant John Gorman. Admitted the act, but justified the murder because the Sergeant had 'been keeping company with and debauching his wife, while Buckley was on guard'. The Sergeant had promised his Company Commander he would desist but had not kept his promise. Found guilty. Sentenced to death but pardoned. *Lydia Buckley (his wife)* — 'Drum'd out of the Fort' at the Cart's Tail, duck'd and sent to Boston for trial by the civil magistrates.[22]

Although some army officers considered the embarkation of the wives helped recruiting or at least prevented desertion, others believed that army women debauched the troops or spread venereal diseases. For instance, in October 1749 James Wolfe ordered 'If any woman in the Regiment has a Venereal Disorder, and does not immediately make it known to the Surgeon, they shall upon the first discovery, be drum'd out of the Regiment, and be imprison'd in the Tolbooth, if ever she returns to the Corps'[23] General Braddock, three times within one month ordered his soldiers' wives to be examined to ensure they were 'clean' and added that the women who were not so, or who tried to avoid examination, were to be barred from marching with them.[23]

DANGERS OF ARMY WOMEN

As General Wolfe waited to attack Quebec in 1759 we catch glimpses of the dangers and difficulties of the army women. Ensign John Knox, who was able to purchase a commission in the 43rd Foot (Oxford Light Infantry) after his marriage to a wealthy woman in Cork in 1751, wrote:

> 'The swarming flies, short rations, dysentery and scurvy were as plaguing as the painted Red Indians, prowling around the old posts with tomahawks and scalping knives. The only relief was in the almost lethal spirits provided by the women sutlers, whose petticoats and leather stays, hanging up between the trees, drove Wolfe to fury'.[24]

Braddock had been ambushed and killed near Fort Duquesne (modern Pittsburg) in 1755 and his mistress captured by Red Indians, who, after stripping and repeatedly raping her, tortured her to death — and then ate her!

In order to starve Quebec into surrender, the countryside was laid waste. The Governor of Quebec wrote to General Wolfe that if the English did not desist from burning and destroying the country, he would give up all the English prisoners in his power to the mercy of the Indian savages. Wolfe replied that he could do as he liked with the prisoners but he would know that the English had captured a considerable number of 'fair hostages'. The very instant that he tried to carry out his threat of execution 'all the French ladies, without distinction, would be given up to the delicate embrace of the English marines'. Wolfe added in a postscript — 'PS. We have at least three, if not four transports, full freighted with French females, some of them women of the first rank in this country'.[25]

Four weeks later Quebec was captured by the English forces scaling the almost perpendicular Heights of Abraham without detection. Both commanders, Wolfe and Montcalm, were killed.

At home, the public were concerned about the conditions being endured by the army women in America and sent a sum of money for the relief of widows and children of soldiers, who had died on active service. General Amherst asked regiments to send a return showing the number of women and children considered 'proper objects of benevolence and also how they proposed to distribute the money'.[26] Some units sent in nil returns, while others showed up to 12 widows and 26 children each. The 47th Foot (North Lancs.), 17th Foot (Leicester Regiment) and 35th Foot (Sussex Regiment) laid out the money 'for the benefit of those children whose fathers had been killed in action'. The 2/60th devoted 10 dollars towards the payment of fees at the school for soldiers' children founded at Quebec by General Murray and spent the remainder on clothing and feeding its six orphans. The 42nd Foot (Black Watch) supported a charity school for its children.

AMERICAN WAR OF INDEPENDENCE

Following the Seven Years War, the colonists sought their independence in a 'War, which was to start at Bunker's Hill, Boston (1775) and end at Yorktown in 1781'. In 1775, Britain began to increase the number of regiments in North America which took their entitlement of women with them. The West Middlesex Regiment took 60 wives and 400 men.[27] Naturally, as the number of women increased, so did the number of children, until the whole represented a considerable total of camp followers, at a considerable cost to the Government. When the British Army sailed out of Boston in 1776, its 8900 officers and men were accompanied by 667 women and 553 children. The 63rd Regiment of 23 officers and 336 men embarked with their 96 women and 64 children.[28] A detachment of Guards sailed from Portsmouth on 29 April 1776 for America under General Sir William Howe with 86 women and 17 children on board.[29]

It was customary, too, for the German mercenary regiments with the British Army to take their women with them — their usefulness in domestic services outweighing their pilfering, marauding and other acts of indiscipline — and their marital status, since there were plenty of unofficial wives and 'camp followers' with both armies.

A Muster taken in New York in 1781 showed — British Troops 9,686: German Troops 10,250: Civilian Storekeepers, Drivers etc. 3,512: Women 3,615: Children 4,127.

Controlling their respective forces proved difficult for all Commanders and the civilian population frequently suffered from both sides. American troops were accused of plunder and raping women, especially those suspected of being Royalists, while the same charges were made by the Pennsylvania Council against Lord Cornwallis's troops. The Boston Press daily reported incidents between the military and local inhabitants — brawling, drunkenness, incitements to desert and respectable women accosted in the streets. Lord Francis Rawdon, a Captain in the 63rd Foot (and later its commanding officer) thought that Boston girls were less accustomed to such 'vigorous methods' than girls further South and 'don't bear them with the proper resignation', with the result that 'entertaining courts-martial' were a daily occurrence. One of his soldiers, for example, Private Timothy Spillman was court-martialled in January 1776 for 'having committed an assault on the person of Mrs Moore, an inhabitant of Boston, and beating her almost to death'. The punishment was 1,000 lashes.[30]

Worse was the report of small bands of roystering officers roaming the town 'trailing their coats with little credit to their birth or breeding',[31] while another blamed the girls themselves:

'Most of the young ladies, who were in Philadelphia during its 9 months' occupation by the British and wear the present fashionable dresses, have purchased them at the expense of their virtue. It is agreed on all hands that the British officers played the devil with the girls. The privates, I suppose, were satisfied with the common prostitutes'.[32]

Many of the officers, in fact, kept their mistresses with them. General Sir William Howe, appointed Commander-in-Chief in 1775, and grandson of the 1st Viscount Howe and Ruperta (Chap 3 page 33), privately enjoyed the favours of Elizabeth Lloyd, whose husband he placated with the lucrative office of auctioneer and vendue-master in Boston. 'Howe spent the winters in dissipation and the eager pursuit of pleasure'. The King's Own Regiment records that when it was quartered in Boston at the same time:

> 'the Puritan householders had billeted upon them, not only the officers and their wives, but in some cases, their mistresses also. Captain William Evelyn, a grandson of the famous diarist, for example, had formed an attachment with Peggie Wright, a servant in his father's household, and when he sailed for America, she accompanied him'.[33]

In the early months of the War conditions in Boston were reasonable. During the celebrations for the Queen's birthday (1775), 'the wives of the military attended the Balls and toasts organised by the local society, while the men celebrated on the cheap rum, on which they could get drunk for a copper or two'.[33] Because of the prevalence of smallpox, considerable care was taken over the women's billets and three hundred women of the various regiments of the garrison were provided 'with proper places to stay in'. 'Many of them engaged in the profitable occupation of buying and selling rum and, although the practice was forbidden and some were caught and whipped, the business flourished. Some of the women also broke into houses and buildings and helped to spread the smallpox'.[33]

But as the siege continued, The King's Own Regiment records 'The streets were deserted: the bells tolled for the dead: sick soldiers cried out from their tents and there was nobody to help them'. The winter was bitterly cold and all the fuel had been burned. The provost marshal was sent on his rounds, accompanied by an executioner with powers to hang anyone caught in the act of wrecking dwelling houses for fuel. Morale was low: food was in short supply and sickness was rife. General Burgoyne decided to evacuate the town. On 17th March 1776 the whole army, reduced to only 9,200 men, together with the women of the camp, the children and the baggage and thousands of loyalists were embarked for Halifax in 160 vessels — 'The officers, sacrificing all but their most private baggage, were huddled up amidst a throng of both sexes and all ages in ships with top heavy decks and encumbered gangways'.[33]

FAMILY WELFARE IN AMERICA

Little was done for army widows. Some remarried but the rest with their children would be quickly shipped home, there to be left to fend for themselves: after August 1776 they received a token sum, usually a half-guinea, to get them back to their place of origin. The widows and children of officers, on the other hand, were usually able to collect small pensions, authorised by the War Office on 17 August 1776. In 1776 a group of London merchants offered £5 to every soldier's wife who was widowed in America.

When a ship from Boston docked at Plymouth, in September 1775, the townspeople were moved by the sight of about 60 widows and children, some of whom 'exhibited a most shocking spectacle'. Within eight days local merchants had contributed more than £100 towards their relief.[34]

Some army commanders made considerable efforts to help their soldiers' families. One such was General Eyre Massey, commander at Halifax from 1775 to 1778, who had responsibility for probably a greater number of soldiers' wives and families than any other officer in North America at the time. He was genuinely concerned for their welfare and his attitude was reflected in the disciplinary code he established.

> 'While other commanders regularly prescribed the use of the whip on Army women, he seldom if ever threatened them with corporal punishment. He tried to find employment for them to supplement their incomes'. 'If soldiers' wives chuse to go a Hay-making Mr Fairbank will employ them'.[35]

In 1776 General John Burgoyne, commanding the Army in Canada under Sir William Howe's overall command, set off to engage George Washington, commander of the American forces. At the rear were over 1000 camp followers — almost an army in themselves. 'Several of his officers had rashly arranged for their ladies to accompany them on the expedition, headed by the adorable Baroness Riedesel and her three young children, her close friend, the handsome Lady Harriet Acland and the stout-hearted wives of Major Harrage and Lieutenant Reynolds. These ladies deliberately ignored the presence in their midst of General Burgoyne's 'piece of military baggage', Mrs Commissary Lewis. Also in the train were the normal quota of wives 'married on the strength' and the usual clutter of women picked up in the bas-quarters of Montreal and Quebec, willing to face the rigours of the campaign with their men'.[36]

A Regimental History (20th Foot) describes the fate of some of these women.

> 'Lady Harriet Acland, wife of Major Acland of the XX Regiment, became the idol of General Burgoyne's unfortunate army, which surrendered to the Americans at Saratoga and the theme of praise of many a writer, on account of her affectionate solicitude for her husband's safety, endurance of hardship and courage in the face of peril and, despite her delicate form, gentle nature and high birth. She was born on 3 January 1750, daughter of the Earl of Ilchester and married in November 1771. During the American War of Independence, she endured the most severe extremities of cold, wet and hunger, in common with the troops, traversing a vast extent of wild country, till the Americans were driven out of Canada. During the winter of 1776–77 she stayed with the Regiment on the beautiful Lake Champlain with the other ladies of the army, but when her husband was wounded, she crossed the Lake, discovered him in a poor American log-house and there nursed him, until he was well enough to rejoin the army.
> Together they went to New York, where their son was born in 1778, and they returned to England. Her son, John, succeeded to the family title and her daughter married the Earl of Carnarvon. She died on 21 July 1815, one month after the Battle of Waterloo, after 37 years of widowhood'.[37]

Chapter 5

Women Campaign with Wellington

In 1808 Sir Arthur Wellesley, who was created the Duke of Wellington in 1814, landed in Portugal with a small British force of 13,000 men and orders to drive the French out of the Peninsula. They took with them the regimental allocation of women, numbers unknown, since there are no official embarkation lists. The 23rd Foot (Royal Welsh Fusiliers) took 48 women and 20 children, but in 1811 the Duke of York issued a Regulation[1] from his Headquarters at the Horse Guards *confirming that* '6 lawful wives of soldiers were permitted to embark on Active Foreign Service with every 100 men, including NCOs, with rations to be issued to their wives' (i.e. half the soldier's ration and a quarter for each child).

The wives who were unsuccessful in the ballot were granted Travel Allowances ('not exceeding twopence per mile for the wife and 3 halfpence for each child to be paid out of the 'Parish Relief for the Poor' rates') to enable them to proceed to their Homes, or to the places at which they intended to reside, during the absence of their husbands abroad.

Justices or Magistrates had to certify the wife's intended place of settlement and make out a Route Card for her, so that Parish Overseers could pay her mileage 'to the next City, Town or place not exceeding 18 miles'. The woman signed (or made her mark) as a receipt and surrendered her Certificate at her destination to the Overseer, who forwarded it to the War Office for settlement.

The ships, assembled for the invasion, had first to survive the crossing. The soldiers and their wives, battened down below decks in cramped, airless quarters, suffered dreadfully as the little ships, pitched and rolled in the high seas. For the women, the conditions were even worse than for the men. Apart from the lack of fresh air, the leaks and the sea-sickness, there were no washing facilities, save for a bucket of salt water, with buckets for sanitary purposes, and no privacy by day or night.

Not only was there the danger of attack by the French fleet but the very real danger of shipwreck. In February 1811, for instance, 14 wives and seven children drowned with the officers and men of the 11th Foot (The Devonshire Regiment), when their ship sank off the Lizard during a storm.[2]

THE WOMEN

Oman described the women, who followed the Peninsular armies,

'as an extraordinary community — hard as nails, expert plunderers, furious partisans of the supreme excellence of their own battalion, much given to fighting'.[3]

Some were native born, an increasing number were foreigners, some were legal or common law wives, others the usual camp followers. George Bell of the 34th Foot wrote:

'. . . averse to all military discipline, they impeded our progress at times, particularly in retreats. They were under no control. They were ordered to the rear or their donkeys would be shot, to stay with the baggage, under the discipline of the Provost Marshal. Despite the warning, next morning they would pick up their belongings and set off, lamenting their bitter fate, ahead of the column, marauding, preparing their men's meals, before their arrival, plundering the battle-field or searching it for their dead; they were wounded, killed or died of exposure and hunger. Collectively and individually, they formed cameos of the Peninsular campaign, a colourful kaleidoscope of the romance and tragedy, devotion and self-sacrifice, the hardships and endurance of women at war'.[4]

Godfrey Davies[5] gives a vivid picture of one of Wellington's Divisions as it set off on its marches through the Peninsula — the infantry and cavalry regiments, then the batteries of artillery, the wagons of stores and equipment.

'Last would come the baggage train of almost interminable length. Portuguese carts with their solid wheels and a thousand mules or more carried the divisional equipment. With the train came the camp followers, including the soldiers' wives and children, some on foot, the more fortunate on mules or asses, leading pet sheep, goats and dogs. Many of the women wore shabby red coats, the property of former husbands or taken from corpses on the battlefield, beribboned old bonnets that partly covered dishevelled hair, skirts repaired by multi-coloured patches, and perhaps, top boots. On their backs, they carried knapsacks, to which babies might be strapped. Children old enough were running beside the carts, hoping for a lift, though to carry passengers was forbidden by General Orders. In addition to the English women were their Portuguese or Spanish sisters, some married to soldiers and others more or less permanently attached to them.'

Their marauding or scavenging for food was one of the main charges against the women for 'ill-discipline' and Wellington was accused of flogging them. Wellington wrote to Lady Salisbury.[6]

'There was no order for punishing women! But there was certainly none for exempting Women from punishment. It is well known that in all armies the Women are at least as bad, if not worse, than the men as Plunderers! and the exemption of the Ladies from punishment would have encouraged Plunder'.

The supply of bread to the troops was an army contract and Wellington tried to prevent the women and camp followers purchasing bread in the villages within two leagues of any of the army camps.

'Any woman who disobeyed this instruction will not be allowed to receive rations and any bread found in her possession will be confiscated'.[7]

Wellington had also to stop the women riding on the regimental baggage wagons and on the carts provided to carry tents and hospital stores, which delayed these supplies from reaching the troops.[8] But more difficult was the problem of knowing how many women and children were actually present in the country. In September 1810 he required regiments to send to his headquarters a Return (Form 12) giving Woman's Name: The name, rank and company of the husband: her own age, height, colour of hair, eyes and complexion: the number, sex and ages of their children: and on Form 13 the same details for women and children returning to Britain, together with details of Parish and County to which they were going and details of marriages and children born, since the regiment embarked for overseas.[9]

There are few contemporary accounts of the lives of soldiers' wives in the Peninsula: one exception was Private James Anton, who reached the rank of Quartermaster Sergeant in the 42nd Foot (Royal Highland Regiment, later the Black Watch). At about the end of 1812 he was permitted to marry Mary, an equally frugal and hardy peasant girl from Edinburgh, 'who shared with me in all my fortunes, over field and flood, in camp and in quarters, in war and in peace, without any unpleasant reflection at her own share of suffering'.[10] As a private soldier, his views on marriage, the selection of women to go with their husbands overseas and on their married life during the campaign are especially valuable. He recorded that only four women were permitted to follow each Company and that when the regiment reached Ostend even that number was suddenly reduced to two women per Company.

'Half the women of the regiment were thus left stranded, penniless and friendless, in a foreign port, and saw their red-coated husbands march off into space with many a backward look at their weeping wives'. But the hardy women of the barracks were not easily defeated. They had been only two days in Ghent, said Anton, when the women left at Ostend found their way to the regiment. They had marched on their own account in the regiment's track, and presented themselves bedraggled and footsore at its quarters in Ghent. The authorities were inexorable, and the weeping women were again conveyed back to the same place from which they escaped, and there closely watched. But woman's wit and wiles proved too much for the sentinels. In a week or two the forsaken but enterprising wives eluded the vigilance of the sentries, and joined their husbands once more; and 'as no official reports were made to their prejudice, they were allowed to follow the fortunes of their husbands during the campaign'.[11]

Surprisingly, considering his own wife's devotion and sufferings, he gives as his opinion that women ought not to be allowed to accompany their husbands on campaign.

> 'If any exception is made in one single instance, it only gives room for pressing and almost irresistible applications from others, and throws the performance of a very painful duty, namely refusing permission, on the officers commanding companies. Every private soldier conceives that he has a good right to this indulgence for his wife as the first non-commissioned officer in the regiment and certainly he is right: she will prove much more useful than one, instead of being serviceable, considers herself entitled to be served,

assumes the consequence of a lady without any of the good qualifications or
accomplishments of one, and helps to embitter the domestic enjoyments of others, by
exciting petty jealousies that otherwise would never exist'.[12]

The Antons spent their first night in the Pyrenees in a tent with 11 soldiers.
They all lay down with their feet pointing to the centre. All retained their
clothes and equipment, using their knapsacks for a pillow and their blankets,
half under and half over them. 'This being her first experience of a bivouac,
Mary often sighed for the morning'.[13] Next day, James Anton, helped by the
soldiers, erected a hut of tree branches to give his wife and himself more
privacy.

As the weather worsened, a second and more substantial hut than the first,
was constructed, complete with fireplace. Alas! their first meal was interrupted
by the drum, the camp was struck and they marched away to fight the battle
of the Nivelle (November 1813). Anton wrote afterwards:

'On leaving the camp, many of the married people set fire to their huts, but I left mine
with too much regret to become its incendiary: and my poor Mary shed tears as she
looked back upon it, as a bower of happiness, which she was leaving behind'.[13]

WIDOWS REMARRY

Before a battle, the married men would take leave of their wives and
children, but, relates Lieutenant William Grattan,[14] although these were
touching sights, the women were accustomed to scenes of danger by many
experiences and regarded the battle as an opportunity for plunder, so that the
suspense of waiting was more than compensated by the gaiety of his return
with his loot. 'Or, if, unfortunately he happened to fall, his place was sure to be
filled by someone of the company to which he belonged, so that the women of
our Army had little cause of alarm on this head. The worst that could happen
to them was the chance of being in a state of widowhood for a week'.

Many of the women were, in fact, widows, twice or thrice over — 'for when
a married man was shot, and his wife was a capable and desirable person, she
would receive half a dozen proposals before her husband was 48 hours in his
grave', commented Grattan.

Schaumann, Assistant Commissary General with the 18th Hussars, tells the
story of the wife of Sergeant Dunn of the 68th Foot, killed at the Battle of
Salamanca. The poor woman was nearly frantic when she heard her husband
was no more. Her loss certainly was great: but in less than a week, she took up
with a sergeant of the same company, whose name was Gilbert Hubbs, with
whom she has lived ever since. She had had a number of husbands before.[15]

For a widow to marry again did not necessarily imply indifference to her
husband's death. A wife's life was hard enough, especially on a campaign
overseas, but an unprotected woman's fate was desperate. She was not entitled
to any rations, and had to rely on what she could earn in the regiment or
scrounge from the men. Even if she had money, there might not be provisions

for sale. During the period after the battle of Talavera, provisions in the Guadiana valley were particularly scarce. Schaumann noted that the soldiers' wives, who were normally decently clad and faithful to their husbands, were riding hungrily in rags on starving donkeys, offering themselves to anyone who would pay for their favours with half a loaf of bread.[16] Sergeant Donaldson wrote that, even in quarters, they were assailed by every temptation that rank and money could devise but especially in a starving condition they were taken advantage of by villains who made their chastity the price of feeding them. Anton commented:

> 'The only protection a poor soldier can offer to a woman suddenly bereft of her husband, far from her kinsfolk, and without a residence or home, would under more favourable circumstances, be considered as an insult, or extremely indelicate'.
> 'I make free to offer this remark, in justification of many a good woman, who, in a few months, perhaps weeks, after her sudden bereavement, becomes the wife of a second husband: this is, perhaps, the only alternative to save a lone innocent woman's reputation: and the soldier, who offers himself, may be as little inclined to the connection through any selfish motive as the woman may be from any desire of his love; but the peculiar situation in which she is placed renders it necessary, despite the idle remarks that may be made, to feel grateful for a protector'.[17]

Sometimes a wife proved unfaithful, as Sergeant Edward Costello of the Rifle Corps related.[18] One evening, he was chatting to a Sergeant Battersby and

> 'a very pretty-looking English woman that passed for his wife, when up marched a tall, handsome grenadier of the 61st Foot. He sat down beside the woman, who became pale and agitated, as he asked 'Nelly, how can you stoop so low as to seek the protection of such a man as this?' glancing contemptuously at Battersby. 'He treats me better than you did', she replied. 'Maybe, but why leave your three year old child. I cannot look after her'. The argument continued until, at length, the grenadier rose to depart. 'So you are determined to continue this way of living?' he cried. His wife (for such she was) nodded, at which he plunged his bayonet into her heart and would have killed Battersby also, had he not been overpowered. He was sentenced to three months solitary confinement but after a month was returned to his regiment. Both he (Bryen, by name) and Battersby were killed in action during the campaign'.

Costello survived to become after 30 years' service a Yeoman Warder of the Tower of London. He married twice — the first time secretly, after eloping with a French girl, despite Wellington's orders that 'no British soldier should be allowed to marry French women'.[18]

Some of the worst conditions for the families were experienced during Sir John Moore's 200 mile withdrawal over the mountain roads to Corunna (1808). Winter had set in with frost and snow and there was everywhere a shortage of food and fuel. The columns of soldiers struggled on day after day, with the French cavalry in hot pursuit, cutting down the stragglers.

The route over the mountains became marked by bodies of men, women and children and of animals, dead from exhaustion, starvation or the cold. Worst of all were the sick and wounded, carried in bullock carts, but left to their fate, when the bullocks died from famine and exhaustion.

Rifleman Harris of the Rifle Brigade wrote:

'On the road behind me I saw men, women, mules and horses, lying at intervals, both dead and dying; whilst far away in front, I could just discern the enfeebled army crawling out of sight, the women huddled together in the rear, trying their best to get forward amongst those of the sick soldiery, who were now unable to keep up with the main body'.[19]

Ensign George Bell records the wonderful story of how the stout little Irish woman, 'as broad as a turtle', Mrs Commissary-General Skiddy, carried her sick husband, Private Don Skiddy of the 34th Foot, and his rifle and knapsack, 'for many a weary mile', nursing and sustaining him during the long retreat from Burgos. Her feat became a legend with the Peninsular army'.[20]

OFFICERS' WIVES

Some officers, too, took their wives with them on the Peninsular campaigns, since there were no regulations governing the numbers of officers' wives permitted to accompany their regiments. Wives travelled and were fed at the officers' own expense. Some stayed with their children in Lisbon during the war, where Wellington established his Headquarters and opened a school at Belem for army children in 1811. The wives hoped to see their husbands during leave periods or when they were billeted for any length of time in a town. 'Some of them', according to one report, 'deprived of their natural protectors and no longer bound by the social conventions of their native land, gave vent to their passions. Some took to drink, others to flirtations and intrigues'.[21] But one captain's wife, relates Captain John Harley of the 47th Foot, was so attached to her husband that she determined to join him in the field, even though the Army was besieging distant Burgos at the time. When she found him, he had to borrow money, to send her back to the safety of Lisbon, because his pay was in arrears. Several weeks later, the Army retreated from Burgos and overtook her, walking barefoot and without horse, attendant or money. She had lost her purse and been robbed of her horse and clothing by the Portuguese boy, her husband had paid to attend her.[22]

Colonel Lejeune described in his Memoirs[23] an officer and his family he saw when a prisoner at Elvas in Spain —

'The captain rode first on a beautiful horse, warding off the sun with a parasol: then came his wife, elegantly dressed, with a small straw hat, riding on a mule and carrying not only an umbrella, but a little black and white King Charles Spaniel on her knee, while she led by a blue ribbon, a tame goat, to supply her with milk. Beside madame walked her Irish nurse, carrying in a green silk wrapper a baby, the hope of the family. Last in the procession came a donkey loaded with the voluminous family baggage, which included a tea-kettle and a cage of canaries: it was guarded by an English servant in livery, mounted on a sturdy cob'.

No wonder Wellington objected strongly to ladies at the front — and all forms of impedimenta!

Susanna Dalbiac joined her husband Charles's Regiment, the 4th Dragoons (Royal Irish), in which regiment her father had served and in which her eldest brother was then serving as a Captain. She nursed the sick and wounded and her own husband, when he was ill with fever. 'She always sleeps in her colonel's tent, when the regiment is in bivouac, but was not afraid to sleep in the open and in the pouring rain with nothing but a blanket to cover her, beside the malarial infected Guadiana river', noted Lieutenant Colonel William Tomkinson in his diary.[24]

Tomkinson retired on half-pay, after serving throughout the War, and in 1836 married Susan of the Egerton family, Oulton Park, Chester. They had four sons and two daughters. One of the sons, who also became a colonel and commanding officer of the 1st Royal Dragoons, edited his father's diary.

Susanna Dalbiac won the high praise of General Sir William Napier in his well-known History of the War in the Peninsula.[25] She would ride at the head of her husband's regiment on campaign, 'deep in the midst of the enemy fire, trembling, yet impelled forward by feelings more imperious than terror, and stronger than the fear of death'. Ensign Bell, later to become a Major General, wrote 'there was no man present that did not fight with more than double enthusiasm seeing that fair lady in such danger on the battlefield'.[26]

The wife of Major Anthony Bacon (17th Lancers), Lady Charlotte Harley, a superb horsewoman, rode with him on his campaigns in the Peninsula and at Waterloo. Theirs was a romantic marriage, for neither had any money but their devotion to each other became a legend. They were never apart. Her mother was Lady Jane Oxford, 'a very beautiful woman but of dubious reputation'. Among her lovers were the Prince Regent and Lord Byron and from the suspected variety of their fathers her children were known as the 'Harleian Miscellany'.[27]

Another Peninsular veteran was the wife of John James, 6th Earl Waldegrave, a major in the 15th Dragoons. 'Lady Waldegrave, who accompanied her Lord throughout the war, was the perfect heroine . . . she had a splendid figure and was one of the best riders I ever saw. . . . Her conduct was the theme of the Army and she won universal praise and admiration', wrote Ensign Gronow of the 1st Guards Regiment.[28] She was exposed to many risks in the cavalry charges, led by her husband, and on one occasion she was nearly taken prisoner. Courageously, she aimed her pistol at a French Cavalryman, who was threatening her; he lowered his sword and allowed her to escape.

A number of officers, who had money and influence, went home on leave. 'Some officers went to England for the purpose of seeing their own wives; that was prudent', remarked one army correspondent. 'Some went to see other men's wives — and many went to prevent other men seeing their wives'.[29]

General Sir Thomas Picton, the able but foul-mouthed commander of the 3rd Division, who would lose his life at Waterloo, had little sympathy with any of them — 'Soldiers haven't any business wiveing', he commented. 'But if ever I come to it, I'll marry the youngest tit I can get'.[30]

A fellow Divisional Commander, General Charles Colville, did survive the campaign and married in 1818 Jane Mure, a girl young enough to be his daughter and sired twenty five great grandsons, all of whom fought in one war or another — 18 in the Army, six in the Royal Navy and one in the Royal Air Force.[31]

MEDICAL ARRANGEMENTS

In 1812, James McGrigor arrived in Lisbon to assume responsibility for the health of Wellington's army, shortly after his marriage to Mary Grant and the birth of his son.

> At any other time', he wrote, 'this appointment would have gratified me to the full extent of my ambition; but the happiness I had enjoyed in the married state, made it now a sad and painful change to me. The announcement was a sad blow to my wife, who at once determined to be my companion in Spain. I had however seen enough of ladies on service in the field to decide me against that step and I knew well, that with the care of my wife and child, I could not do my duty in the way I determined it should be done, while I remained in the service'.[32]

Prior to his arrival, the British Army, unlike the French, had no mobile field units nor ambulance-wagons near to the battlefields, so the wounded were sent back to the large hospitals far to the rear on foot, by bullock cart or on improvised stretchers. Without anaesthetics, the sufferings of the wounded were appalling. Yet the soldiers considered it a point of honour to show no sign of suffering, however great the pain. Such bravado was exemplified by Lord Fitzroy Somerset, one of Wellington's Aides and married to his beautiful niece Emily, and who was later, as Lord Raglan, to command the unfortunate army in the Crimea. As his arm was carried away after amputation, he shouted 'Here, bring the arm back! There is a ring my wife gave me on the finger'.[33] The Earl of Uxbridge (Henry William Paget) had his right leg amputated after the Battle of Waterloo. He did not flinch during the operation. It was said of this illustrious family in the 19th Century that all their men were heroes and all their women angels, for they had a long and glorious tradition of service to their country in the armed forces of the Crown and of both marrying and begetting beautiful women. 'One Leg', created the first Marquess of Anglesey after the battle, married twice and had 18 children, while his eldest son, Henry, Colonel of 42nd Foot, married three times and had 11 children.

Whenever a battle was fought near a large town, the surgeons would seek out houses or barns, in which to operate and to house the wounded. The local women would come to help, as, for instance, in 1812 at Salamanca, where the women in the city prepared large quantities of lint and rags as dressings and many Spanish girls came to the battlefield in the evening to help the walking wounded.

But there was another side to the battlefield scenes —

> 'It was marvellous how quickly the dead, and often the wounded, were stripped on the battlefields by camp followers of both sides — even of their false teeth.'[34]

'When the Roll was called after the battle, the females who missed their husbands came to ask the survivors for news of their fate', wrote Rifleman Harris. One such was Mrs Joseph Cochan, whose husband was killed at the battle of Rolica. They took her to where he lay. 'She embraced a stiffening corpse, then took a prayer book from her pocket and, kneeling down, repeated the service for the dead over the body'. That night she lay with some other females in like circumstances with her husband's Company in the open heath.[35]

McGrigor quickly established a chain of hospitals throughout the Peninsula and used commissary transport to evacuate the wounded. So successful were his arrangements that he earned Wellington's highest commendation for his medical staff and himself — a landmark which was to lead to the creation of the Royal Army Medical Corps in 1898. He also started a Benevolent Fund and Widows' and Orphans' Fund, which continue to flourish today.

THE SOCIAL ROUND

British officers mixed freely with Spanish and Portuguese society and there was no shortage of dark-eyed senoritas willing to keep rich, young officers warm in bed, as Ensign Bell related.[36]

> 'There were many pretty Spanish girls in the town, all fond of dancing, in which we often indulged of an evening. Every young fellow had his sweetheart and many a tear was shed as we moved on'.

Dances were arranged by regiments all over the Peninsula and these were highly popular with the Portuguese and Spanish ladies. Some of the fiery dances and dancers certainly impressed the love-lorn soldiers — and even the British Ambassador, Sir Robert Ker-Porter, who, after watching an exhibition at a Ball in 1808, remarked on

> 'the dancer's great dexterity in keeping time not only with her castanets, but also with the silent movements of her bottom, which in elasticity far exceeded the quickness of her feet . . . and a frequent repetition of the amusement took place during the evening'.[37]

In 1810, during the inactive winter months in Lisbon, revelry abounded after the hardships of the campaign.

> 'The sums of money taken from the officers by wanton girls, the prettiest of whom came from Andalusia, is almost unbelievable', wrote a German chronicler.[37] 'The disorder reached such a pitch, especially between the common prostitutes and the drunken English soldiery, that Wellington had several shiploads of the most brazen girls sent away'.

When Wellington entered Madrid in 1812, 'every window and balcony was filled with beautiful women who showered down flowers upon our heads.' The bells rang and life was gay, recorded the 51st Foot, who organised a grand ball, 'the officers having provided the ladies with shoes and stockings.'[38]

The same thing happened in 1813 when the Headquarters was at St Jean de Luz. A number of soldiers married local girls, some deserting to remain behind with their senoritas. About 700 Portuguese and 400 Spanish women had attached themselves to the army stationed around the town, some having formed permanent relationships with the men. Wellington again had to order them back to the Peninsula, but as so often happened, the women disregarded these orders and were soon back again.[39]

Schaumann also noted that Allied Officers were rarely deprived for long of female society. He had 'plenty of love affairs in Spain'. In one town alone he had affairs with five different women. Two of those were daughters of a wealthy landowner and were 'very responsive'; one was the wife of a Spanish colonel; the fourth, 'a pretty girl, who paid him many visits', and the fifth, the wife of an organist who 'always availed herself of her husband's duties in the Church, in order to come to him'. He was not so lucky, he admitted, with the Basque girls 'and had to console himself with the beauties among the soldiers' wives'.[40]

Another amorous escapade featured 33 year old Lieutenant William Kelly, 40th Foot (2nd Somersetshire Regiment), who eloped with Anna, the 18 year old daughter of a Portuguese General. The family protested to Wellington, demanding the immediate return of their daughter and Kelly's punishment. Wellington, at first, supported the request, 'provided the daughter should not be confined to a convent', the usual fate of erring ladies of noble families. He ordered Kelly's arrest, 'as I cannot allow any officer to be guilty of such a breach of the laws of Portugal, as to carry away a young lady and retain her in the cantonments of the army contrary to the wishes of her parents'. When he learned they had been married, however, he refused to intervene and the bride's mother swore she would kill her daughter and get Kelly and the priest transported for life. But the Kellys had seven children: the priest was dismissed the service: William died in 1836 a Barrack Master in Jamaica. Anna was disinherited and died a penniless widow in Dublin.[41]

THE SACK OF BADAJOZ

The darkest side of the Peninsular War was associated with the capture of Badajoz, the strongest fortress on the Spanish frontier with Portugal, in 1812. The British lost 5,000 men and hundreds of dead, dying and wounded soldiers lay before the breach in the walls. It was still the accepted rule in siege warfare that, if a governor did not capitulate after a practicable breach had been made, the attackers could enjoy the rights to pillage, rape and kill. For two days, the soldiers sacked the town, as no town had been sacked by British troops, since the days of Cromwell in Ireland.

The soldiers ran amok, crazed with drink and revenge, plundering, murdering, raping, sparing neither priests, nor nuns, women nor children.

The soldiers were joined by bands of camp followers, women, or 'tigresses in the shape of women', for, if possible, they were worse than the men.

> 'Every kind of outrage was publicly committed in the houses, churches and streets', said Captain Robert Blakeney of the 28th Foot (Gloucestershire Regiment). 'The infuriated soldiery resembled a pack of hell-hounds vomited up from the infernal regions rather than the well organised, brave, disciplined and obedient British Army, they were 12 hours previously .... I beheld the savages tear the rings from the ears of beautiful women, who were their victims, and when the rings could not be immediately removed from their fingers with the hand, they tore them off with their teeth'. 'The appalling shrieks of hapless women, recalled the regions of the damned'.[42]

Wellington, shocked by these shameful scenes, 'ordered the Provost Marshal into the town with orders to execute any man he may find in the act of plunder'.[43] He erected a gallows in the Central square and hanged several plunderers, in order, with the help of his officers and fresh troops, to restore order and discipline.

Ensign George Bell gives us another realistic and colourful picture of the looting and the camp followers, after the capture and plunder of Vitoria in June 1813.

> 'Around the town lay the wreck of a mighty army and plunder accumulated for years, torn with rapacious hands from almost every province in Spain. Waggons and carriages of all descriptions — cattle, arms, drums, trumpets, silks, jewellery, plate and embroidery, mingled in strange disorder. Here were wounded soldiers, deserted women and children of all ages, imploring aid and assistance and seeking protection from the British. Here a lady upset in her carriage, in the next an actress or *femme de chambre*; sheep, goats and droves of oxen roaming and bellowing about, with loose horses; camp followers were dressed up in the State uniforms of the King Joseph's Court; the rough class of women, drunk with champagne and Burgundy, and attired in silks and Paris dresses — once envied, perhaps in a Palace. The pride of France was, indeed, levelled in the dust after this defeat. Oceans of women — wives, actresses and nuns — were captured.
>
> A French officer watching the scene from the neighbouring heights remarked bitterly to Schaumann — 'No wonder you won, for you have an army, while we are nothing but a travelling brothel'.[44]

A ROMANTIC STORY

The morning after the seige of Badajoz provided one of Military History's great romantic stories. Two surviving officers of the 95th Foot (The Rifle Brigade), Harry Smith and Johnny Kinkaid, were discussing the previous night's terrible events, when they saw two ladies, dressed in black silk, white gloves and stockings, their faces covered with their mantillas, approaching from the devastated city.

The elder explained she was the wife of a Spanish officer, their house had been destroyed, their belongings stolen and their lives and persons in danger. Their earrings had been ripped from their ears by some drunken soldiers and, faced by further outrage, she claimed the protection of the British officers, if not for herself at least for her sister, recently returned from a convent. Kinkaid wrote 'she stood by the side of an angel — a being more transcendingly lovely I had never before seen. A lovely face, set on a long graceful neck, surmounted by a figure cast in nature's mould, rounded slender breasts and hips, with small, typically Spanish feet, which one soldier called 'kissable''. Kinkaid had fallen in love with her at first sight, but while he stood bedazzled, his brother officer moved more quickly and 'a more impudent fellow stepped in and won her', he later recorded.[45]

Captain Harry Smith, also of the Rifle Brigade, had also fallen instantly in love with the dark-eyed Juana Maria, then just 14. She was a Catholic and he a Protestant but they married and their love was to survive many a campaign and enforced separation. 30 years later he wrote 'From that day to this, she has been my guardian angel. She has shared with me the dangers and privations, the hardship and fatigue, of a restless life of war, in every quarter of the globe. No murmur has ever escaped her'.[46] His child-bride became the joy and pride of the Light Division: she survived the Peninsular and Waterloo campaigns and accompanied her dare-devil and fervent lover-soldier-husband 'the only thing on earth my life hangs on and clings to', on most of his 400 skirmishes, sieges and actions in North America, Africa and India (where she rode into the battle of Maharajpore, sitting astride an elephant). Finally, Lady Juana Smith accompanied Sir Harry to the Cape, where he became Governor. Her memory and fame are recalled by the town named after her, Ladysmith, which withstood the siege of the Boers, nearly 30 years after her death in 1872. Her husband died 12 years earlier at the age of 73. Kinkaid died, still a bachelor, at the age of 75.

EVACUATION OF WOMEN

In April 1814 Wellington entered Toulouse, after the last battle of the Peninsular War. Napoleon abdicated and was exiled to Elba. Wellington said farewell to his troops; his camp followers went home. Lieutenant Colonel William Tomlinson of the 52nd Foot thought the Spanish and Portuguese women who had suffered, marched, cooked, washed, danced, loved and plundered for the soldiers should be allowed to go with them. But it was not to be. Wellington, in his Orders of 26 April 1814, decided

'as the only means of avoiding eventual distress' that the greater part of the 'foreign women, with reasonable provision, should accompany the Portuguese troops to the rear .... But there will be no objection to a few of those, who have proved themselves useful and regular, accompanying the soldiers to whom they are attached, with a view to their being ultimately married'.

Lieutenant Gratton[47] gives a vivid picture of the plight of these women —

'The English, Irish and Scotch were sent to England and proper attention paid to their wants and comforts. Several of the most effective regiments embarked for Canada and, as the war between England and America was at its height, restricted to a certain number of soldiers' wives. But the poor faithful Spanish and Portuguese women, hundreds of whom had married or attached themselves to our soldiers and who had accompanied them through all their fatigue and dangers, were, from stern necessity, obliged to be abandoned to their fate. These faithful and heroic women were now, after their trials, to be seen standing on the beach, while they witnessed with burning hearts the filling of those sails, and the crowding of those ships, that were to separate them for ever from those to whom they had looked for protection and support'.

WELLINGTON'S SOCIAL LIFE

Wellington was feted in London and honoured with a dukedom. He was made Ambassador to France and bought a home for the Embassy from Napoleon's youngest sister, the beautiful Princess Pauline Borghese (It is still the British Embassy today). He was glamourised by Parisian society and his name romantically linked with some of the most beautiful among them — Madame de Récamier, the opera singer Madame Grassini and Mademoiselle Georges, the actress. He was still only 46 and in the prime of life, a handsome and successful Commander and it was no secret that he was unhappily married. 'His wife, Lady Catherine Pakenham, had been betrothed to him, before he had first sailed to India, but her parents did not consider Colonel Wellesley (as he was then) a good enough match for their daughter and refused their consent — only sanctioning the marriage after his successful career in that country and not before, unknown to Wellington, she had promised herself to another suitor. This partly explained a complete estrangement between them and his extensive relations with other women'.[48] But Wellington believed that a man's private life was his own affair and did not like women to distract him, or his officers, from their duties. He limited one officer's request for leave in Lisbon on the grounds that '48 hours was as long as any reasonable man can wish to stay in bed with the same woman'.

THE END OF THE WAR

Napoleon's escape from Elba in February 1815 halted efforts to draft a peace treaty and Wellington was recalled to command the European forces against him.

While Wellington awaited the French attack on Brussels, his army was billeted in the capital and in the villages around. Brussels was an enchanting city, full of British tourists and visitors. Every night, all the famous places were alive with smart young women dressed in the latest fashions, dazzled by the young, single and wealthy officers of Wellington's army. There were also the officers' ladies, billeted in the best hotels, and the soldiers' women, living in whatever accommodation they could find or afford in the villages around Brussels, but usually with their regiments.

For the society women, the highlight of the occasion was the celebrated Ball, given on 15 June by Charlotte, Duchess of Richmond, (daughter of the Duke of Gordon) who had taken a house in the fashionable quarter of Brussels with her General husband and 15 year old son. The (4th) Duke of Richmond was Colonel of the 35th Foot (The Royal Sussex Regiment) and was to have had command of the Reserve, if it had been formed. Their eldest son, who had been one of Wellington's ADCs during the Peninsular War, would serve, during the Battle of Waterloo, as ADC to the Prince of Orange. He married (1816) Caroline Paget, the daughter of the First Marquess of Anglesey, who, as Lord Uxbridge, commanded Wellington's cavalry and horse artillery during the battle.

Sergeant Wheeler, a veteran of the Peninsular campaign, was billeted with his Regiment (51st Foot) in the village of Waterloo and wrote to his parents that he did not intend to get entangled —

> 'there are some very pretty young women here, some of them are got very much attached to our men, and I doubt not when we move, there will be an increase in the number of women. I must here observe that your humble servant does not intend to get entangled with any of them'.[49]

Sergeant William Lawrence, having marched through the city of Brussels with his Regiment (40th Foot), sat in a cowshed on the eve of the Battle watching the local peasants, regimental supernumeraries 'and the army women and children and the ladies of easier virtue' making their way out of the battle area. He would survive the battle and marry a pretty Parisian fruit-seller, after receiving his Colonel's reluctant permission — 'at least she will do to teach the soldiers French', he said.[50]

One who would not survive the battle was General Sir William de Lancey, Wellington's Quartermaster General, an American born in New York, who had been knighted for his services in Spain. A few weeks earlier, he had married a Scottish girl, Magdalene Hall, but Wellington had summoned him from his honeymoon to draft his orders for the battle. He was to die in his wife's arms, despite her efforts to save him, a week after the battle had been won.[51]

Another who scoured the battlefield in search of her husband was the distraught wife of Major Hodge of the 7th Hussars. She did not find him. When the Prince Regent heard of her sad story, he sent for her and made her son a page of honour at his Coronation (as George IV). In due course the boy followed his father's profession in the Cavalry and, as Lieutenant General E C Hodge, led the 4th Royal Irish Dragoon Guards in the charge of the Heavy Brigade at Balaclava.

After the battle, Wellington was once again faced with the problems of evacuating the Army's women.

> 'All women belonging to British regiments, beyond one for each 25 men, are immediately to be sent from their regiments to Ostend for the purpose of being forwarded to their respective homes', he ordered.[52]

They were provided with passages and allowances but 'rations are not to be allowed for more than one woman for every 25 men' (increased to 6 per 100 men on 28th December 1815).

A few months later (Cambrai, 13 November 1816), Wellington was dealing with another matrimonial problem — the women who had been left behind were crossing the Channel to join their husbands, forming the Allied Army of Occupation. He asked Commanding Officers to caution their NCOs and soldiers against inviting their wives to come and join them without the Commanding Officers' permission.

'Those who evaded the police at Dover or Calais were not to be given rations, quarters or any of the benefits accorded to a soldier's wife, who is permitted to be with a regiment'.[52]

Finally, on 6 January 1818, an Order was issued asking Commanding Officers

'to take care that NCOs or soldiers sent to England do not take with them from this country any woman who is not married to the person with whom she may cohabit and any soldier taking a woman to England must have a certificate stating that she is his wife'.[52]

Clearly the Army was having problems administering its women. As Colonel Gurwood comments in his Introduction to Wellington's Dispatches[52] in 1837:

'It requires no small nerve to enforce in a campaign all the necessary orders relative to this class of appendages to an Army'.
'The Ladies no doubt will be shocked at the Duke's severity towards them and exclaim What! not allow the poor women to buy bread, not to quit the camp without a certificate of virtue, not to repose their weary limbs on the clothing carts; and Oh! the monster, like Aeneas, enjoining his faithless followers to abandon their French, Spanish and Portuguese Didos on the banks of the Garonne, to seek other protectors! and assuming a despotic authority, without either Alexander, or Caesar, or even Bonaparte as a precedent, presumes to interfere with the sacred rites of martimony . . . . . and dictates to his Amazonian followers how they shall marry and be given in marriage!'
'But', he concludes, 'those officers who have seen the sufferings of women and children, as for instance, in the retreat to Corunna, must temper discipline with humanity and ascertain every defined precedent relating to the women of an army to guide them and those interested in their safety and comfort'.

Chapter 6

Matrimony by Regulation

The wars against Napoleon had been costly and the Government was faced with a huge national debt: so, until the Crimean War, there was little money to spend on the well-being of the soldier. As Fortescue commented —

> 'Soldiers might have their uses in war, but in peace, they were simply an evil. What matter if they were worse paid than others of the same social standing, if they were shamefully overcrowded in their barracks, if their food was the derision of paupers and felons, if they were condemned to almost perpetual exile, for the most part in deadly climates, and supposing that they survived 21 years' service, were turned loose on the world with broken health and a miserable pittance of sixpence a day. They were British soldiers and must expect nothing better'.[1]

If there was little money for an army which had served its country well, there would be even less for his family. Despite the country's growing humanitarianism and awareness of the need for social reforms, the Army's attitude to the soldier's wife and children would remain much as it had done during the previous century. As for its attitude to marriage the following Standing Orders of the 73rd Foot,[2] written in 1858, might well have been written by Major Wolfe at Culloden, one hundred years previously.

MARRIED MEN, WOMEN AND CHILDREN

1. Officers must discourage the men as much as possible from making improvident marriages and ascertain the character and condition of the women before they recommend any men for permission to marry.

2. NCOs and soldiers are not to marry without the consent of the Commanding Officer. Any individual infringing this order will subject himself and his family to great misery: his wife will not be allowed in Barracks, nor have any privileges of soldiers' wives nor be recognised in any way.

(A Private soldier in the King's Own Regiment was sentenced by court martial in 1828 to receive 150 lashes for this offence).[3]

3. Any soldier's wife found drunk, or disorderly, or spreading malicious reports of each other, or bringing liquor into Barracks, will be turned out of Barracks forthwith.

4. *Medical*

The women and children will attend the medical inspection once a week, or oftener if required.

5. *Church*

The women and children will attend regularly their respective places of worship every Sunday. An absence report will be sent in every Monday morning, signed by the Quartermaster.

STANDING ORDERS OF THE 52ND LIGHT INFANTRY IN THE 1860s

> The regiment cannot furnish employment for more than a few women. The small
> quantity of accommodation in barracks, the difficulty of procuring lodgings, the
> frequency of moving, and inconveniences attending marches and embarkations, are to
> be urged as dissuasives against imprudent marriages.

From 1816 each regiment had to keep a register in the Orderly Room, in
which the 'marriage of every NCO and private and the baptism and age of
every legitimate child' of the regiment were to be recorded. Abroad,
Chaplains had been required to record details of births and baptisms,
marriages, deaths and burials since 1796 but in 1824 the Duke of York, as
Commander in Chief had to remind them despite 'the Orders already in force,
great inconvenience has arisen from the want of regular Marriage and
Baptismal Certificates from Foreign Stations, of Officers and Soldiers, and
their Children'.[4] They were reminded to send half-yearly a copy of the
Regimental Registers of Marriages and Baptisms to the Chaplain General's
Office.[4]

An Army Chaplain[5] summarised the regulations and the Army's attitude to
marriage with sarcastic realism —

> 'St Paul tells us that marriage is honourable in all: but the authorities at the Horse
> Guards affirm that marriage is honourable only in the case of 6 soldiers in every
> Company who have received the permission of their commanding officers, and decidedly
> to be disapproved of and discouraged in the case of all others.'

Thus by Army Regulation and Regimental Order the authorities made it
perfectly clear, as they had done for the past 150 years, that while they could
not deny a soldier's legal right to marry, they would control the number of
authorised marriages by insisting on the prior permission of their commanding
officers. There would be a Register of applications and a regimental
establishment based on the number needed within a Company or Troop for
domestic chores. The authorised few would be given privileges, ('the comforts
and advantages which Her Majesty's Bounty and the custom of the Service
extend to married soldiers and to their wives of good characters'), denied to
those wives not officially recognised 'on the strength' ('under no circumstances
to be allowed accommodation in barracks or to participate in any of the
advantages granted by the Regulations to married soldiers').[5]

The numbers could be varied for home service, garrison service abroad, for
India and for the Guards' regiments, where

> 'a larger proportion of men was allowed to marry, because they served largely in the
> London area and were only sent abroad in an emergency, and because, as the élite of the
> army, they recruited a higher calibre of men, who could be accordingly trusted in
> matrimony'.[6]

In practice, marriage regulations were often ignored by the over-riding
needs for recruiting up to authorised establishments. For example, General

Eyre,[7] Commandant at Chatham, in evidence to the Royal Commission on Recruiting (1861) said

> 'It is astonishing what a number of married men enlist. It is well known that the recruiting parties in many instances are aware of this, and tell them to swear they are single, and in the end the wife and child appear . . . . We enlist for India *married* men at the rate of 6% (through the Recruiting Depot at Warley, Essex) but none for the Home Army'.[8]

Queen's Regulations 1865 stated quite clearly that

> 'married men and widowers with a child or children are not to be enlisted without special authority, whether they have served in the Army before or not'.[9]

But after 6 months any attestation was void and the man was deemed to be duly enlisted.[10]

It also proved impossible to prevent soldiers marrying without the Commanding Officer's prior approval. A Commanding Officer had no power to forbid Banns or interfere with marriages in civil places of worship in Great Britain. Nor were soldiers' marriages at home likely to be solemnised by Army Chaplains, 'since none of the military chapels were consecrated or registered for the celebration of marriages.' However, overseas, such ceremonies were most likely to be performed by Chaplains to the Forces, who would first check the local marriage regulations to ensure that the procedures were legal. If a chaplain, other than military, performed such a ceremony, the soldier was required to produce a signed certificate to the regiment to enter into the Regimental Marriage Register. In both these events, the Commanding Officer would be aware of the marriage and take appropriate action.[11]

MARRIED ACCOMMODATION AROUND 1850

During the first half of the 19th Century, there was to be an increasing public outcry against the marriage policies of the Army and its provisions for the married families. Later, we shall look at the circumstances of the 'unofficial' wives, but for those wives officially recognised by the Regulations to live with their husbands and children in a 'curtained-off' corner of the barrack room conditions were pretty primitive, as contemporary writers reveal —

> 'What shall we say of the feelings of a newly-married bride till she has become utterly hardened, while a dozen men, every night and every morning, are stripping and dressing in her very presence?, asked one Journal.[12] Or shall we ask what the husband feels when his duty comes for guard, and he is forced to leave his wife alone in such a place? But worse, when the poor wretch brings into the world her husband's child with the regimental hospitals reserved exclusively for soldiers and (unless she has her child in a crowd) she must seek retirement, provided she can afford to pay for it, outside the barrack-gates.'

Charles Dickens wrote in 1851

> 'Notwithstanding the proverbial popularity of the military amongst womankind, an

average of only 5 to every 95 private soldiers are allowed to enter into the bonds of matrimony. The soldier's weekly stipend of seven shillings and sevenpence does not hold out a very flattering prospect of wedded bliss and even with his free lodgings and military uniform, his 'pay and allowances' leave him with too little to marry upon'.

However justified the limited numbers might be, at least those officially recognised should be provided with decent accommodation for his wife.

'At present the soldier's wife only shares the accommodation afforded to her husband's comrades: sleeping in the common barrack-room amidst whole companies of soldiers, she is obliged to dress and undress in public. Soldiers' daughters of 17, 18 and 19 are also to be found sleeping almost side by side with the male inmates . . . . . Ere long the bride's shame breaks down: she who was innocent is now a slut'.[13]

MORE SOLDIERS SHOULD BE ALLOWED TO MARRY

The United Services Gazette in the 1850s believed that more soldiers should be allowed to be 'officially recognised', but equally that those who married 'without leave' should be severely punished.

'It is *not* distinctly laid down as a Military Law, that only a certain number of men shall be allowed to marry. The consequence is that a considerable number do perpetrate matrimony, and, thus, when the order arrives for the departure of the Troops, some of the women must be left behind to go to their parishes, or depend on their friends, seek a livelihood in any channel, or starve'.[14]

'The Soldiers' wives have hitherto been looked upon by most Commanding Officers as an encumbrance with their quarrels and complaints, their occasional want of care and cleanliness, and sometimes their habits of dissipation, to say nothing of the impedient they offer to quick movement by increasing the baggage excrescence . . . . Under a more general recognition of marriage in the ranks, and a species of surveillance exercised over the object of a Soldier's choice, the evils will be partially corrected and what has become almost a curse to the efficiency of the Regiment may become a blessing'.[15]

But, in addition, the Soldier's wife must learn to respect herself and to become to the utmost of her power a useful member of the military community.

The Herald of Peace[16] argued that the marriage policy of the Army denied many women the opportunity to have a family and directly contributed to vice and immorality.

'Few soldiers can marry, and of those who do, a very small number are allowed to take their wives with them, when they leave the country. A large proportion of women must remain single, deprived of family and social comforts. Such an unnatural state of society causes much misery, crime and immorality. Barracks or quarters are centres of vice, from which it radiates over miles of town and country a halo of disease and misery'.

Charles Dickens agreed —

'*The public policy of this country was to debase the wife of the common soldier, for the direct purpose of making marriage odious to his eyes*', he thundered. 'We are convinced that the English private soldier is improved in quality by the possession of a decent and an honourable domestic tie'.[17]

He hoped that the new barracks being built at Aldershot would put right this public wrong to the soldier. We shall see in Chapter 10, if that hope was fulfilled.

BARRACK REFORMS

In 1854 a Commission was appointed under Lord Monk to look into Barrack Accommodation[18] and that provided for married families — one of the several commissions looking into living conditions in the Army 'which stands at almost the head of unhealthy occupations in the United Kingdom with a mortality rate double that of the civilian population'. The Commission found that the majority of commanding officers disliked the practice of allowing married women to live in barracks, whether in 'married corners' or in separate barrack blocks.

> 'The separation of married couples from the unmarried men, at night, is strenuously recommended on the grounds of decency and is preferable to the alternative of excluding the women altogether . . . . . . Nothing has a more direct influence in demoralising the lower classes than their being huddled all together in one common sleeping room and in some instances in one bed. A living room, two bedrooms and a little scullery are about the minimum accommodation for a man with a wife and family.'[19]

The Barrack Accommodation Committee recommended that, for reasons of discipline, it was better to provide separate quarters for married families *in barracks* rather than outside. The women, too, would be more readily available for domestic chores. Each married man, who was permitted to live in barracks, should be provided with a separate room in a part of the camp away from the unmarried soldiers and no other women, beyond those officially provided with accommodation, should be allowed to live in camp. Whilst such a policy would be costly, the Government would save the lodging allowance permitted to married soldiers, amounting in 1855 to £8000 in the United Kingdom alone.

By 1857 there were only 20 out of 251 military stations in the United Kingdom with separate married quarters, as distinct from the families living in barrack rooms. These provided for 541 soldiers and their families. The Army Sanitary Commission (1857–58) considered this to be insufficient and recommended 'suitable provision be made for NCOs' and married soldiers' quarters'. But progress in building additional quarters would be slow, since funds were always insufficient. Some of the first official married quarters were built in London in 1860 as part of the newly constructed Chelsea Barracks and Queen Victoria personally demanded the building of married quarters in Windsor.[20] But the 1861 Report of the Barracks and Hospital Improvement Commission could still state —

> 'We have seen married mens' beds in the mens' barrack rooms without any screen. At Chatham, at the time of our enquiry, there was a married NCO or soldier in every barrack room among the men: and not infrequently girls from 14 to 16 years of age were thus accommodated'.[21]

In 1867 the Army met some of these criticisms. For the first time, it specified in its Regulations the numbers permitted on the married establishments at home and abroad.[22] In future, the entitlement to be placed on the Married Roll would be given to all Regimental Staff Sergeants, three out of every four or five Sergeants per troop, battery or company, seven per cent of the Rank and File (twelve per cent in India), provided their marriages had the approval of their Commanding Officers, the soldier had completed seven years' service and possessed at least one good conduct badge. The Roll of the married establishment had to be kept in the Orderly Room of each regiment or corps, containing the names of the married soldier, his wife and children (and ages), as verified from the Regimental Register of Marriages and Baptisms. The soldier or wife could be struck off the Roll for misconduct and the family sent home at public expense. The family (defined as 'wife and legitimate children under the age of 14') were entitled to the following advantages:–

Quarters – a separate room (two, if available, for NCOs with large families) or the quarters appointed for four single soldiers, and barrack accommodation, while awaiting embarkation.

Furniture – 'in separate quarters, two bedsteads, two bolsters, four blankets, palliasses, mugs and a broom, bucket, coal-box, pail, mop and table will be provided'.

Lodging Allowance – will be paid when quarters are not provided.

Fuel and Light – will be issued according to regulations or an allowance in lieu.

Provisions – 'Overseas, the wife will receive half a soldier's ration (liquor excepted) and each child under 14 one quarter ration. Such issues will be continued up to three months after the death of the soldier or wife pending the family's return home.' At home, when soldiers were compulsorily separated from their families for more than four days, a ration allowance of 3d per day was paid to the wife and $1\frac{1}{2}$ to each child. On board ship, the allowance was doubled or free rations provided.

OTHER BENEFITS

Apart from an increase in the lodging allowance to 6d per day, these regulations remained in force for the rest of the century. But the women and children on the married establishments received other benefits. Medical entitlements will be discussed in Chapter 10, but here we can note that recognised families could be treated in their quarters, including confinements, and 'some medical comforts' could be prescribed.[23]

Another privilege given to soldiers' families on the married establishment was conveyance at public expense, when the families joined their husbands for foreign service or returned from overseas with or without them, after medical clearance or 'when a soldier dies, deserts or becomes a lunatic or when he is discharged, except by purchase'. With the coming of the railways in the mid-fifties, the families now travelled by rail, instead of by the traditional regimental baggage wagon and so the railway fare of one penny per mile per person over 12 years of age was given and a halfpenny for the 3–12 year olds.

Women and children had to be on board ship and in their berths before the troops embarked and to return from abroad with their husbands 'when the latter are alive and serving'. Sons over 14 and girls over 16 were not provided with free passage but special consideration was given to 'cases in which destitution would result from girls over 16 being left behind on the embarkation of their parents and soldiers' unmarried daughters were to be returned with their parents, if entitled, without any limit as to age, and granted railway conveyance to their homes on landing'.[24]

MARRIED QUARTERS

The Guards claim the distinction of being the first to provide separate married quarters for their soldiers, as a result of an outbreak of cholera in 1830. Some of their soldiers' wives were billeted in the cholera-infected areas and were brought into the barracks and placed in separate married blocks as an emergency measure. In 1845, the 11th Hussars were also allocating designated barrack rooms to its married couples, where only married families were accommodated and other regiments began to do the same as an alternative to the 'married corner'. But the barrack rooms were often overcrowded, badly ventilated and insanitary and encouraged disease and the Guards refused to admit women into their barracks at Portman Street, London, because they feared the spread of disease.[25] In 1852 a group of officers of the Household Division raised £9000 by private subscription and built the Victoria Lodging House, a hostel for 56 married families in Francis Street, Vauxhall Bridge Road, who were charged two shillings and sixpence per week for two rooms and a kitchen.[26] This first project for permanent soldiers' married quarters was an instant success, although the War Office insisted on buying them out, on the grounds that it was illegal for officers to rent accommodation to soldiers, however small the rent and philanthropic the venture. But the practice of providing *married quarters* for soldiers had been established and would soon become official army policy.

Many voices, both inside and outside the Army, were campaigning for better accommodation for married families. Captain Hugh Scott, for example, who had retired from the 92nd Highlanders, proposed the formation of a commercial company for the purpose of building model lodging houses for the families of married soldiers. These would be in the vicinity of barracks and regularly inspected by the orderly officer. Good conduct and regular payment of rents would be the test of admission, the children would be regular pupils at school and wives at Divine Service every Sunday.[27] His plan did not materialise but that did not stop his campaign for better accommodation and a better marriage ratio —

'The moment you begin to stop what are called imprudent marriages you create and foster immorality. If the present restrictions were removed, a higher class of woman would come into the army'.[28]

EMPLOYMENT FOR WIVES

The basis for the Army's administration, discipline and welfare of the soldier was the regiment — and it was to the regiment that the Army turned for the well-being of its women 'on the strength'.

'As soon as the knot is tied, the wife becomes an institution. She is part of the regiment and has a recognised rank and privileges in it', wrote an Army Chaplain.[29]

One way in which the regiment could help the recognised wife to gain self-respect and become a useful member of the community was through work and gainful employment, especially as a soldier's pay was rarely sufficient to support a wife and child.

'Without her earnings at the wash-tub, they could not live, and some soldiers frankly avow that they chose their wives, as a carter would choose his horse, with an eye to strength and endurance', wrote Patrick Benton in 1871.[30]

Work for the regiment was almost invariably given to those 'on the strength' and to women 'of good behaviour'. It was expected as a condition of permission to marry and of those provided with barrack accommodation. Refusal to work or bad behaviour could lead to their being turned out of barracks and to loss of employment respectively. The regiment thus had a cheap and ready supply of women to do its chores and the commanding officer a method of disciplining them.

Washing was, as we have seen, the traditional task of the women on the strength, for which each soldier paid sixpence, earning a woman on average four shillings a week. The officers' washing was done by the Sergeant's wives or by their servants, if married. Wash places were provided but there was no allowance for fuel, which the women had to supply themselves. The state of the wash-houses in Aldershot in 1858 was described as cold and ankle-deep in mud. There was no drying room attached to the wash-houses and, therefore, when the weather was wet, the officers' linen shared the fate of the men's: that is, it was hung on lines round the central stove in the huts used night and day by the married people.[31]

Some of the more dependable would be employed as maids and nurse-maids with officers' families and sometimes work for the wives, widows and daughters of soldiers could be found outside the unit lines — in the Army clothing factories at Woolwich or repairing tents and bedding at Aldershot.

The Daily News argued that there was plenty of work for soldiers' wives to do rather than consigning them and their children to the tender mercies of

Bumbledom and the Poor Law Commissioners.

> 'They might make uniforms, shirts and stockings for the Army, lint and bandages for the military hospitals, and for those wounded in the field. Many a poor girl who followed her husband to Varna or Constantinople during the late war in the Crimea never got any farther and either died there of want and misery, or years after might have been found tramping about the towns of Russia and Turkey in a condition to which even death had been a relief'.[32]

Nursing and teaching, especially for the better educated, became increasingly available in the latter half of the century. Instructions concerning the engagement and duties of matrons and head nurses employed in regimental hospitals were first issued in 1812 and contained a clause as late as 1838 'preference should be given to the wife of an NCO or soldier of the Regiment'. They were supposed to be 'sober, careful, cleanly and accustomed to the charge and management of sick persons', in contrast to nurses in civil hospitals who were notorious for their drunkenness and promiscuity.[33] But despite the recommendations of Florence Nightingale, the general use of women in military hospitals was resisted by the War Office, because of the impropriety of nursing large numbers of men suffering from venereal diseases.[34] No such opposition was forthcoming for the employment of women in hospitals and wards for wives and children and in some regiments midwives were employed and paid out of regimental funds. In 1884 Army Regulations[35] authorised the pay of a matron and midwife in military hospitals 'at no more than two shillings per day' and the Army Medical Department started schemes for the training of army wives in midwifery to be used in regiments.

Teaching in the Army's schools, both at home and abroad, was another source of employment for the wives and daughters of soldiers and NCOs.[36] Regimental schools were officially recognised in 1811 and by the middle of the century were to be found wherever the Army had a garrison, run by the schoolmaster sergeant and by schoolmistresses appointed in 1840, if qualified 'to instruct the Female Children of Our Soldiers in the 3 R's, in housewifery and needlework and to train them in habits of diligence, honesty and piety'. By 1858 there were 12,000 children in the regimental schools, the Infants and Elder girls being taught by the schoolmistress, often married to the schoolmaster. In 1861, the Newcastle Commission noted that

> 'the supply of trained schoolmistresses to regiments is difficult. There are abundance of candidates for training, chiefly wives and daughters of NCOs, and generally of a low standard of educational qualification, although often possessing those personal qualifications which are more important'.

The Regulations of 1863 improved their pay and raised the age of pupil teacher assistants from 15 to 17. A new class of Assistant Schoolmistresses was created, 'being selected NCO's wives with the same pay and conditions as pupil-teachers'.[37] In March 1865 there were 443 female teachers employed in army schools, 'all well qualified for their positions.' An example was Mrs Woodman of the Buffs, who had been left a widow with three children at the age of 24. She remarried (Mrs Pemberton) and became a qualified Army Schoolmistress in 1874, teaching with the Artillery Brigade at Portsmouth on a salary of £30 per annum, plus 8/6d per week for lodging, fuel and light allowance.[37]

The Royal Commission of 1870 noted that the attendance at school of the children of NCOs and soldiers, married with leave, was compulsory. The attendance problems which plagued civilian schools did not exist for the Army!

> 'All married soldiers shall send their children to the school of the Regiment or Garrison', stated Army Regulations, 'on pain of being liable to be deprived of the privileges attendant on the residence of their wives in Barracks'.

At this date there were 20,000 children in the Army's 172 schools at home and in the colonies.[38]

THE UNRECOGNISED WIFE

Whilst the Army helped with the accommodation and employment of those 'married on the strength', its marriage policy had always been, as we have seen, to refuse to recognise and thus to help those who had married (or concealed the fact on attestation) without official permission.

> 'A soldier encumbered with a wife and family almost always loses zeal', stated the Quarterly Review in 1846, 'and if he marry without the permission of the commanding officer, he loses flesh also. Whenever you see a miserable half-starved looking creature in the ranks, you may put him down as one of the unfortunates, whose wives are not recognised in the corps'.[39]

It was difficult to discover (1863) how many soldiers in a regiment were married without leave, as they had every reason to conceal the fact. 'Such marriages are prudently ignored and every precaution is used to deter the men from contracting them'.[40] Every month the Pay-sergeant warned them, on parade, of the consequences of marrying without permission (struck off the list of applicants and debarred for the future).

> 'But passion is often stronger than prudence and it is only when a regiment is ordered on foreign service that the actual number of such marriages becomes known. Without adequate support, they go, with their children, 'upon the parish' or receive what little help (money, food, clothing) the regimental funds can provide', wrote an Army Chaplain.[40]

A Field Officer, with much regimental experience, argued that:

> 'One cannot restrict human nature by regulations .
> Soldiers will marry when they have found a desirable partner for life. The only result of restriction is to bring misery on respectable women and to drive good soldiers out of the service .
> But the social status of soldiers' wives was bad, partly because of the soldiers own

reputation for licentious and immoral behaviour and partly because a large number of them have been either mill-hands, lower class servants, or, we regret to say, regular street walkers'.

Yet, despite such drawbacks, he still believed that a married soldier was better than a single one.[41]

The Army Chaplain[40] did not support the idea of more marriages.

'Few lawyers, doctors or clergymen are in a position to marry, before they are 30 years of age. The average age of our soldiers when they enter the army is 18, and they can always receive permission to marry before they have been 10 years in the service, or return to civil life at the end of that period'.

A much more real and substantial grievance was that, while widows of commissioned officers, who had completed 10 years' service, received a pension equal to a quarter of their husbands' full pay, the widows of NCOs and privates received nothing at all.

'It would be a great boon to a poor woman, struggling with poverty, to receive 6d or 3d per day'.[40]

The Duke of Wellington had had little sympathy for the Army's unofficial wives.

'Let no woman be acknowledged in a corps, who has married a soldier contrary to the will of the commanding officer. Let no aid in money or otherwise be afforded her to follow her husband, and if she do make her way to his headquarters, let nobody connected with the regiment notice her. Such language may sound harsh in the ears of those who do not know the extent of the evil, which a soldier brings upon himself and upon the partner of his folly by marrying without leave'.[42]

Half a century later (in 1866), the *Pall Mall Gazette* took the same line.[43]

'The number of men who, in defiance of the regulations, marry without leave is very large; and the amount of misery to which these marriages give rise can be appreciated only by those who have an intimate knowledge of the case. These women are a perpetual source of anxiety and trouble. Importunate for admission to the charmed circle of privileged wives, they foster discontent in the minds of their husbands, who are daily condemned to see them at a disadvantage with other women, not more honestly married, and enduring very bitter poverty and distress'.

Unfortunately, the chief misery fell on the unoffending woman rather than upon the guilty man — 'These women, won by the smart coat and the flash and finery, are wholly ignorant of military regulations and restrictions and find married life cruelly different from what they had imagined'. Even though conditions had improved and the women were 'no longer subject to those outrages upon common decency which long disgraced the service', her home in the Army was a very miserable one and living on a fixed pay neutralised the improvements of schools for the children at a mere nominal cost, supply of rations at a reduced rate, the recent introduction of regimental canteens and the charitable exertions of self-organised committees of benevolent ladies. It was useless to impose more penalties on those who married without permission, 'because the penalties are already severe and fall on the partner least able to bear additional burdens'.[43]

REMEDIES NEEDED

The Gazette (1866) suggested that length of service and good conduct should determine marriage.

> 'No man should be allowed to marry until he has served 7 or 8 or more years: permission to marry should strictly depend on good conduct'.

Permission to marry should be made a privilege, in reality as well as in name; and the authorised soldier should be able to look forward to a time 'when he will be able to bring his wife to a suitable, respectable home, and to assure her of full recognition by the State of her marriage'. Each garrison should be provided with sufficient quarters to accommodate properly the maximum number of married soldiers and their families: a small allowance, in money or kind, should be made, as in India, to each wife and child: the industrial resources of wife and elder children should be developed: more pains should be taken to establish the respectability of a woman before she is allowed to marry and admitted to these privileges: the children should become the responsibility of the State and the sons enlisted, if possible, into the Army and more consideration should be shown to wives and families, especially when the regiment changed quarters or went overseas.[43]

PUNISHMENT OF WIVES

One further point should be noted in the Army's attempts to regulate marriage and the married women. Its system of awarding certain privileges to those married on the strength meant that such privileges could be withdrawn as a disciplinary measure. Women who broke the regimental rules could be punished, and frequently were, by striking them off the strength and returning them to their homes. They were denied the benefits of accommodation, rations, medical services, employment and schooling for their children.

The Standing Orders of the Queen's Royal Regiment 1877 stated:

> 'Any soldier's wife who disturbs the Barracks, or who is dirty in her habits or who does not behave respectably, will be turned out of barracks and deprived of washing, as will anyone whose children do not attend school. All soldiers' wives living in barracks are expected to attend Church with the Regiment and to appear there decently dressed.'[44]

In most regiments the orderly officer inspected the married accommodation daily; in some 'the colonel's lady, as female commanding officer, has marched the women to church in the same manner as her husband marched the men', wrote a Staff Sergeant in 1871.[45]

The 82nd Foot preserve in their Regimental Museum at Warrington a Punishment Book for Barrack Women which shows how Regulations were applied to the wives. The Book contains 144 entries during the period July 1866 to 31 May 1895, covering tours in India (1866), Ireland, Portsmouth, Natal, Singapore (1888) and Gibraltar (1889–1891). The commonest offences were drunkenness, abusive and obscene language to other women, officers and soldiers, and creating a disturbance, often committed in combination. Other offences were:– having men other than their husbands in their quarters; being out of quarters after 'lights out'; fighting with other women or refusing to clean their quarters properly. Sentences ranged from cautions and reprimands to fines and orders to leave the regiment and withdrawal of privileges:–

> 1867 Mian Mir, India 'Being in the Regimental Bazaar at an improper hour and abusive language to Police Corporal'. Reprimanded.
> 1870 Portsmouth 'Attempting to stab another wife, abusive language and creating a disturbance,' for which the woman was 'turned out of Barracks and struck off the Strength of the Regiment'.
> 1890 Gibraltar 'Allowing single men to frequent her quarter'. Reprimand and last caution.

The disciplinary powers of the Army concerning civilians, including army wives, were codified in the Army Act of 1881, which superseded the earlier Mutiny Acts and Articles of War. We should note also that the Manual of Military Law punished very severely offences against women and children.

As early as 1627 the Articles of War had made rape a capital crime.

> 'If any soldier do force any woman or maid he is to suffer death'.[46]

In 1901 penal servitude for life was the punishment for having carnal knowledge of a girl under 13 and imprisonment for two years, with or without hard labour, for carnal knowledge of a girl under 16, whilst rape, abduction, keeping a disorderly house or procuration of women for commercial purposes and offences against children and servants were explicitly covered under the provisions of Military Law.

One of the most serious offences for an officer was to be convicted of sexual relations with the wife of a soldier, especially one in his own Regiment or Company. For example,

> 'For conduct highly unbecoming in an officer, in having possessed himself of the wife of W.M. at that time a private in the same company to which he, Lieutenant J. is attached, and having detained her in concealment for several months. Finding: Guilty. Sentence: To be suspended from rank and pay for 3 months. 'I confirm the sentence; but in doing so, think it right to declare my opinion of its inadequacy.' Signed G. Hewitt.[47]
> *Case 20*. Colombo 18 February, 1814. Lieutenant R.C. 19th Foot.
> 'For degrading himself, by frequenting the house of a private of the same regiment and associating on terms of undue familiarity with his wife, on several occasions, was sentenced to be suspended from rank and pay for 3 calendar months, and to be publicly and severely reprimanded. The General Officer Commanding in confirming sentence said that the prisoner's conduct was 'Derogatory to his rank and situation and injurious to discipline and subordination of H.M.'s service, for nothing can be more reprehensible or more seriously affect the character of an officer and a gentleman, than demeaning himself by an open and avowed criminal intercourse with a soldier's wife, thus degrading

himself to a level with the soldier, extinguishing all that respect for his officer which should ever reign in the breast of a private soldier.'[47]

THE MARITAL STATE OF THE ARMY IN 1851–1871

The Census Reports for 1851–1871 provide valuable information on the marital state of the Army. 'The conjugal condition of the army differs very much from that of the other professions', states the 1871 Report.[48] 'Proportionally, more officers than soldiers are married, yet the proportion of husbands is less among them than it is among the general population at the earlier ages.' (Appendix A). Complete returns provided by the Commander in Chief from home and abroad showed that on 3 April 1871 the married state of the British Army was as follows:

TABLE 1

Officers   Men

Total	Single	Married	Widowers	%S	%M	%W	Total	Single	Married	Widowers	%S	%M	%W
9,838	6,387	3,287	155	64.9	33.5	1.6	183,769	158,405	24,247	1,117	86.2	13.2	0.6

Source: 1871 Census. Table 131.

The *civilian rates* were single males 27.1%: married 66.1%: Widowers 6.8%. The number and ages of wives and children in the British Army in 1871 are shown in Table 2 (Appendix B).

The Report shows that marriage for the majority of both officers and men was postponed until the 30–40 age group, comparing very unfavourably with the general population. The Army is 'as regards matrimony in the condition of the Roman citizens under Augustus: this is partly due to their duties taking them from home, and partly to the low rate of pay'.[48]

TABLE 2

Proportion of Married Men at each age from 20 to 50 in 1871

Age	Married Officers in 100	Married Men in 100	Married Males in 100 General Population
20–24 inclusive	3	2	23
25–29 inclusive	16	11	60
30–34 inclusive	38	25	75
35–39 inclusive	57	37	82
40–44 inclusive	68	43	83
45–49 inclusive	75	64	84

Source: 1871 Census p.xl (See Appendix A for detailed comparisons of years 1851–1871).

The 1851 Census was the first to survey the 'conjugal condition of the United Kingdom'. 10 years later the Report noted that married women in the 15–55 age groups had increased by 16%, 'chiefly the cause and partly the result of the prosperity of the country.' In 1861 the average age of husbands in England was 43.0 years and that of the wives 40.5: the ratio of widows to wives was 1 to 5 respectively. While the marriage rate was increasing among the general population between 1851 and 1871, the rate amongst officers and men in a much larger army fluctuated considerably, almost certainly caused by the wars of the 1850s, as can be seen from the following Table:

TABLE 3

Year	Number of Officers	Number of Officers' wives	% Married Officers	Number of other ranks	Number of other ranks' wives	% Married other ranks	% Married males (civilians)[49] aged 20+)
1851	6,593	1,675	25.4	136,277	20,755	15·2	62·6
1861	10,262	2,639	25·7	219,299	22,715	10·4	65·4
1871	9,838	3,296	33·5	183,769	24,247	13·2	66·1

Source: Census of Great Britain 1851 Vol I Pt 2. Population Tables (HMSO) 1854 p xlvii.
Census of England and Wales 1861 Vol 3, General Report (HMSO) 1863, p 146.
Census of England and Wales 1871 Vol 4 General Report (HMSO) 1873 p 132.

Trustram found that, of the soldiers quartered in the UK in 1863 the marriage rates were lowest in the Infantry (11%), Cavalry (13%) and highest in the Artillery (19%) and the Engineers (24%).[50]

Whom did the soldiers marry? In general, we know that soldiers tended to marry within other soldiers' families (widows and daughters) and from amongst the poorest women in the garrison towns and neighbourhoods. A large proportion of the wives were Irish, since there was a large number of Irish recruits in the Army and after 1871 a quarter of the home-based troops were stationed in Ireland.[51] The 1871 Census (Table I) confirms this and shows that almost half the soldiers' wives and children were born outside England (Appendix B). In 1861 Colonel Collingwood Dickson, Royal Artillery, said in evidence to the Royal Commission on Recruiting 'I think the women generally of that class in England look more to the future and hesitate to marry a soldier, whereas in Ireland, and indeed in Scotland, they do not think about it; they marry them at once without reflecting. I think that the young women in England are more careful about marrying a soldier'.[52]

78

Judy O'Grady and the Colonel's Lady

Appendix A to Chapter 6

Proportion of officers and men serving in the British Army* who are married compared with the proportion of married men in the general population of Great Britain 1851–1871

Ages	Married Officers			Married Other Ranks			Civilian Married Males		
	1851	1861	1871	1851	1861	1871	1851**	1861	1871
20–24	4.3	3.8	2.6	5.1	2.5	1.5	19.5	22.3	23.0
25–29	15.4	17.2	15.9	14.7	10.5	10.8	53.8	58.7	59.6
30–34	34.8	36.4	38.3	27.9	23.8	25.1	71.0	75.4	75.0
35–39	48.0	55.2	56.6	42.7	37.1	36.6	77.9	81.7	81.8
40–44	58.3	64.7	68.2	54.3	48.3	43.2	80.1	82.6	83.4
45–49	63.9	71.2	75.1	72.5	68.9	64.0	80.6	83.0	84.2
50–54	65.2	71.8	82.0	89.5	84.8	82.8	79.1	81.0	82.1
55–59	68.6	71.3	80.7	81.3	90.4	89.7	76.9	78.9	80.0
60–64	65.8	63.0	50.0	76.5	84.6	78.9	72.0	73.0	73.0
65 +	51.3	55.0	55.0	63.2	78.4	85.0	57.4	67.0	68.0
All Ages	25.4	25.7	33.5	15.2	10.4	13.2	33.2	55.4	55.9

* *Home and Abroad.*
** *Great Britain.*
Source: Census of Great Britain 1851 Vol 2 Population Tables HMSO

1854 p X VII (Table 20).

Census of England and Wales 1861 Vol 3 General Report HMSO

1863 pp 120, 146. (Table 106).

Census of England and Wales 1871 Vol 4 General Report HMSO

1873 pp 63, 132. (Table 131).

(To read Table: In 1851 there were 48 married officers in every 100 officers in the age group 35 to 39 inclusive)

Appendix B to Chapter 6

TABLE 1

Country of Birth of Wives and Children in the British Army 1871 (53)

	Total	English	%	Scots	%	Irish	%	Colonial & Foreign	%
Officers' Wives	3,177	2,284	71.9	259	8.2	541	17.0	93	2.9
Officers' Children	5,914	4,125	69.8	547	9.2	1,113	18.8	129	2.2
Soldiers' Wives	23,637	12,664	53.6	1,715	7.2	7,966	33.7	1,292	5.5
Soldiers' Children	40,985	23,419	57.1	2,922	7.1	12,603	30.8	2,041	5.0
Total Wives & Children	73,713	42,492	57.6	5,443	7.4	22,223	30.2	3,555	4.8

Source: 1871 Census Table 134 Appendix A.

TABLE 2

Number and Ages of Wives and Children in the British Army 1871 (53)

Ages	Officers' Wives & Children				Soldiers' Wives & Children			
	Total	Wives	Boys	Girls	Total	Wives	Boys	Girls
Total	9,091	3,177	2,896	3,018	64,622	23,637	20,351	20,634
Under 5	2,697	—	1,334	1,363	23,546	—	11,710	11,836
5 to 9	1,851	—	903	948	12,584	—	6,283	6,301
10 to 14	1,151	—	559	592	4,658	3	2,277	2,378
15 to 19	271	56	100*	115*	791	591	81*	119*
20 –	629	629	—	—	3,805	3,805	—	—
25 –	967	967	—	—	7,419	7,419	—	—
30 –	658	658	—	—	6,261	6,261	—	—
35 –	441	441	—	—	3,548	3,548	—	—
40 –	246	246	—	—	1,363	1,363	—	—
45 –	104	104	—	—	437	437	—	—
50 –	49	49	—	—	129	129	—	—
55 +	27	27	—	—	81	81	—	—

* *Including a few above 20 years of age.*

Chapter 7

Early Home-Making in India

In 1816 Wellington's army was reduced drastically to 100,000 men and Europe was destined to enjoy 40 years of peace. But there was to be plenty of service in the garrisons overseas for the soldier — in Canada, India, South Africa, the Mediterranean and in the East and West Indies. At home the reduced army was required for duty in Scotland or Ireland or went the rounds of the English garrison towns, spending a year or so in each before marching on to their next duty station. After the exciting campaigns of the Napoleonic Wars, many of the officers returned to the duties and pleasures of country house life, to rural parsonages or to the world of fashion and politics in the towns. The dandies of Regency England continued to seek commissions in the élite Guards' and Household Cavalry regiments, which were stationed mostly in and around London, enjoying the social and military life. Assisting the regular army to maintain internal order and security would be the part-time soldiers of the militia, whose commanding officers were the local squires or lords of the manor, their social superiors, who became their military leaders as a matter of course.

Three-quarters of the infantry regiments would be employed in overseas' stations, chiefly to protect the frontiers of the Empire and to quell any native unrest. The majority of these troops were stationed in India, which would become the largest family station overseas, until the Second World War. It was destined to become the most important 'colony' in the Empire — 'the brightest jewel in the British Crown'. Its very name conjures up pictures of bejewelled maharajahs and their wives in splendid palaces; of warlike hill tribesmen swooping down to plunder a merchant caravan or peaceful village; of rabble-rousers in the teeming bazaars. On the other hand, one sees the sun-topeed British soldiers, the turbanned Indian sepoys, strung out in small garrisons, holding out against massive odds; of relief columns and cavalry charges. One imagines a huge land, of massive population, of exotic sights, sounds and smells; of Himalayan mountains and boulder-strewn hillsides in the north-west; of the jungles and hills of Central India; of the great plains and mighty rivers, the palms and coral beaches of the South. Above all, the popular image is of a land of great extremes of race, religion, language, culture, and of wealth and poverty.[1]

EARLY BEGINNINGS

The Indian Empire grew from a collection of small commercial stations maintained by the East India company, trading from London, under a Charter granted by Queen Elizabeth I dated 1600. By 1857 three-fifths of India would come under its control by treaty, bribery, annexation and open conquest. In 1668 Charles II rented to the East India Company the port of Bombay, which he had received as part of his wedding dowry. Together with Calcutta and Madras, it became the main base for the Company, and Charles sent out four companies of British troops in 1662 (who transferred their allegiance to the Company in 1668) to defend it against its French, Dutch and Portuguese rivals.

All recruits, intended for military or administrative careers, had to be single, were expected to behave themselves and to keep away from the Black Town.

Wives were strongly discouraged and the original charters of the East India Company prohibited women in its factory settlements. But this proved difficult to enforce, when there was such a ready supply of attractive local women from Goa, the progeny of Portuguese traders and settlers. The Company became very concerned about the morals of its employees recruited from England, many of whom took native mistresses, and more especially with the religious consequences of taking wives from the Roman Catholic communities, established around their trading centres of Madras and Bombay. In 1676 the Company's chaplain in Madras complained —

> 'some come out under the notion of single persons and unmarried, who yet have their wives in England and here have lived in adultery'. Others arrived as married couples, 'of whom there are strange suspicions they were never married.'[2]

The Company's solution was to arrange for boat-loads of young, single Protestant girls to come out from Britain for the marriage market and to forbid local marriages without the Governor's consent.

The first records of such English shipments occur in 1671 when 20 'sober and civil' women were sent out to Bombay at the Company's expense, but scandals followed and culprits were warned they would be put on bread and water and shipped back to England.[2] In 1690, the Rev. J. Ovington arrived in Bombay as chaplain to the East India Company and described a situation, which would remain for the next 100 years for the girls coming out to India.

> 'The East India Company allow marriage to their Factors, and Liberty to young women to pass thither and gain Husbands, and raise their Fortunes. As considerable trouble attends the Passage, especially of women, as well as the length of the Voyage, a modest Woman may very well expect, without any great Stock of Honour or Wealth, a Husband of Repute and Riches there, after she has run all this Danger and Trouble for him'.[3]

MARRIAGE CONTRACTS

Women were graded into 'gentlewomen' and 'other women', according to the social conventions of the times. They were not given dowries, but were provided with their 'diet', board and lodging and one set of wearing apparel for the year, while they sought husbands. If they failed to marry within that time, the Company either frowned severely on their morals or threatened to send them home. For the successful, the Company provided marriage allowances or 'jointures' of £300 a year to the husband, which continued to his widow for life. Such 'eagerly sought after prizes' formed the mercenary basis for matrimony which was noted by one wife, writing to her friend Maria in England.

> 'Wives are looking out with gratitude for the next death that may carry off their husbands, in order that they may return to England to live upon their Jointures; they live a married life in absolute misery, that they may enjoy a widowhood of affluence and independence. This is no exaggeration, I assure you'.[4]

Little is known of the lives and fortunes of these women who travelled to India before 1750. Sometimes the Musulmen pirates captured the shiploads and sent them to the slave market at Surat, instead. But having survived the hazards of the voyage, many of the women (and children) who settled in India were destined to suffer the horrors of war and siege at the hands of the French or a native Prince in the colonial struggle for control of India. In 1745 the fate of the women and children captured in Madras is unknown, but many died in the sacking of Calcutta and in the 'Black Hole' in Fort William in 1756. The military commander who recaptured Calcutta and avenged the outrage at the Battle of Plassey (1757) was Robert Clive. The meteoric career of this son of an impoverished squire, who rose from a merchant's clerk to become one of Britain's most successful generals, all in 12 years, is one of the romances of history. He started the rebuilding of Fort William, which became the home of the Calcutta garrison, and set about reorganising the Army and annexing Bengal. The anniversary of Plassey was celebrated with wild festivities, salutes and a banquet, at which

> 'dancing girls entertained the company until supper was announced, when each officer endeavoured to have the lady of his choice conveyed to his room for his subsequent delectation. There was much clamour as to who picked whom. 'I know mine by the ring in her nose' said one officer. While his back was turned, another officer whipped the ring off her nose and carried her off before his face'.[5]

It was the capture of Madras by the French in 1746 and of Calcutta in 1756, which led to the influx of soldiers, both Company's and Royal troops, and with them of European women and camp followers. The 39th Foot (The Dorset Regiment) had formed part of Clive's small force of 3,000 Europeans and sepoys; by 1790 there were 6,000 Regulars under the Company's command. They would remember Clive also for the Military Fund he set up in 1770 for the widows of officers and men who lost their lives in the service of the Army in India. His own marriage to Margaretha Maskelyne, who arrived in Madras at the age of 16 to visit her brother, Captain Edmund Maskelyne, in the company of 10 other marriageable young ladies seeking romance and adventure in India, is recorded in the Register of Marriages kept at Fort St George, Madras. '18 February 1753 at Vepery Garrison Church'. Other entries in the Register show the method of recording local marriages — Private John Fox (72nd Regiment) with Francisco Johnson (a Papist) on 13 April 1789 at Tanjore: Thomas Waterhouse Clarke (1st Battalion Artillery) with Cornelia Leechman (a native) 12 April 1794: Robert Charles (74th Regiment) with Francesca Flovey (a Portuguese woman) 10 January 1795 at Tanjore: Corporal William Wilson (74th Regiment) with Jean Craig (widow of the late Robert Craig (a European woman) 7 October 1793, Tanjore).[6]

WARREN HASTINGS

In 1780 the European inhabitants of Madras suffered the horrors of starvation and another siege at the very moment when the Government was busy giving a grand masquerade ball for a bevy of beautiful girls who had just arrived from England. This time the hero was Warren Hastings, who arrived in India in 1750. He became Governor-General and was to share with Clive, the title of founder of the British Indian Empire. Hastings also married in India — a young widow, Mary Buchanan, whose Captain husband died in the Black Hole of Calcutta. She herself was to die within three years of her second marriage. (Early deaths and remarriage were commonplace — Hastings's own father, a parson, married three times in seven years). But Warren Hastings's second marriage was an even more romantic affair. In 1769, travelling back to India on leave, he met on board the 'Duke of Grafton', Baron and Baroness von Imhoff. The Baron, an army officer in a small German state, was en route for Madras to seek employment in the Bengal Army. Maria and Hastings became lovers, the Baron seemingly more interested in making money than in protecting his wife's virtue. In Madras they formed a '*ménage à trois*', an arrangement so satisfactory that when Hastings left to take up his duties as Governor of Bengal, the Imhoffs followed him to Calcutta. In 1773 the Baron sued Maria for divorce in a German court, almost certainly financed by Hastings himself, and four years later when the process had been completed, Hastings finally married his Baroness 'without any scandal'. Maria was by this time 30 years of age, strikingly beautiful, dressing with taste rather than fashion and of a gay and vivacious disposition. 'Nothing could be more characteristic', sums up the Dictionary of National Biography 'than the quiet tenacity with which Hastings carried on this strange and protracted love affair: indeed it only ceased with his long life'. The marriage was very happy and the two lie side by side in Daylesford Churchyard (Stow-on-the-Wold.) Maria's son, Charles, became a General.

EARLY DEATHS

The women, who survived battles and sieges, were also threatened by their failure to adapt their European habits, diet, drinking and clothing to a tropical climate. They continued to indulge their English custom of eating enormous meals, washed down with great quantities of wine and of dressing in the London fashions. Powdered wigs and ribboned bonnets, hoops and farthingales, flounced petticoats, whaleboned stays and tight pantaloons were quite unsuited to the Indian climate. So, too, was the custom at the end of 18th century of dancing through the night, from 9 p m to 5 a m, during which they literally 'danced themselves into the grave' through excessive physical exertion, followed by the exposure of their heated bodies to the cold, damp night air.

And then there were the endemic diseases of India-fevers, dysentry and cholera. The links between infected water and cholera, mosquitoes and malaria were unknown until the 19th century. Bombay, where the English died like flies, was noted for its bad climate. Madras on the East coast had a better climate, 'the inhabitants enjoying perfect Health, as they would do in England', wrote the Rev. Ovington in 1710; Of Bengal, Captain Alexander Hamilton, writing with accuracy and wit in the early 18th Century stated — 'The Company has a pretty good hospital at Calcutta, where many go in to undergo the Penance of Physick but few come out to give account of its Operation'. Early and sudden deaths by cholera were very frequent occurrences.

In 1843 the 63rd Foot stationed at Bellary in India lost two officers and an officer's wife and 89 other ranks, seven women, five children and from 200 to 300 camp followers in three weeks during an epidemic. Of the 60 wives, who arrived in India with the 74th Foot (H L I) in 1789, only two remained when the Regiment left in 1805.[7]

Another victim of the climate was a descendant of Barbara Villiers. In 1776 Colonel Manson was buried in the South Park Street cemetery in Calcutta, beside his wife, Lady Anne, who had died a few months previously.

> 'She felt herself too good for Indian society, being in fact a daughter of the Earl of Darlington and a great grand-daughter of Charles II by Barbara Villiers. But she consoled herself for her uncourtly surroundings by whist parties that led the fashion in Calcutta. She set afloat the story that Warren Hastings was the natural son of a steward of her father's.'

But 16 months of Calcutta's climate silenced her back-biting for ever. 'After lying speechless through the day, she departed last night at 10 o'clock' recorded a contemporary. 'The poor lady has talked no Scandal since'.[8]

English girls from Britain were not the only source of marriage. The Dutch girls of Capetown cornered part of the market, since many officers of the East India Company spent their leave in South Africa, owing to the leave regulations, which stipulated that all leave at, or eastward of, Cape Colony counted as service with full pay and retention of appointment, while, westwards, both appointment and allowances were lost. General J. S. Rawlins commented that:

'many flocked to the Cape, and spent a pleasant furlough there, since Dutch people are famed for their hospitality and sport and their daughters are exceedingly agreeable and good-looking . . . few young men could resist the charms of the fair maids of Capetown; consequently many a Cape girl married an Indian officer, or civilian better still, as the latter was always worth, dead or alive, £300 a year! and these alliances afforded them much pleasure, as their parents were ambitious and rejoiced to see their girls lifted in the social scale and thus happily united'.[9]

Few officers would consider marriage with Indian women but up to 1800 there was no public opinion against irregular unions or open concubinage with them. Some senior officers and wealthy European officials set up permanent households with the woman presiding over a zenana (seraglio) or having a separate establishment (beebeeghar), where she entertained her consort's guests. General Martin, who joined the Royal Army (see page 86) around 1761, for example, kept four Eurasian concubines, while General John Pater, unable to bury his beloved Arabella in consecrated ground, buried her in a field and built a church over her body.[9] The children were often treated as members of the family and given a good education, many, especially if of a light colour, being sent to schools in England.

LOCAL GIRLS FOR THE SOLDIERS

Since the soldier had to obtain his commanding officer's permission to marry and was constantly on the move, his unions were frequently of a temporary nature and invariably with the lowest classes. If he did marry officially, it was usually with a Christian Eurasian girl.

Alexander Alexander,[10] an artilleryman stationed in Ceylon in 1805, was advised by the old soldiers of the 19th Foot (Green Howards) to take a native wife who would cook for him and purchase better food than he could get in the barrack mess. He erected a hut in the garrison and then chose 'a Singhalese girl of a clear bronze colour, smooth-skinned, healthy and very cleanly in her person and manner of cooking, which was her chief recommendation'. But she wanted money, or clothes and pretended to be sick, lying in bed for twenty-four hours together and [would] neither speak, nor take food or medicine, but lie and sulk'. He tried flattery and cajolery but 'I had not money to satisfy her extravagance, my victuals remained uncooked and the hut in confusion. There was no alternative but to follow the example of the others. I applied the strap of my greatcoat, which never failed to effect a cure, at least for a time'. Alexander was transferred to Headquarters at Colombo and made plans to send his wife there by sea, but, although he continued to send her money, he never saw her again. Later, he heard from his regiment that she had got another husband. Many a poor soldier showed a similar affection for his mistress, wrote another chronicler. One left his slave-girl her freedom and 15 rupees a month: another, when he was ordered inland, left his mistress to his friend.[10]

TWO SEPARATE ARMIES

In 1815, there were two completely separate armies in India — the Royal Army, consisting largely of British troops from home and the Army of the East India Company, part native, part European, recruited, paid and employed separately by each of the three Presidencies into which British India was divided — Bombay, Madras and Bengal — each Presidency having its own Governor and military and civil officers.

The Company also maintained in India at its own expense up to 20,000 Royal troops and by an Act of 1788 up to 12,200 European troops in its European regiments and native regiments under European officers. The officers did not purchase their commissions; promotion was by seniority with none from the ranks. The sons of the great titled and landed families seldom applied, candidates coming instead from the sons of the clergy, solicitors, half pay army and navy officers, merchants, small landowners and officers of the Company itself. Those who entered the Company's service intended to live, marry and settle down in India as their home. Many took up staff, political, or police appointments outside their regiments.

Both armies had a vast, separate army of camp followers, who lived with them in barracks and who accompanied them on campaign — traders, personal servants, mess cooks and waiters, bearers, sweepers, water-carriers and grooms. Although non-combatants, such followers closely associated themselves with their regiments and it became a tradition in many families for son to follow father in his trade with the regiment.

EARLY VOYAGES BY TROOPSHIP

Families journeying to India had to face the dangers and boredom of the 15,000 mile journey via the Cape 'in a sea-prison with a plank between one and eternity', as Ensign George Bell succinctly described it,[11] when he paid £240 to the East India Company to transport his wife, daughter and himself to Madras in 1825 and to cover the cost of the food. Entitled other rank families were provided with free passages and messing. After 1830 the overland route via Alexandria, Cairo and Suez gradually replaced the six months' voyage round the Cape, but, although quicker, it would cost much the same for an officer and his family.

Mrs Sherwood described her journey by troopship, as she accompanied her husband, Captain Sherwood, Paymaster of the 52nd Foot (Oxford Light Infantry) on a four month ordeal to India in 1805.

> 'Those who have not been at sea can never conceive the hundredth part of the horrors of a long voyage to a female in a sailing vessel. Our cabin was just the width of a gun over which the cot was slung, but it could not swing, there being not sufficient height. On entering the cabin, which was formed only of canvas, we were forced to stoop under, there not being one foot from the head or the foot of the cot to the partition . . . We were in constant darkness and we have much putrid water on board'.[12] Food was seldom scarce, but fresh meat and vegetables would run out and scurvy was common.

Dinner for officers and their families was between 1–2 p m and, as the principal recreation, was made to last as long as possible.

One large cabin called the 'cuddy' was the social centre for the families of officers and civilian cabin passengers.

In 1822, the 16th Lancers left Gravesend for India, where the Regiment would spend the next 24 years. On board was Lieutenant John Luard, whose Aunt, Susan Dalbiac, had nursed him back to health, and her husband in Spain in 1812. He was still single, despite three happy years in Ireland, enjoying with his regiment the hospitality of the local gentry and the attentions of the local beauties. 'Several of the officers fell in love', he noted in his diary.[13] 'Lieutenant Harris and I felt very kindly towards a Miss Reynell but she afterwards married Lord Donoughmore: Colonel Pelly married Miss French: Major Persse married a Miss Moore — it was a very hospitable quarter and the officers of the 16th Light Dragoons were paid a great attention.' Only four officers of the Lancers had their wives with them on Luard's ship, but there were several other women passengers on the officers' deck — Miss Gurnet 'a coarse, silly young woman, with an affectation of romance about her', wrote Luard. She was travelling to India with her father in the hope of finding a husband. There was Miss Rowe, 'a half-caste, who nevertheless set several hearts throbbing before the end of the voyage and little Mrs Enderby, who looked like a dry lemon'. The ship's cargo included 44 dozen live ducks and hens, 56 pigs and 70 sheep, so that once the weather grew warmer, the smell between decks was unbearable.

To while away the time the officers played chess, whist or danced on the quarterdeck. 'There were the inevitable shipboard romances, which helped to dispel the boredom but which led to quarrels and jealousy.' Mrs Smallpage, for example, whose husband was a captain in the Indian Cavalry, but who was travelling single, was the object of 'undue attention' from two young subalterns in Luard's troop and Luard had to speak to them most severely, when they proposed to fight a duel for her affections. Mrs Smallpage, said Luard, was 'undeniably attractive, but she was hardly of the social class, from which officers of the 16th Lancers were expected to choose their wives and, in any case, she was a married woman'.

Much the same kind of squabbling went on among the soldiers' families in their primitive accommodation, separated from the men by blankets slung from the bulkhead but expected to use the same lavatories as they did. Down below in the semi-darkness, stifled with heat and nauseated by the stench, mothers gave birth, wrangled amongst themselves or with their husbands, conducted affairs with the soldiers or sailors and longed desperately for the end of the voyage.

When Luard reached India, single English women were still few in number and widely scattered. Liaisons with native women were less frequent among officers and by the time of the Mutiny had become almost unacceptable.

Reginald Heber, Bishop of Calcutta, for instance, could write in 1825:

> 'Connection with native women, though sadly common amongst the elder officers of the
> army, is, among the younger servants, either civil or military, at present by no means a
> fashionable vice'[14]

While William Russell, reporting on India for *The Times* in 1858 noted:

> 'The good old hookah days are past . . . . . The race of Eurasians is not so freely supplied
> with recruits . . . . . There is now no bee-bee's house — a sort of European zenana
> (harem) . . . . . There are now European rivals to those ladies (the native kept women) at
> some stations'.[15]

In 1825, Luard arrived in Meerut, the most popular station in India. He
was 25 and still single but at the age when an officer of his rank and class
started to think of marriage. In Meerut, the senior civilian was Richard
Hastings Scott, the judge and magistrate, and his two sisters Elizabeth and
Maria, kept house for him. They were the 'belles' of Meerut society, and the
target of every unmarried officer of the Lancers but they had opposition in the
person of the garrison commander, General Sir Thomas Reynell — and a
General in love was formidable opposition for a Captain or junior subaltern!
Nevertheless, John Luard was successful and married the 26 year old
Elizabeth in 1826. 'Sir Thomas Reynell was a most generous rival', he wrote
in his diary 'and never altered his friendship for me, and made Elizabeth a
most handsome present of a necklace on her wedding.'[16] They settled down,
high on the social register, to entertain and enjoy married life in such a
fashionable regiment in such a popular station. But after the birth of their
eldest son in 1827, the climate plagued the health of mother and son and the
Luards had to return to England to exchange his commission for a home-
based and less expensive regiment. He was fortunate, for by 1838 he was a
Lieutenant Colonel and his former Regiment, still stationed in Meerut, had
364 out of a strength of 580 in hospital and 48 deaths from cholera. When
Emily Eden visited the European burial ground in Meerut the same year (6
Feb 1838) she could not discover anyone individual who had lived to be more
than 36.

STATION LIFE FOR MARRIED FAMILIES 1830

One of the most vivid and accurate writers on army wives in India during
the 1830s was Emma Roberts (1794–1840).[17] She was well qualified, being
the daughter of a regimental paymaster, Captain William Roberts, and the
niece of a General Thomas, who raised the 111th Regiment in 1794. Her
childhood was spent in Bath, not only a centre of fashion and genteel society
but also home for many an officer's family. In 1828, after her mother's death,
she accompanied her married sister and husband, Captain Robert Adair
McNaghten, to India, as many an impoverished and unmarried girl had done
before her.

'There cannot be a more wretched situation', she wrote feelingly, 'than that of a young woman who has been induced to follow the fortunes of a married sister, under the delusive expectation that she will exchange the privations attached to limited means in England for the far-famed luxuries of the East.'

'Few young women, who have accompanied their married sisters to India, possess the means of returning home: however strong their dislike may be of the country, their lot is cast in it, and they must remain in a state of miserable dependence, with the danger of being left unprovided for before them, until they shall be rescued from this distressing situation by an offer of marriage'.[17]

Emma did not marry. In 1831, on the death of her sister, she went to Calcutta to live and wrote a number of successful books and articles on India, and edited an Indian newspaper. She died in Poona in 1840 at the home of her friend, Colonel Campbell.

During the three years she spent with the McNaghtens in various military stations in Northern India, she observed the life of the soldier and his family:

SOLDIERS' WIVES

'The soldiers' wants are carefully attended to, but their enjoyments are few. They have not many opportunities of forming matrimonial connections with people of their own colour. Many simply vegetate: when a regiment returns home, many volunteer to serve in India, because all links with home have been severed'.[17]

'In no other country in the world can the wives and children of European soldiers enjoy the comforts and happiness which await them in India. The lot of the children is especially fortunate: schools are established in every regiment for the instruction of children of both sexes. The education of persons, belonging to their class in society, can be carried on as well in India as in England; they are taught to make themselves useful; the boys with a view to becoming non-commissioned officers, regimental clerks, etc; the girls to be made industrious servants, and fitting wives for men in a rank rather superior to that from which they themselves have sprung. European ladies gladly take the females into service at an early age, and, if they do not retain their situations long, it is because they are eagerly sought in marriage by their fathers' comrades, or by shop-keepers who chance to be located in their vicinity. The daughters of dragoon soldiers, sometimes aspire to be 'belles'; they enjoy the fashions brought out by new arrivals of a higher class, and do great execution at the balls, which upon grand occasions are given by the élite of the NCOs of the corps'.[17]

Soldiers' wives in India were free from the laborious toils and continual hardships to which they had to submit in countries where the pay of their husbands was inadequate to support them. If sober and industrious, they could easily accumulate a little hoard for the comfort of their declining years.

Acquaintance with any useful art, dress-making, feather-cleaning, lace-mending, washing silk stockings, or the like, might be converted into very lucrative employments. Furthermore, many had the opportunity of becoming ladies'-maids or wet nurses with wealthy families at salaries of 50 to 100 rupees a month, since few officers' wives attached to the King's Army could afford to keep white female servants: 'alas, such unaccustomed luxury made them so lazy, insolent and overbearing that few could be tolerated for long outside the barracks'.

PHILANDERING MALES

The soldiers' wives had to be protected from philanderers and predatory males —

> 'In many garrisons, soldiers have been permitted to construct a theatre for their own performances. Infinite pains are taken to divest theatrical amusements of the danger which might arise from love scenes between married women and gay Lotharios. The soldiers' wives are not permitted to enact the heroines in dramatic entertainments, lest it should lead to deviations from the path of duty: and when female characters cannot be cut out, they are performed by beardless youths — much to the deterioration of the spectacle.'[17]

MARRIAGE AND MOTIVES

Emma gave her opinion of the candidates for marriage and their motives. The popular view of the young ladies who visited India was that they were destined to be sacrificed to some old, dingy, rich, bilious nabob. A few such no doubt existed but generally speaking, these elderly gentlemen had either taken to themselves wives in their younger days, or had become such confirmed bachelors, that neither flashing eyes, smiling lips, lilies, roses, dimples etc. comprehending the whole catalogue of female fascinations, could make the slightest impression upon their flinty hearts.

> 'Happy is the young damsel who can capture such a rare bird, some yellow civilian out of debt or some battered brigadier, who saw service in the days of sacks and sieges, and who comes wooing in the olden style, preceded by trains of servants bearing presents of shawls and diamonds'.

Instead of such antiquated suitors at her feet 'laden with barbaric pearl and gold', she was more likely to be forced into a love match and to select the husband of her choice out of the half-dozen subalterns who might propose; 'fortunate may she esteem herself, if there be one amongst them, who can boast a staff appointment, the adjutancy or quarter-mastership of his corps.'[17]

WEDDINGS

Once a suitor had been accepted, the marriage took place quickly, since weddings involved comparatively little additional expense. The single officers inhabited separate bungalows, but if two shared a bungalow, the prospective bridegroom turned his friend out to make way for the bride. If he were rich enough 'he could be seen at sales (for there was always somebody quitting a station and selling off) purchasing looking glasses, toilette tables and such unwanted luxuries in a bachelor's mansion'. But such items were not considered essential to connubial happiness and frequently the whole of the preparations consisted of 'the exit of the chum and his boxes and the entrance of the bride and her wardrobe, crammed into half a dozen square tin cases painted green'.[17]

The bride's trousseau varied according to the resources of the garrison and the bride's or relatives' purses. Indian pedlars were very respectable people, frequently very rich, whose goods were conveyed in large tin chests upon the heads of coolies. Instead of making a tour of the shops, the lady who wished to add to her wardrobe sent for all the box-wallahs and examined the contents of their chests. The lady sat upon a chair, the merchants and their ragged attendants on the floor and the bargaining began — 'in English, since the recently arrived young ladies would have made small progress in Hindoostanee'. Prices were regulated by stock in hand and the demand. Ribbons were always needed and were therefore never cheap: but rich silks and satins, gauzes and the like, were often sold at very low prices.

For the wedding itself, most of the residents of the garrison were invited to witness the ceremony. The ladies would bring out their best apparel — the splendid, recently arrived dresses from a London ballroom contrasting with the tarnished, faded dresses from Calcutta.

'But', concluded Emma, 'although Indian weddings may be destitute of magnificence, they are generally productive of lasting happiness'. The value of a wife was appreciated not least as a security against boredom on a lonely station'.[17]

THE STEAMSHIP AND THE SUEZ CANAL

In 1836, the East India Company decided to acquire a steam fleet. But it was the Peninsular and Oriental Steam Navigation Company and the Bibby Line which became for so many generations of soldiers links with home, the arrival of the mail, families and friends coming out to India and the periodical six months leave 'on private affairs'. Thus in 1837, the first year of Queen Victoria's reign, it was possible to go from London to Gibraltar (seven days), to Malta (five days), to Alexandria (four days); across Egypt to Suez and thence to Bombay, which would replace Calcutta as India's premier port, after the opening of the Suez Canal in 1869.

Mrs Sherwood described a group of wives returning from India in one of these steamships —

'The voyage from Calcutta was bad and often rough, and Mrs Dawson was buried at sea, having died of drink. Nelly Price got into bad company on board and, when they docked at Portsmouth, decided that a certain way of life was more congenial than the poverty and hardship in England. Many of the returning families landed in a sorry state. Having spent all their money in India, they arrived in England in white muslin gowns, coloured shoes, trailing and shivering along Portsmouth streets'.

OFFICERS' WIVES c. 1850

For the officer at the beginning of the 19th century, marriage was the exception, at least below the rank of major, and married couples often showed a marked disparity in age. The needs of the regiment required that 'subalterns do not marry; captains may marry; majors should marry and colonels must marry'. Although many senior officers still lived in open concubinage of long standing with Indian women, subalterns chose liaisons of shorter duration and greater frequency. By 1850 in Calcutta and to a lesser extent in the larger stations up country, the moral tone began to change as the 'memsahibs' regarded with horror any sexual attachments to Indian women, not just through female jealousy against attractive rivals, who provided officers with a pleasurable alternative to matrimony and another obstacle to almost the only career open to a lady, but on the grounds of an increasing feeling of racial superiority, widening further the gulf between the two peoples.

'The peppery colonel, with his hookah, his mulligatawny and his Indian mistress became, by the middle of the century, a figure of fun'.[18] Emma Roberts commented — 'It would be naive to suppose, however, that all contact with Indian women ceased but it became less and less respectable to cohabit openly with an Indian woman, while casual affairs became less frequent and less affectionate, not quite the mark of a gentleman'.[19]

There was often intermarriage between army families. In one case six sisters all found military husbands.

Emily Eden, sister of Lord Aukland, the Governor General, spent six years in India with him (1836–42) and wrote:

'I was introduced to an officer's wife, remembered here as a little girl running about the barracks a soldier's daughter: but she was pretty, and, by dint of killing off a husband or two, she is now at 19, the wife of a Captain here'.[20]

In Simla, in 1839, Miss Eden met another officer's wife, Mrs James 'a lady of great beauty', whose subsequent career was to scandalise the world. She was born Marie Dolores Gilbert in the barracks of Limerick in 1818, where her father was an officer in the 44th Foot. He took his family to India and died there of cholera in 1825.

'Her mother (Mrs C —),[20] who is still very handsome herself, sent this only child to be educated at home, and went home herself to see her.
In the same ship was Mr James a poor ensign, going home on sick leave. Mrs C nursed him and took care of him, and took him to see her daughter, who was a girl of 15 at school. He told her he was engaged to be married, consulted her about his prospects and in the meantime privately married this child at school. It was enough to provoke any mother. Mrs J is now only 17, and does not look so old, and when one thinks that she is married to a junior lieutenant in the Indian army, 15 years older than herself and that

they have 160 rupees a month and are to pass their whole lives in India, I do not wonder at Mrs C's resentment at her having run away from school'.

In fact, Mrs James returned to England in 1840, when her husband, Captain Thomas James, divorced her for adultery on the homeward journey with Captain Lennox, ADC to the Governor. She became a 'Spanish' dancer, making her debut on the London stage in 1843 as Lola Montez, where her striking beauty made up for her lack of dancing ability. But the Army had not heard the last of her![21]

Fortunate, too, were army other rank parents with marriageable daughters, as Staff Sergeant J. MacMullen of the 13th Light Infantry found:

'Because of the scarcity of white women in India, he is fortunate a man who has two or three tolerable looking daughters on the eve of womanhood; he requires no fortunes to get them off his hands; but, on the contrary, propitiatory presents shower in upon him from a dozen individuals, all ready to pay handsomely in that way, or any other, for being permitted to marry into his family. Nor need the death of a husband be a matter of much regret to a woman, for she is besieged by admirers, while the tears which decency demands are still coursing one another down her cheeks'.[22]

Soldiers' widows were also besieged from other sources, as Sergeant MacMullen recalled:

'When in Calcutta, I was told it was no uncommon thing for men in the Company's civil employment to come regularly there to inquire, if there were any decent soldier's widows to be had: and I knew one woman personally who was the wife of three husbands in six months, and another who had married her fifth husband, having children by every one of them'.[22]

EURASIANS AND ORPHANAGES

Each of the Presidencies had an orphan asylum, which provided opportunities for the soldiers to find a mate.

Sergeant J. MacMullen, for instance, tells of soldiers of one regiment who found in 1846 an attractive source of supply of:

'very pretty half-caste wives, whom they had got out of the Byculla orphan school at Bombay, where any soldier of good character and possessed of capital to commence house-keeping, may obtain a help-mate. These girls are tolerably well-educated, and would make grateful and affectionate wives, were it not that soldiers in general make such bad husbands. For a while after marriage they may get on pretty well, but they soon become negligent of their household duties, learn to drink and smoke the hookah all day long, becoming slatterns in every way. Half-caste women are almost always passionate and vindictive, readily taking offence, especially if they think that it is offered in consequence of their colour and hence they view the indifference of their European husbands in the worst possible light.'[22]
If an English soldier signifies his wish to marry, wrote an army wife, he is asked three times to tea, where he meets all the marriageable girls, and he may select from among them anyone who pleases his fancy'.[23]

A similar source is recalled by Sergeant Bennett of the 13th Light Dragoons. At Punamali near Madras was a depot, which catered for recruits and time expired soldiers, a hospital for wives and children of soldiers and an establishment 'for rogues, thieves and improper females'. Lastly there were two orphan asylums — one for boys and one for girls, the latter

> 'which seems to have been something of a matrimonial agency. Every soldier of good character has liberty to go and take a wife from them, provided the girl is agreeable: and, when such requests are made, the girls parade for the men's inspection: the girls are seldom found backward when the question is put to them'.[24]

Emma Roberts[25] commented on another source of supply in Calcutta — the orphan daughters, legitimate and illegitimate of Indian residents educated at 'a large orphanage at Kidderpore, one and a half miles from Calcutta'.

> 'This latter class is exceedingly numerous, the girls are frequently without family connections and have little chance of being well-established: some have no support except the Orphan Fund: others, who may be endowed with the interest of a few thousand rupees, become parlour-boarders at schools of various degrees of respectability, where they await the chance of attracting some young officer, the military being objects of consideration when civilians are unattainable'.

Formerly, it had been the practice to give Balls at the establishment at Kidderpore, to which vast numbers of beaux were invited.

> 'But this undisguised method of seeking husbands is now at variance with received notions of propriety and has been discontinued, the Female Orphan School assuming, in consequence, somewhat of the character of a nunnery. In fact, the young ladies immured within the walls have no chance of meeting with suitors, unless they possess friends in Calcutta to give them invitations or the fame of their beauty should spread itself abroad. Every year, by increasing the number of arrivals educated in England, lessens their chance of meeting with eligible matches'.

At Appendix A is an interesting document, which shows the numbers of boys and girls admitted to the Bengal Military Orphanage from 1782 to 1820. It shows that over half the boys joined the Army and half the girls left to get married.

> 'Many of the girls married European soldiers, some became ladies' maids, some the wives of officers, but many their mistresses, owing to the growing prejudice against mixed marriages'.[26]

After 1791, Eurasians, as half-castes were called (officially known as Anglo-Indians in 1911), were no longer appointed to the East India Company's Civil, Military or Marine service, though those already employed were permitted to stay. Colonel James Skinner, who was born in 1778, was the son of a Scots Colonel and a Rajput lady, whom his father 'had taken under his protection, when an ensign'. In 1803, his mixed blood caused his dismissal from the Company; then he joined the British Army and raised Skinner's Horse, which became the finest and senior Cavalry regiment in India. He married a Rajput woman of good family and produced a large family. Lady Eden described him as 'a half-caste, but very black and talks broken English and has his zenana (harem) and heaps of black sons like any other native'. 'He is said to have at least 14 wives and two sons in the Indian Army.'[27]

General Sir John Hearsay, who advised the authorities on the eve of the Mutiny to let the sepoys provide their own grease for their cartridges, was descended from a marriage between a Jat and an English army captain: Lord Roberts, hero of the 1879 campaign at Kabul and supreme commander in the Boer War, was the grandson of a Rajput princess. Half-caste daughters often married English husbands, because of the shortage of eligible wives. They were especially popular with British other ranks, because they were usually very good looking, spoke English, wore European clothes and were on the same social level. But many of these women at a lower social level, the progeny of loose Indian women and soldiers, ended up in the 'red light' districts of their native towns.

Emma Roberts commented on the prejudices against these 'dark beauties which are daily gaining ground', especially on account of their accent.

'There are not many heiresses to be found in India and those who are gifted with property of any kind almost invariably belong to the dark population, the daughters or grand-daughters of the East India Company's servants of more prosperous times, the representatives of Portuguese merchants or the ladies of Armenian families'.[28]
'Marriages between Eurasians and officers were unpopular' wrote the Rev W Tennant in 1803 'because the parties were often excluded from society. Instead, they often became officers' mistresses'.[29]

In 1818, Colour Sergeant Calladine went with his regiment, 19th Foot (Green Howards) to Ceylon

'where to keep myself from doing worse, I made up my mind to take a black girl, and it was not long before I got one. All a man had to do was to get the officer of his company's leave in writing and he was then allowed to be out of the company's mess and sleep out of barracks',

he recorded in his diary.[30]
When he returned home, he had to leave his 'poor little Dingy' behind.

'She cried bitterly, but I believe her sorrow was of short duration, for the next day one of our men, who had volunteered into the 73rd Foot, took up with her. We left behind a large number of black women, some with three or four children, and though they were only blacks, still I conceive they felt as keen a sorrow, as if they had been white. I suppose the 19th Foot left more children than any other regiment leaving the country before, as it was so long in the island, between 24 and 25 years. Some of them were grown up, and girls were married, while boys, who had been brought up at the Government School at Colombo, were filling respectable places as clerks or otherwise had entered the Army'.[30]

The native wives and children certainly caused administrative headaches to the Indian Government. For example — in 1817, when the 66th Foot were ordered to embark for St Helena, the Commanding Officer reported that there were 55 unmarried women and 51 children, natives of Ceylon, who had accompanied the Regiment to Bengal. The Bengal Government thought

'it was improper to leave them to starve or to obtain a livelihood by vice and, however reprehensible the Commanding Officer for allowing so many native women to accompany that Corps to India, the Bengal Governor had, for humanitarian reasons returned them to Ceylon at a cost of 5015 Rupees and claimed compensation from the Horse Guards'.

Other claims arrived for orphan children and unmarried women and their children left destitute by the departure of the 78th Foot and 14th Light Dragoons, together with a request from the Indian Government for a general instruction governing these cases and the orphans of European mothers, who had been put to local schools and charged to Her Majesty's Government. The Commander in Chief replied (1820) that he could only be responsible for those children of soldiers born of European women in wedlock — such orphans could be received in the Military Academy at Chelsea.

> 'But his Royal Highness is totally at a loss for the means of arranging the disposal of the natural children of soldiers by Native women, nor could he entertain the least expectation that His Majesty's Government could be induced to sanction any expenditure for such objects'.[31]

It has always been a feature of army life that soldiers should seek out and marry local girls, whatever their colour, creed, race or antecedents. When Calladine disembarked at Gravesend, he noted among the regiment's wives 'several who had been sent from England as convicts and had got their freedom in New South Wales, where the regiment had been stationed for a few months.'[32]

Calladine did eventually 'become ensnared by marriage'. 'Soon after my return to Winchester, I became acquainted with a very decent young woman, who lived in service near the barracks'. He obtained his Commanding Officer's permission 'after great difficulty, but by perseverance' to marry, which he did 'a month before the Coronation of George IV (July 1820), during which the Regiment sat down with hundreds of well dressed folk at a banquet at Weedon Barracks, 'the NCOs and their wives sitting at a separate table'.

Calladine died at Derby in 1876 aged 83, his wife Ann, having pre-deceased him in 1846. They had 13 children, of whom 11 died in infancy.

PROSTITUTES

The shortage of white women had other consequences for the soldier, which will be discussed more fully in a later chapter. Prostitutes flourished around the barracks and the Army was in a dilemma.

Should the Army recognise a soldier's natural needs and instincts and regulate the prostitutes in regimental brothels, where they could be controlled and inspected or turn a blind eye? This moral question would preoccupy the Victorians. Meanwhile, one officer thought that 'from the hour of their arrival in India, nobody gave a damn about the soldiers' health or morals. For three days after the arrival of a regiment, or a batch of recruits, they had permission to run riot in the bazaars — and they made full use of the licence. Wild scenes of drunkenness, often accompanied by violence to the natives, were frequent.

> 'The authorities considered that a blow-out was a necessary indulgence after the five or six months of confinement on the voyage to India. In the three days' 'terrible saturnalia',

the seeds of mortal diseases were laid, and numbers of men only emerged from their debauch to be conveyed to the hospitals of the garrison, whence they were rarely removed alive.'[33]

SOLDIERS' WIVES DESCRIBE INDIA BEFORE THE MUTINY

Intimate pictures of life in contemporary India can be found in journals kept by soldiers' wives. One such wife was Honoria, who married Henry Lawrence of Lucknow fame. Born in Northern Ireland, Honoria travelled out to India to marry her soldier husband. She wrote in her Journal in August 1837 of the army problem of family separation —

> Major and Mrs Hutchinson have 'a dear little girl of four years old, and it is very curious and pretty to hear her speak two languages with accuracy. English she knows from her parents, and she chatters Hindustani with the servants. She is often my interpreter and translates as quickly as I can speak. Her two elder sisters are at home, and this is the sad part of Indian life. As far as children are concerned, this is dreadful; just as their minds expand, and they require and begin to appreciate parental care, they must be sent among strangers and grow up ignorant of their parents. Or else the wife must leave her husband to be with her children.'[34] (Every woman must face the agonising question 'India or England: husband or child?' wrote Maud Diver.[35])

Lady X, writing home from an isolated garrison, North of Madras, also in 1837, contrasted the army and civilian families.

> 'The civil ladies are generally very quiet; rather languid, speaking in almost a whisper, simply dressed, almost always ladylike, not pretty, but pleasant and nice-looking, rather dull, and give one very hard work in pumping for conversation. They talk of 'the Governor', 'the Presidency', the 'Overland girls' schools at home', and have always daughters of about thirteen in England for education. The military ladies, on the contrary, are almost always quite young, pretty, noisy, affected, showily dressed, with a great many ornaments, and chatter incessantly from the moment they enter the house. While they are alone with me after dinner, they talk about suckling their babies, the disadvantages of scandal, 'the Officers' and 'the Regiment', and when the gentlemen come into the drawing-room, they invariably flirt with them most furiously.'[36]
> The military and civilians do not generally get on very well together. There is a great deal of very foolish envy and jealousy between them'.[36]

In general, the English wives had little to do and little was expected of them. Servants did the housework and, unable to converse with the natives, they had little contact with Indian society. It was a man's world and women, the weaker sex, were unsuited to active work. Lady X wrote:

> 'I asked one lady what she had seen of the country and the natives since she had been in India. 'Oh, nothing!' said she: 'really, I think the less one sees and knows of them the better'.[37]

Gradually a cultural and social gap grew up between the two races.

DRINK

Undoubtedly, the biggest problem of the soldier's wife, according to Reginald Heber, Bishop of Calcutta, was drink. Every morning the European troops in India received a pint of fiery, coarse, undiluted rum — and half that quantity was given to every woman — the cause of their dissolute habits and early deaths. Travelling with the Bishop on the ship to Madras in 1826 were

> '30 invalid soldiers, with some women and children going back with broken health and depraved habits either to England, or which seemed most probably with many of them, to die at sea. The women, in particular, seemed incorrigible in their drunkenness'.[38]

Mrs Marianne Postans, wife of an army officer in India in 1838, thought the soldiers' wives immoral and quarrelsome;

> 'not content with frequent libations of raw arrack, they boil in it spices and green chilis to increase its potency, giving smaller potions of the deleterious compound to their children, who are seen rolling in dirt and squalor about the Lines, exposed to the deadly influences of the tropic sun'.[39]

Because of the great heat, the soldiers' wives were unable to move out of the little room allotted to them in the 'married men's quarters' during the day and, provided for two rupees a month with a Portuguese 'cook boy', who relieved them from the toil of domestic duties,' 'their only outlet was in mischievous associations and debauchery, discontented murmurings and habits of dissipated indulgence', she added.

Sergeant R Waterfield, of the 32nd Foot, deplored the disorderliness and moral laxity of some of the wives in 1846.

> 'When their husbands were away and there was no one to watch over them or keep them within bounds, they come out in their true colours and prove false to all their plighted vows. There were some exceptions, I am afraid but few, so much for matrimony! In short, women on the Lines were more trouble than they are worth.'[40]

Honoria Lawrence observed that some of these wives were little more than children. She recalled one such — a pallid, skinny youngster who said that her corporal husband often beat her because she 'stayed out playing marbles with the boys when he wanted his supper'. Barrack girls were often married off in their early teens to men much older than themselves, who were about to go on active duty, because, one told Honoria, 'if he's killed, I'll get six months' widow's pension'. And then there would always be other men ready to take her, for white women were rare in the ranks. Considering this, and that they were forced to live in the communal rooms 'among drunken and half-naked men, hearing little but blasphemy and ribaldry, and surrounded by influences that render decency nearly impossible', it was, Honoria realised, inevitable that the soldiers' womenfolk earned and kept their bad reputation.[41]

Mrs Postans noted the temptations to which a young officer was exposed on first joining his regiment and the absurdity of expecting him to support 'the style of a scion of the nobility' on an income of 180 rupees a month. When he reached the rank of Brevet Captain, being considered *eligible* at this age, he probably married — to find his expenses considerably increased. His wife required a carriage, horses and ayahs. Mercers' bills drew deeply upon his allowances; his subscription to the military fund more than doubled, and as the years passed, his children were sent to England in search of health and education. Little could now be saved and 'he that hath his quiver full of them' was often constrained to struggle on, against failing health and increasing age, for the sake of the sons and daughters, thus torn from him in their infancy. Should strength of constitution befriend the officer, he might gradually rise through the several ranks of the service, until, as a nervous, querulous old Colonel, he might command a station by right of his seniority; or he might betake the tattered remnants of his existence to be patched up for a few years longer, by the congenial climate of his fatherland;

> 'where the 'Old Indian' shivers in the wholesome breeze, clings to his eastern habits, finds himself a century behind the world and seeks in vain for a companion who remembers the friends of his youth; and so sinks into the grave, his death scarcely noticed, but by the congratulations of struggling junior officers, who, as they receive news of 'another step up the line', count over their chances of promotion and rejoice that an old 'so and so' is gone at last'.[42]

RETREAT FROM KABUL

In January 1842, the Afghans, supported by Russia, inflicted a heavy defeat on the British, which led to the famous Retreat from Kabul. 16,000 men, women and children set off from Kabul under the promise of a safe conduct to march back to India. The retreat became a massacre: one week later Surgeon William Brydon rode into Jellalabad — the sole survivor, except for some 120 men, women and children, who were taken into captivity for nine months. The rest lay dead along the 90 mile route: some killed by the Afghans; the rest frozen to death in the snow. The chronicler of that event, Lady Sale was the wife of Major General Sale, who commanded one of the Brigades, which had been ordered back to India, leaving his wife behind. Romantically, he returned and rescued her.[43]

On 26 July 1844, *The Times* reported the arrival at Lyme Regis of 'Major General Sir Robert Sale, the equally heroic Lady Sale and their widowed daughter, Mrs Sturt and child.'[44] They were received by Queen Victoria at Windsor, who granted Lady Sale a special pension of £500 a year, when her husband was killed in action the following year. She spent her widowhood on a small estate in the Indian hills near Simla. Her daughter remarried and with her second army husband, Major Holmes, was one of the first victims of the Indian Mutiny, when four mutineers rode up and beheaded them, as they sat in their carriage.

On Lady Sale's tombstone is inscribed 'Under this stone reposes all that could die of Lady Sale.'

Appendix A to Chapter 7

Abstract of Children of NCOs and Private European Soldiers admitted to the Bengal Military Orphanage from the commencement of the Institution in 1782 to 31 December 1820.[2b]

		Boys		Girls
1	Admitted	1,464	—	1,395
2	Now in School	270	—	354
3	Transferred to Upper School	1	—	1
4	Died	260	—	256
5	Returned to Parents (or Guardians)	89	—	244
6	Apprenticed	114	In Service	34
7	Drummers and Fifers	693	Married	497
8	In East India Company's Vessels	3	—	
9	Appointed Writers	11		
10	Struck Off	20	—	9
11	Eloped	1		
12	Expelled	2		

Chapter 8

Florence Nightingale and the Camp Followers at Scutari

Forty years after Napoleon's defeat at Waterloo, the British Army with its camp followers, was on the march again. The year was 1854 and the Crimea the destination for the Expeditionary Force of 27,000 men under Lord Raglan. Despite the Regulations forbidding women to go with their regiments on active service, four women per 100 men would be allowed to sail with them, laden like pack-horses with all their kitchen utensils, clothes and personal possessions (see Appendix). This would be the last time that the Army would allow wives to accompany their husbands to the battlefields on a large and organised scale, as they had followed the armies of Marlborough and Wellington. There would be all the usual scenes — of bands playing to marching feet and popular enthusiasm: the tears of mothers, wives and sweethearts left behind, many to face, with their children, a bleak future of separation and destitution. A number of officers' wives would go with them — some like Lady Erroll and Mrs Duberly to follow their husbands throughout the campaign; some to accompany them as far as Malta or to reside in hotels or villas on the Bosporus. Some like Lady George Paget and Lady Ann Carew would go later to visit their husbands or sons or like Lady Blackwood and Selina Bracebridge to provide charitable help to the soldiers and their wives. A steamship firm would organise a fortnight's cruise at a cost of £5 with board and accommodation to the Crimean battlefields, where regimental bands played during lulls in the fighting. There would be the 'glorious charge of the Light Brigade', the horrors of Scutari and the frontline reports from newspaper correspondents, which would reveal to the public the need for Army reforms for the soldier and his family. But all that lay in the future!

On 14 February 1854, huge crowds, occupying every vantage point in Trafalgar Square, cheered as the Coldstream Guards with 32 women emerged at mid-day from St George's barracks (where now stands the north wing of The National Gallery) to march along the Strand and over Waterloo bridge to the railway terminus. Next day, followed the Grenadier Guards, amid 'incessant cheering and martial music'.

> 'Men of the humblest station grasped hands in which the best blood of England flowed. Fair women and brave men waved their parting adieus'.[1]

Then came the turn of the Scots Fusiliers (Scots Guards) and their allocation of wives, successful in the ballot. Their departure from Wellington Barracks had been delayed until 7 a m, so that Her Majesty and Prince Albert (and their children) might see the battalion pass in full marching order before them at Buckingham Palace.

> "The thousands who rose from their beds to welcome and cheer were amply gratified, for a finer set of men could not be seen. But many were the curious scenes on the part of women, who saw husbands, lovers and relations leaving them, perhaps to return no more; and heart-rending and distressing it was in many instances to witness the look of sorrow and woe depicted on their care-worn faces'.[2]

Similar scenes were seen when the 50th (Royal West Kent) Regiment left Dublin.

> 'The liveliest demonstrations of popular feeling were made by the bystanders, while the fair occupants of the windows and balconies waved their handkerchiefs. Many friends of the soldiers, both male and female, bid them adieu with sorrowing hearts and not a few weeping eyes'.[2]

At the ports the transports awaited the arrival of the assembling regiments. At Leith, the 4th Regiment embarked on the 'Golden Fleece' 'with 37 officers, a few ladies, 917 rank and file, and 54 women and 75 children'.[3]

At Southampton, the 2nd Battalion The Coldstream Guards boarded the 'Orinoco' with 30 officers, 854 Other Ranks and 32 women, while the 3rd Battalion The Grenadier Guards took 32 officers, 600 Rank and File and 32 women on board the 'Ripon'. The 'Himalaya' sailed for Plymouth with contingents of Sappers and of the Rifle Brigade and 12 women and 20 children. At Plymouth she would collect 931 All Ranks of the 93rd Highlanders with their 54 women and from 75 to 100 children.[3]

But the tragedies were beginning as *The Times* announced —

> 'One of the Scots Fusiliers (by name Hawkins), who left town on Tuesday morning, left behind his wife (four months pregnant) and two young children in a penniless state. The first announcement of her husband's departure, together with the agony of separation, brought on a premature labour and she was this morning delivered of a dead child. Had it not been for the kindness of lodgers in the same house, she must have perished. She was given one shilling and a loaf of bread by the Union. I am told the husband said, before taking his final leave, that he would have been happier could he have followed them all to the grave, 'ere he quitted the shores of England'.

An officer from Wellington Barracks checked these facts and wrote two days later —

> 'The Guards had no knowledge that this man was married, a fact which he carefully concealed from his Regiment'.[4]

While the Lord Mayor was entertaining Lord Raglan and His Royal Highness the Duke of Cambridge at the Mansion House, the Commander in Chief, Portsmouth, had invited a number of important personages to witness the departure of the 'Vulcan', carrying 26 officers, 37 Sergeants and 715 men of the 2nd Battalion The Rifle Brigade. His guests (some of whom had relatives aboard) included the Duchess of Sutherland, the Marchionesses of Stafford and Kildare, the Earl and Countess of Grosvenor and the Earl and Countess of Erroll.

Eliza Amelia, daughter of General Sir Charles Gore, had married the 18th Earl of Erroll, a captain in the Rifle Brigade in 1848. She had been given permission to travel on the 'Vulcan' with her French maid. The Press takes up the story —

> 'A circumstance of a romantic character occurred on the corps embarking. The wife of a private being prevented going out by the regulations of the service, she dressed herself in Rifle costume, and gun in hand, actually marched into the Dockyard. She was, however, detected getting on board . . . . but we believe the Countess of Erroll interceded in her behalf and she consequently went to sea in the ship'.[5]

Less happily the story continues —

> 'We believe about 200 of the wives and children of this gallant corps are left destitute in this borough by the departure of the Battalion. Many of the wives of the Rifles, being Canadians (the Brigade had recently returned from Canada), they have no parish to be sent to here and must all become chargeable to the local union or starve. The Mayor of Portsmouth has called for Government help.'

During the early weeks of the War, the newspapers were full of patriotic 'appeals for help'.

> 'There is no time to be lost in making provision for the wives and children of the gallant fellows who are now leaving home to fight their country's battles'.[6]
> 'Our head constable informs me that three women belonging to the 28th Regiment, which embarked at Liverpool yesterday, had applied to him to be forwarded to their friends at Plymouth, but he has no funds at his disposal for such cases. This shows the need for immediate action, not for sentimental letters and fancy fairs. I enclose a cheque for £10 as a more practical way of meeting the emergency'.

A lady from Liverpool, 'the daughter, wife and mother of a soldier', sent £1 'as her mite'. A soldier's wife, left with nothing but her needle to provide for herself, one child and another unborn, pleaded for assistance to enter Queen Charlotte's Lying-in Hospital.[6]

After the 93rd Regiment, the 1st Royals and the 8th Hussars had left Plymouth,

> 'the destitute condition of the wives and children left behind by the soldiers ordered to the East is exciting much benevolent sympathy'.[6]

The Duke of Sutherland sent £200. Another correspondent suggested that wives and daughters of the soldiers should be given Government contracts 'to undertake the making up of the clothing of the troops'. The wife of a Captain of Engineers, on the departure of her husband to the Mediterranean, found employment for all the married women of his Company.[6]

The Greenwich Union, to whom three Sergeants' wives had applied for relief 'from pauperisation, discovered that, although their husbands would willingly have contributed to their support', they were prevented from doing so by an Army Regulation which forbade such arrangements until 3 to 6 months after embarkation. Such a regulation should be abolished'.[7]

In Parliament, Mr MacCartney asked the Secretary for War whether the Government intended to provide any short or long term support, 'apart from the Parish workhouse', for the wives and families left behind by the soldiers going to the seat of war.

Mr S. Herbert replied that it would be more humane to reduce the customary allowance of six to four women per 100 men permitted to accompany the Regiment on foreign service. The other two would be given half rations.

'This may seem very hard but the more encouragement you gave the soldier to marry the more you increased the evil of which you now complained and could not remedy'.[7]

Early in March 1854 it was decided to co-ordinate nationally the various local appeals and activities and 'the Central Association for the Aid of the Wives and Families of Soldiers Ordered to the East' was born, with Queen Victoria as patron. The Earl of Shaftesbury in launching the Association said that the sudden departure of 25,000 soldiers had deprived a multitude of women and children of all means of support and some public exertions were needed to relieve their distress. H.R.H. the Duke of Cambridge said the Association could provide shelter, food and raiment.

'The sorrow of separation, the agony of the last farewell, was felt as deeply by the wife of a common soldier as by that of the noblest officer. When the soldier heard that those he had left behind him were well cared for, he would feel more strongly than ever that he had a country worth fighting for'.[8]

Among the second instalment of troops sailing for the East were the 8th Hussars.[9] With the 20 officers and 293 Hussars aboard the five transports was Frances (Fanny) Locke, who married Captain Henry Duberly, the regimental paymaster of the Hussars and youngest son of an ancient and wealthy county family in April 1854. She was 24, the youngest daughter of a wealthy Devizes banker. With her graceful figure and dressed in the fashionable riding habit of the period, she would share with her husband and his regiment the dangers and privations of camp and battlefield in the Crimea and later during the Indian Mutiny. Her exploits, which she would record in two journals, would become legendary.[10] She took on board with the 13 successful 'Hussar' wives the wife of Sergeant Major Williams as her personal maid, when she failed to obtain a place in the ballot. The maid would become a widow at Balaclava!

Six transports sailed from Woolwich with the Artillery and their wives and from Devonport the Inniskilling Dragoons in five ships. Next day, when 200 miles out, the 'Europa' caught fire and 'one woman died with 2 officers and 16 men'. Lost, too, was the Commanding Officer, Lieutenant Colonel Willoughby Moore. His widow went out to Scutari, after his death, and 'devoted herself to the care of the wounded and sick there. She would die herself of cholera and be carried to her grave in Scutari by troops of her husband's Regiment'.[11]

As the transports reached Malta, the local garrison cheered from the battlements. Charles Dickens wrote

'the female population of Valetta and the neighbourhood turned out, to a woman, for an inspection of the newly-arrived troops. The old women are quite interesting for their ugliness, the young ones for their beauty; many of our soldiers will, I fear, leave Malta vanquished men'.[12]

Some of the wives of the officers and other ranks decided to stay in Malta, where they hoped to receive visits from their husbands or await their return: some went home. Eight of the 30 women of the King's Own Regiment, for example, decided to go home. Five were left sick in Malta and only 17 continued with the regiment.[13]

'The leave taking by the officers and men of their wives and families formed a painful contrast to the joy, which otherwise so generally prevailed',

cabled William Howard Russell, *The Times* Correspondent, who was given a passage with the Rifle Brigade on board the 'Golden Fleece'. His graphic despatches from the Crimea would attack the competence and leadership of the military and the health and living conditions of the soldiers and their families. They would reveal the full horrors of the war to Parliament and the people and destroy for ever the romantic picture of war as a gentlemanly contest, in which men died with a last message on their lips for their loved ones at home.

One who did not take his wife with him was the 7th Earl of Cardigan (Lord James Brudenell).[14] He had married Mrs Elizabeth Johnstone, wife of a Captain in the 19th Lancers, after eloping with her to Paris in 1823. She was the eldest daughter of Admiral Tollemache, whose family had made their fortune as sugar planters in Antigua and granddaughter of Lady Aldborough, a celebrated courtesan of her day, who provided shelter for Elizabeth in Paris. She soon found she could not endure being a poor captain's wife after the luxuries of the family mansion, Ham House. Captain Johnstone brought an action for damages against Cardigan for 'debauching his wife'. The jury assessed her market value as £1,000 and Cardigan's offer of a duel with her husband as 'satisfaction' was refused on the grounds that the Captain had already obtained satisfaction 'in the removal of the most damned bad-tempered and extravagant bitch in the kingdom'. Two years later, the divorce having been obtained, James Brudenell and Elizabeth Tollemache were privately married in the Chapel at Ham House. Through his family connections with the Duke of York he obtained a cornetcy in the 8th Hussars and rapidly purchased his way through the commissioned ranks to command the 15th and 11th Hussars despite a series of rows with his brother officers and their wives, who regarded his wife as no better than a whore, because of her conduct towards her first husband, and despite an action brought by Lord William Paget against him for adultery with his wife Lady Frances Paget. He arrived at Scutari as a Major General in charge of the Light Brigade, under the divisional command of Lord Lucan, his brother in law but an old enemy in the service. En route he was entertained by Napoleon III and the Empress Eugenie at the Tuileries in Paris.

When the transports reached Gallipoli, troops and families were landed. Two tents were issued to each battalion for the exclusive use of the women, who erected them and set up their regimental laundries. Some women took service with European families in Constantinople; others just disappeared into the towns. 97 wives, arriving in the 'Georgiana' from Malta, were ordered to re-embark immediately and much to their anger to return forthwith to Malta. A number of army and naval officers' wives took lodgings at the 'Hotel d'Angleterre' at Therapia on the Turkish coast: Fanny Duberly and Lady Erroll landed at Scutari, where all the Turkish women had been withdrawn from the neighbourhood of the barracks to avoid incidents between the redcoats and their suspicious husbands.

Scutari, opposite Constantinople, became the headquarters of the Guards Division and its former Turkish barracks housed the Scutari Hospital. Lord Erroll, who was on the staff of the Duke of Cambridge commanding the Guards and Light Division, erected his green marquee in the middle of the Rifle Brigade camp. This marquee became an object of interest to the men, especially at night, when the lantern revealed through the almost transparent canvas walls, Lord Erroll asleep on his single camp bed and Lady Erroll asleep on the floor. After one violent storm, their tent was one of the twenty blown down during the night. 'Her ladyship had to crawl from under the dripping canvas through the slush in a most sorry plight'.[15]

But the Guards were unhappy about the state of the women, lodged in huts in their camp at Scutari.

> 'Their presence in the British Army, about to take the field in a quarter where no depot or base of operations existed, could not fail to be a misery to themselves, as well as a serious burden of our defective military organisation.' Many were to endure the hardships of the men during the terrible winter of 1854 –55 and to suffer death from hunger, cold and disease.[16]

For once the armies of Britain and France were on the same side and they got on excellently together. The English admired the French *vivandières*, in their smart blue tunics, tight trousers and feathered hats, who sold their wine and provisions to the French troops and accompanied them into battle, astride their lively horses. The Turks, accustomed to women of ampler proportions, with veiled faces, were often embarrassed by the dress and behaviour of the English women, especially of the officers' wives, riding their thoroughbreds amongst the troops, dining in the officers' tents or aboard ship and dressed in the latest fashions shipped from London and Paris.

One commentator noted —

'The fair Creatures of Turkey are much more independent than of yore: the summary punishments of former husbands are now impossible and the ladies have no longer before their eyes the traditional terrors of the sack and the Bosphorus'.[17]

The English wives, for their part, 'were appalled by the sight of young girls, flower decked and painted, with henna-tinged eyelids, flaunting their paltry love affairs in public. One disapproving lady, remembering how strict her own mamma and governess had been, wished she could apply 'a good English birch' to the bottoms of those adolescent minxes'.[17]

The Order came to march from Scutari to the forward base at Varna.

'Down went the canvas homes of the whole brigade and the women of the Regiment loitered about, watching for the unlikely chance of a lightly laden cart to gain permission to ride. The regiments fell in, and the bands played and we all rode off ',

noted Mrs Young, the wife of the surgeon of the 28th Foot (Glosters), in her diary.[18]

Russell drew attention to the mass of unsuitable and excess baggage of the British regiments on the move:

'For 7 or 8 miles the bullock carts piled up with beds and trunks, soldiers' wives and tents offered a striking contrast with the absence of women and the smaller loads of the French troops'.

When the British arrived at Varna, Lord Raglan and the Sultan reviewed the 15,000 British troops to celebrate the Queen's birthday (25 May) — a parade which resembled a fashionable field day in England with the large number of British and foreign ladies 'all dressed in the newest Paris fashions'.[19]

'At this time, when two great armies were on the move and spending millions to save Turkey from the Russian bear, the Sultan was amusing himself with his annual wedding, squandering money, while his soldiers were being cheated of their pay, as he takes a fresh young wife every year according to custom, adding yet one more treasure to his harem'.[20]

At Varna, cholera struck, but soon the Army moved on Calamita Bay and Sebastopol, leaving behind the sick and the soldiers' wives. The 93rd Sutherland Highlanders, for example, left 102 Other Ranks, 20 soldiers' wives and 83 baggage ponies.[21]

But some wives were more fortunate:

'The women of several of the Regiments, who had mournfully followed their husbands to the beach (as they departed for Sebastopol) and rent the air with their wailing, when they heard they were to be separated from those with whom they had shared privation and pestilence, were allowed to go on board, by order from Headquarters'.[21]

Russell goes on to give us one of his rare pictures of the fate of these women in the Crimea —

'It must not be supposed for a moment that these women have ever been neglected, nor have they undergone any hardships, save those inseparable from a camp life. The Government provides them tents and rations. On the march they were carried on the arabas (carts) whenever they wished: the men build them snug houses of leafy branches:

they make little fortunes as laundresses, and until the pestilence smote the army and fell upon them with extraordinary fatality, they seemed the happiest and most contented beings in the camp, where their services, as excellent foragers and washerwomen, were fully appreciated'.[21]

Mrs Fanny Duberly also managed to embark at Varna to join her husband at the Crimean battlefront. Lord Raglan had refused her, and other hopeful ladies, permission to embark with the 8th Hussars on the 'Himalaya'. But her friend Lord Cardigan helped her aboard, disguised as a Turkish woman. Now at 25 years of age, a dashing horsewoman, unconventional in her dress and habits, she wrote home to her sister, Selina, for a regular supply of new and suitable clothes — 'bonnets and petticoats are an abomination'. Instead she asked for three strong and durable riding shirts, six pairs of doeskin riding gauntlets, six pairs of warm stockings, a fur cap and a riding whip. She also asked for a tent lining — to prevent her being a source of entertainment for loiterers in the camp![22]

The British, French and Turkish troops landed at Eupatoria without opposition and marched towards the river Alma and the heights of Sebastopol, where they were destined to spend the cruel winter months, ill-housed, ill-clad and hungry, as the supply system broke down and the mortality rate rose to 35 per cent.

The individual Casualty Returns of the women were not included with those of the men, but sometimes numbers were given — '534 deaths in the hospitals at Scutari, including five women, with nine more women and eight children, a few weeks later'.[23] Colonel George Bell, commanding the Royal Scots wrote;

'Our men dropped like flies, convulsed with cholera, groaning with dysentry, rigid from fever, crying bitterly for water. They are now laid under the sod without funeral parties or firing. The dead are carted out of the Varna General Hospital at night in heaps and thrown into pits prepared for them'.[24]

Conditions were just as bad for the regimental women in his Company lines.

'I had 10 or 12 women who stuck to the regiment throughout the winter. Over there is poor Mrs M —, sitting on her husband's grave. She is always there, shivering in the cold. That bundle of a dirty, wet blanket contains a living creature, once a comely, useful soldier's wife, now waiting for death to release her from her misery. That young woman, once perhaps the belle of her village, now in rags but in good health, is eating her dinner, the broth of a bit of salt pork, with broken brown biscuit pounded into it: a tin plate and an iron spoon is all her fortune'.[24]

For the soldiers the Crimea meant also the frightful slaughter and wounds of battles. First came the battle of the River Alma. Fanny Duberly, on board the 'Shooting Star', heard the Russian guns on the heights above and prayed for the safety of her husband. Lady Erroll, elegantly clad, rode into battle on a scraggy mule, festooned with rifles that her husband's men were too weak to carry. Captain Erroll would be wounded in the battle and they would return to England, where he received the Crimean medal from Queen Victoria. She would become the mother of seven children and Lady in Waiting to the Queen.[25]

Following the battle came the long hours of clearing up the battlefield and burying the dead. One burial party came across a number of ladies' shawls and parasols, a bonnet and, strangest of all, a petticoat left behind by Russian ladies, who had come to watch from a special viewing platform the defeat of the invading armies, through their pearl-handled opera glasses.[26]

After the Alma came Balaclava and the famous Charge of the Light Brigade. To the watching French, the cavalry charge against the Russian guns, led by the Earl of Cardigan, was brave but useless. '*C'est magnifique, mais ce n'est pas la guerre!*' said their General. Then came the battle of Inkerman with its dreadful carnage and battlefield scavenging, as camp followers and shoals of people from Balaclava stripped the dead for medals, the small brass crucifixes and pictures of saints and charms, as momentoes of the fight.[27]

> 'Many a young gentleman', declared Russell, 'would be for ever cured of his love of arms, if he could but see one day's fighting . . . . As to young ladies suffering from 'scarlet fever', who are forever thinking of heroes and warriors and singing of champions, if they could have gazed into the burial pits at those who were about to be consigned to the worm, they would feel the horrors of their hero worship and would join in prayer for the advent of that day, when war shall be no more'.[27]

But it was the breakdown of the medical services, which most infuriated Russell and the public at home, when they read his reports.

> 'There are not even doctors and no nurses, though the French have their Sisters of Mercy in an incredible number. The aged and worn-out Chelsea pensioners are totally useless. The commonest appliances of a workhouse sick ward are absent. There is no linen or lint to bind the wounds'.[28]

The story of Florence Nightingale and how she transformed the nursing services, earning the soldiers' love and gratitude and the memory of the 'Lady of the Lamp', is too well-known to be related here, especially as her concern was for the soldiers — not their wives!

As the battle casualties mounted and the full force of the 'Siberian' winter hit the Army and its camp followers, conditions for the women deteriorated and their numbers dwindled. Balaclava became a sea of mud, a town packed with sutlers, shopkeepers and men of all nationalities battening on the needs of the armies.

> 'Some few of the widows of soldiers, who fell at the Alma, have been sent away from here by the Commandant and if reports speak truly their lives were not very reputable lately, nor are they entitled to public compassion and assistance', reported Russell.[29]

Another correspondent wrote:

> 'Of all the ladies, who accompanied or joined the expeditionary army, only one remains — namely Mrs Duberly, wife of the Paymaster of the 11th Hussars, who is quartered at Balaclava and with whom she may be occasionally seen riding or walking. The aspect of this lady is now grave, though she was in England very fond of life. Many of the wives left

at Malta, Therapia and Pera (suburb of Constantinople) etc. have been made widows by war and climate'.[30]

Meanwhile, in the cellars and sewers below the hospital at Scutari Barracks, some 200 women lived with their children in the most abject misery, having been left behind when the Army had departed for Varna. Many of them represented the dregs of the wives who had once marched so proudly behind the regimental bands to ports of embarkation, now rough, weak, resigned, without any hope or will to better themselves.

'The misery of these unhappy creatures defies all description', wrote Dickens.[31]

Here they suffered and died with their children of fever, hunger and cholera. The only relief for many was drink, for which they stole or sold themselves in the booths and drinking shops, operated by Greek traders, while others worked in the brothels, which sprang up around the barracks. The Select Committee in its Report to Parliament on the Army before Sebastopol 1855 confirmed the terrible conditions in which they lived and *The Times* suggested that the Authorities had made 'a terrible mistake' in permitting the wives to go there. In March 1855 it reported that:

'a house has been taken at Scutari, near the hospital, for the accommodation of the sick wives of the soldiers, capable of containing 35 patients, who would be under the superintendence of Lady Alicia Blackwood. The House has been taken by Mr. Bracebridge at the Commandant's request'.[32]

Lady Alicia Blackwood, sister of the 8th Earl of Cavan, had travelled out to Scutari with her husband Doctor Blackwood, a Church of England minister and two Swedish girls, Ebba and Emma Almwroth, at their own expense, to offer their services to Florence Nightingale. Miss Nightingale was not impressed with enthusiastic amateurs, so she asked them:

'to go to the Barracks, where there are 200 poor women in most abject misery. They are the wives of soldiers, who were allowed to accompany their husbands. They are in rags and covered in vermin. My heart bleeds for them, but my work is with the soldiers, not with their wives'.[33]

There were relief parcels and money sent from charities and newspaper collections at home to be distributed, sick women to nurse, babies to feed and filth and vermin to clean up. The Blackwoods took the upper storey of the large house near the hospital, engaged a soldier's wife as a servant, and set up the 'Chaplain's House', for soldier and wife. There Lady Blackwood laboured with energy and devotion, until the last boat load of 'her women' had left Scutari at the end of the War.

Her first task was to regain self-respect for them, so she erected partitions along the walls of the cellars, where each family could live in privacy. She set up hospital rooms for the disabled and the lying-in. A civilian doctor, Smith, came out exclusively for work in her hospital, with all his expenses paid by a charitable circle in England, helped by some of the more respectable army wives as nurses. She established a laundry under a naval officer's wife, Mrs Kealtey, with wives paid to do the washing and a crèche for the infants. A convalescent Sapper officer ran the Sunday School. She comforted the bereaved and dealt with the women's personal problems. Selina Bracebridge and her husband, friends of Miss Nightingale, organised a regular meals service for the starving women and a Gift Store, through which they could purchase at one-third cost price provisions of food and clothing.

During the early months of 1855, *The Times* was reporting men lying dead in their tents, as snow lay three feet thick outside. There was no fuel and cholera, dysentry, diarrhoea, rheumatism, catarrh and scurvy were on every side. The ladies at home were busy sending out winter clothing, books, writing materials and other comforts but 'these should have been here last November. Pity it is that they cannot restore the dead to life'. Casualty Returns showed more women and children being buried at Scutari, with some officers, at least, being comforted in death —

> 'Brig. General Adams and Captain Glazbrook (49 Regt.), whose wives were with them during the last hours of their lives'.[34]

But in death there was also life. The Rev Edward Eade, Chaplain to the Light Division, reported christening a child, whose parents had both died. 'A soldier's wife has taken charge of the poor little mite, who is doing well and is to be sent to England directly'. At the same time in the French lines —

> 'a buxom French cantinière accompanied her battalion to the trenches, there to supply them with their drinks and to brave with masculine courage the storm of shot and shell. Towards the small hours of the morning, she was taken with the pains of maternity and gave birth to twins. Mother and children are doing well'.[35]

Many of the casualties were evacuated to Malta and to Corfu, where the Medical Officer, Dr James Stuart Barry, offered his hospital facilities to Lord Raglan. Corfu was to be his last appointment — and thereby hangs a story,

> 'currently being discussed in military circles, so absolutely incredible', reported the *Manchester Guardian*,[36] 'were not the Authorities able to confirm its truth'. 'Our officers quartered at the Cape between 15 and 20 years ago may remember a certain Dr Barry attached to the medical staff there, and enjoying a reputation for considerable skill in his profession, especially for firmness, decision and rapidity in difficult operations. This gentleman had entered the army in 1813, had passed, of course, through the grades of assistant-surgeon and surgeon in various regiments, and had served as such in various parts of the globe.
> About 1840, he became promoted to be medical inspector and was transferred to Malta and then to Corfu, where he was quartered for many years. He there died a month ago, and upon his death was discovered to be a *woman*! The motives that occasioned and the time when commenced this singular deception are both shrouded in mystery. But thus it stands an indubitable fact, that a woman was for 40 years an officer in the British service, and fought one duel and had sought many more, had pursued a legitimate medical education and received a regular diploma, and had acquired almost a celebrity for skill as a surgical operator'.

At the post-mortem it was confirmed that the body was that of a perfect female and that there were marks on her having had a child when young. She was born in 1795, the granddaughter of a Scottish Earl and enlisted 5 July 1813, sponsored by the Earl of Buchan (whose name Stuart she bore). While at the Cape she had had a secret love affair with the widowed 49 year old Governor-General, Lord Charles Somerset, brother of Lord Raglan. Her medical degree at Edinburgh University (60 years before a woman was officially permitted to qualify as a doctor (1877)) included midwifery and she had used this skill to aid the army wives throughout her service. The War Office confirmed the facts, however reluctant to admit that one of the most successful army doctors of the period — a medical major general — had been a woman.

In the Crimea, Spring was in the air and the health of the Army and its camp followers improved. Letter writing helped to pass the time of the soldiers and did much to raise their standing at home.

> 'Until recently the soldier has been in popular estimation a hero in time of war, a red-coated pariah when his valour had humbled the enemies of his country on the battle-field. What decent young woman, until quite a recent period, would consent to 'keep company' with a soldier in the English service? Happily within the last 15 or 20 years the system has been changed and his lot improved. The letters written by many of our gallant soldiers from the Crimea are quite a sufficient proof that the army is not what it was when its ranks were recruited from the gaol-yards and the off-scourings of our great towns'.[37]

Soon the visitors were arriving — Lady Ann Carew, with her French maid, to see her son Walter, a cornet in the Blues; Amelia Morris to nurse her husband, wounded in command of the 17th Lancers at Balaclava and many other fashionable ladies to be reunited with their husbands and sons and to dance at the New Year's Ball at the Embassy.

Colonel Edward Cooper Hodge, commanding the 4th Royal Irish Dragoon Guards, strongly disapproved of officers' wives on active service. He wrote

> 'There were a great many ladies in the Crimea in 1855. I fully expect to see excursion steamers from England with Manchester, Birmingham and Liverpool on board'.

Russell noted the arrival of:

> 'Mrs Estcourt, wife of the Adjutant General of the Army and another lady (a relative) from England. Amateurs have not much to expect in the way of comforts here, nor is Balaclava the most agreeable residence in the world during the hot weather'.

A month later the General died of cholera,

> 'after 3 days' illness, soothed by the presence of his wife'. 'The Church at Renkoi has collected money for the wives and children of the soldiers. Two pounds will be given to a poor woman now on her way out from England with her children to join her husband, an NCO in the Royal Artillery, who died during the recent outbreak of cholera. She will have sad news to greet her arrival. Mrs Duberly is going with her husband to visit Omar Pasha, the Commander of the Turkish Forces, at Eupatoria'.[38]

Omar Pasha, a handsome man of about 50, had no family of his own and six months' later was to marry a girl of 14.

Another wife to join her husband was Lady Agnes Paget, one of the acknowledged beauties of the day. She had married Lord George Paget (brother of William of the 'criminal conversation' case (page 106)) just before he sailed in February 1854 in command of the 4th Light Dragoons. His father, the first Marquess of Anglesey (Lieutenant General Henry William Paget) opposed the match, despite his own marital escapades. In March 1809 the General had scandalised London society by eloping with, and later marrying, the Duke of Wellington's sister-in-law, Lady Charlotte, the mother of four children, leaving his own eight children by his wife, Lady Caroline Villiers, daughter of the Prince of Wales's (George IV) former mistress, the Countess of Jersey. Lady Caroline sued for divorce, which cost him:

> '2 divorces, a £24,000 settlement and a duel with Lady Charlotte's brother, Captain Henry Cadogan, who sought satisfaction for his sister's seduction'.[39]

Now he considered his son's choice to be too young (she was 22 and he 37), they were related as cousins and Agnes had little in the way of a fortune. Nevertheless the marriage took place by special licence at St James's, Piccadilly, before Colonel Paget left for the Crimea. Paget's brother officers observed he 'was very down in the mouth: leaving his young wife is telling vastly on him'. Colonel Paget was to lead his regiment with distinction in the Cavalry Charge and become Inspector General of Cavalry, but Agnes was to enjoy only four years of married life, before she died, leaving him two children.[39]

Lady Stratford, the Ambassador's wife, and Florence Nightingale came to visit the hospitals and Alexis Soyer (inventor of the Soyer stove) to show the soldiers how to cook in the trenches. Next day, Florence Nightingale, caught the 'Crimean fever', which nearly proved fatal. Lord Raglan, the Commander in Chief, was not so lucky; he died and his body was taken back to England for a State funeral. Lord Cardigan, on the other hand, who survived 'the Valley of Death into which he led the six hundred' (to use Tennyson's words) returned home a hero. He married, a noted beauty, Adeline Horsey de Horsey, in the Garrison Chapel, Gibraltar, on the death of his first wife (Elizabeth) in 1858. She was barely half his age and had been his mistress for the past two years. In her well-cut silk riding habits, showing off to perfection her fine figure and beautiful legs, she was a natural member of the fast, sporting society around the Prince of Wales, sharing with 'Skittles', the celebrated courtesan, membership of the fashionable and exclusive Quorn Hunt and recognition as two of its finest horsewomen'.[40] Their marriage, in her own words, was a 'veritable romance', but mid-Victorian society disapproved, not so much because he had taken a mistress, which was not unexpected, but because he had married her. He died in 1868, the hero of Balaclava; she erected a monument to him at Deene, lying in full uniform, with a recumbent statue of herself, modelled from life, by his side. She died in 1915, a relic of female beauty from an age when the Duke of Wellington was

Commander in Chief and the pretty horse-breakers were the scandal of Rotten Row. Her Memoirs (1909) gave 'a picture of people who regarded themselves as the cream of the earth and who spent their whole time in hunting, drinking and making love to each others' wives'.[41]

Russell's wife also came out from England to join him — but only for one month. Russell's Editor told him —

> 'If you were an officer with a wife and young family in England, I would never advise your wife's joining you for any length of time and leaving her children, except in the event of your being seriously wounded.'[42]

The Russells spent the month on the Bosphorus at the Hotel d'Angleterre, before he returned to report the final battle of the war.

In September 1855 the French captured the Malakoff fortifications and Sebastapol became untenable. The Russians withdrew from the town, blowing up the defences. But the Allied Armies would have to spend a second winter in the Crimea, before Peace was declared (March 1856). They would spend the winter months improving their conditions — building huts and roads and laying out their camps. At home the public continued to subscribe to The Times Fund and to the Crimean Army Fund, the chief agencies for relieving the suffering of the soldiers in the hospitals at Scutari or in the trenches before Sebastopol, but these needs were rapidly disappearing. So, too, was additional support for The Patriotic Fund, which relieved widows and orphans. But more money was desperately required for the Central Association Fund to care for their wives and families, dependent relatives and motherless children, whose

> 'number now exceeds 7,000 wives and 14,000 children. The proportion of widows to wives is not more than 15 per cent at present and money, furniture, clothing, blankets and shoes are needed. There is no alternative but the workhouse if the Fund runs dry', commented *The Times*.[43]

Major Powys, Chairman of the Soldiers' Infant Home, at Hampstead was also appealing for funds.

> 'In 1815, 600 girls were maintained and educated at the public expense at Chelsea and at the Hibernian School in Dublin. In 1856 none are supported at public expense and when the soldier returns from the Crimea, he will still be compelled to see his daughters growing up to womanhood in the barrack-room, surrounded with temptations which are fatal to her moral and eternal welfare. 100 of these poor girls are sheltered from destruction at Hampstead, the only asylum in the country for the daughters of soldiers, kept to the age of 15, with situations found for them. I call on all the high-born mothers and sisters of officers in the Crimea, soon to welcome their loved ones home, to support it'.[44]

Russell was now writing of entertainment for the troops.

> 'The French organised a Costume Ball for the Allied officers — unfortunately, the fair sex formed but a small proportion of the throng. Between vivandières and shop-keepers I believe the figure of 8 was at last attained, but the fun was kept up to a late hour'.[45]
> 'The 4th Division excelled in attempts to dispel the boredom of winter in camp. It built the Theatre Royal, with dresses, scenery, properties, orchestra etc. The theatre is half-

tent, half-wood, with no boxes or gallery but one large pit fitted with rows of benches, always liable to tip over and deposit the occupants in the mud. The *'corps dramatique'* is entirely of the masculine gender, but we have highly fascinating young actresses and the most seductive soubrettes. Of course, the ladies were got up with an ample amount of buckram and padding and, although they looked rather solid armfuls, one can imagine their power over the hearts of their respective admirers. After the performance, there was a dance on stage, in which the actresses rather detracted from their feminine effect by exchanging their bonnets for forage caps and by placing cigars between their beautiful lips. There were no bouquets for the ladies, not because of any lack of charms or merit on their part, but because of the scarcity of flowers in the camp'.[46]

Three months later he added —

'Theatres are always crowded to excess, nor are they altogether filled with redcoats for now and then a bonnet or hat belonging to an officer's wife may be seen dimly through the clouds of tobacco smoke'.[46]

But the war was nearing its end. Fanny Duberly, who had watched from the Heights of Balaclava the destruction of the Light Brigade and the safe return of her husband, lamented 'Everybody seems to be going home'. When her turn came to return to England, she found her name was known in every household.

The surviving women and children were returning, too. Their numbers who embarked and disembarked to and from the Crimea and the Mediterranean stations were small in comparison to the number of troops engaged, but as can be seen from the figures provided by one military district, they still represented a considerable involvement. Many were the families of militia regiments garrisoning the Mediterranean and Ionian bases (see Appendix A). Some would be German regiments, recruited to serve in the Crimea with the British Army. While they awaited repatriation at Colchester, 150 married local girls in October 1856 in the Garrison Church (64 on the same day, 20 October, as a plaque commemorates). Not only were they charmed by the local beauties but also by an offer for married men to go to the Cape Colony as military settlers![47]

Appendix A to Chapter 8

	Number of Ships	Officers	Staff	Ladies	Children	Sgts.	O Rs	Wives	Children
Embarked	151	1,987	345	105	154	2,464	56,154	1,223	1,224
Disembarked	280	1,775	764	73	109	4,303	74,514	2,275	2,430

Source: Return for the SW. District from the commencement to the close of the War with Russia: Officers, Men, Women and Children passing through — Crimea, Mediterranean and other Stations.

Another Return showed the embarkation and disembarkation figures at Portsmouth 1855–6 as follows:

	Officers	Men	Women	Children
Embarked (8 Feb 1855 – 13 Sep 1856)	1,300	35,322	935	1,128
Disembarked (1 May 1856 – 13 Sep 1856)	2,251	61,498	930	1,028

Source: Portsmouth embarkation and disembarkation Returns from the Army in the East. 13 September 1856 (including Militia, Depot and Garrison troops and families).

India on the eve of the Mutiny 1856

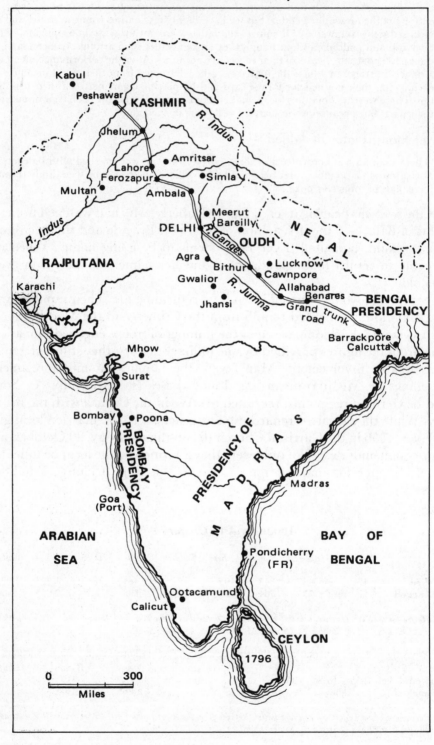

PLATE 1. Tangier c.1665. *Wenceslaus Hollar. (British Museum).*

PLATE 2. Women's duties in camp 1803. *W. H. Pyne. (National Army Museum)*.

PLATE 3. Women beg a lift. Baggage Train 1802. *W. H. Pyne.* (*National Army Museum*).

PLATE 4. Light Dragoon's barrack room 1788. (*National Army Museum*)

PLATE 5. Women and children attend a compulsory drumhead service: 1801. *Thomas Rowlandson. (British Museum).*

PLATE 6A. Women and children on the march. Old Buffs 1808. *Thomas Rowlandson. (National Army Museum).*

PLATE 6B. A woman drummed out of Camp by the Regiment. Hyde Park 1780. (Note the differences in dress and occupations of the other women in the picture). *(National Army Museum).*

PLATE 7. Sarah Churchill, Duchess of Marlborough. (1660–1744). *c.1700 After Kneller. (National Portrait Gallery)*.

PLATE 8. Barbara Villiers, Duchess of Cleveland (1640–1709). *c.1665–75. After Sir Peter Lely. (National Portrait Gallery)*.

PLATE 9. Nell Gwynne (1650–1687) *c.1670. Simon Verelst.*
(Private Collection. National Portrait Gallery).

PLATE 10. Louise de Keroualle, Duchess of Portsmouth (1649–
1734). Her son became the first Duke of Richmond. *Henri Gascars.*
(By kind permission of Christies. Photo: *National Portrait Gallery).*

PLATE 11. Sutler. (Often an Army wife or widow). Forerunner of NAAFI. *(HQ. NAAFI)*.

PLATE 12. Footguards and wives in camp at Scutari 1854. (*Illustrated London News. 15 July 1854*).

The arrival of the 'fishing fleet' caused the utmost
excitement in the garrison.

Jack's own Jill goes up the hill to Murree or Chakrata.

Gossip was elevated from a pastime to an art!

Jack remains and dies on the Plains
and Jill remarries soon after.

The young ladies would have their choice of the
regiments.

'Sweat the sex out of you' was the watchword.

PLATE 14. Massacre at Cawnpore 1857. Nana Sahib butchers the British survivors of the Garrison (mostly women and children) as they take to the boats. *T. Packer. (National Army Museum)*.

PLATE 15. Leave-taking for the Far East 1857. *Henry O'Neil. (Victoria and Albert Museum).*

unless by special authority on the recommendation of the Medical Officer.

4. Great-coats are not ~~to be transferred from one Company to another, nor allowed~~ to be taken by men going on pass or furlough.

5. Officers commanding Companies will inspect the great-coats of their respective Companies weekly.

MARRIED MEN, WOMEN, AND CHILDREN.

1. It is incumbent on the Officers to discourage the men as much as possible from making improvident marriages, and to be very cautious in previously ascertaining the character and condition of the woman, before they recommend any man for permission to marry.

2. No Officer in temporary command is to give a Non-commissioned Officer or soldier permission to marry, except with the sanction of the Lieutenant-Colonel commanding.

3. Non-commissioned Officers and soldiers are not to marry without the consent of the Commanding Officer. Any individual infringing this order will subject himself and his family to great misery; his wife will not be allowed in Barracks, nor have any privileges of soldiers' wives, nor be recognized in any way.

4. Any soldier's wife for [...] or diso[...]

or spreading malicious reports of each other, or bringing liquor into Barracks, will be turned out of Barracks forthwith.

5. The women and children will attend the medical inspection once a week or oftener if required.

6. The women and children will attend regularly their respective places of worship every Sunday. An absence report will be sent in every Monday morning, signed by the Quartermaster.

7. The washing and work of a Company will be distributed among the legally married women of it, at the discretion of the Officer commanding the Company. In general the distribution should be regulated by the number of children in each family, and equally divided amongst the other women, unless they are guilty of neglect or misconduct.

8. No washing is permitted in the Barrack-rooms, nor are lines to be put up for drying linen, except at the appointed places.

9. ~~All marriages, births, and ... will be entered in the Regimental by ... les in the soldiers' small account book~~

The women are expe[cted ... keep their] children clean, and to ma[...] the Regimental School, and to [...] place...ship.

PLATE 16. Standing Orders for the 73rd Foot 1858. (Extract from the personal copy of Lieutenant Hugh Hackett Gibsone, illustrated with Victorian pin-ups. (*Museum of the Black Watch (The Royal Highland Regiment)*)).

PLATE 17. Alice Keppel. Print by Jenkins after Roberts.
(National Portrait Gallery).

PLATE 18. Members of the Women's Army Auxiliary Corps (WAAC) on Paris Plage at Le Touquet 1918. *(Imperial War Museum)*.

Chapter 9

Women Face the Indian Mutineers

On 4 June 1845, Private John Pearman embarked at Gravesend for Calcutta. Pearman's mother had been governess to the children of Mrs Jordan, mistress of the Duke of Clarence (King William IV) and much to her sorrow, her son had enlisted at the age of 24, after a 'tiff' with his employer, 'to travel and to see other countries.' He would become a Sergeant and leave us a graphic account of life in the Queen's Army in India and of events leading up to the Mutiny.

He was now joining his Regiment, 3rd King's Own Light Dragoons, accompanied by 13 'officially recognised' women and 37 children, together with '4 young married women of the 3rd Light Dragoons, who had been smuggled aboard without leave'.[1]

Four months later they would land at Fort William, Calcutta, where the recruits

'died at the rate of two and three every 24 hours. Those that died in the day were buried at sundown and those that died in the night were buried at 5 in the morning. In the space of 12 hours after landing, a soldier of the 80th Foot, (The South Staffordshire Regiment) his wife and baby all died with cholera.'

LIFE AT THE CAPE

When Lieutenant John Luard had arrived in the Cape in 1822, white women were scarce, being mainly the wives of soldiers and local officials. But when Pearman arrived twenty years later, there was a thriving community of settlers along the coast and inland, attracted by the healthy climate and good prospects at the Cape. The constant and increasing demand for wives and governesses led to the foundation in England of societies to encourage emigration

'to places like the Cape, where the men want wives, the mothers want governesses, while the shopkeepers, the schools and the sick will strongly appreciate the exertions of your local societies and heartily welcome your women'.[2]

The main military towns were Cape Town, Pietermaritzburg, Grahamstown, Kingwilliamstown and Fort Beaufort, garrisoned by regular units from Britain and African auxiliaries levied into the Cape Regiment and Cape Mounted Rifles, whose commanding officer, Colonel Somerset, requested a schoolmistress in 1839 for his 213 Army children, most of them the product of local liaisons with Hottentot women.[3] Here, too, were many civil and military officers on leave from India, who retained their pay and allowances at the Cape, and thus became a byword for idleness, profligacy and wealth but whose custom kept the local shop and inn keepers prosperous. Their uniform and wealth dazzled the Colonial women and the Cape's fashionable ladies became, in time, another source of wives for Indian army officers. However, Sir Garnet Wolseley, when Governor there, tried to discourage such permanent liaisons and described them as 'a collection of housemaids with their greengrocer admirers in attendance. Fancy having to make love to such a set for months to come.' But, despite his warnings, many of his officers were carrying on half a dozen love affairs simultaneously.[4]

REGIMENTAL MARRIAGES

Meanwhile, Sergeant Pearman, had arrived in Barracks at Ambala, where 700 women and children and a great number of officers' ladies in the officers' quarters had been assembled for safety on account of the Sikh Wars (1845–9)

> 'We had 14 or 15 widows in the regiment, and most of them were married in a month, after our return to quarters. Soon forgot the ones dead,' Pearman observed.[5]

In 1849 the Regiment was again at Ambala, where

> 'the centre barracks were left to the married sergeants and the Sergeants' Mess Room and the temporary stables were also made into married quarters and the canteens. There were many widows and some young unmarried girls, 14 years of age, who had to get married or 'go off pay' (6 months after the death of their husbands),' he wrote, 'so weddings went on merrily, as they are articles that would not keep, four or five a day. Some women in that country have several husbands, before they are very old. One of my companions had a black wife and wanted to stay in India, so he paid £100 to a soldier in another regiment to change places, when we were leaving'.[6]
>
> Mrs Postans noted in 1838 — 'These speedy remarriages are far from uncommon: frequent cases occur, in which a wife engages herself to a suitor during her husband's life, and trusts to the chances, provided by arrack and climate, for the fulfilment of her contract. Disproportion in age is never considered in a soldier's marriage; a grisly bombadier of 40 unites himself to a girl of 12, with the full consent of her parents, who are probably present at the marriage'.[7]

Mrs Postans's husband died in India and she returned to England. She, too, married again!

General Sir Neville Lyttleton[8] relates the story of another hasty marriage:-

> 'In India burials follow death very rapidly and sometimes a widow's remarriage is equally hasty. One widow attended her husband's funeral the day after he died and on the same day the Colour Sergeant of the Company proposed to her. She burst into tears and the N.C.O., thinking perhaps he had been too hasty, said he would return in two or three days. 'Oh, it isn't that', she said 'but on the way back from the cemetery, I accepted the Corporal of the firing party' — a far less attractive offer!'

LUCKNOW

Early in 1856, the Reverend Henry Polehampton, and his wife Emily, arrived in Calcutta as Chaplain of The East India Company in Lucknow. He was 32, a product of Eton and Oxford and a fine athlete, having gained his rowing blue in the 1846 University Boat Race. In his first letter to his mother he wrote:

> 'Just now Lucknow is full. At Cantonments there are three native regiments. The English Officers of these regiments, with their wives and children, form my congregation there. At the other end of the city is my largest congregation, the 52nd Regiment (Oxfordshire and Buckinghamshire Light Infantry), all English, 1000 strong. We have service in the open air.'[9]

Soon he was in the throes of a cholera epidemic. In a period of six weeks he helped to bury 70 men, women and children of the Regiment. At the end of the year, his son was born. Within a few days he had convulsions and died. A few months later the Mutiny had begun, which Henry would not survive.

CALCUTTA

Another married couple to reach India at this time were Captain Archie Wood (from a line of military forebears) and his wife Minnie. They arrived in Calcutta in November, 1856, tired, unwell and somewhat disillusioned with each other, after a voyage round the Cape lasting 116 days. The cramped quarters of a sailing ship, bad food, poor ventilation and extremes of climate were not the most perfect conditions for a marriage, even for newly-weds! Captain Wood, aged 37, had been home on leave seeking the health-healing waters of Bath and a suitable wife. Within a few weeks of meeting Marie Lydia Blane, aged 20, they were married on 22 May 1856 and en route for India. In her trousseau were various quantities of cotton chemises, flannel vests, silk slips, petticoats with flounced bodices, French stays and corsets, cotton drawers, black silk stockings, costumes, skirts, dresses for morning, afternoon and evening, ball gowns, opera cloak, hats, gloves, shoes and boots for all occasions, riding outfit, parasol and umbrellas. Her husband was equally kitted out for military and social occasions and carried a good gun, revolver, opera glasses, deck chair, map of India and a case of saddlery. They also took out their household linen, curtains and furniture covers, (not to mention the furniture itself and cooking utensils!)[10]

Minnie was entranced with Calcutta, the homes of rich European merchants and officials — two storeyed buildings with deep verandahs, flower-beds, and well-kept lawns, British children at play with their pet dogs and 'ayahs': and Fort William, where scarlet-coated European soldiers paced the ramparts and below British women in crinolines chatted on the dock-side amid the coolies, bullock carts and London built landaus. Soon they would settle down to army married life in a small military garrison at Jhelum — a few months before the outbreak of the Indian Mutiny.

THE INDIAN MUTINY

Whatever the causes of the Indian Mutiny (or Sepoy Revolt, as many prefer to call it) — it was the horrors of the Mutiny which were to preoccupy the British wives, living in Northern and Central India at the time. Some wives and children would not survive it; others experienced the barbarities of war, suffering torture, rape and death (although reports were often false or highly exaggerated), but many were to show great courage and endurance in the face of danger.

The Army officers living in the Company's Lines could not imagine that their loyal and disciplined sepoys would actually rise in revolt against them. Lieutenant Fred Roberts (later to become Field-Marshal Earl Roberts), wrote to his father, General Abraham Roberts, 22nd May 1857, from a Camp near Jhelum.

> 'I am sure you have been astonished at the news . . . . . the mutiny of the Sepoys, all thought so faithful and true, nasty scoundrels. They have shown themselves at heart to be worse than even our enemies. No Sikh or Afghan ever abused and killed our women and children as these wretches have done.'[11]

That sepoys should lay their hands on white women, let alone outrage them, horrified Victorian England and the troops alike.

The Times, for example, carried a 'factual' report from a clergyman, alleging that in Delhi,

> '48 delicately nurtured ladies, mostly girls from 10 to 14 had been violated and kept for the base purposes of the heads of the insurrection for a whole week: after that they were paraded naked in the streets and handed over to the lowest of the people to be mutilated, abused in broad daylight and then tortured to death.'[12]

Reports of murders, massacres and mutilitations were read avidly, as Mutiny erupted over Meerut, Delhi, Lucknow and especially over Cawnpore, formerly the home of two cavalry, three infantry regiments and a lot of artillery and chock full of pretty women, with private theatricals every week, balls, picnics and dinners every evening.[13]

MEERUT AND DELHI

The first British women to meet violent deaths were those in Meerut, a town forty miles north of Delhi, on the night of 10th May 1857. It was the largest military station in the north-west provinces. But, early that Sunday evening, when officers and their families were getting ready for Evensong, hundreds of sepoys ran through the bazaars, burning the bungalows of The Lines, firing and slashing at every European in sight.

> 'No European man, women or child has had the slightest mercy shown them. The terrified women and children of our soldiers were murdered under circumstances of unheard of barbarity'.[14]

Captain and Mrs McDonald were savagely slain and the Adjutant's wife, recovering from smallpox, was burnt in her bungalow. Mrs Charlotte Chambers, a captain's wife, soon expecting her confinement, was raped, her unborn child ripped from her and both thrown in the flames. The mutineers, to gather support for their cause and fearing punishment, fled from Meerut to Delhi.[14]

In Delhi lived their King, Bahadur Shah II, now an important pensioner of the British, but a descendant of the Mogul emperor, Akbar the Great, who had built the Red Fort as his palace in the 17th century. The Fort dominated the city, its massive red walls, one and a half miles in circumference. When I (the Author) visited it daily at the end of 1945 to practise my Japanese on its Prisoner of War inmates, it was a grim fortress indeed. Once it had been one of the wonders of the world, an early paradise of wealth and pleasure for the Emperor and his court. At the time of the Mutiny, the King's wealth had diminished, his palace plundered. The magnificent audience hall and peacock throne of solid gold were set beside dirt and filth. Persian carpets and dirty mats lay side by side on the floor: ivory and silver chairs were covered with rags. This ramshackle court was all that was left of the empire of Akbar, where, wrote a contemporary, incest, murder, poison and torture were daily occurrences; where girls gleaned from the surrounding villages 'danced naked to inflame the passion of old age'; a haven for criminals, a hot-bed of intrigue. Below, the silent river kept its secrets.[15]

Now 82 years old, the King had little stomach to lead a crusade and it was his youngest wife and favourite Begum, Zeenat Mahal, who would urge on the sepoys against their European officers.

This chapter is not a history of the Mutiny but a glimpse of women and children caught up in armed conflict. Such a family was that of Captain Robert Tytler of the 38th Bengal Infantry, his wife Harriet, a Colonel's daughter, born in India, and their two young children.[16] They lived in their cantonment bungalow on a Ridge, overlooking Delhi and the River Jumna, to the North of the Red Fort and the City. On that first day in Delhi, 11th May 1857, they were at breakfast, when a message arrived summoning Robert to his regiment and all non-combatants to Flagstaff Tower, a four-storey building on the Ridge, a traditional meeting place and lookout position for Europeans. When she, the children and her French maid, Marie, reached the Tower, they found other frightened and hungry women, who told her that some 2,000 mutineers from Meerut had poured into the city during the night and were killing every Christian they could find. With their children they had escaped the slaughter in the city. The scene at Flagstaff Tower was described by George Wagentreiber of the *Delhi Gazette*, as 'a Black Hole in miniature'. He had taken refuge there with his wife Elizabeth, youngest daughter of one of the 14 wives of Colonel James Skinner, the famous half-caste leader of irregular cavalry (Skinner's Horse). Thanks largely to her dark skin and

Indian upbringing, she was able to help her husband and baby daughter to survive their ordeals.

In the tiny upstairs room of the Tower, women, children and servants, the remnants of Delhi's European population, huddled together, in the stifling heat: here were widows mourning their murdered husbands, sisters weeping over a brother's death, wives waiting anxiously for news of their men on duty. Only Marie, Harriet's maid, remained irrepressible, flirting openly with the officers.[17]

At dusk, the order was given to withdraw. Some of the women and children escaped to Kurnaul in carriages; Harriet Tytler and the Adjutant's wife, Mrs Gardner, together with a small party of wives and children, fled to the comparative safety of the large military station at Ambala, in rags, penniless, their bungalows and wordly possessions burned. Elizabeth Wagentreiber drove her carriage with her children inside, while her husband fought the way with his revolvers, killing four men and wounding many more.[18]

Later, Harriet went back to Delhi with her husband, gave birth to a son and was the only British woman to witness the whole of the Siege. Robert, promoted Colonel, became the first Governor of the Andaman's Penal Colony, whose highest peak is named after Harriet. Marie married a Sergeant in the 60th Rifles.

Meanwhile, the sepoys had invaded the Eurasian and Indian-Christian quarter of Delhi and massacred the men, women and children on the spot. Some, mostly women, were taken to the courtyard of the Palace and put to the sword and their corpses thrown into the River Jumna. Only one woman escaped, Mrs Aldwell, a Eurasian, who pleaded that she was a Moslem and was spared.

Veronica Bamfield[19] supplies another 'cameo' of the Delhi story —

Captain Forrest was a widower and in 1840 married a fifteen year old girl, who, the following year, produced their first child on the troopship taking them to India. Thus Mrs Forrest was still in her early thirties, when her eldest daughter, not quite 16 years old, became engaged to Lieutenant Montague Proctor of the 31st Native Infantry in May 1857, stationed, like her father, in Delhi.

When the mutineers arrived in the city, Proctor and another officer quickly gathered together a number of women and children, including Mrs Forrest and her three daughters, and hurried them towards the Kashmir Gate. The party had to pick its way over the bodies of people they knew. These had been covered over with pretty ball-gowns, looted from neighbouring houses. Mrs Forrest was shot through the shoulder, but even before the wound could be attended to, she had to be let down over the high parapet on an improvised rope made from ladies' dresses. After walking for seven days, during which they were joined by two Sergeants' wives and their babies, also escaping from Delhi, they reached safety. All the women were in a terrible condition, their bleeding feet bandaged with strips torn from their dresses, their heads protected from the burning sun by pieces of their underwear.

Minnie Wood wrote to her mother from Jhelum on 15th May 1857, to announce the birth of her baby.

> 'In Delhi, Mr Jennings, the Chaplain, with his 20 year old daughter, were speared, as they were returning from church in their buggy. Two of our fellow passengers on the ship have been murdered at Meerut, Mr and Mrs Dawson, I believe, slowly burnt to death in one of the houses the mutineers fired, and would not allow them to escape.' The letter continues in Archie's handwriting. 'The Mutiny is spread from Barrackpore, 15 miles from Calcutta, up to our Frontier station Peshawar. At Delhi, the mutineers have butchered every white man, woman and child in the city. More than 50 women and children, Christians, who took refuge for safety in the King's Palace there, have all been murdered. Such revolting atrocities, etc., have never been heard of before. Minnie is behaving like a soldier's wife. She does not fear much.'[20]

On 11th June 1857, Lieutenant Roberts was writing to his mother (herself the widow of an army officer) from Amritsar.

> 'We don't know exactly, who were killed in Delhi, or who escaped . . . . . A native, who was at Delhi during the massacre, told me he saw eight ladies let out, and shot one after the other; they nearly all had children with them, who were killed before their eyes. If anything has ever helped to keep me from marrying, this mutiny has.'[21]

In fact, 20 years later he married the 10th child of a Black Watch officer and sailed for India with her, 3 weeks later.

CAWNPORE

From Delhi, the rebellion spread along the Valley of the Ganges to Benares, Allahabad and to Cawnpore which was to become in June 1857 'a name for Saxon courage and Hindu cruelty at its highest', — 'a name which afterwards raised so much passion and fury and thoughts of revenge in the mind of the British soldier.

Cawnpore, an important trading centre and military garrison, was under the command of General Sir Hugh Wheeler, son of a captain in the East India Company's service, who had married a daughter of the first Lord Massey. Wheeler had spent nearly all his military life in India, loved the country and its people and had married an Indian woman. Mistakenly, he put his trust in Nana Sahib, the local leader of the mutineers, who bore a grudge against the British for terminating his father's substantial pension from the East India Company on his death — a pension he had hoped to inherit. 'The ladies who had shuddered deliciously at gossip of the Nana's sensual pleasures were now to find a far more sinister side to his character.'[22]

Wheeler ordered some 300 European officers and men and 400 women and children, together with 100 civilians, to move to the safety of some half-built barracks, situated on an open plain outside the city, protected only by a small entrenchment and an earth wall.

Suddenly, in June, Nana Sahib attacked and for 20 days and nights bombarded them from all sides, a single shell killing seven married women of the 32nd Foot. (The Duke of Cornwall's Light Infantry). Then, amid their sufferings from hunger, thirst and the shelling, a message arrived from Nana Sahib offering 'a safe passage to Allahabad'. Wheeler was reluctant to surrender, but was persuaded there was no other way to save the wounded, the sick and the women and children. On 27th June the survivors moved towards the river the dirty, half-dressed memsahibs clinging to the ropes on the elephants, the wounded in the palanquins, their limbs bound up with strips of petticoat and stockings, the thin children in the bullock carts.

As they started to embark waiting boats, the massacre began. Hundreds of concealed rebels opened fire. 'Children were stabbed and thrown into the river. The schoolgirls were burnt to death. I saw their clothes and hair catch fire.'[22]

Another witness, Amelia Horne, the pretty 18 year old Eurasian daughter of a deceased naval captain, who lost her mother and sister in the massacre, wrote —

> 'The cavalry waded into the river with drawn swords and cut down those who were still alive, while the infantry boarded the boats to loot. The air resounded with the shrieks of the women and children, and agonised prayers to God for mercy. The water was red with blood, and the smoke from the heavy firing of the cannon and muskets and the fire from the burning boats lay like dense clouds all around us.'[22]

Of the British who managed to live through the massacre on the river, the men were immediately shot but the 125 or so women and children, later joined by some officers' wives and two captured boat-loads of fugitives, were imprisoned in a small house known as the Bibighar, the 'House of Ladies', originally built by a British officer for his mistress. On 15th July, when news reached Cawnpore, that a relieving force under General Henry Havelock was approaching the city, Nana's men entered the Bibighar and murdered the 212 women and children, while he passed the evening with a nautch. Next morning the bodies were dragged out, stripped of their clothing and thrown down a well.[23] It was this final massacre that inflamed British feelings into a savage thirst for revenge; for when they entered Cawnpore, after driving out the rebels, they found the Bibighar looking like a slaughter-house. When General G. S. Neill, left in charge by Havelock, saw the room for himself, he wrote —

> 'Ladies' and children's bloody torn dresses and shoes were lying about and locks of hair torn from their heads. The floor was saturated with blood . . . who could be merciful to one concerned? Every miscreant, after sentence of death, will be taken to the house and forced to clean up a small portion of the bloodstains; the Provost-Marshal will use the lash in forcing anyone objecting to complete his task — then the culprit is to be immediately hanged.'[24]

REVENGE

They took a terrible revenge. They went on a rampage of slaughter, rape and killing. Hanging was thought too good for the mutineers (mutiny in the Army was punishable by death) and it was usual to blow them from guns.

> 'Our blood is roused. We have seen friends, relatives, mothers, wives, children brutally murdered and their bodies mutilated. As the riflemen charge the word is passed 'Remember the ladies, remember the babies!'[25]

Delhi was recaptured after a desperate siege lasting several months. With the fall of the Red Fort all effective resistance ended. The old King and Queen Zeenat Mahal surrendered; he was sentenced to exile and with his Begum ended his days in a tented camp in Rangoon. His palace was looted by the troops; thousands of corpses were carted away and buried. The Shah's two sons, who had ordered — and witnessed — the wholesale murder of the surviving European and Eurasian men, women and children, held captive in the Palace, were shot, partly on the evidence of Mrs Aldwell, who, after escaping the massacre, had been condemned to death, accused of being a Christian in disguise. She had been rescued by the sepoys of the 38th Native Infantry.[26]

Amelia Horne survived. When the massacre in the river at Cawnpore began, she watched the other members of her family being slashed, burnt or drowned and was herself knocked into the water by a sepoy's musket. At the last moment she was hauled out of the river by an Indian trooper who, in the general confusion, managed to carry her off on his horse and hid her in a nearby shed. Later, she was forcibly 'converted' and married to the trooper, who made her accompany him on his various campaigns. Eventually he allowed her to escape to Allahabad, where five months later she married a railway superintendent.[27]

One other survivor was General Wheeler's youngest daughter, Ulrica, aged 18, whose supposed fate was enacted in theatres and described in books all over the world. It was said she had killed her captor and then thrown herself down a well. Many years later a priest in Ambala came upon an old lady in the bazaar, who told him on her death-bed, she was Miss Wheeler. She had agreed to become a Muslim and had married the young sowar, who had saved her from massacre; he had been good to her.[28]

LUCKNOW

For events during the siege of Lucknow, we are fortunate to have the eye-witness accounts of Lady Julia Inglis,[29] daughter of the first Lord Chelmsford and wife of Lieutenant Colonel (later General Sir) John Inglis, commanding the 32nd Foot in Lucknow. He took over the command of the garrison, after the death of Sir Henry Lawrence, whose wife, Honoria, had died three years earlier in 1854. Julia, who had three children under five years of age, gives details in her journal of the daily domestic events of the siege.

'Eleven ladies and 15 children crowded into Lawrence's house, guarded by the most mild-looking sepoys, who used to amuse themselves during the day by playing with the children. I used to watch them and could hardly fancy they were murderously inclined.'

While they waited Mr Polehampton preached a beautiful sermon. Next day all the women and children left the cantonment for the City Residency, which was being prepared to withstand a siege. During the month of June, before the siege began, Lady Inglis gives us a picture of the women and children scattered about in various houses and buildings, of Julia starting her own ladies' mess, of 'the women of the 32nd Foot' and 'the artillery women', of half-caste clerks and their families and of Christian drummers and their wives, all living apart. Mrs Bruere, wife of the major commanding the 13th Native Regiment, 'was spending the night in cantonments contrary to orders' and had to be smuggled out of the house by her husband and sepoys and hidden in the ravine till morning. Julie and her children slept on the flat roof in the open air, while at dawn, the other ladies and children joined them for a breath of air. In the rooms below, trials took place of native prisoners, many of whom were sentenced to be hanged. 'We could see them chained in couples sitting on the ground.'

Lady Inglis was suffering from smallpox on the day Sir Henry Lawrence received news of the capitulation and massacre at Cawnpore. He immediately sent all the European women and children into the Residency and when the rebels attacked it on 30th June 1857, the most famous siege in British military history began. On the second day, a sniper's bullet mortally wounded him.

The prospect facing the British families, joined by more and more families escaping from outlying stations, was grim. At best they could hope that the siege would be short and that food and drink would last. At worst they faced a savage death.

Amid the flies, mosquitoes, the terrible heat, the sick, the wounded and the dying, the women played their part magnificently. Emily Polehampton and some of the officers' widows turned to nursing the increasing numbers of casualities ('1st July: Miss Palmer had her leg taken off by a round shot today') and the serious illnesses among the children from the poor food, smallpox, scurvy and cholera ('loose teeth, swollen heads and boils'). There were several suicides ('several of the ladies had poison at hand') and the stench of imperfectly buried bodies was everywhere. 26th July 'Mr Lewin of the Artillery was shot dead at the Cawnpore battery today. He left a young widow: their only little girl, one of the prettiest children I have ever seen, had died from cholera at the commencement of the siege'.[29]

The 23 year old Katherine Mary Bartrum[30] dedicated her little diary to the memory of her husband Captain Robert Henry Bartrum of the Bengal Medical Service and to their son Robert. At the outbreak of the Mutiny, they were in Gonda, a military station 80 miles from Lucknow, 'where we have been living for the last 8 months the peaceful and retired life of an Indian officer's family in an up-country station.' Their peace was shattered on 22nd May 1857 'by the alarming news of the massacre at Meerut and Delhi of all the European inhabitants of those stations.' In a letter to her father she writes:

'For many nights we have scarcely dared to close our eyes. I have kept a sword under my pillow and dear Robert had his pistol loaded. My husband always consoled me with the promise that should things come to the worst he would destroy me with his own hand rather than let me fall into the power of those brutal sepoys'.

Sir Henry Lawrence, 'our wise commissioner', ordered all ladies and children in outstations to go to Lucknow for safety and Mrs Bartrum and her son went with them to the Residency. In her diary she records her feelings 'Often I had contemplated death with my husband but not separation from him' and tells of the deprivation, horrors and casualties, during the siege, including the death of her own husband, 'shot just as he gained the gates of the Residency of Lucknow' with the relieving force under Sir Henry Havelock. Katherine escaped from Lucknow, and returned home to Bath, after a terrible march to Calcutta, where her baby 'Bobbie', sickened and died.[31] She subsequently married a Nottingham physician.

As the relief force under Generals Havelock and Outram approached, Brigadier Inglis had 'upwards of 120 sick and wounded and at least 220 women and about 130 children' on his hands and when the three months' siege ended, the surviving women and children were escorted to Cawnpore and thence by bullock cart and rail to Allahabad and so on to Calcutta by boat and steamer. There, Lady Inglis, once again the Colonel's lady,

'gave the women and children, who were left of the 32nd, a dinner. It was anything but a festive sight to me. There were now only 17 women and nearly all were widows, and every child present had lost one or both parents'.[32]

Sir Henry Lawrence's epitaph reads

'Here lies Henry Lawrence who tried to do his duty. May God have mercy on him'.

The Reverend Henry Polehampton, who had officiated at the wedding of Archie and Minnie Wood, had also died, of cholera, having been weakened by a shot wound. His brief life as a Mutiny chaplain had been an example and inspiration to all. The Alam Bagh cemetery, five miles out of Lucknow on the Cawnpore Road, records the death of Major General Sir Henry Havelock.

'Destined to relieve the brave garrison of Lucknow and to die in the moment of his greatest triumph. His monument was erected by his sorrowing widow and family'.[33]

Beside him lie the bodies of Mr Polehampton, Robert Bartrum and about 400 other Europeans, victims of the Mutiny.

THE AFTERMATH

The churches and churchyard cemeteries of almost every town and outpost in Northern and Central India record the massacres that took place — Agra,

Banda, Benares, Cawnpore, Delhi, Jhansi, Lucknow and Meerut — to name but a few.

> 'Captain Alexander Skene, Mrs Skene and two children; Mrs Brown, wife of Captain Brown and Miss Brown, his sister. Murdered at Jhansi in June 1857' (together with the other 65 European officers, 13 women and 18 children and near where the young, attractive Ranee, leader of the mutineers, was struck from the saddle and killed, 'fighting and dressed like a man',[33] in red tunic and trousers, white turban and a magnificent pearl necklace.)

At the well of Cawnpore, the mass memorial reads:

> 'Sacred to the perpetual memory of a great company of Christian people, chiefly women and children, who near this spot were cruelly massacred by the followers of the rebel Nana Sahib of Bithur who cast the dying with the dead into the well below on the 15th day of July, 1857'.

A regimental tribute simply records:

> 'Women and children of 32nd Regiment, Killed 16th July 1857'.[34]

On 1st January 1859, the Crown assumed control of India by Royal Proclamation, delegating its authority to a Viceroy. The Company's European regiments were converted to the Queen's service (and numbered 101st to 109th Foot). Henceforth, more battalions (and thus more 'women') would be garrisoned there.

The Mutiny was over also for Minnie Wood but her troubles were not at an end. Her last letters home (June–August 1860) spoke of her poverty and Archie's increasing debts and the gradual break-up of their marriage. 'My husband tells everyone he married me, because he thought I was an heiress'.[35] Soon she left India with her children and returned to her mother at Bath. Divorce followed. Both remarried into military families, Minnie returning to India as a Colonel's wife and Archie to command his regiment and marry a widow.

Going in the opposite direction were the Duberlys, once again on their travels — this time bound for Bombay, via the Cape, in the company of the 8th Hussars, aboard the new steamship 'Great Britain'. They arrived in December 1858 after a voyage of 70 days. Soon the regiment was on the move — to face $11\frac{1}{2}$ months and 2028 miles of marching through the hot weather and monsoon floods with the Rajputana Column. Fanny would cover 1800 miles in the saddle and with her husband would perform one of the greatest feats of endurance in the Army's history.[36]

They left India with the 8th Hussars in 1864 and settled in Cheltenham, highly regarded by families returning from India for its gentle climate and spa waters. Fanny died there in 1903, aged 73.

One other who survived the Mutiny was a Mrs Heddick, one-time governess to the two children of the Duke of Cambridge, who went to India with her husband and became a Regimental schoolmistress. Two who did not survive were the Schoolmaster and Schoolmistress remembered in an altar memorial to the massacre at Cawnpore.[37]

And what of Sergeant Pearman of the 3rd (King's Own) Light Dragoons? He had returned home with his Regiment in June 1852, before the Mutiny began. As he disembarked at Gravesend he found the port

'full of fathers, mothers, sisters and sweethearts and hundreds of girls and pick pockets'.

He was posted as an Instructor to Sandhurst and then joined the Buckinghamshire police after 13 years' service. At the age of 34 he married a Berkshire girl, much younger than himself, who bore him 11 children.

'What is marriage', he asked, 'but a life of trouble and care, and in most cases of the poor, a great deal of poverty? Mine was not a boyish love; it was the love of a man to do my duty and take care of her. When I took my wife from her father's home, although I knew my wife never had much affection for me, I swore to God to do my best to maintain her in comfort and this I have done and with the help of God will continue to do'.[38]

Chapter 10

Aldershot and Degradation

In 1854, a few months before the start of the Crimean War, the Army purchased 8,000 acres of heathland as the site for the future Aldershot Camp. It was within easy access of London and perfect for assembling and training a large military force. Soon the workmen and thousands of troops moved in, followed by the drink and vice vendors, the hucksters and prostitutes, who set up a 'shanty area' beside the growing Camp and Town to cater for their off-duty fun and recreation — 'a sexual paradise' for the crude labourers and soldiers in the drinking booths, squalid 'love-tents' and darkness of the nearby bushes.

In 1856 Charles Dickens gave his impressions after a month's stay in the area:–

> 'To describe the Camp at Aldershot is unnecessary: its position on the dark heath, its long lettered avenues flanked by black wooden huts, its lines of fluttering linen, its schools, parade grounds and canteens have become familiar to us. What I want to draw to the attention of at least every wife and mother in England is the demoralising misery to which this camp exposes their sister women.'[1]

In the Camp lines were Married Huts, with high windows, a door at either end and a cooking stove in the centre. Along the sides of the huts were iron bedsteads arranged in pairs, where a minimum of five married couples with their children were partially screened off from the next family by regimental blankets, a scanty sheet or two or by a woman's dress.

> 'Where families are more crowded, ten men, ten women and eight children are to be found occupying one hut, such attempted preservations of decency are impossible. The double beds nearly touch each other, without even the scantiest attempt at screen or curtain'.

The Camp had no accommodation for sick women or children. Since lodgings were unobtainable in the neighbourhood, those women who could not travel to their homes were forced to stay in the crowded huts. He saw one such wife of an NCO, with a young family, daily expecting her confinement. She occupied a hut with 20 men and the space between beds scarcely allowed standing room, let alone any privacy. He saw another delicate looking creature, who had lately given birth to a dead infant, cowering over the central stove, amid the soldiers' washing, crying children and men sitting on the benches, cursing and quarrelling as they awaited their mid-day meal.

> 'The result of this degradation', said Dickens 'is that the modest innocent girl soon succumbs to the shame and obscenities around her and step by step she becomes the drunken, dissolute, fear-inspiring and slatternly brawler of our barrack yards. What good are chapels and schools before this systematic training in depravity?'.

UNOFFICIAL WIVES

Outside the Camp was a district known as West End, where in rows of shoddily built little houses dwelt most of the wives of soldiers, who had wed without 'official' permission. Since the pay of the privates was so small, these wives and their children were desperately poor, their ragged clothes often clumsily converted from the discarded uniforms and underwear of their fathers. Most were sustained by scraps of food that the soldier-fathers had managed to save from their own meals in The Camp or to scrounge from their comrades in the regimental cookhouses.

> 'These women and girls had sacrificed so much to romance in defiantly wedding such poor men, that their physical looks and general appearance quickly and sadly deteriorated and they were shunned by many Aldershot townsfolk, who regarded themselves as greatly superior to such degraded females'.[2]

THE TOWN

If Aldershot's West End was sordid, the centre of Aldershot itself, which replaced the earlier shanty town on the heath from 1860 onwards, was worse. By day Aldershot seemed provincial and respectable, despite the 130 drinking houses to supplement the Regimental and Garrison canteens: but by night it became a vulgar, boisterous fun town, shunned by all respectable women and girls.

> 'Despite the good work of the Military Police', noted *The United Services Journal*[3] 'the vice and depravity fill the thoughtful with horror at the vile wretches (pimps, prostitutes and publicans) who trade upon the soldiers' passions, or their miseries.'

A police inspector who conducted the reformer William Acton round the area in 1857, pointed out

> 'a range of cottages, with lights in their windows, each room containing a man and a woman. The price of the rooms was twopence: the majority of the women rented the rooms from publicans, who not only insisted on the daily payment of their rent but also required their tenants to serve in the bars to induce the soldiers to drink: only after the tattoo had sounded at 9.30 pm were they permitted to leave the pubs to pursue their own business. They could only obtain a bare subsistence by taking home 8 or 10 soldiers each night'.[4]
> 'Badly built houses of the most inferior sort, ill-constructed drainage, fetid pools of refuse water in the low-lying parts, dear provisions and every low temptation: such is this degrading town for wives and families of soldiers, not on the strength of regiments, or married without leave, or of pensioners or widows and orphans of men sacrificed to war or climate. What a contrast', concluded *The United Services Journal*,[5] 'from the wives and

families of men on the strength of regiments, who are treated with every care and consideration by the authorities and well looked after by their own regimental officers' ladies.'

It is not surprising that mission work, established by the combined efforts of some military ladies, aided by others resident in the neighbourhood and the local authorities, found this a fruitful field for help to the soldier and his family. One who established a tradition of voluntary help for the soldier[4] and his family, which survives to this day was Louisa Daniell, widow of an Indian Army Captain, who in 1865 built the first Soldiers' Home and Institute and with her sister Georgiana opened such inexpensive recreational and canteen centres in other military garrisons. At weekly mothers' meetings the semi-starved women were served with free tea and buns, learned to sew articles, which were sold to supplement their family incomes, and their children put to school.[6]

During the years spent by Mrs Daniell in Aldershot, the exploitation of the women 'off the strength', and especially of their teenage girls, was a scandal. Many were enticed by their conditions and low wages into prostitution in London and other garrison towns.

A soldier of the East Kent Regiment described his experiences at Chatham and Aldershot, where

'dozens of these unfortunate women waited outside the barracks. I found that to be able to boast of a frequent connection with them was considered to be a most manly thing by a great many of the men . . . . The most common crime was 'drunk and absent': men would get half drunk at one of the many drinking dens in the place and then stay out all night with some woman.'[7]

CONTAGIOUS DISEASES ACTS

The Army Sanitary Commission of 1857 found that the Army's mortality rate was double that for the average male population in England. It also noted that one third of the hospital cases in the Army were caused by venereal disease.[8]

Historically, prostitution has been a fact associated with army camp and garrison from Roman Chester to Victorian Aldershot and whenever and wherever a camp or garrison was established, at home or abroad, brothels and drinking places have sprung up around them. The Military Dictionary of Major Charles James in 1816 defined Women of the Town as

'common prostitutes, such as infest the streets of every capital and large town, especially the seaports of Great Britain. On the continent these dangerous animals are always under the strictest regulations and police surveillance.'[9]

It was also a social evil in 19th century England, especially in London.

As we have already seen, the Army restricted matrimony, while recruiting large numbers of virile, healthy young men and concentrated them, often in isolated places, away from other amusements and activities and left them with long hours of idleness and boredom. The not unnatural result can be seen from a letter in *The Times*, dated 20th February 1857,[10] written by Alexander Henderson, the Presbyterian Chaplain at the Curragh Camp, outside Dublin:

'To call the earnest attention of the British public to the wretched daughters of guilt and misery, who, sunk in degradation, prey on the young innocent soldiers in the Curragh Camp.' All the roads leading to the Camp are infested day and night 'by these sad specimens of depraved and degraded humanity.'

THE ARMY'S ATTITUDE TO PROSTITUTION

The Army up to the second half of the 19th century had taken a practical, rather than a moral view of prostitution and the soldier's sexual needs and activities, both recognising and tolerating them. But increasingly its image came under mounting public criticism, as Church and social reformers attacked both the country's Victorian attitudes to prostitution, male 'double' standards and the Army's ambivalent practices and increasing cases of venereal disease, hospitalising more and more of its soldiers. There was a Victorian view, supported by the Army's military commanders and medical officers, that the lower classes, from which the soldiers came, could not be expected to control their 'animal passions', because of their baser natures and the conditions in which they lived. So the soldier had to be protected from the consequences of indulging in his natural instincts, especially from the resultant venereal diseases, which rendered ineffective so many of its men. Should the Army continue to ignore the problem or regulate brothels on the Continental fashion?

The Times and the medical *Lancet* carried out a vigorous campaign for lectures to troops on the dangers of venereal disease and for special hospitals for prostitutes. Miss Nightingale, on the other hand, preferred improvements in the soldier's environment and condemned efforts to inspect prostitutes as

'morally disgusting, unworkable in practice and unsuccessful in results'.[11] *The National Review*, 1863, sympathetic to the soldier's plight explained that the soldier led an abnormal life. His unvaried diet, the monotony of barracks life, and the dullness of garrison duty were enough 'to drive men to intemperance and debauchery.'[12]

THE WHITBREAD COMMITTEE

In 1862, a Committee[13] was appointed under Samuel Whitbread to enquire into the prevalence of venereal disease in the Army and Navy and report on the continental system of the regulation of prostitution. Some form of regulation existed in India, Malta, Hong Kong, Aden, Gibraltar, and South Africa. The Committee found

'a disgraceful and alarming amount of prostitution around UK army camps and in the ports, with 422 hospital admissions for every 1000 men, with an average of 22–23 days' duration or the equivalent of 2417 men per annum, equal to the loss of nearly 3 regiments. The beerhouses around the military camps were little more than brothels in disguise'.

It asked the Government to grapple at once

> 'with the mass of vice, filth and disease which surrounds the soldiers' barracks and the seaman's home, which not only crowds our hospitals with sick, weakens the roll of our effectives and swells the list of our invalids, but which surely, however slowly, saps the vigour of our soldiers and our seamen, sows the seeds of degradation and degeneracy and causes an amount of suffering difficult to overestimate.'[13]

The Committee recommended that voluntary hospital care for prostitutes be provided, rather than the compulsory examination and detention of diseased women favoured by the War Office and the commanding officers and in force in continental armies.

In 1864, the Government passed the first of its three Contagious Diseases Prevention Acts to meet this specific military problem.

Under the Act a Justice of the Peace could order a woman believed to be a 'common prostitute' in any one of 11 military garrisons to be taken to a nominated hospital for medical examination. If the woman preferred, she could undergo a voluntary examination. If found diseased, she could be detained in hospital for up to three months or until she was cured, and could be imprisoned for two months, if she refused examination. Her expenses were paid by the Services. The 11 towns were Portsmouth, Plymouth (including Devonport), Woolwich, Chatham, Sheerness, Aldershot, Colchester, Shorncliffe, The Curragh, Cork and Queenstown.

Another Act in 1866 included Windsor in the list, and provided for the registration of prostitutes and their compulsory regular medical examination, increased imprisonment to six months and provided moral and religious instruction, while the women were detained in hospital. Finally, in 1869, six more towns (Canterbury, Dover, Gravesend, Maidstone, Southampton and Winchester) were added to the list, making 18 in all, and detention was increased to nine months.

The Broad Arrow summed up the results of this legislation in 1875.

> 'There is copious evidence that throughout the length and breadth of the British Empire, wherever troops have been stationed, the Contagious Diseases Act has done its work well ... Whilst the real abuses of the Act are few and far between, their benefits are great and immeasurable'.[14]

The Army, too, was satisfied with the legislation. Its Medical Department Report[15] for 1866 gave its reasons:—

> 'The experience obtained in Belgium, in Malta and Gibraltar made it obvious that the prevalence of these diseases was a matter within our control, if the subjects of them were placed under a similarly strict surveillance. Unfortunately, the matter was approached from its moral or religious, instead of its physical aspect and many persons were reluctant to legislate, despite the facts and notoriety. Acts of Parliament, of course, can neither enforce morality nor prevent crime but they can do much to diminish mortality and sickness, by prohibiting the sources of contagion from spreading diseases and by confining them in hospitals until cured'.

The Report noted that the pay, position and comfort of soldiers had vastly improved in the last few years, offering a better livelihood and an improvement in the quality of recruits. But such improvements could not, by themselves eradicate immorality and disease.

'The life of a soldier is altogether peculiar: he enters the army as a very young man, and is not an old one when he leaves it. During this period the passions are not by any means at their weakest, and the soldier leads a life of enforced celibacy for the benefit of the State. It would be incompatible with the nature of his occupation for every soldier to be married, even were it practicable to find sufficient barrack accommodation. Every one will perceive that such a state of things is likely to entail a good deal of immorality'.[15]

LOBBIES FOR REPEAL OF THE ACTS

The lobby in Parliament for the repeal of the Acts became increasingly powerful, claiming that the laws gave legal sanction to vice, were medically ineffective and contrary to commonly held views on morality. The voice of Mrs Josephine Butler, secretary of the Ladies National Association was added in 1869. She denounced the Acts, both at home and in India, to the Royal Commission[16] appointed in deference to public agitation. She attacked not so much the soldier who used the prostitute but the authorities who assumed that sin was inevitable and that women must gratify male sexual appetites.

But the Commission argued the case for double standards —

'There is no comparison to be made between prostitutes and the men who consort with them. With the one sex, the offence is committed as a matter of gain; with the other, it is an irregular indulgence of a natural impulse'.[16]

Many abolitionists attacked the idea of a 'celibate' army and the military attitude to marriage.

'Military debauchery has become a recognised national institution — and a costly one, too! . . . When military regulations are framed expressly in the interests of the licentious and when a benevolent Government spends enormous sums of money in providing its faithful servants with medically certified harlots, how can it find either time or money to provide them with wives?'.[17]

Aldershot was cited as an example of immorality, not only encouraged but actually caused by the Army, which seemed to prefer its soldiers to live as immoral single men than as married family men. Florence Nightingale called the Aldershot harlots 'War Office prostitutes'[18] and sarcastically observed that 'prostitutes who survived five years in the regimental brothel should receive good service pensions'.

'Furthermore', recorded the surgeon at the Aldershot Lock Hospital, 'many of the most confirmed prostitutes who have been repeatedly in this and other hospitals are married (to soldiers without leave), deriving very little assistance from their husbands; and their previous bad character being known, little honest employment is open to them, and they are often compelled, in a manner, to prostitute themselves for necessary food and shelter'.[19]

'The C.D. Acts and all that they represent must go — the special police, their unhappy wards — everything. There was a time in English history when women plying their trade were taken up and sent to Bridewell. Let us have that old fashioned time back again and abolish the distinctive moral character of military towns as such'.[20]

Ultimately, the abolitionist movement won the day and successfully secured the Repeal of the Acts in 1886. But the problems were shelved not solved. Social attitudes would change and the introduction of Salvarsan during World War I would help to control venereal disease. Education and improved recreational facilities would improve the lot of the soldier but society in general still regarded him as a 'poor profligate wretch' and his profession a disgrace for any respectable son or husband to follow.

UNOFFICIAL WIVES

The Army's biggest social problem was still its 'unofficial' wives, who, in common with all lower class women, suffered from poor food, low wages and the fear of large families, desertion and widowhood, together with the burdens of heavy household duties. But to these were added the extra burdens of being a part of the Army, even if not recognised by it. There were the frequent moves, the constant upheaval of home and chattels, the absences on duty, the fears of separation by long overseas postings, the higher mortality rates and probabilities of disease and sickness and the fewer job expectations in isolated garrisons.

> 'The unrecognised families can have no rations. Some soldiers' wives may manage to obtain an honest living: but the majority — and it is no use blinking the fact — obtain a living which is not honest, and which cannot be considered reputable by any stretch of charity.'[21]

But the War Office rejected the notion[22] that the Army should provide for the soldier's wife, whether at home or abroad, in peace or in war. In 1855, Lord Panmure, Secretary of State for War, argued that the Government made every effort

> 'to discourage, while they cannot prevent, the marriage of soldiers, whose pay is calculated as only sufficient to maintain their health and military efficiency, and as regards whom the law provides that he shall not be liable to be taken out of Her Majesty's Service for not maintaining his wife and family, which his pay will not enable him to do, while on home service. Every soldier's wife must therefore depend upon her own industry for her maintenance, whether her husband is in this country, in a colony or at the seat of war.

Any attempt to offer a maintenance for a soldier's wife would only be an encouragment to marriage and deprive the woman of any incentive to work to support herself in her husband's absence. The regiment could provide help for the wife 'on the strength' — such wives had 'the privilege of washing for their respective companies'. Some cooked or sewed: the more respectable were selected to be maids or nursemaids in officers' homes. Those left behind, or not on the regimental strength, were not the Army's responsibility.[23]

RESPONSIBILITY FOR THE MAINTENANCE OF WIFE AND FAMILY

Traditionally, as we have seen, the soldier 'with too much wife' had been able to avoid his marital responsibilities by enlistment and overseas' service.[24] The deserted wife, unable to support herself and her children, had to seek Poor Law relief from her own or her husband's parish. The soldier, by an Army Order of March 1826, could not be compelled to hand over any portion of his pay to support his family. Furthermore, in 1837, a clause was added to the Mutiny Act (Section 40) under which

'no soldier shall be liable to be arrested or taken out of His Majesty's Service by reason of the Warrant of any Justice or other process, for not supporting or for leaving chargeable on any Parish, Township or Union, any Wife or any Child or Children.'[25]

During the 1860s the bastardy clause of the Mutiny Act was attacked in press and Parliament as immoral and unjust in law.[26] These 'legalised seducers' — the dissipated man, tired of his wife and careless of his family, the youth who has been successful in the crime of seduction and incurred the responsibilities of maternity

'may escape, with the greatest ease, by a visit to the nearest recruiting office, all the obligations of his position and cast the burden of their maintenance on the long suffering rate-payers.'

Furthermore, argued the Shield,[27] the Mutiny Act was a frequent and immediate cause of prostitution. A great many women became prostitutes through starvation, because, having married soldiers without the permission of the Colonel, they were left in the seaport and garrison towns with no means of support, either for themselves or their children.

CARDWELL'S AMENDMENT

In 1873, Cardwell amended the 40th clause of the Mutiny Act —

'A soldier shall be liable to contribute to the maintenance of his wife and of his children, and also to the maintenance of any bastard child of which he may be proved to be the father, to the same extent as if he were not a soldier, save that he could not be imprisoned or taken out of Her Majesty's service in consequence of such liability'.

Thus, noted *The Times*

'it would be no longer possible for a poor deluded servant girl, who had married a soldier without leave from his commanding officer, to learn from a magistrate that the law could not enforce her claim or that of her baby to maintenance. Military immorality would not have the premium of immunity, and the ratepayers would not be bound, as they were now, to provide the entire cost of the illegitimate offspring of soldiers — estimated at some 2000 annually.'[28]

But, despite the pressure of press, public and Members of Parliament and the Act's amendment, it was not until the Mutiny Act of 1883 that such payments were made obligatory and the number of army wives on poor relief began to decline. But the Army continued to argue their need for a soldier to have sufficient pay to be fit for duty and for the Act to be inapplicable once the soldier had been ordered overseas. As the Judge Advocate General told the House: The liability of a soldier was not the same as that of any other man. A soldier had a two-fold liability: he was under an obligation to support his wife and family and he had to serve his Queen and Country. The business of the House was to try as far as it could to reconcile the two obligations.[29]

REGIMENTAL ASSISTANCE AND VOLUNTARY HELP

Almost every regiment had established a long tradition of assistance to their soldiers' families through funds provided by the officers and ladies of the regiment, although practices varied between regiments. Help in the form of clothing, maternity aid and travel allowances were usually, but not exclusively, provided for wives on the regimental establishment, lest help to unrecognised women should be construed as supporting improvident marriages. Regimental schools were also provided at State expense for their children.

The Guards, as we have already noted, had such traditions. In 1861, they established a Home for the maintenance and education of the daughters of serving and former other ranks in the Brigade, hoping thereby to remove girls from the barracks and to give them training for domestic service. 60 years later[30] they were still maintaining the senior 28 girls free of charge and the junior 24 at a cost of £4 each per annum, the girls being drawn proportionally from the five regiments. The Brigade also provided work for wives on the strength by the making and repair of clothing and subscribed to several London hospitals to pay for the sick and pregnant wives.[31]

In 1900, Lady Arthur Paget, wife of the Colonel of the Scots Guards, raised £6000 by means of an entertainment at Drury Lane Theatre and Lord Cheylesmore £10,000. These sums were amalgamated into the Paget Trust Fund

> 'to relieve distress among past and present other ranks of the Brigade, their wives, widows and children.'[30]

Officers' wives have always played a key role in helping the soldiers' wives and children in their regiments (and sometimes necessitous officers' families as well) by visiting married quarters, arranging charitable fund raising occasions and by distributing clothing and necessaries. Such efforts were directed by the Commanding Officer's wife and the remaining wives, assuming their husband's rank and status, worked in nurseries, in bazaars, providing outings and on duty-visiting rosters. In the larger garrisons, such as Woolwich and Aldershot, the help was organised on a larger scale. For example, in 1862, the Woolwich Garrison built a Garrison Female Hospital with 25 beds for 250 'in' maternity cases and 1200 'out' patients (of which 600 were maternity) annually, with Lady Wood, the General Officer Commanding's wife, heading the scheme. *The Times* for 28th November 1864, announced the First Annual Report of the Association for Providing Lodgings for Soldiers' Wives and Families at Aldershot at a cheaper rate than the high rents ordinarily available.

> '99 wives and 72 children have been benefited by the lodgings, since these were opened, and all the tenants continue to express their satisfaction with the quarters provided for them. There is a rule most rigidly adhered to by the committee, which excludes from the benefits of the association the wives of soldiers married without leave; but if a sufficient number of women married with leave do not apply for the lodgings, then those married without leave, who can obtain recommendations from their commanding officer, are admitted.'[32]

Heading the list of subscribers were the Earl of Shaftesbury, Miss Nightingale and a number of Senior Army Officers.

NATIONAL APPEALS

During wars, as we have already noted in the Crimea, national appeals under Royal patronage, centrally launched and administered, provided funds for the Soldiers' wives and children and especially for widows and orphans. In 1858, during the Indian Mutiny, funds collected at the ports of embarkation proved inadequate to relieve

> 'the appalling cases of distress, resulting from the removal of 40,000 soldiers from our shores'.[33] So a 'Central Association for Improving the Condition of the Wives and Families of Soldiers and Sailors' was formed with the Queen as patron.'

As the Duke of Cambridge said

> 'The object is not to encourage sloth and idleness but to encourage the honest and hardworking: to obtain employment for such as are in a position to work for their living: to send the children of the Association to school.'

WIDOWS' PENSIONS

The Press had taken up the special case of the soldier's widow during the Crimean War. Pensions for officers' widows and orphans had originated in the 18th Century, as we have seen, but the soldier had to wait nearly 200 years before his widow received any financial recognition. *The United Services Gazette*,[34] for example, wrote in 1867.

> 'The soldier's widow gets no pension, his orphan children no allowance: he may have won the Victoria Cross or he may have given up his life for his Queen and Country in some pestilential foreign station: but if he has not saved his tardy prize money or his miserable pay, there is no resource for his widow or his orphans but the workhouse or the road'.

The first provision was made in the 1881 Regulations, by which the widows of NCOs and men killed in action or dying as a result of wounds became eligible to receive a gratuity of one year's pay.

THE PATRIOTIC FUND

The best known, largest and most enduring of the military charities (founded 1854) was the Patriotic Fund for helping

> 'those who by the loss of their husbands and partners in battle, or by death on active service in the Crimea, are unable to maintain or support themselves'.[35]

If a woman remarried, she ceased to be eligible, 'or if by profligate conduct she dishonours the memory of her husband or if, when capable of service, she remains idle or will not go to service'.[36] Places were found in the Royal Cambridge Asylum for Soldiers' Widows, founded in 1851 by the Duchess of Cambridge, for 50 widows, helped by regimental funds and officer subscriptions. During the 1860s and 1870s the Fund was helping an annual average of 3000 soldiers' widows and some 3900 children, whose fees were paid at local schools or orphanages.

In 1857, the Commissioners opened and endowed the Royal Victoria Patriotic Asylum at Wanstead for the education of 300 daughters of soldiers, sailors and marines, to train them in domestic service and some as pupil teachers. The Reverend Grant, who inspected the Patriotic Fund's schools, had one criticism of the high standard of education provided — 'servants read too many books and write too many letters.'[36]

In 1862, a similar school was opened at Wandsworth for 224 boys to provide industrial training in shoemaking, tailoring and carpentry, a quarter of whom entered the Navy or Army.

By 1873 the contributions to the Patriotic Fund had reached one and a half million pounds. 133 widows and 127 orphans of officers were in receipt of allowances, 15 boys being supported at Wellington College. 3024 soldiers' widows and 3928 orphans were being helped, while 659 boys had been apprenticed to trades and 1354 girls had entered domestic services. Some 2000 orphans of officers and men who had served but not died in the Crimean War had been placed on the books.[37]

As Colonel James Gildea, the founder of The Soldiers' and Sailors' Fund (later SSAFA) announced at one of its Branch meetings in 1893 — The soldier's

> 'heart will be stouter, his arm will be stronger,
> When he knows that his children are clothed, taught and fed;
> That his wife lives in dread of the workhouse no longer,
> To the shame of the country, for which he has bled'.[38]

THE CARDWELL REFORMS OF 1870

In 1870, Edward Cardwell, as Secretary of State for War, introduced an Act which carried out major reforms in the Victorian Army — the abolition of purchase of commissions, the amalgamation of the Horse Guards and War Office and short service engagements for the soldier. One of the effects of the latter, whereby the soldier served six years with the colours and six on the reserve, (later changed to seven and five respectively), was to restrict marriages in the Army further until the First World War.

As the 1871 Regulations[39] made clear —

> 'The married establishment at home and abroad (India excepted) shall consist of (A) All staff sergeants and 50% of sergeants and (B) 7% of corporals and privates (reduced to 4% in 1876).[40] But all rank and file included under (B) must have completed 7 years' service and be in possession of at least one good conduct badge to be eligible to have their names placed on the rank and file list of the married roll. No NCO or soldier will be placed on the married roll or be entitled to any of the advantages of these regulations, unless he has obtained the consent of the commanding officer to his marriage before it took place.'

The Army intended by these regulations that a young man between 18 and 23 should be excluded from any entitlement to be 'officially' married, a privilege reserved as a reward for the longer serving soldier.

As a company officer of 18 years' experience expressed it in *The Broad Arrow*:

> 'A soldier understands pretty plainly that when he enlists he sinks his 'civilian' rights so far as marriage is concerned, and soon discovers that by good conduct and service alone will he have any claim for leave to marry, and though this does not tend to make the Service popular, it makes it more efficient'.[41]

Another officer[42] set out the three courses open to a soldier in 1875: —

> 1. Marry without leave and thus bring misery to himself and his wife; an infantry private, who has no good conduct badge clears about 3/6d a week, out of which he has to provide his wife and children with food, clothes and lodgings. He is not allowed to sleep out of barracks or be 'out of mess' (i.e. loses the value of rations of $4\frac{1}{2}$d per day).
> 2. Marry with leave on the understanding that he must wait his turn to be placed on the marriage establishment. He is allowed to sleep out and claim the ration allowance but otherwise the wife is ignored by the regiment and the State. She is, however, infinitely better off than those married without leave.
> 3. Wait patiently until there is a vacancy on the married establishment before taking unto himself a wife, when he will be comparatively well off — provided with one small room (or quarters appointed for 4 single soldiers or lodging allowance instead): cease to belong to the mess and may take his rations either in money ($4\frac{1}{2}$d) or in kind ($\frac{3}{4}$ lb meat and 1 lb bread). He receives free fuel and light, furniture and bedding (but excluding sheets).

MEDICAL CARE FOR WIVES AND CHILDREN

Medical care for the soldier's family dates from the second half of the 19th Century and owes much to Florence Nightingale's work for the soldier and his family, to which she devoted her life on her return from the Crimea. With her old friend Sidney Herbert and the new Secretary of State for War, Lord Panmure, she planned and worked for the Royal Commission on the Health of the Army and on the Royal Sanitary Commission on India. She advised the War Office for many years on nursing and hospital services.[43]

Before 1860, all sickness amongst the wives and families of other ranks, including confinements, had been treated in quarters (officers, their wives and children were invariably treated privately). In 1824, for instance, the Regulations for Army Hospitals authorised the Regimental Medical Officer to supply authorised wives and children with medicines from the regimental chest and to visit and prescribe for them. Apart from this 'indulgence', they were expected to provide for themselves or rely on the charity of individual officers or help from the regimental fund. For the unauthorised wives and the destitute there were the medical services provided under the Poor Law either in workhouses or through home attendance.

By 1860 the Army had become concerned about the danger to soldiers of having women and children with infectious diseases in crowded barrack rooms and with 'the universal deficiency of accommodation for the sick wives and children of married NCOs and Soldiers'. The Report of the Barracks and Hospital Improvement Commission in 1861 set out the situation as it then existed.

Some accommodation for the authorised 6% of married soldiers had been specially provided at several stations but no such married provision existed in the great majority of barracks.

> 'Soldiers' wives and children have, therefore, to be lodged wherever sufficiently cheap lodgings can be obtained, quite irrespective of the healthiness of the house or neighbourhood, and when a family so circumstanced is overtaken by sickness, or in cases of childbirth, the regimental medical officer has to attend the cases, irrespective of distance and convenience. He can supply medicines, but not diets or medical comforts, unless the sick woman or child be in hospital. At present there is no hospital accommodation for these cases, and as the soldiers' resources are too limited to meet such expenses, his family is exposed to privation at the very time when it can least be endured'.[44]

The Report showed that in 10 major stations[45] covering 5,095 wives and 6,750 children, 396 women and children were constantly on the sick list and requiring medical attendance, medicines and diets, besides some 1,100 confinements per annum. No hospital accommodation existed for such cases, except at Aldershot. At Fermoy, for example, sick women and children were seen by the medical officer at the dispensary, if they were able to present themselves; if not, they had to be attended in a crowded barrack-room, without the least privacy, husband, wife, children, sick or well, sleeping together in one miserable bed, or in some wretched, ill-ventilated, overcrowded lodging-room, far away from the barracks, hospital or medical aid. No provision existed for confinements.[46]

GARRISON HOSPITALS

But now these wretched conditions were to change and improvements made, at least for those on the Married Roll. In 1860, as we have noted, the first hospital for wives and children of NCOs and men was provided at

Aldershot and later at other stations such as Woolwich and at Fort Pitt (Chatham) a hospital for female infectious cases.[47] By 1866, the Herbert Hospital was completed in Woolwich with Mrs Shaw Stewart (who had been in the Crimea with Florence Nightingale) and eight lady nurses on day duty and quartered in the Female Infirmary. In July 1879, the Duke of Cambridge opened the hospital named after himself in Aldershot, built, like the Herbert, to Miss Nightingale's pavilion specifications (instead of the old 'corridor' type), with airy wards and plenty of sunlight.[48]

We have already noted (Chapter 6 p 68) that the Army Regulations of 1864 authorised free medical attendance and medicine for entitled women and children, provided they lived within one mile of the military hospital or dispensary. The same Regulations permitted confinements to be admitted to Army hospitals, 'if no midwife or private doctor could be called in to the home' and, as recommended by the 1861 Hospital Improvement Commission, in the larger garrisons, family hospitals or family barrack wards were authorised to provide treatment and diets for authorised wives and children at public expenses.

With the health and safety of the troops in mind, the 1871 Regulations for Married Soldiers stated that

> 'cases of scarlet fever and smallpox, when occurring in barracks or huts, will always be admitted into these hospitals, with the view of preventing, or limiting the spread of such cases. All other infectious maladies will, as a general rule, be treated in quarters (exceptions can be authorised by the Principal Medical Officer) but infectious cases will never be treated in hospital under the same roof with lying-in women'.[49]

In exceptional circumstances or to protect the troops and their families against the spread of contagious diseases, the wives and children of soldiers not on the regimental Married Rolls could be admitted to hospitals upon the daily payment of one shilling for a wife and sixpence for each child. Where hospitals had not been provided, barrack rooms could be set aside as wards, with equipment, fuel and light, for the reception of sick women and children on the married roll, whom it was deemed expedient to remove from their quarters, provided the expense for diet and nursing was not charged to public funds.[49]

In 1873 the regimental hospital system, which had existed for over 200 years and in which army wives had served as 'nurses' before nursing became recognised as a profession, was abolished and replaced by station and garrison hospitals with an Army Hospital Corps established to man them, which in 1898 became the Royal Army Medical Corps. In 1878, the Army accepted full responsibility for family medical care, as the Regulations specified:

> 'Hospitals for wives and children are provided and equipped at certain stations by the special authority of the Secretary of State. A Medical Officer is specially appointed to their charge and provided with a staff of female attendants. Up-patients in the maternity wards will be required to assist in cleansing the wards and in attending their fellow-patients'.[50]

In 1880 a maternity and child-care service was undertaken and women were admitted for the first time to hospital before confinement, a practice still not common in civilian hospitals, as late as 1900. But if the wives were within three months of confinement neither they nor their husbands were allowed to travel on Her Majesty's ships (1881).

ARMY NURSING SERVICE

In 1881 *The Times* and *The Daily Telegraph* carried advertisements for a limited number of Nursing Sisters to be trained in military hospitals. 'Preference will be given to widows and daughters of officers of HM Services'.[51] Thus was born the Army Nursing Service, which in March 1902 was expanded by Royal Warrant into the Queen Alexandra's Imperial Nursing Service (QAIMNS), with Queen Alexandra as its first president.

The actual building of the military hospitals was slow and by 1883 only 10 had been provided, but

> 'the effects of better medical care and better accommodation were plainly felt and can be
> seen in the significant drop in illness and mortality rates amongst soldiers' families',

comments an authority on Queen Victoria's army.[52]

In 1898 (the same year that Agnes Keyser, mistress of the Prince of Wales, established with his help the well-known King Edward's Hospital for Officers and later of their dependants), another hospital was opened in Aldershot for the sole purpose of caring for the wives and children of the Army. Princess Louise Margaret, Duchess of Connaught, and daughter-in-law of Queen Victoria, opened the hospital, which bears her name. The Hospital was provided with the usual surgical and medical wards and with a special ward for maternity cases and another for children. In 1926 another wing was opened by Queen Mary for the families of officers, whose medical welfare during the 19th century had been the sole responsibility of the officers themselves. Five years earlier, in 1921, a Military Families' Nursing Service had been founded, which was later amalgamated with the QAIMNS, and proved a great value to the army families, providing them with a complete hospital cover, and, in turn, the nurses with a welcome alternative to an exclusive nursing service for men. The final link was provided by the post-World War II National Health Service, whereby all treatment for all ranks was free and available to all army wives, irrespective of rank.

Chapter 11

The Memsahibs

During the reign of Queen Victoria, thousands of British women went out to India to live, work and to die, as wives, mothers and sisters and later as teachers, doctors or missionaries. Many were army wives, following their husbands to a land, which became for them a second home. Historians, like Correlli Barnett, have blamed these memsahibs for exacerbating racial prejudices and dividing Indian society by their failure to understand Indians, speak any of their languages and by maintaining their inappropriate customs, arguing that

> 'in the early 19th century, Indian mistresses brought officers and men closer to Indian life: later stern memsahibs, stiffly corseted with Victorian morality and etiquette, and, resentful of the voluptuous competition of sari-clad brown bodies, stopped all this, with lasting damage to British relations with Indians'.[1]

Writers, such as Rudyard Kipling who was born in Bombay in 1865, have written realistically of army life in India, portraying the typical memsahib as a snobbish and selfish butterfly, flirting, and flitting from bridge, tennis and garden parties to dinners and dances in the delightful hill stations, while her husband slaved at his job in the heat of the plains.

> 'From pedestals of sober respectability, Englishwomen have passed judgement on us', wrote Maud Diver. 'They have denounced us as idle, frivolous and luxury loving'.[2]

Nevertheless, many of these women, loyally and stoically accepted their share of the white man's burden and lightened it with their quiet humour, their grace and often with their youth.[3]

THE FISHING FLEET

With the opening of the Suez Canal, officers were able to spend their year's leave in England and return with a wife or fiancée, instead of waiting for the arrival of the 'fishing fleet', with its annual shipload of marriageable young girls, hoping to find husbands among the European civil servants and army officers. Those travelling alone were advised to stay in their cabins, Bible in hand, to avoid the temptations of the East and the shipboard romances — not for nothing was the British India Shipping Line known as the 'bibi' line, the

Hindustani word for 'woman' or 'mistress' coinciding with the Company's 'B.B.' monogram. For a girl, of Victorian England, without dowry, rich relations or beauty to make a suitable match, India offered, as soon as she landed, proposals of marriage

> 'from old and young, military and civil, nobles and commoners. She was counselled not to dance with anyone below a very senior civilian or a military officer with a staff appointment'.[3]

Thomas Hood satirised these ambitious husband-hunters with

'My cousin from Hyderapot' —   *'With boots and shoes, Rivarta's best,*
'She's married to a Son of Mars,   *And dresses by Ducé,*
With very handsome pay,   *And a special licence in my chest* —
And swears I ought to thank my stars   *I'm going to Bombay'.*
I'm going to Bombay'.

The arrival of a young lady in the station was likely to cause the utmost excitement amongst officers and wives alike.

> 'No sooner is it known that Miss So and So is coming to the station than everyone begins to speculate whom she will accept', wrote Doctor Gilbert Hadow.[4] 'For it is taken as a matter of course that all the bachelors will propose without loss of time (irrespective of suitability and antecedents). There is something very absurd in the race for a wife out here'.

At least, while the race lasted, it helped to relieve the boring sameness of the days, and to provide a diversion for officers from pig-sticking and big game hunting in the foothills of the Himalayas or drinking and womanising in the hill stations of Southern India.[5]

The interest of the ladies was equally intense but for different reasons, as Lady Angela Falkland, wife of the Governor and a daughter of William IV and Mrs Jordan noted in 1848:–

> 'The arrival of a cargo of young damsels from England is one of the most exciting events that mark the advent of the cold season (in mid October) with its 4 months of concentrated gaity of dances, balls and picnics. It can be well imagined that their age, height, features, dress and manners become topics of conversation, and as they bring the lastest fashions from Europe, they are objects of interest to their own sex'.[6]

She added that the ladies of Bombay were more rank conscious than those at home!

The young girls would be shown off to their best advantage at the regimental Balls — as Emily Eden relates of two girls just arrived from England to join a married sister, wife of an officer in the Lancers.

> 'They are such pretty girls and have brought out for their married sister, who is also very pretty, gowns and headdresses like their own. These three are the only young ladies at the station, so I suppose they will have their choice of the three regiments. At regimental balls there might be six dancing ladies for every 25 men, so that the couples had to dance first on one side, then on the other in the quadrilles, until the fair few were exhausted. It was an artificial situation for both sexes that resulted in a number of hasty and ill-considered marriages'.[7]

STATISTICS

The massive Report of the Commission on the Sanitary State of the Army in India 1863 gave the military population statistics and conditions after the Mutiny. The 1861 Census had revealed that the English population in India was 125,945, consisting of 84,083 European officers and men of the Army, 22,556 civilians and 19,306 British-born women and girls, of whom 9773 were 20 years of age and above, including 7570 wives, 1140 widows and 1001 unmarried women.

> '786 wives under the age of 20 make the number of wives of English origin, under the age of 45, to be 7626, scattered all over British India'.[8]

— a very small number indeed, compared with the men!

MORTALITY RATES

Despite their being exposed to many of the same insanitary influences as the soldier and officer, the mortality rate of the English officers' wives and widows between the ages of 20 and 40 did not exceed 14 in 1000 — about the same as it was in London during the last century .... Young children were easily affected by the climate but their mortality rate was lower than that of children generally at home.

> 'But as age advances, large numbers are sent home at great expense; if they remain, they suffer from impaired health'.[9]
> 'The wife and children of the NCO and soldier do not fare so well, as the provision for their accommodation is inadequate.[9] The women are exposed to great hardship; they die at the rate of 35 per 1000, including women of English birth and Eurasians. In the lower orphan school of Calcutta, the mortality was double or treble the English rates; but more favourable results are obtained at the Lawrence military asylum in the hills'.[9]
> This school was founded by General Lawrence at Sanawar in 1847 — 'to give to all orphan and other children, the offspring of European fathers and European mothers, both of Her Majesty's and the Honourable East India Company's army, whether Catholics or Protestants, an asylum from the debilitating effects of a tropical climate and the demoralising influence of barrack life, wherein they may obtain the benefits of a bracing climate, a healthy moral atmosphere and a plain, useful and above all religious education, adapted to fit them for employment suited to their position in life'.[10]

EURASIANS

At the Census (1861) 11,636 women above the age of 15, of English origin, including 8356 wives, were enumerated, and 98,888 men.

> 'Hence a certain number of soldiers marry Indian wives. The sons and daughters of the two races, known as Eurasians or East Indians, or half-castes, amount to considerable numbers.'

They exceeded the English in Calcutta at the Census of 1837 by 3138 English to 5981 Eurasians.[9]

MARRIED QUARTERS

Great improvements had been made in India of late years in providing quarters for married NCOs and soldiers, stated the Report,[9] usually consisting of separate huts or bungalows, of two or three rooms, built in the patchery, a court belonging to the barrack (the origin of 'the married patch'?). In about 20% of the stations no separate quarters had yet been provided; and families were lodged in barrack rooms divided by mats.

> 'There are 2 or 3 instances in which married people occupy the same rooms as single men, separated from them by mats.'

At two-thirds of the stations the married accommodation was said to be sufficient, some having from 80 to 120 separate married quarters.

> 'The general sanitary condition of the married quarters is the same as that of the station, but the men living in patcheries with their families are much more healthy than men living in barracks.' 'Occasionally, from want of care, considerable overcrowding took place in these quarters and in one instance at least, it led to frightful results. In Dum Dum (Calcutta) where a large number of women and children were lodged together in barrack rooms, without proper space or ventilation or other sanitary arrangements, there were 64 deaths in 5 months amongst 554 women and 166 deaths of children out of 770, compared with an annual mortality rate of 44 women and 84 children per 1000 in Bengal. The diseases of which so many perished were dysentery, fever and cholera, caused by intemperance, immorality, reckless exposure, unwholesome food, want of cleanliness, personal and general, and a polluted atmosphere. The effluvia from the privies were perceptible in the barrack rooms'.[9]
> 'Every station has one or more female hospitals for the sick of soldiers' families, generally under the same management as the regimental hospitals at the station, and they are in most cases supplied with matrons, native nurses and midwives. The attendance and nursing is generally considered sufficient but the buildings are not so in all cases'.[11]

MARRIED STATE OF THE ARMY IN INDIA 1861–71

The Report provides some invaluable statistics of the married state of the Army in India, 1861–1871.

Table I (at Appendix A) shows the percentage of British wives, widows and single women, of military and of the civilian officials in each age group. In general, the married rate for officers is higher than for soldiers in the Royal Army, but both are less than those for the East India Company's troops and still less than that of the civilian population, while the respective proportions of the unmarried are large compared with the unmarried population of England.

For example, for every 100 officers and soldiers in the Royal Army between ages 30–34 29% and 15% were married in the Army respectively, 36% in the East Indian Army and 51% in the civilian population.

The 1871 Census gives the Number and Ages of the Wives and Children of the Royal Troops in India on 3 April 1871. The Royal Troops numbered 4091 officers and 57,807 men, the European Forces of Her Majesty's Indian Army having been amalgamated in 1861–2.

TABLE 2   *British Army Wives and Children in India 1871 — Number and Ages*

	Officers' Wives & Children				Soldiers' Wives & Children			
Ages	Total	Wives	Boys	Girls	Total	Wives	Boys	Girls
Total	2,469	910	797	762	17,762	6,565	5,592	5,605
Under 5	673	—	359	314	6,275	—	3,163	3,112
5–9	503	—	248	255	3,595	—	1,810	1,785
10–14	279	—	136	143	1,271	3	594	674
15–19	125	21	54*	50*	448	389	25*	34*
20–24	225	225	—	—	1,545	1,545	—	—
25–29	282	282	—	—	2,202	2,202	—	—
30–34	181	181	—	—	1,477	1,477	—	—
35–39	116	116	—	—	682	682	—	—
40–44	48	48	—	—	203	203	—	—
45–49	27	27	—	—	53	53	—	—
50–54	5	5	—	—	9	9	—	—
55+	5	5	—	—	2	2	—	—

* Including some above 20 years of age.
Source: 1871 Census Appendix A Table 136 and p 309.

The Report on the Sanitary State of the Army in India (1863) compared the annual mortality rates for married officers (2·7%) and unmarried 3·8%) in Bengal (similar statistics for soldiers have never been provided). 'These figures are remarkable, since the unmarried officers are younger than the married'. The married ensigns died at the rate of 1·6% annually compared with the 3·6% of the unmarried ensigns.[11]

EPITAPHS

Statistics do not convey the personal tragedies, which are often found in epitaphs on tombs, such as:–

> *A Husband's Sadness —*
> 16 years a maiden,
> one 12 month a wife,
> one half hour a mother,
> and then I lost my life.

or *The Grief of Major Eagle's Wife —*

> 'Silent grave, to thee I trust
> This precious pile of worthy dust,
> Keep it safe in the sacred tomb,
> Until a wife shall ask for room.'[12]

or the grief of an army widow, whose entire family was wiped out in the space of a few days at Dharmsala —

'Lieutenant Francis Tigue Reilly died 13th July 1875, aged 45. Died between 6–10th July 1875 Edmund Patrick aged 5, William aged 3 and Mary Agnes Alice aged 1 year'.[12]

Or for Elizabeth Smith, buried at Jaunpore 22nd February 1829, aged 14 years 9 months and 21 days — already the widow of Fife-Major John Smith, 16th Native Infantry Regiment —

— or the accidental humour caused by the stonemason on the grave of a soldier, who died in the United Provinces, 'Craving a large widow and family to mourn his lot'.[12]

LIFE IN THE CANTONMENTS

All the Army wives lived in the cantonments, the most fortunate in their white-washed bungalows, with safety-wire covered windows and little garden patches, where a few English flowers struggled to survive. Because of the constant moves, furniture was passed on to the next family, household goods were sparse, and auctioned when the family left, to be replaced at the next station. Bedrooms were spartan with wooden framed beds, laced with webbing, cotton mattress and sheets and a bathroom, containing a zinc tub, earthenware water jars and a 'retiring room' or lavatory. The best part of each bungalow was the verandah, on to which all the main rooms opened: there at sunset, the best time of the day, the family gathered to drink, smoke, chat and play.

The day followed a routine of

'up at 5 am; ride to 7 am; breakfast on the verandah, cold bath, dress and receive visitors 10-12 mid-day; tiffin, followed by the siesta hour, when silence fell on the whole cantonment; bath and dress again for evening walk or ride; everyone gathered at dusk to gossip until dark and the evening meal; songs, drinks, a few yarns and so to bed'.

Thus one army woman described her day. Variety came in the form of letters from home, visits of itinerant traders selling Persian carpets and knick-knacks from Calcutta or to mend the kitchen utensils or furniture. Talk was always of money, promotion, leave and home. This monotony was the life the wives accepted, devoting themselves to their husband and children, enduring the heat and boredom and many finding early graves in the process.

With so much time on their hands, British women in India became notorious for gossip, elevating the passing on of juicy pieces of scandal from a pastime to an art.

'In other parts of the world, they talk about things; here, they talk about people . . . . . all the interminable gossip about marriages and no-marriages, and will-be-marriages and ought-to-be-marriages, and gentlemen's attention and ladies' flirtings, dress, reunions and the last dinner party'.[13] wrote Peregrine Pultuney in 1844.

Mrs Colonel Elwood said the same thing in 1830 when she described the 'scandal point' at Breach Candy near Bombay, where the English community met every day to discuss

> *'Who danced with whom and who is like to wed,*
> *And who is hanged, and who is brought to bed'.*[14]

As a result of the Mutiny, the Lines of the European or Queen's regiments were separate from those of the native regiments, with barracks for the soldiers and huts for the sepoys. Every station of reasonable size had its officers' messes, theatre, assembly rooms, hospital, court-room, Anglican church and Roman Catholic chapel and well-stocked burial ground, a botanical garden and main street, usually called The Mall, with a few shops, customarily owned by Eurasians or Jews. The Mall would be watered every afternoon, so that the dust would not ruin the ladies' bonnets, when they took their evening walks and drives. The soldiers had their own bazaars, crowded with shopkeepers, prostitutes and thieves, in which they spent most of their time, when not asleep on their beds, drinking and whoring. Most sepoys were married and were permitted to live on the station with their families, widowed mothers and other dependent relatives. The European wives took their social position from their husbands and adopted the hierarchy of civil servant, military, businessmen, missionaries, police and the shopkeepers and clerks, when they met at supper parties, picnics, croquet and tennis meetings.[15] This was especially important at the table for

> 'India is the land of dinners, as England is the land of five o'clock teas,' wrote Maud Diver.

Whether she be the Colonel's lady 'dining the station' or a subaltern's wife with a party of six or eight, every good hostess was expected to know who went first into dinner and where to place everyone at table.

Frank Richards observed the same social hierarchy on regimental occasions:

> 'The same wide gulf that was fixed between officers and men also separate their women-folk. I often did a grin at some Battalion outdoor function, such as Regimental Sports, to watch the ladies, according to their different social classes, collect in groups apart from one another; one group of officers' wives with the Colonel's wife in command, another of senior NCO's wives with the Regimental Sergeant Major's wife in command, and then the wives of the sergeants, corporals and privates, each group parading separately. It was class distinction with a vengeance'.[16]

RECREATIONAL NEEDS OF THE SOLDIER

The Commissioners also considered the recreational needs of the soldier in India:—

> 'All stations were provided with the usual ball games, skittle-alleys, libraries and sometimes a theatre but his duties were over by sunrise and, during the hot season, he was confined to his barrack until late in the afternoon. He had a heavy lunch, drank spirits and a quart of porter and 'lies on his bed and perhaps sleeps most of the day.'

The soldiers, for all practical purposes, were entirely idle and their amusements, such as they were, were always connected with drink. They were led into vice and intemperance. Because there were few European women for the British troops to meet socially, they sought native women for their pleasure with the concomitant risk of venereal disease.

> 'Venereal disease prevails to a very great extent in the Army, and at almost every station. The proportion of venereal cases constantly in hospital is usually from 20 to 25% of the total sick. At some of the larger stations it very much exceeds this amount, reaching 50% at Bangalore. Men become unfit for service and in others their constitution is undermined.
> There is no subject so difficult to deal with as this: and almost every plan for lessening the evil has been tried and found to fail. They all resolve themselves into two classes, namely, repressive measures of police, or marriage and moral restraint'.[17]

Many of the witnesses recommended the establishment of lock hospitals, which had been introduced into India many years before the Report but their use had been discontinued after a while. Doctor W. Maclean stated in his evidence:

> 'In the 1830s every station had its lock hospital for the treatment of prostitutes, but prejudices against them had led to their abolition. The consequence is that the prostitutes are now under no control'. He knew of one Queen's regiment 'where one woman in the course of two nights had utterly destroyed 10 men — they were no longer fit for duty'.

The Commission noted that among native regiments, where marriage was not restricted,

> 'this disease is much less frequent than in European regiments in which marriage is restricted'.

Many experienced officers considered the proportion should be increased.

> 'Married men are generally the most healthy: they are the best soldiers and many of them are an example in a regiment; but, when the regiment goes on foreign service, only a certain proportion of women can be taken with it and, thus, as far as India is concerned, any large increase in the proportion of marriages would lead to wives and children being left behind, and exposed to much temptation and possibly to distress, while the domestic tie cannot fail to be weakened by long protracted absence'.[17]

REMEDIAL MEASURES

There was, however, urgent need for some remedial measures. The rate of infection amongst the troops in all three Presidencies was so high in 1860 (345 cases per 1000 of the strength in Bengal, 249 in Madras and 314 in Bombay) that the Commission 'after considering the various plans, which have been adopted in different countries', decided that none were so likely to diminish 'this great scourge of the soldier in India', as the reorganisation and improvement of the measures formerly adopted in the three Presidencies. Thus the Report added its weight to the medical authorities and social reformers, who wanted legislation on similar but not identical lines to those adopted in the United Kingdom.

In addition to the control of prostitution and disease, the Army and the authorities in India had to face the additional factors of climate, different social customs and moral standards among the indigenous population and the prestige and standing of a ruling race. The Army's attitude had been to attempt to isolate the soldiers by providing cantonments away from the towns and villages, and by providing regimental brothels or 'Lal Bazars', where British white troops were expected to satisfy their sexual needs away from the dangerous diseases and oriental vices of the native bazaars. But the increasing number of young, virile, unmarried soldiers coming to India, recklessly disregarded the dangers and heedlessly pursued the local women. The officers, on the other hand, were increasingly expected to shun their Indian mistresses (bibis), socially accepted in the first half of the century, and content themselves with the white women, who were arriving in increasing numbers, after the opening of the Suez Canal in 1869.

THE SOCIAL GAP

The social gap between the two races widened during the second half of the century. Part of the blame was placed on the 'memsahibs', who as wives hastened the disappearance of the Indian mistress: as hostesses, they fostered the development of exclusive groups and, as women, they were thought by British officers and upper class Englishmen to be in need of protection from lascivious Indians, who practised child marriages[18] and polygamy and at receptions usually left their wives at home, it was said, in order to ogle the white women guests. On the other hand, Indians were often shocked by European social habits of eating, drinking, and personal hygiene and by the indecorous behaviour and dress of their wives — baring the upper body and dancing in public.

Emily Eden, for example, commented:

'the Sikhs who were invited to a Government House Ball at Calcutta knew the English custom of dancing sufficiently to understand that the ladies were ladies and not nautch-girls'.[19]

Between the two ethnic groups were the half-castes or Eurasians (later known also as Anglo-Indians), who threatened to bridge the gap. Bishop Heber wrote of them

'I never met with any public man connected with India, who did not lament the increase of the half-caste population, as a great source of present mischief and future danger to the tranquillity of the colony'.[20]

They were excluded from the Army's commissioned ranks, because they were not gentlemen and were, as such, not accepted by the British officers and other ranks and were despised by the Indian soldiers. They could not be medical officers, because it was not acceptable for an English lady to be physically examined by a coloured doctor. Similarly, Indian princes, as members of a ruling class but not of a ruling race, threatened the social hierarchy, if they married a white woman and especially when, towards the end of the century, when they were acquiring Western education and tastes, they moved in 'high society in Europe'.

> 'But of all the areas of sexual behaviour, which embarrassed the authorities, relations between British soldiers and Indian women proved the most troublesome',

concluded Ballhatchet in his study of 'Race, Sex and Class under the British Raj'.[21] The Authorities in India would continue their attempts to regulate prostitutes and brothels, by registration, inspection and detention of girls in hospitals on the same lines as under the Contagious Diseases Acts in England between 1864 and 1886. But, as in England, these attempts would be criticised as immoral, inhumane and ineffective, and as sacrificing Indian women to British lusts. All three Presidencies, alarmed at the rising numbers of cases of venereal disease re-established Lock Hospitals (where prostitutes were detained until cured) and organised 'Lal Bazars' in regiments, where carefully selected and supervised native girls were installed for the exclusive use of British soldiers. In 1864 the recommendations of the Royal Commission[22] for improved occupational and recreational facilities for the troops were approved and one for the return of the lock hospital system was incorporated into the Cantonment Act of 1864, whereby local governments could make rules 'for inspecting and controlling houses of ill-fame and for preventing the spread of venereal disease'.[22]

The arguments for an increase in the married establishment were rejected on the grounds of cost. Cynics could retort that it was cheaper to provide prostitutes than wives! In 1868 the Indian Contagious Diseases Acts extended the compulsory registration of brothels and prostitutes, their periodical medical inspection and compulsory treatment to the principal ports and to the major cities like Calcutta and Bombay.

REPEAL OF THE CONTAGIOUS DISEASES ACTS IN INDIA

As in the United Kingdom, Gladstone, the military authorities and the Government of India came under great pressure to repeal the Acts. The Royal Commission appointed in 1871 to consider the British Acts, also heard evidence concerning the Acts in India. The Baptist Missionary Society gave evidence and accused the Army in India of detailing an establishment of prostitutes for each newly arrived regiment, of housing them in the bazaar, where they were attended by the regimental Surgeon and of placing them under a head woman 'who procures a greater or less number of women according to the character of the corps'.[23] The Commander in Chief, after consulting the 65th, 85th and 92nd Regiments of Foot, recently arrived in India, denied the allegations and 'of patronising prostitution'—

> 'The military authorities anxiously strive to mitigate the evils of prostitution, yet no act of theirs can justly be interpreted as encouraging vices. It is not the practice of prostitution that is legalised, but the attempts to avert its consequent and accompanying disease'.[24]

The successful campaign to repeal the Acts in the United Kingdom in 1886 led to increased efforts on the part of reformers to obtain the repeal of the Acts in India, especially after one of them, Alfred Dyer, went to India to investigate for himself the Army's practices and published his findings in The Sentinel in 1888. He related how registered prostitutes were being accommodated in tents in prominent positions in regimental lines, that regimental funds were being used to make their accommodation more attractive and comfortable for their 'European only' clients and that officers were requesting 'younger and better looking' replacements.[25]

These revelations were confirmed by a Memorandum issued from General Roberts's Army Headquarters in Simla:

> 'To arrange for the effective inspection of prostitutes attached to regimental bazars (brothels), whether in cantonments or on the line of march'.
> 'To have a sufficient number of women in the regimental bazars (in proportion to the number of men who visit them); to take care that they are sufficiently attractive, to provide them with proper houses, and to insist upon means of ablution being always available'.
> 'Any reasonable expenditure on these suggested measures will be sanctioned from cantonment funds.'[26]

When this became known in London, Mr McLaren (Crewe) asked the Under Secretary of State for India whether

> 'in furtherance of the instructions in this Memorandum the officer commanding the 2nd Cheshire Regiment at Solon caused a requisition to be sent to the Cantonment Magistrate at Umballa on 6th August 1886 stating that the strength of the regiment was 400 men and that 6 additional women were now required for it. Some of the women now with HQ of the 2nd Battalion Cheshire Regiment are not very attractive and application has been made for others, but up to date none have arrived; therefore it is presumed a great difficulty exists in procuring the class of young women asked for'.[27]

As a result of the public uproar which followed, the Contagious Diseases Acts in India were repealed in 1888.

But by 1896 the rate of venereal disease had risen to 522 per 1000 (i.e. 'over half the British Army in India had venereal disease') and once again the Indian military authorities were forced to amend their Cantonment rules for the compulsory regulation of prostitution, 'so successfully practised in the French and German armies in Europe'. Lord Roberts made a powerful appeal in the House of Lords for support for these measures.

> 'I am aware that opponents say the Acts are contrary to morality and that, in all justice, the sinner should be allowed to reap the punishment of his sin but I cannot understand

why one should not take measures to prevent the spread of an evil, which involves disease
and misery on innocent women and children'.[28]

The Archbishop of Canterbury suggested a larger number of men should be
allowed to marry, but Lord Clarina, who had commanded regiments in India
and elsewhere, disagreed.

'One cannot provide a regiment, 1000 strong, with 1000 wives and supply transport for a
couple of thousand children. If 200 were allowed to marry what would become of the
remaining 800?'[28]

Perhaps the last word should be given to the ladies. On 25th May 1897 *The
Times* published a memorandum in favour of Regulation by a large number of
titled ladies, doctors, matrons and Miss Nightingale (who had formerly
opposed such measures).

'We desire to express our anxious hope that effective measures will be taken to check the
spread of contagious diseases among our soldiers, especially in India. We appreciate and
respect the opinions of those who, notwithstanding the appalling statistics recently
issued, are opposed to us on this subject. We believe that they hold, in all sincerity, that
the evil of rendering vice safer and the risk of degrading women outweigh all other
considerations, but, speaking as women, we feel bound to protest against these views. We
feel that it is the duty of the State, which of necessity collects together large numbers of
unmarried men in military service, to protect them from the consequences of evils, which
are, in fact, unavoidable in such a community and under such circumstances. And with
the deepest earnestness we call on the Government to do all that can be done to save
innocent women and children in the present and future generations from the terrible
results of vices for which they are not responsible'.

Frank Richards, a private soldier of the Royal Welsh Regiment, who served
for many years in India and wrote a 'classic' on his experiences there at the
turn of the century, relates:–

'At Meerut, Kilana and Agra were brothels reserved for the use of white troops. The one
at Agra was about three-quarters of a mile from the Barracks. In this brothel, or Rag as it
was called by the troops, were between thirty and forty native girls, whose ages ranged
from twelve to thirty. This number was considered sufficient for the fifteen hundred
white troops that garrisoned Agra. Each girl lived in a separate shack of her own, which
was made of plaster and mud with a hard-baked mud floor. The only furniture was a
native rope-bed with no bed-clothes, a large earthenware vessel for holding water, and a
small wash-hand bowl.
Natives who passed through this street were not allowed to stop and talk to the girls; if
any one of them did, the Regimental Police would give him such a thrashing with their
sticks that he would remember it for a long time. The Rag was opened from twelve noon
to eleven at night, and for the whole of that time the girls who were not engaged would
stand outside their shacks soliciting at the top of their voices.[29]
'Everything possible was done to prevent venereal disease. Each girl had a couple of
towels, vaseline, Condy's fluid and soap — they were examined two or three times a
week by one of the hospital-doctors, who fined them a rupee, if they were short of any of
the above requisites. If he found that any one of them had the disease he had her
removed to the native lock-hospital. There was also a small lavatory erected in the street,
which had a supply of hot water; it was for the use of any man, who was not satisfied with
the washing he had done in the girl's room. There was always a number of men in
hospital with venereal, but it was very rarely that they contracted it in the Rag. It was
generally caught from half-caste prostitutes or native girls outside. If a man hired a

gharri to go for a ride somewhere, the driver would immediately say: 'Sahib, you want nice Bibi, me drive you to bungalow of nice half-caste, plenty clean, plenty cheap, only charge one rupee, Sahib.' In the evening a man could not take a walk anywhere at a distance from the Barracks, without hearing the familiar cry of 'jiggy-jig, Sahib?'

INDIAN ALLOWANCES

The Royal Commission of 1863 had also been concerned about the 'terrible results' of abandoning their women, when a regiment went into the field —

'If the women were properly cared for when they were left behind and had money given to them to provide themselves with food, a great deal might be done to remedy the present evil'.[30]

European soldiers were permitted to marry native women, who received from the Government $2\frac{1}{2}$ rupees a month, half the European wife's allowance, on the grounds that having 'been born in India and habituated to live chiefly on rice, the wants of half-caste women are much less than those of European women'.[31]

By 1861, these rates had risen to 8 rupees (16 shillings) for a European or Eurasian woman and to 13 shillings for a native woman, with 5 shillings for each child under 16 years of age. The European Regiments had adopted the Sepoy system of authorising a member of his family to draw by 'pay certificate' part of his pay, when he was away on duty. By 1870 The Indian Government had authorised rations for a soldier's family, when he was absent on field service, had provided him with married quarters, some barrack furniture, bedding, blankets etc, and if he died in India, his widow could draw his family allowance for 6 months, unless she remarried or was supplied with a passage to England within that time. Although these privileges only applied to the 'recognised' 12% of wives (exclusive of Sergeants', all of whom were allowed to marry), they met some of the Commissioners' concern and provide one major reason for the greater popularity of service in India compared with the UK.[32]

According to the Commissioners,[33] 'the sons and daughters of the two races, known as Eurasians, or half-castes, amount to considerable numbers'. They seldom went to England with their husbands, though they had the right to do so. Usually the husband volunteered to serve with another regiment and on retirement took a job and settled in India.

PROVISIONS FOR OFFICERS' WIVES AND FAMILIES

For the officer's widow and children,

'provided the officer were killed in action or died within 6 months of being wounded, she received a gratuity of one year's regimental pay and $\frac{1}{3}$ of the amount for each legitimate child under age and unmarried'.

If the officer had no wife or child his mother received the widow's equivalent pension annually. But

> 'widows cannot claim pensions as a right', stated the Regulations. 'Pensions are granted as rewards for good and faithful military service rendered by deceased officers! They are only conferred on fit and deserving objects, are withheld from widows in wealthy circumstances and are liable to be discontinued altogether in case of misconduct'.[34]

The widow forfeited her pension, if she remarried, and lost her eligiblity, if her husband was 60 years of age, when he married her or if he had been guilty of bigamy or if either party were 'in a disreputable state of separation' at his death. The pension varied according to rank and cause of death: a captain's widow, for example, received in 1850 a pension of £50 per annum or £70 if he were killed in action or died of wounds, with a compassionate allowance for each child of £9 or £12 each. In India, each Presidency of Bengal, Bombay and Madras ran a voluntary subscription fund, with monthly payments for the different ranks of officer and for married and single states. These annuities could be transferred to the widow.

In 1872 the fund was designated 'The Indian Service Family Pension Fund'.[35]

THE HILL STATIONS

By 1870, the 'Fishing Fleet' had overfished the waters and many had to return home as virginal, or at any rate as unmarried, as they had come. Writers now drew a different picture. Instead of recording that a certain Miss X had married within a few weeks of landing and received a settlement of some thousands of rupees; or that Miss Y had received 3 proposals of marriage at her first Ball,

> 'Now the young ladies droop and languish', wrote General Rawlins 'and nobody comes to woo; and charming girls spend four or five years in India and then return as spinsters to their mother country . . . . . for most officers now select their wives on furlough or on home leave in England—
>> 'Now sail the chagrined fishing fleet
>> Yo ho, my girls, yo ho!,
>> Back to Putney and Byfleet,
>> Poor girls you were too slow!'[36]

Furthermore, the young officers were encouraged to self-denial and to 'sweat the sex out of them' by healthy out-door exercise. F. Yeats-Brown, who joined his regiment in India in 1905, described (Bengal Lancer) his life 'as sexless as any monk's. The subaltern, like the priest, had work to do, which he could scarcely do, if hampered by family ties'. The Colonel would watch whether his young officers spent their leave chasing mountain sheep in Kashmir with a gun or chasing the ladies in Mussoorie — a hill station noted for its Eurasian girls hoping to make a good match.

Between 1815 and 1947 the British would create over 80 hill stations on the lower mountain ranges and increasingly the wives turned to these hill stations, which, from April to October, offered them an escape from the heat and exhaustion of the plains, and healthy recreation in the lovely climate and surroundings in the hills. Simla became the official hill station for the Bengal Government (and in 1863 the summer capital of British India), Poona for Bombay and Ootacamund for Madras, Naini Tal for Lucknow and Darjeeling for Calcutta. Central and provincial governments moved there and took the whole machinery of administration with them — files and clerks. Officers, too, joined their wives and families whenever possible, taking eight weeks' leave and leaving their wives as 'grass widows' (the origin of the term) for the rest of the time. Social life flourished with dinner parties, dances and amateur theatricals; in the afternoons, race meetings, polo matches, dog shows and at all times, endless gossip.

A contemporary described the hill-stations as a world of 'duty, red-tape, picnics and adultery; where every year someone or other lost his or her reputation or became involved in a scandal'. Maud Diver put the blame on amateur dramatics and the army officer.

> 'The grass widow in the Hills has pitfalls to contend with; and perhaps the two most insidious are amateur theatricals and the military man on leave. These two factors are accountable for half the domestic tragedies of India. The proverbial relation between Satan and idle hands is too often confirmed in the Himalayas; and for a woman who is young, comely and gifted with a taste for acting, Simla is assuredly not the most innocuous place on God's earth. Here frivolity reaches its highest height and social pleasures are the end of everyone's existence'.[37]

Flora Annie Steel, who spent 22 years in India as the wife of a District Officer, blamed the women for the scandals.

> 'The majority of European women in India have nothing to do. Housekeeping is proverbially easy and she has few companions of her own sex, no shop windows to look at, no new books to read, no theatres, no cinemas. Above all, in many cases, an empty nursery'.[38]

Dickens wrote in 1858

> 'All the chief hill stations have a bad name for gambling, intrigue and dissipation of every sort. Half the scandal in India may be traced to these places' — and most of the court-martials.[39]

Kipling gave his view of hill station married life:

> 'Jack's own Jill goes up the hill
> To Muree or Chakrata
> Jack remains, and dies in the plains
> and Jill remarries soon after.'

Maud Diver sought to redress the balance.

> 'To assert that social morality is lower in India than in England is unjust and untrue. Upper class women in England are more strictly encompassed by 'the conventions' than Anglo-Indian. Moreover, in a country where men and women are constantly thrown together under conditions which tend to minimise formalism and conventional restraint, where leave is plentiful and grass widows — willing and unwilling — abound, it is scarcely surprising that the complications and conflicting duties of married life should

prove appreciably greater than they are elsewhere. If Jill's conduct is not always exemplary, she is not always as frivolous as Kipling depicts. Many wives do stand by their husbands through bitter and sweet, through fire and frost and some blame must be attached to the husband; if he is careless of his wife's reputation or through indolence, indifference or a mistaken notion of unselfishness, he leaves her too entirely to her own devices'.[40]

Colonel S. Dewe White of the Bengal Army (1844–1866) said Simla was used by officers

'aspiring to get a civil or military appointment, to curry favour with the great . . . Here the place-seeker would stick during the whole period of his leave, taking every opportunity to ingratiate himself with all who could do him a good turn'.[41]

Some officers even sent their wives to do the job for them. One subaltern, found guilty in Simla of conduct unbecoming a gentleman for seducing the wife of his commanding officer, was ordered to be dismissed from the Service. The Commander in Chief, General Sir Charles Napier, reviewed the sentence and decided to quash it on the grounds that 'the fruit stolen by the officer had not required much plucking'.

At a later date, Private Frank Richards gave one of his own vivid pictures of life on the plains, for the soldier's wife, as well as the officer's —

'A few married women were left each year on the Plains at Agra during the summer, but those that had young children were generally ordered to spend the whole of the summer in the Hills. Children born in Barracks were referred to as 'barrack-rats': it was always a wonder to me how the poor kids survived the heat, and they were washed-out little things. It was rarely that a woman was sent to a Hill-station without her husband, but if that happened, and if she was young and pretty, she would be sure of an invitation to all the dances and social functions held by the NCOs there. She would have to be very level-headed and virtuous to resist all the temptations that came her way, especially if her husband did not join her with the half-time relieving party. Six months in India is a hell of a long time for husband and wife to be parted . . . . But I never heard of a divorce among the Rank and File; a murder would have been far more likely'.[42]

RACE AND CLASS IN INDIAN SOCIETY

Problems over race, colour and class in India came to a head at the end of Queen Victoria's reign and especially under her Viceroy, Lord Curzon (1898–1905).

Curzon criticised the immorality of some of his senior military and civilian officers for living openly with native women in India and Burma.

'You cannot prevent young English bachelors from consorting with native women. But you can, and ought to prevent the open practice of these relations by men in responsible positions.'[43]

He was quick, too, to condemn the ill-treatment of Indians by the military. When, for instance, he discovered that the officers of the West Kent Regiment had hushed up the systematic rape of a Burmese woman in Rangoon by some of their drunken soldiers and that the officers of the 9th Lancers had shielded two of their troopers who had beaten to death an Indian cook for failing to provide them with a woman, Curzon ordered the West Kent Regiment to the most unpleasant station available — Aden — and stopped all leave for the Lancers for a year.

> 'The English may be in danger of losing their command of India, because they have not learned to command themselves', he wrote.[44]

But when Richard's battalion went to Burma, they found a different social scene. Many officials, including British officers, kept Burmese mistresses and married Burmese women — customs which had lasted longer in Burma than in India, because there were fewer white women, no caste and no purdah, and because inter-racial liaisons were not regarded as shameful. The Burmese women themselves were attractive, proved good wives and housekeepers and had greater social freedom than in India. Rangoon offered many opportunities, too, for the soldiers.

> 'We were allowed out in Rangoon. The soldiers said that it was the finest place in the world and that it was impossible for a man to go wrong, either in his choice of a woman or a bottle of beer.'[45]

Queen Victoria's long reign was now at an end and one-third of the British Army was stationed in India. The British Empire was at the peak of its power and India 'the chief jewel in the British crown'. Delhi, the former capital of the great Mogul empire, would replace Calcutta (1911), as the capital of British India, and the Great Durbars of Edward VII and George V would show the British Raj in all its splendour. During the next century, India would gain its independence but would remain, until after the Second World War, home for the largest number of soldiers' wives, outside the United Kingdom.

Life at the end of Victoria's reign for the memsahibs was very different from that of their earlier sisters. The rapid development of rail and road communications meant that they were more mobile, less at the mercy of geography and climatic conditions and less likely to vegetate in some remote out-station for months on end. Electricity improved their household management, new medical discoveries made them less susceptible to illness and early death, whilst the broadening of education and social opportunities allowed them to take up many professions.

> 'Today more than half the English women in India have spent their girlhood and early childhood in the country', wrote Maud Diver in 1900. 'The present generation are much too spirited and fond of healthful excitement to subside into the luxurious and slothful habits of the poor native harem ladies and have little in common with the lolling, vapid, washed-out, poor useless creatures most of their predecessors in old Anglo-Indian times certainly were. But this is not a fair judgement on many of those ladies of yesteryear — the lackadaisical and the adventurous, the tough and the timorous, who served as 'wife' and 'mother' and 'hostess' and 'housekeeper', while her husband served in India, who endured and suffered on the plains or escaped occasionally to the hills. Many of the Army families, as well as the British civilian community could proudly claim to number among their forbears, soldiers killed in the retreat from Kabul, grandmothers who had survived the Mutiny and relatives scattered all over India, part of the social and administrative life of the country'.[46]

TABLE 1   *Percentage of Married, Unmarried and Widowers, at each age,*
of British subjects in India 1863

Ages	Royal Troops						East India Company's Troops			British Civilians in India		
	Officers			Soldiers								
	Married	Single	Widowers	Married	Single	Widowers	Married	Single	Widowers	Married	Single	Widowers
Total of 20 and upwards	19.2	77.5	3.3	6.5	93.0	0.5	28.8	69.3	1.9	45.4	50.1	4.5
20– ,,	2.8	97.2	—	1.7	98.2	0.1	5.1	94.9	—	12.7	86.9	0.4
25– ,,	13.0	86.1	0.9	6.9	92.7	0.4	19.2	79.7	1.1	31.8	66.7	1.5
30– ,,	29.2	69.2	1.6	15.7	83.0	1.3	36.9	61.5	1.6	51.8	44.6	3.6
35– ,,	42.5	50.2	7.3	21.9	75.1	3.0	53.2	43.5	3.3	66.1	29.2	4.7
40– ,,	49.2	39.9	10.9	18.9	75.9	5.2	71.9	24.1	4.0	70.5	21.7	7.8
45– ,,	55.2	27.6	17.2	10.7	75.0	14.3	77.5	14.5	8.0	72.3	18.0	9.7
50– ,,	55.9	20.6	23.5	—	—	—	72.3	13.7	14.0	73.8	14.1	12.1
55– ,,	53.8	23.1	23.1	—	—	—	88.1	4.8	7.1	71.9	13.2	14.9
60– ,,	66.7	33.3	—	—	—	—	79.5	7.7	12.8	72.8	10.2	17.0
65– ,,	33.3	44.5	22.2	—	—	—	73.7	10.5	15.8	72.5	6.9	20.6
70– ,,	—	—	—	—	—	—	100.0	—	—	61.8	2.9	35.3
75 and upwards	—	—	—	—	—	—	—	—	100.0	58.3	12.5	29.2

Note: The Table may be read:— of 100 officers aged 20 and under the age of 25, there were 2.8 married and 97.2 single.

Source: Table 29 p XCVII Report of Commission on the Sanitary State of India 1863.

Chapter 12

Regimental Ladies

'Let no one assume that matrimony for officers is encouraged — very far from it', wrote Captain Cairns[1] in his account of social life in the British Army at the end of the 19th Century.

> 'It is recognised that human frailty is such that some allowance must be made for senior officers, but the married subaltern is not likely to find himself popular, and, unless a very good chap, may receive a strong hint to remove himself and his bride to some other regiment. The Colonel should be married — a bachelor colonel in the mess is not always a joy forever; majors, especially if grumpy and livery in the mornings, may be married: captains should not be married: and subalterns must be bachelors — though, sad to say, they often prove quite as susceptible as their seniors.'

Field Marshal Sir Garnet Wolseley writing of his life in Montreal said:

> 'Altogether, it was a paradise for young officers, the only trouble being to keep single. Several impressionable young captains and subalterns had to be sent home hurriedly to save them from imprudent marriages. Although these Canadian ladies were very charming, they were not richly endowed with worldly goods. One old general was fond of saying 'when I was young I fell in love with every pretty girl I met, but providentially none of them would have me'.'[2]

Major C A Barker of the Royal Irish Fusiliers was of the same opinion:

> 'whilst it is detrimental to a corps to have a large proportion of its officers married, it is advantageous to have a few. But an officer should not rush rashly into matrimony the first time he is taken with a pretty face.'

He ought to have at least five years' service before he got married and, to prevent imprudent marriages, it would be well to adopt the rule which prevailed in both the French and German armies of allowing no officer to marry, until he could show that he and his future wife would have an income, which would permit them to live in a manner befitting their position — in England it should not be less than £500 a year.

> 'In the usual 'happy-go-lucky' way we have in England, there are no regulations on the subject at all and more than one case has been known of a newly-joined subaltern driving up to the barracks of his regiment with a perambulator on the top of his cab'.[3]

The reasons against early officer marriages were largely professional and financial. Matrimony interfered with a subaltern's training and could prove disastrous to his career: not every new wife increased the harmony of regimental life, while coping with regimental expenses and with the scale of mess hospitality was a financial problem for the less wealthy officers, who had to seek service abroad, usually in India, where they could enjoy the sport and social life of a gentleman at much less cost.

Throughout the nineteenth century, commissioned rank remained almost exclusively the preserve of the upper class, which, as late as 1912, formed over 40% of the Army (see Appendix A Tables I and II). Studies into the social origins of British Army officers[4] show that before 1856 influence and wealth were the prerequisites for the grant of a commission and then up to 1870, wealth and a public school education. The leading families of the aristocracy were all inter-related by marriage and their family connections spread downwards to the lesser nobility and the gentry. Thomas showed that during the eighteenth and nineteenth centuries the largest proportion of marriages between peers and 'commoners' was to the daughters of landowners, which included many Army officers (40%), with an increasing proportion (27%) towards the end of Victoria's reign to daughters of the Armed Forces, mostly Army (ie: within a broad class of gentlemen).

Against this background the sons and daughters of the landed classes could meet and mingle with those of the wealthy commercial and professional families. An appropriate marriage contract would realise the aspirations of a middle class wishing to climb the social hierarchy and ensure at the same time the continuity of the landowner's family estates and hereditary titles by an infusion of mercantile wealth, talent and beauty. Their younger sons would seek careers in commerce, law, the Army and the Church. For the Army, as we have noted, early marriage would be discouraged, but the pattern was the same. When an officer decided to take a wife, his choice would almost certainly fall on a girl within the same social spectrum as himself, while she would have to conform to the standards and expectations of the regiment and with the life-style of her husband and his brother officers.

REGIMENTAL LADIES

Edith Cutbell described[5] the regimental ladies, of whom she was one in 1894.

> 'There is probably no married life in which a wife's existence is more thoroughly merged into her husband's career than that of soldier's wife, from the Generals down to the sergeants, for under the present short-service system, the married private is fast dying out. Regimental life, with its fun and its worries, its network of red tape, its iron bonds of discipline, its unwritten code of 'noblesse oblige', its traditions and its taboos, has to be lived to be realised and can only be appreciated in full by those who have 'soldiered'
> ....'
> 'It is impossible to imagine a greater change, not to say shock, than that experienced by the clergyman's daughter from the even tenor of a vicarage life, the squire's from a quiet country home, or the London girl from the mill-horse round of recurring seasons transplanted into regimental life. In all the golden glamour of the honeymoon, when other brides have their husband-lovers at their feet and reign a rule supreme, the

soldier's wife has instantly to learn that she can never be first. Military and social obligations are paramount'.

Other brides could choose their residence and enjoy the delights of building their nests. But the soldier's wife had no such choice — of home, furnishing, decorating — even the wedding presents had to be selected for their portability.

When the nursery days were over and school became a problem, the poor mother had to give up either husband or children in a sacrifice to duty.

'The little bones of many of our children whiten our every station and they sleep in our military cemeteries all over the world. They are part of the price we pay for our great Empire.'

But there was a bright side to the picture.

'Leaving out of the question the officer's lady, who puts in a few weeks with her husband's regiment, the Hussars, between the London season and a round of country-house visits, or the Honourable Mrs X whose further 'foreign service' is with the Guards at Dublin, it is certain that Mesdames Fuse and Pipeclay have a much better time of it than their sisters, Mrs Briefless in a London flat or the parsoness at a country vicarage. The better a regiment, the more of a happy family it is, and the newly-joined bride, if she be nice and cheery, willing to make the best of things, places and people, finds herself at once well received by her husband's brother officers, however much they may regret that she has robbed them of a good fellow.'

There were no secrets in a regiment. Everyone knew everyone else's business. When the husband was away on duty, his wife had to have an escort. This was made easy by the unwritten army command, proved like all rules by occasional exceptions.

'Thou shalt not flirt with thy brother officer's wife'.
'But this rule does not apply, however, to the wives of other regiments and to those with a penchant for it; the career of a soldier's wife offers every opportunity for indulgence in the gentle art of 'dangling'.'

And one day she might climb the steep ladder of promotion — and become as old a soldier as her husband. Mrs Proudie in all her glory could not compare with the Colonel's lady.

'The senior officer flings his mantle over his better half and she ensures that she does not only get the corners of it.'

Regimental ladies had to learn by heart the 'table of precedence' and the Army Lists and have everyone's rank and length of service at their fingertips.

'It is worth while having borne the burden and heat of the day to be able to receive the guests at a regimental ball, or to go down first at a ladies' mess dinner. When flirting days are over and active participation in sport or dancing no longer practicable, senior regimental ladies can drill the adjutant socially or break in the subalterns.'[5]

HIGH SOCIETY

When Edward VII came to the throne in 1901 he had been the leader of society for the last 20 years of Queen Victoria's widowhood. He had gathered around his London home at Marlborough House, a 'set' of aristocratic young men and women 'of pretty faces and large fortunes', picked almost exclusively from the 600 families which formed London Society, who, while they did not flout conventions in public, had little use for morality in private. Among them was the Countess of Warwick (descended through her mother from Charles II and Nell Gwyn), whose father, Charles Maynard, was Colonel of the Blues and Colonels Oliver Montagu and Seymour Wynne Finch, who would succeed him as Colonels of the Royal Horse Guards and who were 'in the centre of the Marlborough House set'.

Daisy Warwick described this Society and its morals in her autobiography[6] —

> 'I remember smart young men about town, who had no profession other than perhaps soldiering .... They would have died rather than have dishonoured a girl of their own class, but they fixed their eyeglass in the other eye when the woman was married, or when they 'looked after' a maid of low degree. The Blues and the Guards mostly supplied London ballrooms with eligibles; Society girls, if not as innocent as they were 'pure', were often unbelievably ignorant, even of the physical facts of marriage. As wives, they accepted without question the code of their day as unchanging and unchangeable. Nearly all the young men had mistresses, so most bridegrooms had a second establishment to pension off or maintain. The only thing that mattered was that there should be no scandal'.

The Marquess of Hartington, for example, eldest son of the 7th Duke of Devonshire and twice Secretary of State for War, set up the celebrated courtesan 'Skittles' in a house in Mayfair. Born Catherine Walters (1839–1920), she was, according to *The Times*[7] 'a charming creature, admired and envied by the fashionable world' and by the crowds who flocked to see her ride daily in Hyde Park in her skin-tight riding habits. *The Daily Telegraph*,[7] on the other hand, called her 'a lewd woman, with a pretty body, which she sells to the highest bidder, enabling her to dress splendidly and drive handsome equipages in Hyde Park'. When Hartington wanted to marry her, his father packed her off to Paris, with £500 a year, to avoid such a family scandal.

Then there were the London Season and the big country house parties, where the hostess's chief preoccupations were to include a good selection of mature and attractive wives on her party list and to ensure the right bedroom arrangements, 'according to currently desired proximities', for the expected extra-marital activities of her guests.

> 'When the nursery had been sufficiently stocked up with a few sons to carry on her husband's name and inherit his estates, a kindly husband might discreetly look the other way — in the direction of other wives, in fact![8] 'As cultivated courtesans', wrote Mrs Gerald Paget[9] 'we practised upon other men the arts which had been taught us by our husbands'.

The Prince's amorous initiation had been 'stage-managed' by a group of subalterns in the Grenadier Guards, after a mess night, during his 10 week infantry training course at the Curragh Camp, near Dublin. They smuggled nightly into his bed an attractive young actress Nellie Clifden, reasoning that the 19 year old Prince should enjoy similar delights as themselves.[10] In 1898, now 57, while inspecting the Norfolk Yeomanry, he first met Mrs George Keppel, the wife of one of the officers on the parade, younger brother of the Earl of Albemarle. The Prince requested she be presented to him, as his eyes travelled approvingly over Alice Keppel's lovely face and fashionable curved figure. She was 29, with a small budget and expensive tastes. Within weeks she had become the Prince's mistress and remained so for the next twelve years, until his death, 'the most perfect mistress in the history of royal infidelity', writes Edward's biographer Giles St. Aubyn.[10]

Both the Keppel families had long traditions of military service. George, her husband, as a younger son, became an officer in the Gordon Highlanders and Colonel commanding the 2nd/4th Battalion The East Lancashire Regiment, during the Great War. The First Earl of Albemarle had accompanied William of Orange to England and received the earldom and large estates in Ireland for services to the crown. The second Earl was Colonel of the Horse Guards and served at the battles of Dettingen (1743), Fontenoy (1745) and Culloden (1746), becoming Commander in Chief of the Forces in Scotland. The family home at Quidenham in Norfolk was bought in 1762 by the third Earl with the money he had been awarded as Commander in Chief of the landing force during the Seven Years War, in which he and his brother, Admiral Keppel, had jointly captured Havana. Alice Frederica Keppel was the eighth child of Admiral Sir William Edmondstone, ADC to Queen Victoria and married to the daughter of an Army officer'.[11]

Less conventional marriages were made by the 'Bilton sisters', daughters of a Sergeant of the Royal Engineers, who with his wife performed at The Garrison Theatre, Woolwich. The 1890s was the age of musical comedy and of the Gaiety Girls, two of the loveliest of whom were Belle and Florence; both, like Camille Clifford, one of the Gibson girls, whose husband was killed in action in 1914, married into the aristocracy, where beauty sometimes triumphed over wealth and caste. In 1884, Kate Vaughan married Colonel Wellesley, a nephew of the Duke of Wellington: Denise Orme married Lord Churston in 1908 and in 1913, Olive May became Lady Victor Paget and so the sister-in-law of the Marquess of Anglesey.[12] But Society did not always approve of such marriages — nor did the Army! When Captain Maurice Brett, the son of Viscount Esher, married the Gaiety Girl Zena Dare, for example, he had to resign his commission in the Coldstream Guards, although he later became a Lieutenant Colonel in the Black Watch. The military hierarchy, especially the Brigade of Guards, continued to look askance at actresses and chorus girls as far as marriage was concerned — until the Second World War. An Adjutant of the Life Guards, for instance, married the film star Madeleine Carroll just before 1939 and, as a matter of course, had to give up his appointment and retire from the Army.

Another source for suitable marriages was the American heiress, the 'dollar princesses', who came to Europe seeking aristocratic titles. So successful were these heiresses that by 1915 no less than 454 had married into the European aristocracy.[13] Jennie Jerome of New York married Lord Randolph Churchill and became the mother of Winston Churchill and Consuelo Vanderbilt became the Duchess of Marlborough. Another was Minnie Stevens, who married Colonel Arthur Paget of the Scots Guards, the grandson of the first Marquis of Anglesey, whose family had been associated with the officer corps for generations.

Actresses, too, especially beautiful ones, as we have seen, could enter into the aristocracy, but not if they offended the officer's code of honour, as *The Times* reported —

> 'We understand from undoubted authority, that immediately on the marriage of Lieutenant George Trafford Heald with the Countess of Landsfeldt (Lola Montez), the Marquis of Londonderry, Colonel of the 2nd Life Guards, took the most decisive steps to recommend to Her Majesty that this officer's resignation of his commission should be insisted upon, and that he should leave the regiment, which this unfortunate and extraordinary act might possibly prejudice'.[14]

'Having developed her talents for dancing and amorous adventures', Lola Montez had achieved further notoriety through her liaison with the infatuated King Ludwig of Bavaria, who showered riches on her and created her Countess of Landsfeldt. She practically ruled the country, until banished in 1848. When she married Lieutenant Heald, she was prosecuted for bigamy, as her divorce was not yet final. She fled to the continent with her second husband, bore him two children and wounded him with a stiletto in Barcelona. In Madrid he left her — but not to return to his Regiment! On Heald's death in 1853, she married a Mr Hull of California but quickly deserted him, to die in New York in 1861 a penitent working for female outcasts.[15]

MATRIMONIAL CAUSES ACT 1857

The most important piece of legislation for women during Queen Victoria's reign had been the Matrimonial Causes Act of 1857, which made divorce easier and cheaper, but which accepted, until 1929, the double standards of adultery, whereby a husband only needed to prove simple adultery, whereas a wife had to prove adultery, compounded with desertion, cruelty, incest or rape, before she could obtain a divorce. The Act also allowed a legally separated wife to obtain legal ownership of her own earnings or of money bequeathed or gifted to her. The year before the Act, Charles Dickens had likened Victorian husbands to gaolers, who held their wife's person, property and reputation in a conjugal prison, built by society and the law

> 'in whose cells lie more broken hearts than ever the dungeon held. If the marital gaoler be a man of coarse or fickle passions, if he be a man without conscience or honour, of

violent temper, depraved habits, of reckless life, he may ill-treat, ruin and destroy his prisoner at his pleasure — all in the name of the law, and by virtue of his conjugal rights. The prisoner-wife is not recognised by the law, she is her gaoler's property, the same as his dog or his horse; with this difference, he cannot openly sell her. She has no property. All that she possessed before her marriage, and all that she may earn, save or inherit after her marriage, belongs to her husband. He may squander her fortune at the gaming table, or among his mistresses: he may bequeath it to his illegitimate children, leaving his wife and her children to beggary: he may do with it as he will. A marital gaoler may entertain as many ladies light-of-love as he pleases. He may support them out of his wife's property, he may even endow them with that property after his death and leave his lawful lady and her children to want and misery — and the wife has no remedy. The relief of divorce was not instituted for her'.[16]

Many Victorian women could not hope to find husbands and had to seek a livelihood; for them career and work opportunities increased during the century. For the upper classes and educated girls of military families the governess and teaching offered the most scope, although their status and pay were poor. Nursing was also a popular profession.

'Many are ladies by birth and education', wrote Charles Booth[16] in 1892, 'daughters of clergymen, military and naval officers, of doctors, farmers and tradesmen and of artisans are found side by side in all the great metropolitan hospitals. Many of those who would formerly have sought places as music teachers or nursery governesses have been absorbed in this way'.

Large numbers of women were finding employment in offices and shops, while increased mechanisation in factory and commercial house offered unskilled and routine jobs for women, on lower rates of pay than men.

But marriage remained the goal for most girls and here the daughters of army families had an obvious advantage, since they lived in a male-dominated society, where single men far outnumbered single women, whether at home or in the overseas garrisons all over the world. But even the Victorian servants could find a potential husband among them —

'Policemen and soldiers were the usual objects of the maids' affections, with soldiers particularly notorious for hunting up these women, especially nurse maids, who feel flattered by the attention that is lavished upon them, and are always ready to succumb to 'the scarlet fever'. The soldiers, for their part, were only too anxious to take advantage of the situation, for the average ranker could not afford to employ professional women to gratify his passions. He is only too glad to seize the opportunity of forming an intimacy with a woman who will appreciate him for his own sake, cost him nothing but the trouble of taking her about occasionally, and who, whatever else she may do, will never by any chance infect'.[17]

Sergeant Mole of the 14th (King's) Hussars found that one of the chief benefits of promotion was that a Sergeant 'could always get the choice of an upper servant in one of the tip-top families or a tradesman's daughter'.[18]

AUTHORISED WOMEN 1890

For Other Ranks, the Army was slowly increasing its provision for the soldier 'married with permission', while restricting still further their numbers on the Married Roll (See Appendix A, Table III) Cardwell's six year short service engagements made the large proportion of soldiers ineligible to be considered for the marriage establishment, which the 1890 Regulations, for example, laid down for an Infantry regiment as 'all Warrant Officers and 50% of the NCOs may be married and 4% of the rank and file'.[19] No soldier was allowed 'to enter the blessed state', unless he had seven years' service, five pounds in the savings bank and two good conduct badges (and the commanding officer had satisfied himself as to the woman's character).

New Regulations authorised

> 'better housing — windows with sashes to increase ventilation, the provision of a larder or food store, slop sinks, a fire-place in all bedrooms, water closets in each quarter and paving and asphalting of the ground in front of buildings to protect women and children against wet and damp'.
> Quarters of different size were allotted according to seniority and size of family — two rooms (exclusive of scullery) to an NCO or man with two children: three rooms for three to five children and four rooms for six or more children.[20]

His household effects, all liberally stamped with the Government broad arrow, comprised two narrow and extremely hard iron beds, palliasses and bolsters stuffed with straw (pillows were considered superfluous luxuries), sheets and blankets: a small deal table, form, stool, a couple of coal-boxes, zinc bath tub, large tin pail, poker, fender and fire-shovel.

> 'During the absence of a soldier on active service, or ordered away without his family, the family may, if they have no home to go to, occupy quarters until the quarters are required or until the family can make alternative arrangements'.[20]

VOLUNTARY AGENCIES

The British soldiers' proclivities for matrimony are proverbial, 'wrote Private Wyndham.[21] Whatever the Regulations, many continued 'to commit matrimony without leave' and required help from regimental funds or voluntary agencies. One such agency, which is still serving the Army today was the Soldiers' and Sailors' Families Association, founded in 1885 by Major (later Colonel Sir) James Gildea,[22] the Royal Warwickshire Regiment, to look after individual Service families and aged parents, whether such families were officially recognised or not. Queen Alexandra presided over the Association for 31 years and has been succeeded by Royal Patrons to this day.

STATISTICS ON THE SOCIAL STRUCTURE OF THE ARMY AND ON MILITARY MARRIAGE

Social Structure
Studies[23] confirm that, broadly speaking, the social structure of the officers of the Army (by percentages) was as under:

TABLE 1

Army List Year	Aristocracy	Landed Gentry	Middle Classes
1780	24	16	60
1830	21	32	47
1875	18	32	50
1912	9	32	59
1930	5	6	89
1952	3	2	95

Source: Razzell – British Journal of Sociology xiv (1963) Table 7 p. 253.

TABLE 2
Spiers, in his analysis of the military leadership at the beginning of the three major wars, identified more clearly the elements of the middle class group and demonstrated the importance of 'internal recruitment' within the Armed Forces.

	1854	1899	1914
1. Landed Aristocracy (Peers and Landed Gentry)	38–46	38–51	33–42
2. Internal Recruitment (Sons of Serving and Retired Officers, Orphaned etc)	22–18	23–19	23–25
3. Professional Classes (Clergy, Doctors, Barristers, Surgeons and Higher Civil Servants)	15	21	26
4. Others (Merchants, Teachers, Engineers, Small Farmers and Estate Managers)	15	15	15

Source: Spiers – The Victorian Army.

TABLE 3

Marriage at the Turn of the Century
Numbers of officers, other ranks, wives and children on the official married rolls in the United Kingdom and India.

United Kingdom

Year	Officers	Other Ranks	Women	%	Children
1890	3,963	100,120	10,591	10.1	21,371
1900	3,996	132,921	9,148	6.6	18,156
1910	4,712	123,318	13,235	5.5	24,354

India

1890	1,948	67,456	3,127	4.5	5,867
1900	1,780	60,553	2,908	4.6	5,376
1910	2,365	72,491	4,137	5.5	6,678

Source: Army Medical Department Reports on the Health of the Army, 1890 (Vol XXXII), 1900 (Vol XLII) and 1910 (Vol LII).

TABLE 4

Countries of Birth, Officers and Soldiers 1901

England & Wales	%	Scotland	%	Ireland	%	Other than United Kingdom	%	Total
177,313	71.9	21,955	8.9	30,888	12.5	16,557*	6.7	246,713

* Includes 12,246 whose birthplaces were 'not stated'.

Source: 1901 Census. Appendix A. Table 50.

Chapter 13

War and Stagnation

The Great War and the years of peace which followed proved a brief but significant interlude in our continuing story of the Army's attitude to marriage and its 'women' but their impact on the status and rights of women in general were to be profound and lasting.

WAR DEMANDS THE WOMEN

When Britain declared war on Germany on 4th August 1914, most people thought the War would be over by Christmas, but before it ended in November 1918, the whole nation had been mobilised, including the soldier's wife and sweetheart — and often his mother and sister too! Kitchener's 'Call to Arms' produced about $2\frac{1}{2}$ million volunteers in the first 18 months for his 'New Army', as the British Expeditionary Force took its place alongside France on the Western Front. So great was the demand for men, both for the war industry, as well as for the battle front, that, increasingly, women were needed to fill the gaps on the Home Front and to provide the nurses, drivers and canteen workers overseas.

> 'They turned into a generation of redoubtable grandmothers, or more precisely, maiden aunts — because most of the men of their age group, whom they might have married, never came back from the War. Some did marry, but the others were not content to return to the old life of busy idleness nor to sit around mourning their lot as the 'surplus women'. They shortened their skirts, bobbed their hair, flattened their chests, and, having proved beyond argument during the war that women could do anything, set out to carve themselves a place, in what was still a man's world'.

Breeched, booted and bobbed, they worked as military chauffeurs, land girls, railway, munition or social workers, bus conductors, postmen and teachers.

> 'They won the vote and the right to work in the face of formidable opposition and the obdurate philosophy that a woman's place was in the home, even though such hopes as most marriageable girls had had of husband and children lay buried with their men on some far-off battlefield.'[1]

When the troops left for France, they carried in their Pay Books a message from Lord Kitchener.

'Your duty cannot be done, unless your health is sound, so keep constantly on your guard against any excesses. In this new experience you may find temptations, both in wine and women. You must entirely resist the temptations and, while treating women with perfect courtesy, you should avoid any intimacy. Do your duty bravely. Fear God. Honour the King'.

The VADs arrived in France to staff the Base Hospitals. The matron at the General Hospital at Rouen told them precisely what she expected of them —

'Remember you are on Active Service. You are not allowed to go out to luncheon or dinner nor to go riding, driving or boating with anyone of the opposite sex — and, above all, no dancing! You must always be in camp by 7 pm. If you do not obey these regulations you will be sent home at once.There are plenty of girls waiting to take your place'.[2]

SOCIAL PROBLEMS

At home, *The Times*[3] was reporting in April 1915 'The New Social Problem' of

'the large numbers of unmarried girls and women in this country who are expecting to become mothers . . . . . A great wave of emotional nonsense has been set in motion. In the excitement created at the outbreak of war, many young girls lost their balance: there was a weakening of parental control, a lowering of ideals. 'These poor girls had so little to give and they gave their all' — is a foolish excuse. The babies are not those of men of the Regular Army but of the Territorial or New Armies. Billeting is much to blame'.

Behaviour and moral patterns were relaxed and tacitly it was admitted that a girl might go further with her boy friend than she normally would, since she might not see him again. C E Montague records that, while the first volunteers of Kitchener's New Armies followed his advice in their Pay Books, 'hundreds of reputable women and girls round every camp seemed to have been suddenly smitten with a Bacchantic frenzy', which Mrs Helena Swanwick of the Women's International League explained, as

'the natural female complement to the male frenzy of killing. If millions of men were to be killed in early manhood, or even boyhood, it behoved every young woman to secure a mate and replenish the population, while it was yet time'.[4]

In October 1914, Parliament had authorised Separation Allowances for the dependants of soldiers mobilised for the War[5] and concern was expressed not only over the problem of 'war babies' but also over Government proposals to pay the same allowances to the unmarried as to married women —
'The State should not support concubines' was the cry. But Separation Allowances could be withdrawn for misconduct, as the Under-Secretary of State made clear —

'Separation allowances or pension may be withdrawn on clear proof of serious misconduct, such as immorality definitely established, conviction on criminal charges, gross neglect of children or persistent drinking, especially where such drinking results in the neglect of children. The allowance or pension to the children is not withdrawn'.[6]

The main effect of paying separation allowances to the dependants of a National Army was to end the distinction between wives 'on' and 'off' the strength and to change for many the traditional poverty and hardships of the soldier's unrecognised woman.

In April 1915 the most important of the voluntary women's organisations, the Women's Legion, was formed by Lady Londonderry to release soldiers from cooking and support services to combatant duties. The Legion was organised into Canteen, Ambulance and Cookery Sections.[7]

In February 1915 the Women's Police Service was instituted to discourage 'provocative loitering near military centres' by young women struck with khaki fever' and, in May, the shortage of munitions led to the establishment of a special Ministry of Munitions, which took over and built its own munition factories, built accommodation for the largely female workforce which it directly recruited, and suspended many of the trade union practices which sometimes served as a barrier to the employment of women. There was no conscription of women during World War I, but so great was the manpower shortage and so insatiable were the demands of the trenches that in August 1915 all persons, female and male, between 15 and 65 had to register particulars of age and occupation in a National Register.

In the home, every women seemed to be knitting Red Cross comforts for the men, but Mrs Alec-Tweedie, authoress and well-known champion of women's rights, believed strongly in the capabilities of her sex in taking over men's jobs to release them for the Front and had little time for men, who would keep them as ornamental appendages.

> 'Men liked women to be incapable before the war, hence the number of senseless fluffy dolls. Men now expect women to be capable of everything during the war, hence the number of wonderful women to be seen everywhere. The same women, merely changed. Today, women are crews, not merely passengers, for they man the oars!'.
> 'Women have shown the world what is in them. They have done everything but fight, and they are ready to do that, too, if the country wants them. National work will not end with the war. That end will be the dawn of a new era, a breaking with old conventionalities, the awakening of a new industrialism, the rebuilding of homes, the remodelling of nations. There will be much to do to bring renewed health, happiness and a better civilisation. Fighting men and Soldier-women will each and all have a place in that reconstruction'.[8]

Who will deny that she was right?

FRANCE

In the shell-scarred towns and villages behind the lines, the soldiers sought rest, baths and a few days' recreation from the trenches. Lieutenant Gerald Brenan bicycled over to Armentières for a meal and

> 'to flirt with the French waitresses, who were not yet browned off by the sight of men in khaki. In the courtyard a group of soldiers waited their turn with one of the waitresses on a heap of straw on the cobble-stones!'[9]

The author's father was also at Armentières in June 1915, a subaltern with the Cambridgeshire Regiment. In May 1916 he was injured by a grenade in the Festubert Line and invalided home. His Commanding Officer recorded in the Regimental History:

'If officers and men had been addicted to drink, or the women living in the villages where we were billeted had been immoral, the fact must have come to my knowledge. I marvel at the unadulterated rubbish written on the subject by a number of war novelists and the credulity of the section of the British public that is stupid enough to swallow this fiction. The fighting soldier was not addicted to sexual immorality. Occasionally cases came to my notice, but less frequently than in times of peace'.[10]

For many soldiers marriage was the answer —

In 1915 there was an amazingly high marriage rate of 19.5 marriages per 1000 inhabitants, but marriage in haste often meant divorce at leisure, for between 1910 (596) and 1920 (1629) there was a three-fold increase in the number of divorces 'made absolute'.[10]

In 1916, the Government passed the Naval and Military War Pensions Act, transferring responsibility for the relief of the wives and families of soldiers from voluntary bodies like SSAFA to the newly created Ministry of Pensions. For example, during the first two years of the War, SSAFA had made grants of over $£2\frac{1}{2}$ million to 718,000 wives, $1\frac{1}{2}$ million children and nearly $\frac{1}{2}$ million other dependants. Queen Alexandra still saw the need for SSAFA to supplement State aid — a role SSAFA has continued to this day.

LIFE IN THE WOMEN'S SERVICES

By tradition, the Army had been reluctant to use women in any other capacity than as nurses, but their work in the munitions industry forced the Army to employ them as cooks and waitresses in Britain[11] in 1915 and abroad in 1917 — in the new Women's Army Auxiliary Corps[12] (WAAC).

The WAAC was organised in four sections — Cookery, Mechnical, Clerical and Miscellaneous — to do

'all kinds of work, which a woman can do as well as a man, and some which she can do better'.

Women were recruited into the Women's Royal Naval Service (WRNS) and finally into the Air Force as cooks, waitresses and drivers. The popular verdict was that —

'The WRNS uniform was neat and sedate: the WAAC uniform serviceable, but that of the Air Force was decidely ornamental'.[13]

Between 1917 and 1919, 100,000 women would pass through the Auxiliary Services, 57,000 of them in the WAAC, which was honoured on 9 April 1918 when Queen Mary became their Commandant-in-Chief.

A former WAAC described her life at the large Reinforcement Base at Etaples.

'Much to my surprise we were informed that we could make friends with the troops, but were advised to choose carefully. I had not anticipated that this would be allowed, but like many other girls it was here that I was to meet my future husband'.[14]

There was no 'social intercourse' between officers and other ranks and there were all sorts of restrictions on the freedom of all members of the various uniformed women's organisations. They could invite and entertain friends of both sexes in the Camp YWCA, 'the nearest thing to home', but the girls were expected to chaperone each other and to be escorted back to camp on late duties.

'Paris Plage (Le Touquet) did become a centre for numerous scandals', wrote Lady Angela Forbes,[15] 'but the morals of the WAAC contingents were unfairly criticised'.

A Government Commission, sent over to France in 1918 to investigate complaints, agreed that accusations of immoral conduct on a large scale amongst the female auxiliaries were unjustified. 'A vast superstructure of slander had been raised on a small foundation of fact'. Many officers and YMCA officials spoke with warm appreciation of the advantage to the soldiers of the possibility of frank and wholesome comradeship of women of their own race and the graver social dangers, which such comradeship tended to avert.

'The scandalous tales in connnection with the WAACs had emanated, in more than one sector, from some of the low-class French estaminets, whose custom among British soldiers has suffered considerably, owing to the better type of companionship now available for the men'.[16]

But in France the Army did try to halt the increase in VD cases by denying leave for a year to any officer or soldier who contracted VD (1917) and by placing out of bounds even the licensed brothels or *maisons de tolérance* (1918).

THE END OF THE WAR

Suddenly, the War was over. The crowds cheered and sang and flocked to Buckingham Palace and Trafalgar Square to sing 'God Save the King' and the Marseillaise.

But with the dawn came the problems of demobilisation and the resettlement for the soldier and his family. In 1920 Haig's Officers' Association appealed for £5 million to assist 25,000 unemployed officers, as well as 33,000 disabled, 10,000 widows and 8,000 orphans.

For the thousands of widows of the war dead, trips were arranged to the 500 British cemeteries, handed over in 1921 to the care of the Imperial War Graves Commission. Each grave had its neat headstone, bearing the Regimental badge, name, rank and date of death, with the inscription 'Their name liveth for evermore'.

The unhappiness and frustration of women before the War, due in large measure to the greater number of women in the population, was now even greater after the War. The balance of females over 14 years of age rose from

595 per thousand persons to 638: there were more spinsters than ever and now more widows — 43 per 1000.

> 'More women and girls had to face the prospect of forced virginity and parents the long boredom of old age without grandchildren'.[17]

For women in general, there was unemployment. 'Doing a man's job' deprived a man and his dependants of a wage and a livelihood. *The Times* drew attention to the growing resentment against women in work, which was to last between the two Great Wars, after thanking them for helping to save Britain from defeat by their efforts.[18] Britain could be as ungrateful to its women, as it had often been to its soldiers!

There would be many changes for women in the post-War years in their struggle for emancipation and recognition — changes in legal rights, in personal freedom and employment prospects.

> 'Soon women would be smoking cigarettes in public, drinking cocktails or beer, skirts over their knees, calling each other bi-sexual names like Bobbie, Billie, Jackie and Jo and sitting in the same room with men and even at the same table, supervised by a man or woman according to suitability, not only in the new departments, but also in the old-established offices of Whitehall.'[19]

The Army now returned to regimental life and soldiering for the Regular Officers once again became the occupation of a gentleman, which married well with the social and sporting life of the countryside, smartness on parade and stiff regimental custom and etiquette.

> 'Once again the Army would be outside the mainstream of the nation's life and thought — a colonial gendarmerie, as in the 1890's, with no major role to play or plan for'.[20]

POST-WAR DUTIES

The activities of the Royal Berkshire Regiment illustrate the Army's role immediately after the Armistice. In 1920 the 1st Battalion was at summer camp at Karind, beyond the Persian frontier, with regiments and detachments from most British units in Mesopotamia and the wives and children of the entire Mesopotamian Force.

> 'Canvas shops sprang up, sports grounds were cleared, 'mutti' tennis courts constructed, a YMCA started, and restaurants opened. Weekly dances were inaugurated and bathing began in the nearby river. Even the 'married families' were soon happily inured to domesticity in a tent. In brief, everything in the Persian garden was lovely, when out of the blue came a bombshell — 'Prepare to move immediately to North Persia on active service scale'. For the married families and the soldiers this idyllic life in the lands between the Tigris and the Euphrates, of Baghdad, Babylon and of peoples stretching back to the beginnings of recorded time, was over, as the troops prepared to protect Teheran from the Bolsheviks', chronicles the Regimental History.[21]

Meanwhile, the 2nd Battalion was posted to Portobello Barracks, Dublin —

> 'as dreary and depressing a collection of buildings as any other barracks of the period, hardly improved by the defence measures considered necessary — blocked gates, walls

crowned with broken glass, long stretches of barbed wire and sentries patrolling the fences. For this was the time of 'the troubles' in Ireland — of Sinn Fein and the IRA commanded by Michael Collins, when no one could be trusted — the artisan working on your car, the girl who sold cigarettes, or the man sitting next to you on the bus.

The married families — especially those in civilian houses — lived anxiously. Early one Sunday morning in November 1920, 20 British officers living in lodgings were called upon by Sinn Fein gunmen and murdered in front of their wives. After this murder-raid all families were brought into barracks, and given accommodation in the single officers' quarters'.[21]

Between 1926–1928 the 2nd Battalion was stationed in Wiesbaden as part of the British Army of the Rhine, sharing the occupation duties of the Treaty of Versailles with the French Army.

'The families were billeted with German families in the town, where a good German maid would willingly perform all the household duties for 30 to 40 marks a month (at 20 marks to the pound sterling). English cigarettes were sixpence for 20, beer was threepence a pint, boots and shoes ten shillings and sixpence a pair and a suit of clothes was considered extremely dear at eight guineas. There were family picnics in the woods and excursions on the Rhine, whilst the soldiers found pleasure in the local beauties, the Wein-Stuben and the Karnival season'.[21] 690 British soldiers of the Occupation Force married German women.[22]

MARRIED REGULATIONS

Between the Wars, the Army would change little in its attitude to marriage or in its provisions for married families. In 1923, for example, placement on the married quarters roll and entitlement to marriage allowance were still 'a privilege',[23] and only permissible for those soldiers who had attained the age of 26 years and whose wives and selves were of good character and conduct.[24] Permanent sleeping out passes for a married soldier or widower with children required the Commmanding Officer's approval and were only given to men who were

'regular in their duties, orderly in lodgings or quarters, exact in dress and who would never leave their quarters after tattoo, except on duty or with leave'.[25]

Misconduct, for which wives could be removed from the married quarters roll, was defined as

'not only immorality but any serious breach of Army Regulations or Standing Orders applying to them and any other improper or irregular conduct of which they may be adjudged to be guilty by the Commanding Officer'.[25]

Such Regulations were still in force 12 years later in precisely the same words.[26]

THE MARRIED STATE OF THE ARMY

The Table shows the total number of officers, other ranks, and other rank wives and children on the married rolls and in the United Kingdom and India for the years 1921 and 1931, taken from Army Medical Returns. These reveal that 6.9% of the Army's Other Ranks were officially married in 1921 and 9.6% in 1931. The figures for the United Kingdom and India respectively were 7.5% (1921) and 11.5% (1931): India 7% (1921) and 7.5% (1931).

Army Strengths 1921 and 1931

	1921				1931			
	Officers	Other Ranks	Other Rank Wives	Children	Officers	Other Ranks	Other Rank Wives	Children
Home and Abroad	13,897	239,525	16,588 (6.9%)	24,684	10,966	181,508	17,465 (9.6%)	28,056
United Kingdom	7,651	127,922	9,662 (7.5%)	15,349	7,216	99,362	11,406 (11.5%)	18,413
India	3,122	58,681	4,158 (7%)	5,567	2,319	55,842	4,172 (7.5%)	6,621

Source: Report on the Health of the Army 1921 p. 27.
Report on the Health of the Army 1931 Vol. LXVII pp. 64 & 89.

At Appendix A to this chapter a Table can be found, taken from the 1921 and 1931 Census Returns, giving the married and single numbers and percentages for the different age groups.

The Table shows that only 17% of the total Army was married in 1921, falling to 12% in the smaller army of 1931, as compared with a constant 60% of the civilian population for the equivalent age groups.

At age 25 and over, 31% of the Army were married in 1921, falling to 12% in 1931, rising to around 50% at age 30 and over as compared with 65% of the civilian population.

The trend for later and fewer marriages in the Army can be seen clearly.

Married Quarters: Between the Wars (1921–1939) the Army suffered from the effects of the country's economic depression, resulting in manpower, pay and maintenance cuts and delays in its building programmes for barracks and married quarters until the reforms of Hore-Belisha in 1937. Many temporary war-time hutted camps continued to be used with huts converted into make-shift married accommodation. One such was the Royal Tank Corps camp at Bovington, which, an unmarried soldier complained, was losing its attractive backwoods atmosphere as perambulators, well-fed women and overdressed children took over the roads and paths once sacred to athletes.[27]

Medical: In September 1924 the Army officially recognised Mother and Child Welfare Centres, hitherto financed by voluntary agencies. SSAFA paid for trained nurses as Health Visitors for families in Egypt, Malta and China, as well as at Home. By 1931 there were 56 such Centres at Home (and 13 unofficial ones) and 16 overseas.[28]

CHILDREN'S SCHOOLS

Another benefit for the married soldier was free education for his children in Army schools, at home and abroad.

190 Army schools were operating throughout the world in 1920, under the newly formed Army Educational Corps, which replaced the Corps of Army Schoolmasters.

The majority of these schools were overseas in India (60), in the British Occupation Area on the Rhine (20), in Egypt (13), Far East (9) and in the Colonies of Gibraltar, Malta and West Indies. The 5000 children in 66 Army schools in the United Kingdom were largely in such garrison towns as Aldershot, Chatham and Woolwich and in London and Dublin. Officers generally preferred the continuity of United Kingdom civilian boarding schools for their children.

One such school was established in Singapore in 1919.

> 'The garrison school is situated in Tanglin Barracks, $3\frac{1}{2}$ miles from the town of Singapore and occupies a good position, adjoining a large recreation ground. The married quarters are within a short distance of the school, consequently children are seldom late and very rarely absent. One building, formerly a church, and still used as a chapel on Sundays, accommodates infants and elder children, a wooden partition separating one school from the other. Usually the Mistress, if single, lodges with one of the married families living in quarters, but Tanglin is an ideal station for a Mistress married to an Army Schoolmaster'.[29]

The schoolmistress was one of 261 Army Schoolmistresses, not uniformed as were the Army nurses, but governed by War Office regulations and employed in Army schools at Home and overseas. In 1927, in recognition of their long (since 1840) and devoted services to the Crown, they received the honour of being called after their patron, Queen Mary, Queen's Army Schoolmistresses.

INDIA

India was to be the largest and most important overseas Command for the British forces and for their families during the inter-war years and the most popular with the British Army. The winter capital was Delhi and the summer one Simla.

India was divided into Northern Command (Peshawar, Rawalpindi, Lahore, Meerut and Lucknow Divisions) and Southern Command (Quetta, Mhow, Poona and Secunderabad Divisions) with the garrisons of Burma and Aden.

Life in the hill stations followed an annual pattern, with one battalion allotted a station each alternate year, whilst a second remained on the Plains. The annual migration took place every April and the return to the Plains in October.

The move to the hills followed a well recognised pattern. First, the Garrison Engineer and his staff would go, even before the snow had melted, to prepare the buildings and installations. Then the married quarters would be allocated, based on unit strength returns, and families would take what 'moveables' they required for the five months' stay — at least for many of the wives, who would remain with the children after their husbands had returned to duty.

For the children, the schoolmaster and mistress opened up the hill station schools (the first of which had been built at Mussoorie by Major General Biddulph, RA in 1876).

> 'From the spur of the Murree Hills may be seen on a clear day the Hill Stations of Upper Topa, Murree, Juldana, Barian, Kyra Gali and Kahanspur. At these places are Army schools varying in the numbers of children attending from 7–70'.[30]

With the constant moves of schools and children continuity of education was one of the biggest problems facing the teachers (as it is today!)

Residental boarding schools gave a more stable environment but the frequent moves of army children meant constant attention to the basic skills and much dedicated teaching! An ex-army school child summed up the problem with truth and wit:

> 'One young lady, who began her school career at the Infants' School in Kahanspur, India in 1930, was a 'Reorganised' child in the Punjab in 1932, a Mixed Infant in Norwich in 1933, who left her Record Book behind in Kowloon and her tonsils in Ambala and attended 3 different schools in 1935, is credited in her Record Book and Medical History Sheet (now arrived from China) with being somewhat backward, but a pleasure to teach in Swahili; weak in Mathematics, but good at skipping. At the age of 12, after 13 schools in 6 and a bit years, she can read with tolerable fluency, but weeps over sums a child of 9 at home would call 'money for jam'; can sing a little, sew a little, skip magnificently, has a few words of alleged Chinese, rather less Hindustani, and a disarming smile'.[31]

BRITAIN

In England, in 1935, SSAFA was celebrating its 50th Anniversary. Its Guide listed details of over 700 funds, organisations, institutions or schools available to help service or ex-servicemen and their dependants. The Dublin Branch spoke of the great poverty in Ireland, the low standard of living and the enormous size of their families (12 to 14).

Much had changed, however, for the better for the wife, mother or widow. Legislation had given equal facilities for divorce in 1923; equal guardianship of the children and the first progressive improvements in widows' pension rights in 1925; and in 1927 the right to legitimise a child by marriage to the father. The Adoption Act of 1926 replaced the voluntary work in finding homes for 'war babies'. Legal adoption 'first became a fashion and then a passion' in Britain, with waiting lists of eager childless parents, and gave a girl with an illegitimate baby the choice of handing it over for a better future with adoptive parents than having to catch up with and marry an unwilling father or of trying to support the child herself on inadequate means.

JO—G

MARRIED OFFICERS

In 1938 there were changes for the married officer. He was not permitted to be married 'on the strength', until he was aged 30, nor could he receive a marriage allowance; but he could live in sin! The effect of these changes was set out by Major G F Ellenberger, of the King's Own Yorkshire Light Infantry.[32]

> 'An officer officially married at 30, at which age he becomes entitled to Married Quarters. The Captain with less than 11 years' service finds himself in much the same financial straits as a newly joined subaltern! However inexpensive their tastes, the married pair must have a private income. If, however, no MQs are available for them, they will still be more out of pocket, since lodging and furniture allowance (45 shillings and sixpence a week) will hardly suffice to provide them with a suitable, furnished house, including rent, rates and water, in the neighbourhood of a military garrison. By the time the husband has 14 years' service (some 4 years after the age, at which he is officially recognised as being married), they should need little besides his pay and when, at the age of 37, he gets his majority, they should be freed from all financial anxiety — always provided they have no children!'.

Army Quarters were allotted in accordance with rank, not the size of family and were unduly cramped for all but the childless!

But his greatest concern, as a married man, was the education of his children. Most officers would have been educated 'on approved lines' at expensive 'prep' and public schools!

> 'Naturally he would expect, and was expected, to give his children the same sort of education as he himself had enjoyed. This would cost him anything from £150 to £200 or more for each child, but as a major with 22–27 year's service he received an annual salary of £611.7.6. (together with an issue of rations for himself and free quarters, fuel and light for his wife and self or cash allowances instead worth £210), out of which to educate perhaps 2 or 3 children'.[32]

But such complaints over conditions of pay and quarters for the married officer would fall on deaf ears, for the trumpets of war were sounding for all army families all over the world.

Army: Ages and Marital Conditions 1921 and 1931 (Officer and Other Ranks Combined)

England and Wales: Males per 1,000,000   Appendix A to Chapter 13

Age	Army (Officers & Other Ranks) 1921							Army 1931							Civilian Males 1921				Civilian Males 1931			
	Single	%	Married	%	Widowed	%	Total	Total	Single	%	Married	%	Widowed	%	Single	Married	Total	%	Single	Married	Total	%
Under 15	63	100	—	—	—	—	63	24	24	100	—	—	—	—								
15+	28,185	99.6	115	0.4	2	—	28,302	4,045	4,039	100	6	—	—	—	4,542	18	4,560	—	4,267	12	4,279	—
20+	77,943	94.7	4,839	5.3	50	—	82,832	49,351	48,247	97.8	1,098	2.2	6	—	3,143	676	3,819	17.7	3,663	587	4,250	13.8
25+	15,809	69.9	6,711	31.0	106	—	22,626	24,330	21,285	87.5	3,014	12.5	31	—	2,360	4,493	6,853	65.6	2,701	4,908	7,609	64.5
30+	7,801	50.6	7,460	49.4	167	—	15,428	5,929	2,840	47.9	3,047	52.0	42	—								
35+	3,933	39.1	5,957	59.2	178	—	10,068	3,295	866	26.3	2,396	72.7	33	—	989	5,450	6,439	84.6	788	5,375	6,163	87.2
40+	941	28.4	2,291	69.0	86	2.6	3,318	1,382	269	19.5	1,094	79.2	19	—								
45+	256	20.2	970	76.3	45	3.5	1,271	512	84	16.4	421	82.2	7	—	675	4,679	5,354	87.4	625	4,884	5,509	88.6
50+	73	16.9	332	76.9	27	6.2	432	205	20	9.8	180	87.8	5	2.4								
55 & Over	19	—	83	75.5	8	—	110	34	3	—	29	85.3	2	—	379	2,857	3,236	88.3	452	3,514	3,966	88.6
Total	135,023	82.1	28,758	17.4	669	0.5	164,450	89,107	77,677	87.2	11,285	12.6	145	0.2	12,088	18,173	30,261*		12,496	19,280	31,776*	
%	82.1%		17.4%		0.5%				87.2%		12.6%		0.2%		39.9%	60.1%		60.1%	39.2%	60.8%		60.8%

* N.B. Add 1718 Widowed and 1833 respectively.

Source: Census England and Wales 1921 Appendix C Table II and 1931 Appendix B Table II.

Chapter 14

The Second World War

During the Second World War (1939–1945) the whole country was mobilised for the war effort with the result that nearly all women became soldiers' wives, mothers, sweethearts or daughters. Many thousands joined the uniformed branches of the Services and then became soldiers' wives as well. The wives and children of regular soldiers, caught overseas by the War, were dispersed, sent home or remained to help the war effort locally. Some were captured, killed or suffered at the hands of the enemy. Most children's schools closed overseas and the children, usually with their mothers, were evacuated — as, for instance, from Burma to India and from Singapore to India or Australia. Schools closed in Ceylon, Hong Kong and Gibraltar. In Bermuda, the schools remained open and the Army wives knitted and collected funds for the troops. South Africa received many evacuees and the Service children attended the local fee-paying schools free of charge.[1]

In Malta, despite the air attacks, three army schools remained open — and two Headmistresses were decorated for gallantry.

There were three Queen's Army Schoolmistresses (QAS) in Burma, when the Japanese attacked. One left Rangoon in February 1942 on a hospital ship, which took off the last of the women and children to Calcutta. The other two joined a party of women and children trying to escape by train and boat through Mandalay and down the Chindwin river — then by elephant and on foot to Imphal before entraining for Calcutta.[2] Another QAS. Mrs Mamie Colley, an army wife herself, who was teaching in an army school in Singapore when it was captured, spent $3\frac{1}{2}$ years in Japanese captivity in Sumatra with 700 other women and children. There she taught the Junior class, sitting on sacks in the rice store, Arithmetic, Geography, English and Nature Study.

> 'There were no text-books or writing materials, so most of the work was oral and we relied upon our memories. Teaching had to be fitted in between other camp chores, such as wood-chopping, lavatory and drain cleaning, rice washing and cooking, water-carrying and so on. As we become weaker and beset with the varied ills, the camp life became more demanding and teaching had to be abandoned'.[3]

In her group of 15 women, she was one of only five to survive, serving after the War in Aldershot, Kenya and Somalia, until her retirement in 1951, after 25 years with the QAS.

'I learned to live a day at a time. Yesterday is past, forget it and tomorrow is but a dream, so live for this day', became her practical philosophy. We shall meet Mamie again, later in the Chapter, when her experiences became part of the television series 'Tenko'.

INDIA

By contrast, the War was hardly felt in India in the early days. For the white population life continued as usual on the sports field, at the Club and in the round of social entertainment. Most had kin in Britain — parents, wives, children at school, sons in the Armed Forces and even daughters in uniform. Regiments arriving from England were genuinely shocked at the peacetime standards which continued to exist. Christmas was celebrated with the customary festivities, canteens and leave camps were opened for the soldiers, but their biggest problem was the lack of white female companionship. Many had enlisted at 18 and were now in their early twenties, having spent half a dozen years abroad without having spoken to a white woman — and now they would have to spend years abroad with the same problem. The Anglo-Indians provided the only change of society for the off-duty soldier and it was not long before Army HQ in India relaxed its attitude to such associations. It decreed that

'in future there was to be no impediment put in the way of mixed marriages: such wives were to be admitted to barracks and free rations were to be issued. Some units took considerable advantage of these new orders'.[4]

It warned that venereal disease was rife in India and that promiscuous intercourse should be avoided. It commented on one of the characteristic features of the status of women in India — the practice of purdah.

'In the unsettled past, women came to be regarded as prizes of war and, as a consequence, many women, even of Hindu families, came to accept purdah. It gave them safety, though it kept them in seclusion. But during the last 25 years, the status of women has been gradually changing. Those with a good modern education are now leaders of Indian womanhood, especially in Welfare work amongst their less fortunate sisters and some professions such as education and medicine are opening up for them. Some have joined the Women's Auxiliary Corps, India.'[5]

THE BLITZ

In England and Wales, the Government put into effect on 1st September 1939, its plans to evacuate mothers and children from danger areas to reception areas. Parents tearfully waved goodbye to their children, carrying their small suitcases, packets of sandwiches and gas masks, and escorted by their teachers and by members of the Women's Voluntary Service.

The University of London too was dispersed with parts, including King's College, going to Bristol. There also went the Drama and Music Departments of the BBC, together with all their announcers, actors and actresses and the

BBC Symphony Orchestra to establish war-time variety, music and children's broadcasts.

The years 1940–41 are chiefly remembered in Britain for 'the Blitz' — as the Germans' heavy air attacks on London's East End and upon such provincial cities as Coventry and Southampton were known. Those attacks really put the civil population into the front line of the war'— for the first time in our history there were many soldiers serving overseas who were far safer than their womenfolk at home. With undaunted courage and good humour, the women settled down to run their homes amidst the devastation and the disruption to their war work caused by the damage to transport, water, gas and electricity.

In December 1941, the conscription of women was introduced, with exemptions for married women, not living apart from their husbands, and for mothers with children under 14. In fact, only the 19 to 24 age groups were called up and given the choice of serving in the Women's Services (WRNS, ATS or WAAF), civil defence or certain specified civilian jobs. But conscription played only a minor part in women's employment during the War, for even in the Services, the majority of women were volunteers, as in World War I. Women took over many jobs, traditionally performed by men, and expanded their own forms of employment, in nursing, teaching, offices, canteens and shops. Many joined the Land Army, war factories and Government departments, or enlisted in Lady Reading's Women's Voluntary Service (WVS) to take part in communal feeding and emergency meals for the homeless, or social welfare work — in fact, women could be found in every non-combatant occupation.[6] Princess Elizabeth joined the ATS in the Spring of 1945, trained as a driver and became a junior officer.

1941–1943 AUSTERITY

1941–1943 was a period of 'austerity', as the effects of German submarine and aerial warfare began to lead to food shortages, rationing and queues for such 'luxuries' as cigarettes and eggs. Fashion was one of the first casualties, when clothing became functional and 'utility' patterns had to conform to the rules and regulations of the Board of Trade, which limited the amount of material for each garment. Clothes were rationed by coupons and a points scheme — 7 points for a dress, 18 for a coat or suit — with a total of 50 coupons per person per year. People converted lawns and flower beds into vegetable gardens, 'dug for victory', and collected scrap and salvage to recycle paper, cans and materials. It was a time of 'make do and mend', of jumble sales and clothing exchanges, communal feeding, of salvage bags and 'pig bins' in every kitchen.

But the Government and the people could still hope and plan for better times to come. In December 1942, the Government published the Beveridge Report, identifying the five Giant Evils — Poverty, Disease, Ignorance,

Idleness and Squalor with suggestions for social reform in housing, education, health and employment with the institution of children's allowances, a comprehensive health service and the avoidance of mass unemployment, which together with the 1944 Education Act would be the major legislative issues for Post-War Britain.

SINGAPORE

While Britain faced air raids and austerity at home, and dreamed of the future, British women and children in Hong Kong, Malaya and Singapore were facing fire, death and internment at the hands of the Japanese. Singapore was considered to be an impregnable fortress, the Gibraltar of the Far East, and when it fell in February 1942, Winston Churchill described it as 'the worst disaster and largest capitulation in British History'.

> The wives of the military in the battle areas, in the face of a particularly brutal enemy were a special cause of anxiety.[7] Mamie Colley gave a vivid picture of the problems —
> 'When the war with Japan began, I was in Singapore at the Alexandra School, situated on one of the Island's highest points and a fine target for bombers. Many families were leaving Singapore for England, Australia or India, leaving many married quarters vacant, some of which we utilised. By the middle of January 1942, school numbers were greatly depleted and I taught 15 older children in a married quarter in Tanglin barracks. On 30 January, we received urgent notice to leave immediately.
> Getting to the docks was a nightmare, with destruction by bombing on the way and chaos on arrival. Huge clouds of smoke rose from burning shops and buildings. We had to make a detour to avoid an unexploded bomb on the docks and pick our way over masses of debris and hose pipes to the ship's side. It looked as if the whole of Singapore's women and children had congregated there. After many weary hours of waiting, 1500 passengers, mostly women and children were embarked'.[8]

Mamie escaped on the 'Mata Hari', which was forced to surrender to Japanese warships off Sumatra. After $3\frac{1}{2}$ years in Japanese prison camps, she survived the War to settle in London. Some ships reached safety in Australia and India; many did not survive.[9]

Many of those who died or who suffered captivity were women. The wives of Servicemen who died were taken from their jungle resting places and reburied in the War cemeteries of Singapore and Batavia (Djakarta), Java, by the Commonwealth War Graves Commission. Civilian wives, on the other hand, are recorded in the Roll of Honour of Civilian War Dead 1939–45, kept in Westminster Abbey.

The key to the Japanese treatment of women prisoners is partly contained in their belief that women are inferior to men and partly in their martial code of Bushido, which teaches that it is better to die with honour than live, a captive, in shame. A Japanese who surrendered was considered by the military to have died — a philosophy which made the Author's job as an interrogator, extracting information from Japanese prisoners, relatively simple. Since the Japanese soldiers (and officers) received no advice on their rights as a POW nor training on what information to give (Name, Rank and Number), once they discovered they were not going to be killed and were treated reasonably well, they would talk freely on military matters. To the Japanese, white women especially were an embarrassment as well as a nuisance; they were humiliated but the Japanese 'did not take advantage of them in the Hong Kong Internment Camp,' wrote Mr F.C. Gimson[10], 'though I regret to record that there were some women only too willing to receive their attentions.'

For their part in the defence of Singapore, thousands of Chinese were rounded up by the Kempeitai, the women and young girls raped and the men beheaded in their presence. Many Chinese and Malay girls were forcibly taken from Penang for the Japanese Comfort Corps.[11]

EGYPT

If 1942 had begun with disaster in Singapore, it was to end with the victory of Alamein, which turned the tide of war in our favour.

By June 1942 Rommel had driven the 8th Army back to a defence line at El Alamein, blocking the gateway to the Nile Delta, but only 60 miles from the main port at Alexandria, where Helen Long, a nurse at the 64 General Hospital described the social life, enjoyed by the Service girls and herself, even though her hospital would soon become a clearing station for the wounded of Alamein.

> 'Alexandria was attractively cosmopolitan, sophisticated and full of restaurants, bars and night clubs. Allied uniforms were to be seen everywhere. It was 'the thing' to be tanned, bleached, sandy and randy! In Cairo, we sat on the balcony of Shepheard's sipping cocktails, gin slings and freshly crushed lime drinks and swatting flies. At night the sky was ablaze with stars and the lights of Cairo. The great pyramids were bathed in moonlight. So we fell continuously in and out of love, flirting outrageously in our little white dresses, living only for the moment'.[12]

As Barbara Cartland remarked — In the War, love was about the only thing left unrationed — and the men, too, found time to enjoy themselves.

But General Alexander put an end to such junketings, when he ordered key personnel to leave Cairo and moved his Headquarters to Mena Camp in the Desert.

> 'There were too many opportunities for the 8th Army to surrender to the curiously seductive and nostalgic charms of Lili Marlene. It was all too much divorced from the battlefield',[13] wrote the Commander-in-Chief.

As General Montgomery said in his Order of the Day before the Battle of Alamein —

> 'The sooner we win this battle, which will be the turning point of this war, the sooner we shall all get back to our families'.

He knew that the soldiers were worried about the safety of their homes and families, during the air raids in Britain and about the three months' delay in mail reaching them. They were worried about other things, too.

THE ALLIED FORCES

During the War, Britain was 'host' to the troops of many nations — Free French, Poles and troops from the Dominions, Canadians, Indians, Australians — thousands of men in a variety of uniforms, far from home, seeking recreation and female companionship — which had a great effect on the social scene, especially in London. But it was the 'American invasion' of fun-loving and free-spending 'GI's, which captured the women-folk and upset the British troops overseas. They feared their wives and sweethearts were succumbing to the cigarettes and fully-fashioned nylon stockings of their American rivals and had no illusions on how these 'bribes' had been obtained. Their Allies were 'all right, except that they are overpaid, over-sexed and over here.'

One woman wrote:

'With their smooth, beautifully tailored uniforms, one could hardly tell a private from a colonel. They swaggered, they boasted and they threw their money about, bringing an enormous lift to the female population. How they could shoot a line and how we loved it. They were equipped moreover to the eyebrows with scented soap, cigarettes, food, sweets and nylon stockings and dozens of other things we had not seen for years. After jitter-bugging all night with them to their top line bands, I returned home laden with enough soap, cigarettes and candy to stock a shop.'[14]

A Home Office Circular of 1943 pin-pointed another concern of the Serviceman, whether at home or overseas.

'Some British women appear to find a peculiar fascination in associating with men of colour. The morale of the British troops is likely to be upset by rumours that their wives and daughters are being debauched by coloured American troops.'

Barbara Cartland, a WAAF moral welfare officer, maintained that it was the white women who ran after the black troops, not vice versa, resulting in some 1500 coloured babies being born in Britain during the War.

'Women would queue outside the camps, they would not be turned away: they would come down from London by train and they defeated the Military Police by sheer numbers'.[15]

Some 70,000 GI's would take their 'war brides' back to the States after the War. Altogether, more than 100,000 girls married servicemen from Allied or Dominion countries but there was a widespread and sometimes bitter ill-feeling against Service wives and women who associated with them or succumbed to Italian Prisoners of War.

'Yet society tacitly acccepted that husbands serving abroad had a right to girl-friends or prostitutes, while looking askance at many excellent young mothers, who were unable to stand the loneliness at home; and hasty war marriages, on embarkation leave, sometimes between comparative strangers, with a few days or weeks of married life, often left both parties with little sense of responsibility or obligation towards each other'.[16]

In 1942 the birth rate of 156 per 1000 was the highest since 1931 and the trend continued upwards until 1947 (20.6 per 1000). So did the boom in marriages to record a United Kingdom record of 22.1 per 1000 in 1939–40 as the following statistics show:–

United Kingdom Marriages 1938–1945   **Thousands**

	1938	1939	1940	1941	1942	1943	1944	1945
Number of Marriages	409.1	495.1	533.9	448.5	428.8	344.8	349.2	456.7
Persons married per 1,000 pop.	17.2	20.6	22.1	18.6	17.7	14.1	14.3	18.6
Divorced Women	4.2	5.5	5.4	4.8	4.8	5.5	6.5	9.0
Widows	18.0	18.5	20.0	21.4	21.9	21.4	22.6	28.5
Spinsters	387.0	471.2	508.6	422.4	402.0	317.7	320.2	419.3
Females under 21	67.6	97.3	129.3	116.0	117.1	93.9	90.5	108.3
21 and upwards	341.6	397.8	404.7	332.4	311.8	250.9	258.8	348.3

Source: Registrars General HMSO1951.

The rate of births among married women fell during the War, but the number of illegimate births per thousand single or widowed women very nearly tripled to record 16.1 in 1945. 'Spinsters, nearing middle age, who kicked over the traces,' wrote one observer.

In due course, the War would take its toll of marriages in a huge increase in the divorce rate, clogging up the peace-time procedures for applications for divorce and leading to long delays in dealing with them.[17] Between 1942–July 1945 there were 48,500 applications from Servicemen for assistance with divorce proceedings through the Command Legal Aid schemes.

> 'A tragic but symptomatic feature of the disturbance brought about by war in the field of family relations'

said the Chancellor. Only 5200 cases had reached the courts by the end of 1945 and of these 3000 had not been completed.[17]

FAMILY RECREATION

Boredom, the enemy of good morale, had to be combatted, both for the civilians and the soldier, so the Authorities harnessed the world of entertainment to the war effort. Tommy Handley, Vera Lynn and Henry Hall became household names on the BBC and cinemas, theatres and dance halls re-opened (sometimes with restricted times of closing to disperse audiences before the nightly air-raids). The Windmill Theatre, with its popular nude shows, 'never closed', while the Stage-door Canteen and the stars and big bands from America, like Glenn Miller, Judy Garland and Bob Hope, provided a tonic to British as well as American audiences. The converted

Drury Lane Theatre (Covent Garden) became with Hammersmith Palais and The Paramount, Tottenham Court Road, London's most popular Dance Halls.

For British troops and their families ENSA (the Entertainments National Service Association) provided 100 shows a week by Christmas 1939 and at its peak in 1944 employed 4000 artists in 13,500 stage and 20,000 film shows a month, with concerts, plays, ballets and dance bands travelling to hospitals, units and garrisons at home and overseas. Started by Basil Dean, the Director of Entertainments for the Navy, Army and Air Forces Institute (NAAFI) and run from its Headquarters in the Theatre Royal, Drury Lane, when Ivor Novello's play 'The Dancing Years' became an air-raid casualty, ENSA attracted stars like Gracie Fields, Vivien Leigh, George Formby, Charlie Chester and Frances Day, in shows which varied from a couple of unknown comedians to full-scale West End productions under a Jack Hylton, an Adrian Boult or a Geraldo.

The Author was one of the Unit Entertainment Officers, appointed by commanding officers, to organise the transport and reception of such parties visiting Battalions. In Ireland, he had only an improvised stage and make-shift dressing rooms in an enlarged Nissen hut. The ENSA party was collected in Army trucks and entertained after the show to a meal and drinks in the Officers' or Sergeants' Messes. At Wrotham in Kent, there was a huge, purpose built Garrison theatre, seating 2000, which attracted the more sophisticated and full scale play, ballet or variety show, with well known comedians and a chorus line. The majority of the audience preferred variety, comics and long-limbed dancing girls, but ovations were given to two unknown artists for a 1½ hour 'show', by an isolated unit of 50 men and women in uniform.

Dedicated to the Serviceman and his family, NAAFI grew rapidly during the War.

> 'From a small distributive organisation it grew into a Canteen Colossus with a trade of £200 million, a staff of 120,000 in 10,000 establishments in over 40 countries, serving 5 million customers'.[18]

Many of its employees died on Active Service, spent years as Prisoners of War or were decorated for gallantry, running clubs, shops and canteens in barracks and camps exclusively for the benefit of the Serviceman and his family.

During the War, the NAAFI girl proved her worth. In 1939, 55% of the NAAFI staff were women; by 1943 the percentage had risen to 85. The girls came from every class and background — from shop, restaurant, office and factory. They included Servicemen's wives and debutantes, raw teenagers from school and sophisticated models. They were all trained as members of the Auxiliary Territorial Service (ATS) and, like the men, were subject to military regulations and discipline.

THE SECOND FRONT

By 1944, the build up for the expected invasion of Europe was almost complete and Southern England was declared a restricted area. General Montgomery had ordered that no wife was permitted to live within 10 miles of her husband's unit, unless she was normally resident in the area or employed there.

After the fierce fighting in Normandy, the victorious Allied Forces swept through France, Holland and Belgium; they were welcomed everywhere with delight and relief in villages and towns for which their fathers had fought in the First World War. On Sunday evening, 3rd September 1944 the Guards Armoured Division entered Brussels to end four years of German occupation, bestiality and plunder. The tank crews were mobbed by waving and cheering people; in the Place de Brouchère crowds shook their hands, and excited women, many dressed in astonishing dresses in the national colours, hugged and kissed the men in their black berets.

> 'The countries of Continental Europe suffered the trauma of forcible invasion by foreign troops, which, for the female population could, at worst, mean rape or harassment: at best sexual liaisons formed by women to protect their loved ones or to curry favour with their conquerors — 'horizontal collaboration', as the French called it,' wrote Arthur Marwick.[19]

In Naples, for example, women of all ages and class turned to prostitution as a means of supporting their families, while in liberated Europe the girl-friends of the former German conquerors were paraded with shaven heads and beaten bodies. In Berlin and elsewhere, the Red Army would earn a grim reputation for drunken and savage sexual assaults, while returning Dutch Prisoners of War would find their wives entertaining Canadian soldiers.[20]

But the mood was to be very different when the troops crossed the Rhine and entered Germany. In March 1945 orders were issued that there was to be no fraternisation with the German population and in a broadcast later General Montgomery explained the reasons —

> 'For the second time this century your country has declared war on Europe. When your leaders once more unleashed this war, you applauded them. Once again, our soldiers have seen their comrades shot down, their homes in ruins, their wives and children hungry. They have seen terrible things in many countries, where your rulers took the war. That is why our soldiers are not behaving in a friendly way towards you.[21]

General Eisenhower said much the same thing.

> 'Non-fraternisation need not continue for years: sooner or later we have got to find some answer through education and example. We cannot build on hate. But first the criminals must be punished.[22]

BELSEN

There was little sympathy for the plight of Berlin or for the German people in Occupied Europe, especially as the horrors of the concentration camps were discovered. On 19th April 1945 Brigadier Glyn Hughes, the senior Medical Officer at British 2 Army HQ, described the camp at Belsen as:

'the most horrible, frightful place I have ever seen. There was a pile sixty to eighty yards long, thirty yards wide and four feet high of the unclothed bodies of women, all within sight of several hundred children. There was no water. There were 28,000 women, 11,000 men and 500 children in the overcrowded camp, with thousands of typhus, typhoid and tuberculosis cases. The German Commandant, Joseph Kramer, a sadistical, heavy featured Nazi, was quite unashamed as he drove me round the camp in a jeep and passed the compounds filled with the dead and dying'.[23]

Several years later, when Station Commander of the British garrison at Hohne (now renamed from Bergen-Belsen, the former SS barracks and Wehrmacht Training School, where Kramer and the infamous Irma Grese — his female counterpart — had lived and where the United Nations Relief and Rehabilitation Administration had housed the survivors from Belsen), the Author had the pleasure of meeting Glyn Hughes and of going with him to the site of the former concentration camp — now a National Memorial. The picture of the scene was still fresh in Hughes's memory as he described how the British soldiers with bayonets fixed, had paraded thousands of German prisoners and officials to see the conditions of the camp for themselves and then forced them to help SS women guards to carry the dead to huge pits, dug out with bulldozers, to create common graves. The camp was then burned down to prevent the spread of infection. Now, those pits are grassed over and are marked by mounds of earth, each having a small notice describing the number of dead buried beneath it. A great Jewish memorial stands at the head of the camp and trees have been planted to create some semblance of a garden of rest. The birds have, at last, returned to the place where once 'no birds sang'.

The end of the War in Europe came swiftly. General Montgomery accepted the German surrender on Luneberg Heath and the 8th May 1945 was celebrated as the official Victory in Europe (VE) Day.

But the War was not yet over and the final celebrations had to await the Japanese surrender after the Americans had dropped the atomic bombs on Hiroshima and Nagasaki in August 1945.

With the Japanese surrender came a considerable deployment of Allied troops throughout Malaya, Singapore, Hong Kong and the Dutch East Indies and the release of thousands of Allied prisoners of war and civil internees. Their care was the responsibility of an organisation known as RAPWI (Recovery of Allied Prisoners of War and Internees Organisation) although, in many cases, British, Indian and even re-armed Japanese units had to be used to secure their initial release from camps deep in the jungle in areas dominated by armed Indonesians who were bent on seizing control of their country through Independence (Merdeka) from the Dutch.[24] One of the largest of the internment camps was at Tjideng, a residential area in the middle of Batavia, surrounded by high double bamboo stockades. Here, amongst a large number of Dutch internees, were many British and Allied women and children. Instead of the end of the War bringing them immediate release from some four years of privation, they were destined to spend more months in the overcrowded camps before they could return home. The Author (a qualified Japanese interpreter) was commanding an Interrogation Unit in Djakata (Batavia), at this time and so had a first hand opportunity to come into contact with many of these unfortunate people and even to employ one or two as typists as they awaited repatriation.

They were attractive Eurasian girls, who looked upon Java as their home, products of the Dutch policy of intermarriage with the native population — a policy in direct contrast with our own in India and Malaya. Colour had not been the problem in the Dutch East Indies that it had been in India and Singapore and the departure of the Dutch from Java and Sumatra was the loss of 'home' for many, as well as of an empire. But some of them caused resentment before they left by becoming British officers' mistresses,

> 'often women who were known to have been living with Japanese officers and who now hoped to 'escape retribution'. Others rushed into hasty affairs which they later had cause to regret, when a good marriage broke-up as a result,[25]

recorded Daphne Jackson, a London secretary who had married her 'boss' in Java and been interned there.

DEMOBILISATION

After the War, the troops were demobilised by age groups, but Churchill believed the women ought to be treated differently from the men. In a note on Release on 5th July 1945, he had written to the Cabinet —

> 'They do not mutiny or cause disturbance and the sooner they are back at their homes the better.'[26]

Many of the new measures in social services, housing and education in the nation at large would be reflected in the post-war Army, bringing many improvements in the lot of the soldier's wife and family. Compassionate leave, the DILFOR scheme to bring wives to the bedsides of dangerously sick husbands, airgraph letters, family radio programmes, SSAFA's work in reconciling broken marriages, the hostels and camps for army wives and children had been introduced during the War and most would continue in 'Operation Union', whereby the Authorities tried to keep families together in the post-war armies of occupation, through their housing, medical and education services. The Army would be largely demobilised and reduced to its peace-time establishments and changed from a pre-war regular army of volunteers to a 1946–50 Army largely composed of conscripts. Many of the wives and children would become unwilling members of a military community and all would face housing shortages and domestic upheavals, as the post-war military deployments took effect.

Little did the Author know, when he returned to London University in 1946 to complete his professional qualifications, that he would spend the next 30 years of his life tackling some of these problems and experiencing with his wife and children the life of a married soldier 'following the drum'.

Chapter 15

Post War: The Families Return Overseas

With the War over and demobilisation well under way, the Army settled down to its peacetime roles — as an Occupation Force in Germany and to garrison duties in the Mediterranean and Far East. In August 1947, the British flag was pulled down in Delhi, as India gained her Independence, and a few months later the troops left Palestine, 30 years after wresting it from Turkey. But even though Britain's former Empire was much reduced, the wives and children of her Army looked forward once again to joining their husbands and fathers in garrisons all over the world. In June 1944, the families had already started to return to Gibraltar. By March 1946, schools were being hastily opened in private houses, converted barrack blocks and requisitioned buildings in Rome and Naples and in Tripoli. From the beginning of 1946, the trickle of reunions began in earnest, a trickle which would become a flood during the next three years, stretching accommodation resources to the limit and providing Army commanders and their welfare, medical and educational services with many family problems and much improvisation. Families left England on board troopships for the Middle and Far East stations or boarded the 'Medloc' Express, one of the finest troop trains ever organised by an army, to join husbands, who had moved up through Italy with the 8th Army and were now stationed in Austria; in Klagenfurt, set among lakes and hills, in Vienna with its woods and palaces or in Graz looking down from the Alps to the plains of Hungary below. By the end of the year there were Army families in Burma, Singapore and Hong Kong and in Egypt and Cyrenaica and in early 1947 the children were even at school in Japan.

BRITISH ARMY OF THE RHINE

The first wives and families arrived in Germany in the middle of 1946 and lived in requisitioned houses or flats. They were the forerunners of what was to become the principal family station outside the United Kingdom, at first known as the British Zone of Occupied Germany, an area extending from the lines of communication in the Low Countries to the British Sector of Berlin and incorporating Hamburg, Hanover, the Ruhr and Düsseldorf. They found appalling conditions — the German towns had been heavily bombed, road, rail and sea transport was paralysed, industry was at a standstill, local government hardly existed and the local police had disbanded themselves and gone into hiding. Tens of thousands of Germans lived in underground hovels or roamed the countryside in droves seeking food and shelter, among them many war criminals hoping to avoid arrest. Millions of German soldiers were prisoners of war and scores of thousands of refugees had fled before the Russians in the East into the British Zone.

By October, 1946 468 wives and 514 children of soldiers had been accommodated and 771 wives and 848 children of civilians in the Control Commission or British Military Government, responsible for creating order in the British Zone out of this chaos.[1]

Mr Frank Buckley, one of the founder members of the British Families' Education Service (BFES), gave the Author his impression of life in Germany at this time —

> 'My first impression was one of appalling destruction. Whole towns were in ruins; supplies of gas and electricity were limited and water had to be boiled before use. The only transport seen on the roads belonged to the Army, the Control Commission or Military Government. The German population was apathetic and bordering on starvation. There were few shops and those which remained had nothing to sell. Money had no value, barter replaced currency and the black market was everywhere.
> The British families lived in requisitioned houses among neighbours, who were sometimes hostile and very rarely friendly, but life for them, after the austerity of wartime Britain, exceeded belief. They were provided officially with domestic help — cook, housekeeper, boilerman — and drink was cheap. Consequently, they could enjoy the social round. Anything of value could be purchased for the price of a few cigarettes. The fathers held responsible and well-paid positions in 'Occupied Germany': their children were intelligent and rapidly matured socially. A nine year old could mix a gin and tonic, as expertly as his parents. He could sail, ride or engage in a host of out of school activities. How could such children take their schooling seriously!'.[2]

By the end of the summer of 1947, 220 teachers, mostly recruited from the UK but with some Service wives, were at work with 4,000 children, spread over 70 locations in improvised schools from adapted, requisitioned houses, flats and German barracks. With the families so widely scattered, secondary schools had to be centralised and two boarding schools were opened, with marvellous recreational facilities — one at Wilhelmshaven in the former German Naval Barracks, the other at Plön, in the once German U-boat Training School, with Colonel Spencer Chapman, who had made his name fighting the Japanese in the Malayan Jungle,[3] as its first Headmaster.

For many British statesmen and leaders worse than the food situation and the economic problems in Germany was 'the appalling moral vacuum which had been created 18 months after the end of the War'.[4] Despite warnings, prosecutions and confiscations, a vigorous Black Market existed everywhere and moral principles had long been abandoned. In Hamburg, according to one MP, human life was at its lowest.

'The only people who remained physically mobile were workers in heavy industry, and those who had bodies or possessions to sell: the others were too feeble to walk about'.[5]

Many Germans were selling their only capital assets — clothing, books, pictures, ornaments, carpets, furniture and jewelry — in order to live. They scoured the countryside to barter for potatoes, eggs and meat from the farmers. The women slept with the Occupation soldiers in return for candy, chocolate and cigarettes from the PX and NAAFI canteens. The fortunate obtained jobs as cooks, waiters and cleaners in army billets and messes. In the American Zone 'the black market thrives, of which the all-pervasive American cigarette is one of the major causes'.[5] For the Berlin Black Market teenagers were sent out to solicit for cigarettes for trading for goods and food, while their mothers and elder sisters of every walk of life 'drank, necked and jitterbugged with their foreign 'schatzes' or struggled with their G-strings in the strip-tease joints and basement bars'.[6]

The non-fraternisation regulations had soon proved unworkable and had been abandoned in October 1945. It is easy to understand why German *Fräuleins* were in such demand with the young, victorious soldiers, far from home and family ties and well provided with the good things of life and why even nice girls discovered their bodies afforded the only real living.

> 'No soldier needed to be without female company, if he carried a few packets of cigarettes, or a can of bully beef or a pair of silk stockings in his knapsack — She was often unemployed, homeless, usually hungry, cold in winter and lonely. Their men were dead, missing or POWs or wounded, maimed or penniless. Some had children to look after. So they would become mistresses for a night, a month, for ever in return for cigarettes or a warm bed. They had no future and they had lost their self-respect.'[6]

In June 1946 the 2nd Battalion The Gloucestershire Regiment left Soest in Germany to drive through the Soviet Zone of Occupation to the British Sector of Berlin. There, the Battalion hoped to settle down in Spandau to its ceremonial and operational duties, while the families would be able to enjoy the wonderful leisure activities and night life of the former German capital. Tim Carew related what happened.[7]

> 'Excitement among the married families was intense and the married quarters were designated. For the first time since 1939 families would be part of the Battalion; the quarters were spacious, domestic help seemed to pose no problems; there would be schools, playgrounds and entertainment in plenty'.

But these plans and hopes were short-lived; orders were received to leave Spandau for the West Indies, where during their last stay between 1817 and 1822, the Regiment had lost 7 officers and 356 other ranks. This time it was to be a different story.

> 'Kingston, Jamaica, was to be for the soldiers and their families a source of never-ending wonderment. Most of the wives had spent the War years in conditions of severe food, clothes and fuel rationing, of austerity, discomfort and danger. Now, suddenly, they found themselves in a land untouched by war, where the shops were crammed with goods, either long forgotten or unrecognisable; where the sun shone all day and cool

breezes rippled in from the sea at night; where household chores were cut to a bare minimum, for there were servants for all — cooks, houseboys, cleaners, laundrymen and nannies, who spoiled the children atrociously!'[7]

The main barracks were at Up Park Camp on the outskirts of the capital: there was another Camp 3900 feet up in the hills at Newcastle, where companies in rotation could escape from the heat of Jamaica. The leave camp was at Montego Bay, which was not yet the exclusive playground for the very rich, it was soon to become. For the married and single alike in the Regiment, it was to prove a wonderful recreation centre during the years 1947–1949.

AFRICA AND THE MEDITERRANEAN

In 1948, the Chief Education Officer in the Middle East reported that he now had 2000 children on roll, with every month seeing more and more families arriving in a Command, which encompassed the Canal Zone, Cyrenaica, Greece and Cyprus, Mauritius and Malta. Consequently, school rooms had been established on the top floor of the railway station at Benghazi, in private houses in Greece and Cyprus and in newly completed schools in the Canal Zone, with secondary schools at Fayid and Moascar. In East Africa, the Army had opened schools in Mombasa, Nanyuki and MacKinnon Road. One who enjoyed the life abroad was a Queen's Army Schoolmistress, who wrote,

'A couple of weeks ago I was posted from Palestine to El Ballah, which is just a tented camp in the Egyptian desert, but there are some compensations. The Camp is run by POWs and we have nothing to do for ourselves. They make our beds, 'do' our tents, clean our shoes. The food is quite good and inside the camp there is a cinema, two halls where they hold concerts and dances, 3 shops and a NAAFI'.[8]

Other families 'trooped' by air to West Africa, after documentation at the London Assembly Centre, deep under Tottenham Court Road in the former George Street air-raid shelter. First stop was Gibraltar, followed by a 12 hour flight across the Sahara Desert — a long haul, especially for children and mothers. West African Command was composed of Gambia, Sierra Leone, the Gold Coast and Nigeria, with military traditions stretching back to the 18th century, when British soldiers had garrisoned forts like Fort James on the Gambia river and military posts along the coast to protect the lucrative slave trade. In 1948 there were no European units in British West Africa, so the wives and children arriving there belonged to commissioned officers, Warrant Officers and Sergeants serving with the locally recruited West African Forces and were based, mostly in Bathurst (Gambia), Freetown (Sierra Leone), Accra, Kumasi and Takoradi (Gold Coast) and Lagos, Kaduna and Kano in Nigeria, places separated by hundreds of miles. West Africa had not been a 'family station' during the 19th century, when it had been regarded as 'The White Man's Grave'.

Because there had been few white women in Africa during the 19th century, concubinage was customary, as in India, with girls often provided by local chiefs, 'as a compliment to the Europeans', as the traveller William Smith[9] found in 1846.

> 'The beautiful proportions and exact symmetry of the girl provided for me was such that I was able to forget the complexion of my bedfellow and obey the dictates of all powerful nature. Greater pleasure I never found'. 'If any white man has a fancy to any of them', wrote another[10] 'and is willing to maintain them, they will make no scruple of living with him in the nature of a wife, without the ceremony of matrimony'.

Purchase a dusky helpmate unreproved, but a white man would 'lose caste, if he espoused even an educated negress'.

Life and conditions in Africa had been hard for wives before the First World War and an army wife wept, when she saw the first home prepared for her, wrote Harold Bindloss'.[11] It consisted of two rooms with mud walls and a small verandah. The child mortality rate was particularly high and health a problem.

> 'Where it is dry and free from malaria', he wrote 'you may see Englishmen thrive and grow bronzed, broad shouldered and wiry: but the wives and daughters almost invariably weaken and whither and drag out their lives in chronic listlessness'.[11]

In contrast, the modern army wife found European homes in Africa spacious and airy. Her main problems were to keep her servants up to the mark and dealing with the high cost of food and living. Although conditions and health had improved and tours were short and inter-tour leave invaluable, the education of the children was interrupted and doctors still advised parents not to keep young children in the Command after the age of nine years. Thus it was that, despite the greatly improved living conditions, many a soldier and his wife breathed a sigh of relief when Ghana gained her independence in 1957, Nigeria in 1960 and Sierra Leone in 1961.

FAR EAST

In 1948 the Chief Education Officer in the Far East was also reporting that his schools were 'overflowing, despite the bandit operations and terrorism in Malaya'. Because families were so scattered in Malaya, a secondary boarding school was established in the hill station known as the Cameron Highlands. Bren carriers had to be used to escort the locally based children to and from school. Writing home to a still austerity-based England of living conditions in Singapore, a Queen's Army Schoolmistress had this to say:

> 'The cost of living is high and most commodities are scarce but your eyes would pop out if you could see the amount of tinned food in the shops — all the Heinz 57 varieties and then some! I pay the cook 60 dollars a month and the amah 40 (1 dollar = 2 shillings and four pence)'.

Married accommodation, whether army owned or privately rented, was in such short supply and the family waiting lists so long that the Author converted the former Guard Room of the 15 inch gun battery at Changi into his first army married home. Built to protect the naval base, it had been blown up before Singapore had been surrendered to the Japanese. For this sub-standard but delightful quarter he paid the token rent of one dollar a month!

HOUSING PROBLEMS IN THE UNITED KINGDOM

Meanwhile, the families at Home were also facing considerable housing problems. To help to overcome the shortage of quarters, 19 military families camps were established around the country. Some consisted of wooden or Nissen huts, built during the War to house a greatly expanded army; others were requisitioned hotels with all modern conveniences.

The Army was very conscious of its housing shortages (and would be for many years to come). In stark contrast to its policies of the pre-World War II days, its long-term aim was to provide modern accommodation for every entitled Regular married soldier and his family. If only the Army had had a fixed number of garrisons, all static and permanent, its housing problems would not have been difficult to solve, even with the wartime back-log of building and modernisation and the post-war shortages of labour and materials! But with the Army's re-deployment and consequent loss of married accommodation in India, Burma and Palestine, the build-up of Malaya and Singapore and of the garrisons in the Middle East, with more married soldiers than ever before being stationed there, together with changes of unit locations at Home, the Army's problems were enormous. Furthermore, since the War, the official marriage age of officers had been lowered from 30 to 25 and that of men from 26 to 21, thereby greatly increasing the number of all ranks, eligible for married quarters. In 1949 the Army established a five-year programme aimed at providing about 10,000 quarters for married Regulars in the United Kingdom with extensive building and hiring programmes overseas, wherever the permanent size and location of the troops could be predicted with reasonable certainty.

An example of the Army's problems is well illustrated by the situation in Colchester, where 100 houses had been completed in the form of a well planned family village, some distance from the nearest barracks, to form a landscaped garden suburb of two and three bedroomed houses, each with sitting room, dining room and kitchen annexe, built-in cupboards, bathroom and toilet, with gas and electricity. In contrast, were the married quarters in the Cavalry Barracks, two miles away. Built 50 years earlier, their

'sloping eaves darkened the narrow windows of the upper floor homes, while a gaunt iron verandah, running the length of the block, overhangs the ground floor. Solidly built and snug, they, nevertheless, lack today's essential amenities. The living room is heated by a closed-in black kitchen range and a gaunt boiler in the kitchen provides the only hot water supply. The walls are of painted bare brick and the floor is bare concrete. There are no wash basins: the bath has to be filled with buckets from the boiler. The back windows look across a small patch of bare earth into the neighbour's kitchen.'[12] Such old-style married quarters for soldiers' families could still be found in many post-war barracks.

EGYPT

In 1951, Egypt's abrogation of the 1936 Treaty, led the Army authorities to reduce the number of families in the Canal Zone and to redeploy the remainder from their rented accommodation in the towns into War Department accommodation in the 'safe areas'. Children had been stoned in a school bus in Moascar and hooligans had burnt and looted the NAAFI shop in Ismailia.

The events in Egypt doubled the number of families in Cyprus and led to many wives being separated from their husbands. But the Army in Cyprus had had a housing problem even before the troops began to stream out of Egypt — a problem which it was hoped the rising cantonments of Dekhelia and Episkopi would solve.

The site of the new garrison at Dekhelia, some seven miles from Larnaca and 18 from Famagusta was begun in 1953. When completed it had barracks, married quarters, schools, clubs, churches, playing fields, cinemas, a hospital and a town centre with shops, a bank, post office and market, all within sight of the Mediterranean. Families could visit Paphos, where, according to tradition, the goddess Venus, wearing nothing but a few drops of salt water, rose from the waves to come ashore. Or they could wander round the 1500 year old ruins of Salamis, an important Greek and Roman settlement and port. Lying north of Famagusta, it is historically associated with Caesar and Cleopatra and with St Paul.

When Libya was granted her independence by the United Nations in 1951, she asked Britain to help her guard her 1000 mile Mediterranean coastline, as she had done since 1943, when the 8th Army captured the towns of Tobruk, Derna, Barce, Benghazi and Homs — all of which became post-war army family stations. In Benghazi, headquarters of Cyrenaica District, the Army built its first pre-fabricated aluminium hospital, made in the United Kingdom and shipped in wooden crates to be assembled by local labour. 100 new married quarters were also erected and another 130 at Tripoli.

MARITAL STATE OF THE ARMY 1950

No longer did the Army set out to discourage marriage, as it had done before the War; instead it sought to regulate it —

'he is only entitled to recognition as a married man and to allowances and other privileges as such, when he conforms to certain regulations'.[13]

An officer had to be 25 years of age and a man 21 to qualify for a marriage allowance and married quarters. To qualify for the marriage allowance, a soldier had to make a weekly allotment from his pay, whilst the size of the quarter depended on rank,[14] with allocation being made on a 'points scheme', weighted for rank, number of children, length of service and length of separation.

In 1951, there were about 18,500 Married Quarters in Britain, with most (8300) in Southern Command. About 2250 were officers' quarters. Additionally, there were hired quarters — 1200 for officers and 500 for Other Ranks, again mostly in Southern Command, where the bulk of the married families lived.

In 1950, statistics for the Army, which included National Service men, showed that 68% of the Regular Officers and 9% of the National Service officers were married, (Table IA at Appendix A) compared with 38% of the regular other ranks (Table IB) but, as would be expected, about 90%–96% of the senior ranks of both regular officers and Warrant Officers were married.

The high rates for Short Service Officers (82%) and Other Ranks (61%) should also be noted. (Appendices A & B). On the other hand, the married rates for regular subalterns (10%) and corporals and private soldiers (30% and 22% respectively) were comparatively low'.[15]

In 1953 one of the Army's major problems was the increasing 'wastage' of Regular NCOs leaving the Service. The two most often quoted reasons were lack of stability and shortage of married quarters, both factors affecting married men and most Regular NCOs were married. In the belief that the NCO's decision was largely influenced by his wife's desire for a contented and united married life, Headquarters British Army of the Rhine (BAOR) decided to ask the wives for their ideas on how to induce NCOs to stay in the Army. Prizes were offered and over 100 entries received.[16]

The winners, the Royal Engineers' Wives Club in Düsseldorf, raised eight major points — stability, housing, children's education, welfare, cost of living, pay, promotion and security on completion of service.

'Security is a basic feminine need. It is the threat to this natural instinct that makes Army life unattractive to wives. A husband may be posted at short notice to a place his wife cannot go. She faces eviction from her quarters and possible life in a hostel. Her children's schooling is interrupted. If she follows her husband she has to store her furniture or sell it at a loss and then buy afresh at her new home — and repeat the process in a year or two. A wife with a young child may be left to cope alone with the problems of packing, removal and documentation'.[16]

Suggestions for improvement were — the Army should provide storage facilities for family belongings in Britain: a return to the pre–1929 system when postings between home and overseas were on a reciprocal basis of family for family, single soldier for single soldier, with husband and wife travelling together and a guaranteed three year tour: build more quarters and return to the Married Quarters Roll, which ensured that, if the husband were posted to a family station anywhere in the world, he would occupy a married quarter (its drawback was the limited number on the Roll!): the provision of mobile caravan 'colonies', Army Building Loans and Savings schemes, secondary boarding schools at Home and guaranteed employment on a soldier's retirement.

Some of these suggestions were more idealistic than practical but others would be implemented by the Army. However, as we shall see, the problems would remain.

THE OFFICER AND HIS LADY

In 1946 a War Office directive stated that the Royal Military Academy, Sandhurst would open on 3rd June 1947 'as the chief means of training cadets for regular commissions in the Army'. Most commissions went to public schoolboys although, increasingly, places were offered to entrants from the State schools. Education, rather than land ownership, would dominate the officer structure, 'although the sun had yet to set on the English Gentleman', concluded Razzell[17] twenty years later.

With the decline in the aristocracy and the landed gentry and with the broadening of the officer corps through the widening of the range of school and university entrant, so too did the social structure of those women who married officers change and broaden. Class today is less significant than education: more important is general suitability to the family of the regiment and to the demands of Army life. Many officers continue to select their wives from within the Services, but amongst the ladies of the regiments and corps will be found a cross section of society, with the professional groups well represented.

Some officers' wives originate from the country, in which the husband has been stationed, for instance in Germany, but their numbers are not so significant as amongst the other ranks' wives, where in many regiments former foreign nationals may constitute a large proportion of the soldiers' and NCO messes.

WELFARE

During the Second World War, Commanding Officers had been largely relieved of their responsibility for handling the family welfare problems of the huge civilian army by specially appointed Army Welfare Officers. On 1st April 1947 they resumed their traditional role. SSAFA retained one senior full time representative in each major command overseas in a consultative capacity. Another change was brought about by the National Health Service Act of 1946, which provided a district nursing service in the United Kingdom, a service which included the care of young children, preventive medicine and home hygiene, duplicating the service provided by SSAFA for army families in quarters since 1895. The War Office asked SSAFA to continue to provide their Nursing Sisters overseas, where medical and dental care of soldiers' families remained an Army responsibility. Similarly, in 1948, after running its own schools for over 200 years, the Army handed over all its day schools (but not its boarding schools) in the United Kingdom to the Local Authority. Its Queen's Army Schoolmistresses, founded in 1840, were gradually replaced by United Kingdom based teachers on short-term contracts, supplemented by qualified local civilians and army wives, for its schools overseas.[18]

In 1956, in conjunction with the British Legion and 18 other organisations, SSAFA mounted a vigorous and successful campaign for the improvement of all forms of war pensions. Now, when an Other Rank's widow qualifies for a pension, after her husband has served for five years from the age of 48, she receives his three months' salary and half his pension. Officers' widows were similarly treated.

NAAFI

The changes in social habits and the greater general affluence created demands from the consumer, including the soldier and his family, for a wide range of commodities in shops and markets. NAAFI introduced a number of changes in its shops and trading practices to meet these demands. During the 1950s NAAFI introduced self-service shops, computerisation, coin-machine catering, canteens converted to social clubs, dividend stamps as an alternative to discounts, instalment credit and other measures.

As a contemporary NAAFI publication explained:

> 'The money NAAFI pays into unit and central funds has helped make possible welfare amenities for the soldier and his family, which the Services could not otherwise have provided — swimming pools, ski slopes, theatre and disco equipment, mini-buses, washing machines etc.'[19]
> 'Through its 400 family shops, its 400 clubs and canteens, its 270 Service shops and over 100 other trading establishments (mobile shops, canteens, petrol stations and sub post offices) families can now buy cars and caravans, houses and household goods under hire purchase or discount schemes, insure themselves and their property or order goods by Mail Order. NAAFI will cater for a children's party or a wedding banquet, book tickets for theatres and entertainments, provide a self drive car at the port of disembarkation or arrange flowers through Interflora to mark a birthday or family event'.[19]

NAAFI claimed to be highly competitive, at home or abroad, with prices that 'are rarely beaten'. With wives and children outnumbering the men, NAAFI had over the years increasingly given itself a new look orientated more towards the families and their needs.

NAAFI kept its shops overseas stocked with the latest fashions. Whilst some wives would slip over to Britain from BAOR on 'shopping sprees', most wives depended on these shops to keep their wardrobes up to date. Fashion shows were held at Rhine Army Headquarters in Rheindahlen and in the major garrison towns on social occasions, so that not only the wives but the teenagers and the Women's Services could sample the latest creations of the fashion houses.

Visiting British Forces Educational Service Schools in Germany, the Author once asked the Senior Mistress in one of the largest secondary schools about her problems with teenage girls. She said she had occasion to invite the mother of one of the schoolgirls to discuss the shortness of her daughter's mini-skirt, which even in the Mini era was causing raised eyebrows amongst the teaching staff. When the mother arrived, she found she had an even greater problem on her hands for the mother, wife of a senior officer in the Garrison, was wearing a skirt even shorter than her daughter's!

ENTERTAINMENT

The most popular forms of family entertainment, during and immediately after the War and especially overseas, were the cinema and radio (and later television). The Army Kinema Corporation (AKC) began in Nissen huts in 1946 but soon its 'Globe' cinemas were providing nine programme changes each fortnight for soldiers and their families all over the world, some cinemas having such exotic names as the 'Sampan' in Singapore or 'The Jerboa' in Berlin. Prices were cheap and this non-profit making organisation helped to support the Army Widows Fund, amongst other charities, with its 'profits' ploughed back into a variety of welfare projects. Bingo was never such a popular family attraction as at home, but television rentals were highly successful. In 1969 the Ministry of Defence ordered the amalgamation of the AKC with its RAF equivalent, in the interests of economy.

From the former headquarters of the AKC in London's Dover Street, the Combined Services Kinema Corporation controlled 155 cinemas, two ten-pin bowling alleys, a television rental service and a film library for smaller units in addition to a maintenance service for projectors and associated equipment. But the AKC will long be remembered by army families for providing many a happy evening's entertainment in its cinemas world-wide — in the open air in Aden, air-conditioned in Malaya and Singapore or centrally-heated in BAOR — or through a mobile unit in some remote location at Home.[20]

On New Year's Day 1944, the British Army opened its first broadcasting station in Algiers: from there it spread throughout the world, with the British Forces Broadcasting Service in the Middle East and British Forces Network (BFN) in Germany, before they were united in one system — the British Forces Broadcasting Service (BFBS) — with a central headquarters in London. The BBC provided parts of the programme, some was produced locally and some came from its London Headquarters in Dean Stanley Street. 'Woman's Hour', by popular request, retained a regular spot during the afternoons.

We have already noted the foundation of the Royal Military Asylum, in Chelsea in 1801, as a residental school for the orphaned sons of soldiers and its removal, as The Duke of York's Royal Military School, to its present site at Dover. Like its sister schools, the Hibernian in Dublin (closed in 1922) and the Queen Victoria School, Dunblane (opened in 1908 by King Edward VII as a memorial both to his mother and to the Scottish soldiers and sailors who died in the South African War) 'Dukies', as it is affectionately known, was originally intended for boys who would follow their fathers into the Army. Today, there is no such obligation, although many of the boys still do so, nor are they all orphaned — indeed, the school is now open to the sons of all army soldiers and officers. Former pupils may be found in all walks of life throughout the world.

The School still retains the best of its military traditions, such as its CCF activities and Sunday Church parades in uniform, its world famous military band and its annual Trooping the Colour ceremony, which the boys command themselves, carrying the Colours they were first awarded in 1825.

THE CHANGING SCENE — THE ADVENT OF AIR TROOPING

The movement of families by troopship had been a very familiar feature of army life, and a most enjoyable one in most cases, but by the middle of the 1950s it was no longer economical to run specialised ships for this purpose and, in any case, the age of air movement had arrived. Now that India had gained independence, the importance of the large and expensive garrison maintained in Egypt to secure the Imperial life-line had diminished. In 1955 the decision to evacuate the Canal Zone was announced and the trek towards Port Said began — an operation that involved the movement by road, air and sea of some 80,000 servicemen and women, 50,000 vehicles and more than half a million tons of stores. Wives continued to join their husbands until the final evacuation and the schools, clubs, cinemas, canteens and bathing beaches and other amenities provided for the soldiers and their families, many of whom were to find new homes in Malta and Cyprus, were retained until, the evacuation completed, there was only a trail of deserted camps to show where so many thousands had lived in a great military community.

At the same time as we were evacuating Egypt, 15,000 Servicemen and their families were being transported annually each way by air between Britain and Singapore. 20 aircraft a month, operated by a charter company, Airwork Limited, were used to cover the 8000 miles in 4 days, compared with the 22 to 30 days required by sea, and at less cost. The stops were Rome, Nicosia, Bahrein, Karachi, Delhi, Calcutta, Bangkok, Singapore and Hong Kong.

The wives going on to Hong Kong discussed their accommodation in the colony, where 700 army families lived in married quarters and had another 1000 on the waiting list, most in private accommodation. Some were going to live in Kowloon Tsai, an army colony on the outskirts of Kowloon, complete with eight-storey blocks of flats for 30 married officers and 118 men, a NAAFI shop and playgrounds within a few minutes' walk of St George's Secondary School, opened in 1955. Others were bound for Sek Kong Families' Village, six miles from the Chinese frontier, where 200 army families (with 300 children) lived in bungalows spread out over the Colony's largest peak, with views over the Bay to China. Sek Kong was a self-contained village with shops, church, club, hospital, primary schools and a cinema-theatre. A Committee, which included army wives, looked after the welfare of the villagers. The village had its own bus for taking fathers to work, children to school and for trips to the beaches and shopping in Kowloon and its own local newspaper to serve a total population of about 1300.[21]

RHEINDAHLEN

As this chapter has sought to show, the whole status of the soldier's family and its place in military garrisons overseas had changed to so marked a degree once the Second World War had ended that it is almost impossible to comprehend fully the sufferings and privations endured by military wives and their children even as late as the turn of the century. There have been many reasons for this but the chief of these must be the impact upon society of the social revolutions of two world wars and, later, the economic demands of young people reared in a climate of prosperity quite foreign to the families of whom we have read in earlier chapters. Perhaps these higher living standards are best exemplified in Rheindahlen in West Germany, for some forty years the site of the great international headquarters of NATO's Northern Army Group and of the British Army of the Rhine. Only a few miles from the town of Moenchen Gladbach, Rheindahlen was the first military town to be built in Germany and the task of construction took only 19 months from start to finish. In addition to the vast central headquarter block, with its 2000 rooms, housing British, German, American, Dutch and Belgian staffs and with the Headquarters of the Second Allied Tactical Air Force and RAF Germany alongside, there is a massive complex of married quarters and supporting amenities in what looks like a beautifully landscaped town. There are hostels for newly arrived families, over 40 German shops in addition to a rash of NAAFI shops and supermarkets, petrol stations, cinemas, a theatre, swimming baths and playing fields, a hospital, churches for many religious denominations, riding stables, cycle tracks and an internal bus service. What would Marlborough, who camped on this site with 19,000 soldiers on his way to Blenheim, have thought of all this or the soldiers of Julius Caesar's XIVth Legion, who lie buried beneath its foundations — symbols of an earlier occupation? More particularly, for it is with the army's womenfolk that this book is concerned, what would the women who accompanied Marlborough's regiments have thought as they watched their modern counterparts living a life of ease and luxury with every possible amenity available to them and with their children provided with first class primary and secondary education?

Families can cross the border into Holland to shop for fresh vegetables, journey down the Rhine to Heidelberg or the Black Forest or travel further afield to holiday in France, Italy or Spain. Truly, the Army could advertise amongst its many attractions 'Wonderful opportunities for family travel'.

LORD NUFFIELD

In 1957 the Army paid its tribute at a dinner at the Grosvenor Hotel in London to a man, who had done more for the welfare of the soldier and to promote the happiness of his family than any other individual in history. Lord Nuffield at the age of 80 had subsidised the Armed Services to the tune of some £2 million. From a Trust Fund established in 1939 by shares in his Morris Motors industry, Lord Nuffield had provided sports courts and equipment, 'radio and television sets, camping and stage equipment, swimming pools in Singapore and Gibraltar, Malaya, Aden and the United Kingdom, the Junior Officers' Club in Eaton Square and the United Services Club in Portsmouth — to name but a few. His wartime clubs and rest centres were to be found everywhere — from Iceland to Baghdad, Rangoon and Singapore. The best known was the Nuffield Centre near Piccadilly during World War Two, which incorporated the bombed Café de Paris next door, and which was removed to its present location, Gatti's Restaurant, in 1948. Where once officers of the Edwardian Army escorted their ladies and show girls to the Restaurant to dine and dance, the servicemen of the 1950s and their wives and girlfriends watched the stars of film, radio, stage and television in the Centre's theatre or danced there nightly, after a meal in the restaurant or a drink in the bar.

> 'Few soldiers and their wives and children, certainly those who served throughout World War Two and since, have not enjoyed hospitality, comfort, entertainment or recreation from the benefactions of Lord Nuffield, the motor millionaire',[22]

recorded *Soldier Magazine*, reporting the Army's appreciation and thanks.

TABLE IA   *Officers — The Marital State of the Army on 30 November 1950 was:*

		Regulars				Total officers*			
	Rank	Married	Single	Total	% Married	Married	Single	Total	% Married
1.	Lt Gen & above	24	1	25	96.0	25	1	26	96.2
2.	Major General	103	12	115	89.6	104	12	116	89.7
3.	Brigadier	382	25	407	93.8	385	25	410	93.9
4.	Colonel	456	59	515	88.5	472	60	532	88.7
5.	Lt Colonel	1,733	209	1942	89.2	1,892	224	2,116	89.4
6.	Major	4,433	935	5,368	82.5	6,245	1,121	7,366	84.8
7.	Captain	2,838	1,643	4,481	63.3	8,245	2,736	10,981	75.1
8.	Subaltern	282	2,506	2,788	10.1	1,252	6,492	7,744	16.2
QM Class 9.	Lt Col & above	110	—	110	100	119	1	120	99.2
10.	Major	785	21	806	97.4	1,196	38	1,234	96.9
11.	Captain	368	14	382	96.3	1,269	66	1,335	95.1
12.	Subaltern	38	1	39	97.4	187	13	200	93.5
	Total	11,552	5,426	16,978	68.0	21,391	10,789	32,180	66.5

* Married includes widowed or divorced. Total includes Short Service, XR, National Service & Others.
Source: War Office AG Statistics 1950.

TABLE IA   *Officers – Non Regular (continued)*

	Married	Single	Total	% Married
Short Service	9,172	2,041	11,213	81.8
X.R.	170	16	186	91.4
NSM	302	3,095	3,397	8.9
Others	195	211	406	48.0

TABLE IB   *Other Ranks*

	Regulars				Total Other Ranks			
Rank	Married	Single	Total	% M	Married	Single	Total	% M
1 WO1	3,182	371	3553	89.5	3,416	395	3,811	89.6
2 WO11	6,346	1,026	7,372	86.0	6,869	1,159	8,028	85.6
3 S/Sgt	5,064	1,315	6,379	79.2	5,857	1,552	7,409	79.0
4 Sergeant	11,500	6,138	17,683	65.2	14.982	8,995	23,977	62.5
5 Corporal	8,578	11,675	20,253	42.4	11,673	16,600	28,273	41.3
6 L/Cpl	3,948	9,354	13,302	29.7	5,461	21,819	27,280	20.0
7 Private	16,377	57,582	75,959	22.1	24,264	231,255	255,519	9.5
8 Boy	1	3,802	3,803	–	1	3,802	3,803	–
Total	54,996	91,263	146,259	37.6	72,523	285,577	358,100	20.2

TABLE IB

Non-Regulars (continued)

	Married	Single	Total (M&S)	% Married
Short Service	13,570	8,801	22,371	60.7
N.S.M.	3,957	185,513	189,470	2.1

Source: War Office AG Statistics 1950.

Chapter 16

The Swinging Sixties

THE PERMISSIVE SOCIETY

The 1960s will be remembered by historians as the years of social change, when a permissive society, led by the young, revolted against established traditions and authority. Many of the Victorian attitudes to women and marriage were transformed and a greater equality of the sexes and of the social classes was gained. The grounds for divorce were made more 'realistic', abortions were permitted and 18 year olds obtained the vote. Hair crept down to the shoulder, skirts crept up the leg and everyone wanted to be young. Mary Quant replaced Christian Dior as the arbiter of fashion and Carnaby Street 'gear' was sold by 'dolly' assistants to the affluent young of a classless society. In 1966 came the mini-skirt, which forced the Chancellor of the Exchequer to change the purchase tax regulations to prevent older women buying the tax-free garments meant for 14 year olds, and 'Swinging London' was advertised by United States tourist agencies as the centre of the cult of youth. Neil Armstrong made his 'great leap for mankind' on the moon and the Russians launched the first woman into space. The Beatles and the Rolling Stones topped the Pop Charts, Sean Connery played James Bond and television replaced the cinema in popular entertainment. On stage 'Oh! Calcutta' banished the Censor and 'Hair' set new standards of public nudity. The Mods fought the Rockers and both fought the London Bobby, as crime rates and vandalism soared. Women burnt their 'bras' and went on the 'pill': women 'libbers' interrupted Miss World contests and even the Bunny Girls went on strike. The 'topless' waitress made a brief appearance, before being chased away by the law, only to reappear on Page 3 of *The Sun* newspaper.

CHANGES IN THE ARMY

These, and other, pressures would be felt within the Army and on the soldier's family. At the end of the decade in 1969, the Northern Ireland Riots created unpopular tours of duty for the soldier and even more unpopular unaccompanied tours for his family. But the 'Sixties', for the families and for the Army generally, were years of expansion and consolidation, after the ending of National Service. There were new programmes for the building of married quarters, the remodelling of barracks, the extension and provision of garrison shopping and recreational facilities at home and abroad. These links between family welfare and a contented wife, with recruitment and re-engagement success rates, were reinforced by the Army — and the married officer and soldier were to enjoy increased pay and allowances. Above all, despite the loss of India and other garrisons in the Commonwealth, there was still the possibility of overseas' postings and of world-wide travel for the soldier, his wife and children.

A ROYAL ARMY WEDDING
The decade was to have for the Army a romantic beginning, when a Royal Prince and serving Army officer married the daughter of a Colonel of The Green Howards, who traces her ancestry back to Oliver Cromwell. *The Times* of 9th June 1963 reported:

'Yesterday, the sun shone and the bells of York Minister rang out as HRH The Duke of Kent married Miss Katherine Worsley.
To the triumphant notes of the toccata from Widor's Fifth Symphony, the newly married couple left the church through a guard of honour provided by the Duke's regiment, The Royal Scots Greys. It was the first Royal wedding the Minster had seen for 633 years'.

A NEW DEAL FOR MARRIED FAMILIES

The Army's 'New Deal for the Sixties' was announced by a committee under Sir James Grigg, a former War Minister, which examined *'the factors bearing on the willingness of men and women to serve in the Armed Forces . . . . . in an effort to make the Service more attractive than ever before to all ranks and their families'.*[1] Pay and soldiers' and family pensions would be raised, and automatically reviewed at least once every two years, beginning on 1st April 1960. There would be increased rates of disturbance and education allowances. There would be greater opportunities for promotion within the ranks and to commissioned rank; Officer recruitment would be widened and officers would be offered the choice of early retirement around 40 or of continued service to age 60. Unnecessary parades, including pay parades, would be abolished.

The Committee and Parliament were greatly concerned at the continuing shortage of married quarters for the increasingly married Regular Army. Secretary of State for War, John Profumo MP was able to announce, on the eve of SSAFA's 75th Anniversary of its Foundation;[2]

'The Army has now a new building programme, the greatest programme of the kind we have ever undertaken, and its emphasis is very largely on married quarters'.

True to its promises, in 1961 the Army started to rebuilt completely, and for the third time, the military town of Aldershot, a community of 20,000 people. Down came the old barracks and the grim Victorian terraced married quarters, to be replaced by new, architect designed and planned, married estates, complete with shops and playing areas for the children — all located in the central town area for the convenience of the families. The Louise Margaret maternity hospital was provided for army wives and Service women.

Similar 'face lifts' were given to other well-known Army Garrisons — Chester, York, Colchester and Catterick. In London new barracks were built at Chelsea for the Foot Guards and at Knightsbridge for the Household Cavalry. On Salisbury Plain barracks and married quarters were modernised or built at Bulford, Tidworth and Warminister. The REME Barracks at Arborfield was modernised, the old stables of 1914–18 vintage were pulled down and the married quarters area was rebuilt.

Gibraltar, too, received a major redevelopment in a 10 year programme, designed to move the garrison from its former old and scattered buildings in the city to a new military town to be erected at Europa Point on the southern tip of the Rock. There would be built a Fortress Headquarters, barracks, stores, messes, clubs and a cinema. There would be blocks of high rise flats for junior ranks and houses for the senior NCOs and officers on Buena Vista plateau. 'Bleak house' built in 1828 as a fever hospital for officers became Gibraltar's Army Education Centre and home for its annual Drama Festival. There was a new Primary School overlooking the Mediterranean, with marvellous views across the Bay to Spain.

The Times[3] reported in 1962 that the Army in BAOR was facing a serious housing shortage, 'which is going to mar Christmas for many British Service families'. An estimated 4000–5000 families lacked army accommodation.

The families of 58 officers and 2265 other ranks were waiting in the United Kingdom to join their families in BAOR and 50 officers' families and 2572 other rank families were living in German privately rented accommodation, hotels or hostels. To help to reunite families, 200 family caravans had been bought, others hired and more were being arranged. Parliament promised that by 1964 some 20,000 married families would be provided for by the Army at home and abroad.[4]

MARRIAGE AND THE MILITARY SALARY

At this time, too, Parliamentary Questions were being raised about the Army's restriction on marriage for its young officers to the age of 25 — a concept now out of keeping with the increasing national tendency for earlier marriage:

> 'Officers ought to be entitled to Family Allowances at age 23 at least' argued *The Times.*[5] We give them responsibility for handling expensive RAF fighter planes and Army Centurion tanks at that age. Surely we can trust them to handle a wife'.

In April 1970 the Army introduced the most radical reform of its pay system in its long history — the Military Salary. This measure, which abolished

Marriage Allowance, meant that all men, whether married or single, would now receive the same rates of pay and allowances, the rents charged for soldiers' married quarters would be based upon council house rents with an additional charge for the provision of furniture, maintenance and rates; officers' charges would be on a pro rata scale based upon the size of the quarter, as determined by the size of the family and not by the rate of pay or the rank of the individual. Pay was to be equated to comparable civilian rates with an added factor — known as the 'X' Factor — to reflect the special conditions and hazards of Service life. For the first time, the soldier in barracks would make a contribution towards his bed and board. The entitlement of Field Officers (ie: those of the rank of Major and above) to batmen in married quarters was abolished except for Lieutenant Colonels and above in command.[6] The Separation Allowance of four shillings a day, which had been introduced in 1966 for officers and men separated from their families by duty outside the United Kingdom for periods of over twelve months, was retained. All married men would now be entitled to married quarters but priority for allocation of quarters in areas where there was a shortage would be on a points basis, weighted by rank, age, length of separation, length of service, number of children and other factors. The concept behind all this was an attempt to equate army conditions of service, in so far as the special circumstances of the soldier's life would allow, with those of the soldier's civil counterpart. That so dramatic a change was felt to be necessary reflects the care with which the Army Board at that time was considering those factors which most affected the problems not only of recruiting good young men for what had now become a highly professional all Regular Army — but of keeping them in an army that was becoming increasingly heavily married. Furthermore, as the national standard of living had improved and the growing influence of the media was increasing the expectations of the average citizen, the Board recognised the importance of catering for these new circumstances, if the soldier and his family were to feel that the Army was offering them an attractive way of life and recognising their family needs. A further factor was the concern felt in some political quarters that there was a danger of the Services becoming too divorced from the rest of society and this attempt to equate pay and conditions with those prevailing outside the Services was one measure designed to help break down the barriers. Once again, one is driven to reflect what an almost unbelievable change had been effected in the lot of Judy O'Grady since the turn of the century — and indeed, in that of the Colonel's Lady, now living in very much more democratic circumstances than even in 1939.

Some indication of the impact of the increase in military families to be found in overseas garrisons, even before the advent of the Military Salary, can be seen in a comparison of the numbers in army schools overseas in 1956 and 1966.

	1956	1966
BAOR	13,267	25,676
Far East	6,031	16,739
Middle East	3,196	6,994
Elsewhere	1,738	3,631
Totals	24,232	53,040[7]

THE PERFECT ARMY WIFE

One army wife published an article in *Soldier Magazine*[8] on the sort of wife that was needed to cope with the modern Army — and a military husband!

'It is my firm belief that all girls should go on a course before marrying soldiers. Most of them have the mistaken idea that life in married quarters will be just a continuation of life under mother's roof, only in a different part of the world. They need to enter this new adventure with an open mind and be ready to start life afresh. I have been in quarters a good many years and seen happy newly-weds turn into disillusioned 'naggers', merely because the wife could not, or would not, adapt herself to new conditions'.

The first hard lesson to be learnt by a Service wife was that she took second place in her husband's life. 'The Army is his first love and his ever-demanding mistress'.

So heavy will be his duties at times that she will plead with him to return to 'Civvy Street'. But when she watches him take part in a large parade, pride for her man, and something of his pride for the regiment, will touch her woman's heart.

She will need to be a good actress and disguise her real feelings. When schemes or courses drag him away, she must be totally self reliant, 'ready to cope alone with the children, sudden illness and the pay that doesn't arrive, especially in a foreign country'.

The third essential was to be a versatile housekeeper. A wife should not be dismayed by houses that were far too large or far too small. Married quarters went from one extreme to another. One day it might be paraffin stoves and straw mattresses, tomorrow an electric cooker, a refrigerator and a maid.

'And keep the spring-cleaning till the manoeuvres start — it's a good antidote for loneliness. Each house will have the same styles of furniture and curtains — but what a difference a good wife can make with her own 'bits and pieces'.

Among other things, a soldier's wife had to be a good mixer and willing to join in the social life of the camp. Her neighbours would come from all walks of life — different classes, different creeds, different colours: some amusing, some irritating, 'like those who try to wear their husband's rank'.

'Travelling? — Yes! About the only thing I haven't travelled in is a tank and it would never surprise me, if one pulled up at the door.' Every soldier's bride should know that abroad there might be little or no local transport, so every regiment provided a taxi-service to all the necessary places. 'You have to take lessons in how to be ladylike, while clambering in and out of an army truck in a tight skirt.

'She must also be an adventurous wife — ready at a moments' notice to start a new life in a different place' — Berlin, for example.

FAMILY LIFE IN GERMANY

Berlin is a very popular station, despite its being an island in the middle of the Russian Zone, 100 miles from the West German border. The 3000 British troops in the central sector (French in the North and Americans in the South) either live in the former German Barracks in Spandau or in the Montgomery Barracks, close to the Berlin Wall, as The Queen's Regiment did in 1970. The Author's daughter, Jacqueline, and her husband Captain Michael Jarratt, lived in a married quarter in the Barracks and from their bedroom window they could see the East German Guards surveying with their binoculars the 'Death Strip' dividing the two nations. The wives of The Queen's Regiment ran their clubs, library and playgroups, visited the opera and restaurants in East Berlin or shopped in the famous Kurfürstendamm, Berlin's equivalent of London's Oxford Street.

In 1962 Edinburgh House was opened as a 100-bed non-profit making hotel, to become known to thousands of married Service families, who were lucky enough to spend a leave or duty 'visit' in it.

Connecting Berlin with the Western Zone are links by road and rail. Every morning the Army's military train would set off punctually at 8 a m from Charlottenburg Station on its 145 mile return journey through East Germany to Brunswick — a 4 hour daily journey it had made since 17 December 1945. Strict security was maintained by the Duty Officer commanding the train, accompanied by his Warrant Officer and a Russian speaker from the Berlin interpreters' pool. Door handles were wedged inside and passengers were forbidden to leave the train in transit or to use cameras or binoculars during the journey. Once in the British Zone, such restrictions were lifted and the Serviceman and his family could once again live and travel freely in a land, which was home to many. But, despite determined efforts by the Authorities and by regiments to make the wives, especially, feel at home in Germany, many army garrisons still appear as isolated communities in a foreign land, separated by language and social customs, as indeed do many of the American Air Force bases in Britain. Young wives, often away from home for the first time, especially if they have young children to look after, find life is often inward looking and bound by the perimeter of the Army camp or married 'patch'. The Army tries hard to encourage families to mix with their German neighbours on social occasions; Anglo-German societies exist and language classes flourish in most garrisons.[9] There are skiing trips, sailing expeditions, buses to local shops, school visits, extensive holiday opportunities and many families, especially those of officers and senior NCOs, take full advantage of these and other cultural and recreational facilities.

FAMILY ENTERTAINMENT

One of the greatest boons to the military families in BAOR, and especially to young wives with children or separated from their husbands by official duties, was the introduction of the English television service in the early 1970s. At peak viewing periods, it has been estimated that the programmes are watched by audiences of 80% of the British military population — thus reducing boredom, loneliness and welfare problems and raising morale.

Also popular are the live variety shows provided by the Combined Services Entertainment (CSE), which took over from ENSA in 1946. CSE sponsors some 54 shows and 500 artistes a year in BAOR, Gibraltar and Cyprus and these are especially welcomed in 'unaccompanied' stations, such as Northern Ireland and Belize (and later in the Falklands). From 1966 the Head of the Service was Derek Agutter, father of actress Jenny, who held its auditions (at which only about 10% made the grade) in the King's Buildings in Dean Stanley Street.

'They have to have youth (anybody over 25 is a geriatric): a good voice and figure and, most essential, the ability to socialise in the various clubs and messes after the shows. Some acts we audition would not be suitable for family shows. Swinging breasts and high-kicking girls may not go down well in Cyprus or BAOR but are fine for unaccompanied troops in Belize, N. Ireland (or the Falklands)', he told *Soldier Magazine*.[10]

THE 1970s — THE ARMY AND ITS FAMILIES IN A CHANGING WORLD

1970 was to be a year of particular significance for the soldier and his family for the decision of the British Government to withdraw its garrisons from East of Suez and to concentrate its defence resources upon its priority role of support for the North Atlantic Alliance, taken in 1968, began to take effect. Indeed, within a very few years, the Army had withdrawn either into the Strategic Reserve and the Home Army or into BAOR, leaving only a very few garrisons overseas of which the largest was Hong Kong, though even that was small when compared with the huge deployments in the Far and Middle East Commands of previous years. This new situation marked, of course, the end of all those glamorous overseas postings which had brought so much colour to Army family life, enabling Judy and her children to live in a style and in surroundings which would otherwise have been completely beyond her experience.

SINGAPORE

The disbandment of the Far East Command and the closure of the huge base in Singapore in 1971 meant the loss of what was, perhaps, the most glamorous of overseas postings for the Army family. The post-war Island with its native kampongs, its colonial-type bungalows, each with tennis court and gardens, its single lane traffic in Orchard Road, with its trishas and British-made cars, had been transformed out of all recognition. Today, it is an independent modern city-state with a population of two million and the fifth largest harbour in the world. The Raffles Hotel of Somerset Maughan and Rudyard Kipling was still there, much as they had known it, but now lost among the huge modern hotels and high rise apartments, commercial houses and dual carriageways of this prosperous multi-racial, multi-religious, multi-lingual city, in which Chinese, Malays, Indians and Europeans, live and work together and inter-marry in harmony.

The Army had changed too. In 1947, Singapore and Malaya had replaced India as the major British bases in the Far East. Singapore's naval dockyards and the RAF's airfields at Changi and Seletar had become huge operational stations with wonderful accommodation and amenities for their Servicemen and families. The Army had increased its numbers and facilities, its workshops and depots, so that Singapore had become the largest garrison for troops and the principal home for Service families outside the United Kingdom and Germany. Most of the Army's new barracks, workshops, depots, married quarters, schools, swimming pools and playing fields were located in 2600 acres of former old rubber plantations in the Pasir Panjang and Alexandra areas, near the prewar Military Hospital and Gillman Barracks, scenes of the heroic last stand of the British troops against the Japanese. Here was the beautifully designed and spacious St John's Secondary School, which the Author handed over as the Singapore International School, incorporating the Atlantic College of SE Asia, for 1250 boys and girls of 47 nationalities, with teachers from a dozen countries. Here, too, were the Slim Barracks, home of the Gurkhas and their families, which he had seen completed in 1949. Since then 4000 babies had been born there, some of whom had grown up and returned as young soldiers in their fathers' regiment.

The last Family Guide to be published[11] gave the following advice on conditions in Singapore — very different from 1948! 'When you are posted to Singapore, you are, in fact, being posted to a foreign country. You are there as guests and have no privileged position. You are subject to the law of the land; your wife and children will need identity cards of the Singapore Government; you will need driving licences and will queue like everybody else. You must be careful to respect the religious customs and habits of the Singaporeans.

You will be booked into an army hostel ('The Gap' for officer families: 'The Savoy' for soldiers and their dependants), with a stay of a maximum of a month, whilst you get adjusted, organised and accommodated in your official army house, flat or hiring or private accommodation'.

The booklet contained valuable advice for the ladies on clothing ('Stockings are not worn, except on the most formal occasions') and on shopping ('Housewives have a wide choice of Eastern and Western foods: NAAFI and nearly all shops deliver and accept orders by 'phone').

But no guidebook can convey the true magic of this exciting and colourful city, where East and West meet on equal terms and almost half the population is under 15 years of age. Tourists crowd its many luxurious air-conditioned hotels and join the local residents in their open-air swimming pools, enjoy their Russian, French and Italian cuisines or Malay, Indonesian, Indian or Chinese menus, sip cocktails or iced drinks in Hotel Bars or Expresso cafes, served by uniformed waiters and waitresses or Eastern-type bar-girls, and dine and dance in their night clubs and discotheques. But the real atmosphere of Singapore can be found in the bustle and colour, the sounds and smells of its streets and markets and amongst the tax-free imports and native goods of its stalls, shops and departmental stores. Wives — and husbands — can wander from early morning till late at night amid a babble of language and colourful costume in Raffles Place, Collyer Quay, Change Alley, Arab Street and Chinatown, admiring Japanese cameras, Chinese carpets, Thai silks, Indian saris, jewels from Burma and Ceylon, textiles from America, French perfumes, Balinese carvings, antiques from Communist China and crocodile-skin handbags and shoes from local farms. There is nothing that Singapore does not sell, at prices lower than almost anywhere else in the world, and bargaining is an acknowledged sport as well as an art. The House of Tang in Orchard Road was a shopping paradise with its exquisite ivory, jade, silver and glassware, its embroidered linen and carved teak and rosewood furniture and camphorwood chests. Not to be despised were the Chinese emporiums, exclusively selling from Communist China everything from *objets d'art* to the proverbial kitchen sink or the 'Night Bazaars' unique to Singapore, where street hawkers set up their stalls from 6–10 p m each night in a different district or in front of a different hotel. Here you would enjoy your 'bargain' at half the asking price — only to discover you could have got it cheaper still on the next stall!

Raffles Hotel had changed. In 1970, couples of all nationalities dined and danced, attired in anything from evening gowns, cocktail dresses, trouser suits to Indian saris or Chinese 'thigh revealing' cheongsams, contrasting sharply with the Author and his wife's first visit to Raffles in 1949, when formal evening dress was still obligatory and social barriers predominated. Then, because of the Army's shortage of accommodation, a number of officers and their wives rented rooms in the Hotel, whose management increasingly encouraged Service personnel to patronise its dinner dances and fashion shows, with special concessions on certain occasions. The Tanglin was still an exclusive Club for Europeans, although most officers and their wives were members of the Singapore Swimming Club, and dined and danced at the Cockpit or the Sea View. In 1970, the Cockpit still flourished, the Singapore

Swimming and Tanglin Clubs remained, shorn of their exclusiveness, perhaps overshadowed now by such exotic 'night spots' as the Tropicana, Gino's. Marco Polo or The Orchid Lantern — to name but a few!'

ANOTHER ROYAL WEDDING

But 1974 had a happier memory for the Army, when a Princess married a serving Army officer. 900 Servicemen lined the processional route from Buckingham Palace to Westminster Abbey, where HRH Princess Anne married Captain Mark Phillips, with a Sovereign's Escort of the Household Cavalry escorting the Queen's carriage. Outside the Abbey's Great West Door stood men of the 14/20th King's Hussars and the Worcestershire and Sherwood Foresters Regiment (in which the Author had served during the War), paying their tribute to their Colonel-in-Chief, Princess Anne, and the bridegroom's regiment, 1st The Queen's Dragoon Guards, stationed in Hohne, Germany. But for one couple at least, the royal wedding was not the most important occasion of the day. A Corporal stationed at Soltau married, on the same day, an army teacher from the nearby Gloucester Secondary School at Hohne. Not for nothing is the Army worldwide called 'one family'.[12]

Chapter 17

Judy Comes of Age

In 1975 SSAFA, conscious of the marital and social revolution which had taken place since the Second World War and which was evident in its voluntary work with Army families, devoted much of its Annual General Meeting to 'Marriage and the changing Pattern of Family Life'. O R McGregor, Professor of Social Institutions at the University of London described these changes to the Conference —

'For the first time since the early 19th Century, women have acquired an equal opportunity to marry. In the marriageable age groups there are now rather more men than women and marriage has become universal. Despite the large number of divorces, between two thirds and three quarters of all broken marriages are remade with new partners. There has been a striking fall in the age of marriage. 50 years ago, about 6% of the girls and 1% of the boys married in their teens. Today one-third of girls and 16% of boys marry before the age of 20.

Today, about 85% of all children are born within the first eight years of their parents' marriage. In 1870 women, who married, often had ten children or more. Large families are now the exception but the proportion of childless families has also fallen. About 10% of all marriages with dependent children are single parent families. The Army does not recognise common law wives (although SSAFA does).

Women now constitute about 40% of the labour force. In the 1930's only 10% of all women workers were married. They left school earlier, went out to work and married later: but when they married, they ceased to work and retired into marriage and motherhood. Today over 60% of all women workers are married and the proportion will continue to rise.

There has been a legal revolution in handling broken marriages. The whole of our inherited Canon Law was abolished in 1969, when the Divorce Reform Act redefined the grounds for divorce in terms of the breakdown of marriage, rather than being necessarily the fault of husband or wife. The following year the Matrimonial Proceedings and Property Act gave discretion to the courts as to how they divide up the property relating to marriage. In 1967 the Matrimonial Homes Act gave wives some protection from being evicted from their homes on the breakdown of marriage, while the Guardianship of Minors Act finally gave women equal rights with men as to custody of children, access to them, etc.'

Thus, concluded Professor McGregor —

'I do not see any evidence whatsoever of a crumbling of family life. On the contrary, people are rushing into marriage, often too young and perhaps in too large numbers. Despite the improvements in the legal and social status of women, welfare and social workers are still very much needed, perhaps even more so.'

Mrs Marjorie Proops, the *Daily Mirror* colomnist, said she did not have the same optimistic view of marriage as an institution. She dealt with 40,000–50,000 problems in her columns every year, the majority of which were related to the breakdown of the marriage, and the disintegration of the family. The changing role of women, with their economic, social and employment stresses and their changing attitudes were the principal causes of the breakdown of marriage.

'The more independent women become, the more problems will be created in marriage'.

Mr Philip Goodhart, MP said that many of these changes, trends and problems were relevant to Service life, which was dominated by more separations and turbulence than in normal families, and these were the root causes of most marital breakdowns. Ten years later, when the divorce rate had climbed to one in three marriages, the Marriage Guidance Council [1] would put the Army in a high risk category, second only to the 'caring professions' — doctors, dentists, social workers and clergy!

Parliament and the Army Authorities, also aware of the special problems of Service life and its effect on the family, set up a Committee, [2] (called the Spencer Committee after its Chairman Professor John Spencer, Professor of Social Administration at Edinburgh University) *'to look at the Army's provision for the welfare of its soldiers and families, in relation to the services provided by the local authorities, and to make recommendations for preventing or lessening their social and domestic difficulties'.* As we have seen, the welfare State now looks after its citizens in health, education, housing and employment, assisted by local councils and their social services, and these benefits were available in some measure for the soldier's family in Britain. But overseas, much of this help was lacking, leaving the Army to supplement its medical, educational and welfare services from regimental and voluntary sources. Furthermore, the Army had special problems of its own, caused by its terms and conditions of service and the calls of duty, such as Northern Ireland, which made difficulties for the separated wife and children.

MARRIED FAMILIES — NUMBERS AND LOCATIONS

First, the Spencer Committee noted that the Army consisted of 18,500 officers and 153,000 other ranks (including 900 officers and 4900 OR's in the women's corps), while its dependants numbered 92,000 wives and 156,000 children. Therefore, the dependants far outnumbered the men. 60% of the Army was stationed at home, chiefly in the four major garrisons at Aldershot, Bulford/Tidworth, Colchester and Catterick but the families were widely scattered over the whole of the United Kingdom. For example, the four major garrisons contained less than one third of the 43,000 married quarters in the United Kingdom with over 160 different towns containing 20 or more married quarters.

Although its terms of reference were for the United Kingdom only, the Committee visited BAOR, where 30% of the Army was stationed, with the remaining 10% scattered over the rest of the world. It was alarmed to find 981 teenage wives and mothers in BAOR, many of whose husbands spent long periods in Northern Ireland on unaccompanied tours,—

> 'vulnerable young families, living in a strange land, many of them in high rise flats at some distance from their unit locations and often without the head of the family, and too few social workers operating without the back-up services available from the local authorities in the United Kingdom'.[3]

The National trend towards early marriage was reflected in the Army. Before the introduction, in 1970, of a 'military salary', which made pay the same for the single and married soldier (see page 213), there had been some discouragements to early marriage in the Army. For example, marriage allowance was not provided below the age of 21 for other ranks and 25 for officers. Since 1970, such disincentives had been swept away. Married quarters had become more readily available, with the result that *there was now a marked increase in the number and youth of married soldiers*. Between 1969 and 1974, for example, the percentage of married soldiers rose from 52.6% to 57.8%, despite a 3% fall in the strength of the Army. The proportion of junior ranks married at the ages of 19 and 20 almost doubled.[4]

THE MARRIED STATE OF THE ARMY 1975

The statistics produced for the Spencer Committee (extracts at Appendix A to this chapter) gave valuable information on the married state of the Army in the mid-1970s. They confirmed the trends towards earlier marriage and younger wives amongst both officers and other ranks and showed that, compared with pre-World War II figures, a greater proportion of the Army was married, especially in the Infantry (Table 2). Over 90% of all marriages had taken place *after* the husband had joined the Army. The Committee also found that families with small children now predominated (two-thirds of junior married men had a child under five) and that the average size of a soldier's family was roughly comparable with the figure for the civilian population. However, the proportion of officers with three or more children was significantly higher.[4]

ARMY SEPARATION

The Spencer Committee found that turbulence and separation were the two worst problems affecting Army families, caused by individual and regimental postings, emergencies like Northern Ireland, Belize or Cyprus with their 'unaccompanied tours' and constant training commitments or courses. The average stay in any one station for all ranks was about two years, while the turn-over of married quarters (MQs) in garrison towns was very high, resulting in a very large number of virtually one parent families in them. For example, in Colchester, with some 2000 quarters, there was on average, 3300 changes of occupancy each year. In September 1974 there were 915 wives in them without their husbands.

FAMILY SUPPORT

The Committee praised the Army's traditional system of regimental care and responsibility for the family.

> 'It had served the Army well: in a simpler age it provided an excellent standard of support and even now it exhibits an excellent degree of concern'.[5]

Support for the families started with the regiment, in which officers' wives, led by the Commanding Officer's wife, arranged visits to individual families, clubs for mutual help and playgroups for pre-school aged children. The Chaplain and doctor assisted the families with marriage and medical problems, comforted the sick and bereaved, gave hospital cover overseas but also provided assistance at Home in garrison towns and for families in isolated units.

But the idea of regimental welfare was conceived in the days when soldiers were single and recruited from the ranks of the poor and the unemployed and were fed, clothed and nurtured by the regiment. As the number of married men increased, the concept changed but

> 'it is still a system designed for soldiers and not for the wider needs of families, even with the help of housing commandants and unit families' officers'.[5]

VOLUNTARY AGENCIES

A wide range of voluntary agencies was also available to help in the field of family welfare and community care. The Women's Royal Voluntary Service (which supplied welfare officers both at home and overseas), the Council for Voluntary Welfare Work (a confederation of voluntary religious organisations) and the Youth Services all played important roles as did SSAFA (whose nurses will long be remembered with gratitude by many young mothers). In addition there were substantial non-public funds to provide financial and amenity back-up (eg: The Army Benevolent Fund, the Army Central Fund, the Nuffield Trust in addition to the private funds of Corps and Regiments). In the United Kingdom, the soldier's family could make use of the Social, Educational, Health, Housing and Medical Services and the Employment agencies. In addition they could call upon such organisations as the Samaritans, the Marriage Guidance Council, Citizens' Advice Bureaux and Family Planning clinics. The problem which so often faced the young soldier's family was which of these organisations could best meet their problem and often to decide what exactly was the nature of their problem — money, anxiety, boredom, frustration, loneliness etc.?

MARITAL PROBLEMS

To help to identify and quantify the problems, the Committee carried out a number of surveys, based on questionnaires and personal interviews. They discovered that the young married soldier found life in the Army less satisfactory than did the single and older married soldier, chiefly on account of levels of pay and because of the enforced separations and ensuing loneliness. All enjoyed the travel, the trade and training facilities and the comradeship, but the wife's attitude and expectations played a major role in the young husband's priorities and perspectives. On the other hand, for those contemplating marriage, married quarters was the strongest incentive and the prospect of separation the worst aspect of army life facing the girl-friend. The support and help of parents, both of soldier and wife, were also important factors, especially in providing temporary accommodation and assistance over births. But less than half the parents were within easy travelling distance, so free travel warrants and compassionate leave were important aids to married families. Concern over their children's education worried many wives — especially those of senior officers. Young wives found they could not obtain employment because of their mobility and the isolation of army camps. Many had worked before marriage in offices and factories but now had to take catering or cleaning jobs, often connected with the Army. They looked for a second income to support their families and resented the fact that only menial jobs were available, especially overseas.

Top of the list of marital problems, certainly in the absence of their husbands, were isolation and loneliness, with the attendant feelings of depression, restrictions of social life and boredom.

'I get depressed: worry myself into illness: lost 2 stone in weight: I never go anywhere: just stay in and worry if he's all right'.[6] 'All the evidence suggests that matrimonial and family problems, especially loneliness, form the largest matter of concern for the Army today', noted the Committee.[7]

MARRIED QUARTERS

One of the Army's major problems, as we have seen over the years, was to provide sufficient married quarters, of the right size, in the right place and at the right time, with an army frequently changing in size and in the composition of its married personnel, and with constant redeployments to meet operational requirements. Unlike the other Services, the Army did not encourage early home ownership, as a stable base during periods of separation. Instead it tried to provide, within its budget, fully furnished quarters built to comparable civilian standards, in places where the soldier was located, the balance being made up of civilian hirings.

In 1969, Housing Commandants were appointed to allocate, administer and maintain the quarters and to care for the families in them. In 1973 they were given Senior NCOs of the Women's Royal Army Corps to assist them. In 1980 married women of the WRAC became entitled to married quarters with the Army trying to keep Service couples together during their careers.

CHILDREN'S EDUCATION

The Spencer Committee found the education of their children was of major importance to Service families. It noted

> 'the common concern of LEA's, HMI's, Headteachers, school welfare officers and of many Army parents about the effect of the Army way of life on the education and development of Army children. This anxiety is nothing new: the Plowden Report, for example, drew attention in 1966 to evidence of backwardness amongst Army children and of high turn-over of pupils and teachers in areas with large Service populations. Many LEA's have tried to overcome some of these disadvantages by positive discrimination, by giving their 'Service schools' higher staff/pupil ratios, increased ancilliary staffs and higher capitation rates'.[8]

But not all army children showed signs of disturbed behaviour: much depended on the ability and motivation of the parents, especially of the mothers, in coming to terms with the impact of turbulence on their own lives and relationships and on how well they themselves integrated into Service life.

> 'Many parents prefer a settled UK boarding school education for their children, for which boarding school allowances are available, as an alternative to constant changes of school'.

In April 1975, 73% of the 21,500 claimants for boarding school allowances were officers, 27% other ranks. Parents overseas were also entitled to free travel for their children for two or three visits annually during school holidays: but many parents complained to the Committee that these allowances and free travel passages were inadequate, with the result that they could not afford a boarding education for their children. Each term 3,000 Servicemen's children would join their families in Europe through the Air Trooping Centre at Hendon, with SSAFA escorts if necessary. One experienced traveller told a Soldier Reporter:- 'I have been travelling since I was very young — to Hong Kong, Nepal, Singapore and Kenya and now I'm off to Germany'. He was just 12 years old.[9]

MEDICAL

The Society of Community Medicine believed that

> 'Army families were at a disadvantage compared with civilian families in the fields of health, education and welfare, especially those of junior ranks; when officers' families were affected, it was usually manifested as psychiatric illness in the wife'.

There was also need for family planning facilities to remove marital stress caused by untimely or unwanted pregnancies.[9]

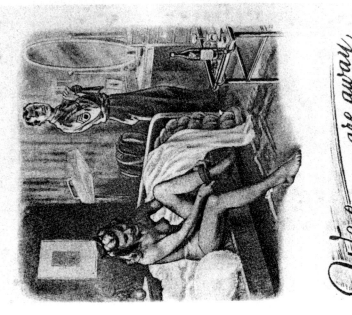

PLATE 19. Leaflet dropped by the German Army over Anzio Beachhead, March 1944. (*By kind permission of the Psywar Society, Birmingham*).

PLATE 20. Families escape from Singapore 1942. *(Imperial War Museum)*.

PLATE 21. Women internees, Tjideng Camp, Batavia, Java 1945. *(Imperial War Museum)*.

PLATE 22. ENSA in Egypt 1943. *(NAAFI)*.

PLATE 23. The Author's first married quarters — the converted guardroom of the Singapore Gunsite.
Insert: Destroyed by the British before the surrender in 1942. *(Author's photos)*.

PLATE 24. Her Royal Highness The Duchess of Kent visits Singapore schools in 1969. (*Public Relations HQ FARELF*).

PLATE 25. Wives at Runnymede Centre, Penang 1969. (*Public Relations HQ FARELF*).

PLATE 26. Larnaca Market, Cyprus 1967. *(C.O.I.)*.

PLATE 27. Shopping in Aden 1965. *(C.O.I.)*.

PLATE 28. Wives run a Thrift Shop.

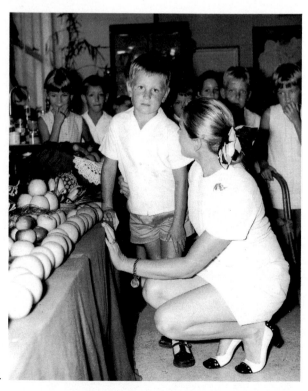

PLATE 29. Harvest Festival.

PLATE 30. Ex-Bombadier Sir Harry Secombe meets the wives.

SINGAPORE LIFE IN THE 1960s
(PLATES 28–31 PUBLIC RELATIONS
HQ FARELF)

PLATE 31. Wives Fashion Parade.

PLATE 32. The Colonel of the Regiment meets the wives in Paderborn. *(Public Relations HQ 4th Division)*.

PLATE 33. 'Exercise Birdwalk'. The wives sample the Malayan Jungle. *(Public Relations HQ FARELF)*.

PLATE 34. Street scene, Hong Kong 1961. *(Public Relations HQ FARELF)*.

PLATE 35. Brunei 1967. Local girls who have married soldiers wave goodbye. *(Public Relations HQ FARELF)*.

PLATES 36 & 37. Wives Clubs in action in Hohne and Fallingbostel 1987. *(Public Information HQ 1st Armoured Division)*.

PLATE 38. Wives shop at the Ismailia NAAFI under armed guard during the troubles in the Canal Zone 1951. *(Courtesy of HQ NAAFI)*.

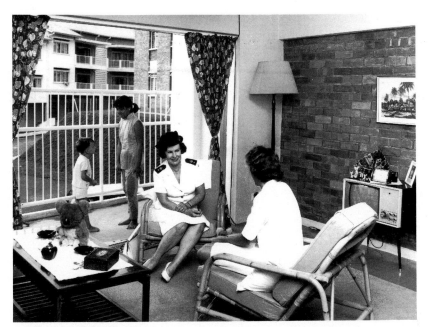

PLATE 39. SSAFA at work, Singapore 1966. Deputy Director, Mrs Phyllis Harvey, visits an Army wife in her married quarters. *(C.O.I.)*.

PLATE 40. 'Goodbye Daddy'. Off to the Falklands 1982. *(NAAFI)*.

PLATE 41. Conference of the UK Land Forces Federation of Army Wives 1985. (*MOD PR*).

PROFESSIONAL HELP NEEDED

The Committee decided that most servicemen and their families coped well with the vicissitudes of army life but complex cases of social distress did arise for both officers' and soldiers' wives, which were beyond the resources of the regiment, however well motivated.

> 'Commanding officers should be given the professional help of fully trained and experienced social workers to complement the regimental system and the family care provided by the officers and their wives'.[10]

Neither SSAFA nor the Local Authorities could give such a service, and therefore *the Committee recommended that the Army should provide such full-time professional social workers within its own organisation for service at home and abroad. The Army*, however, *did not accept this recommendation*, nor one for longer tours of duty to reduce stresses of separation and constant moves and the ensuing problems of 'turbulence'. Instead, the Army decided to improve its existing welfare arrangements and those with SSAFA by the formation in 1978 of the Family Housing and Welfare Service with responsibility for all housing and welfare problems in the Army and for co-operation with the statutory and voluntary agencies in these fields. SSAFA argued that the officers, NCOs and army wives were inherently unsuitable for welfare work of the kind the Army now needed for its families, because they were identified with the establishment and lacked the necessary experience and training.

> 'The Colonel's lady cannot provide for Judy O'Grady as well as she used to do 50 years ago. Mrs O'Grady, like her husband, expects rather more than kindly patronage.'[11]

SSAFA could offer such experienced social workers, abreast of current social legislation and accustomed to working with Local Authorities and the Government and with the voluntary agencies. They had already four highly qualified social workers in the United Kingdom, working in the major garrisons of Tidworth/Bulford, Colchester, Catterick, and Aldershot and 15 in overseas commands, together with some 12,000 SSAFA voluntary workers dealing with Service and ex-Service families. More social workers would be required. But better terms of service, pay, leave, training, uniform grants, overseas allowances and clerical support were needed to enable them to do the job. SSAFA also provided nursing sisters overseas similar to the Local Authority's health visitors.

OVERSEAS TOURS

In 1980, apart from operational needs, the Army had only four overseas stations for families — Germany, Cyprus, Gibraltar and Hong Kong, compared with 40 after the Second World War. This shortage of overseas postings had removed one of the major attractions for both the single and the married soldier, which undoubtedly affected the Army's ability to recruit full career soldiers. The largest and most attractive of these overseas stations was still BAOR, with some 145,000 Service and British civilian personnel spread out over an area the size of England and Wales, stretching from Antwerp to Berlin in some 14 major garrisons and a few smaller ones. The largest garrison was Osnabruck with 10% of the British personnel and the smallest Lubbecke with only 3000 soldiers and dependants. Rheindahlen, near Dusseldorf, was the main Headquarters with only 2000 soldiers but some 6500 dependants and United Kingdom based civilians.

Despite the world of culture, sport and entertainment waiting for them outside the camp, especially if soldiers and families learned to speak the language, however imperfectly, most army camps remained island communities, largely self-sufficient for shopping and amenities. Garrisons varied in the facilities and social amenities available to the families and in their isolation from the German communities.

Munster, for instance, was one of the largest garrisons, with 5500 military personnel and 6000 civilians and dependants. It was a very attractive family station with over 2400 married quarters spread over 17 'patches' — still 300 short of the needs of its increasingly married soldiers. It had a wide range of recreational and welfare amenities of its own to supplement the excellent facilities in the town. At the other extreme was Hohne. This camp was originally built in 1936, to support one of Hitler's main training areas for his Panzer Divisions and today supports a major NATO tank range. To provide much needed entertainment for the 10,000 British, Dutch and German troops and their families in this isolated garrison, the Author who was Station Commander there from 1962–65, converted the Roundhouse, a former German Officers' Mess, into a theatre, seating 1200, with the help of German labour, and brought there well-known entertainers like Acker Bilk, Frankie Vaughan, Larry Adler and Chris Barber with his singing wife, Ottilie Patterson, to supplement the Regimental bands.

Fashion shows were arranged, with local wives and daughters on the cat-walk, to show off the latest NAAFI outfits and a bowling alley (bought from the Americans with some of the weekly Bingo 'takings') was installed. A thrift shop was run, with the help of some of the officers' wives, the 10% profit going to SSAFA's welfare funds. Some families lived within the camp, others in the newly built married quarters in the village of Bergen. Most shopped at the NAAFI and YWCA gift shop or went to Celle or Hanover. There was an AKC cinema and many sporting and social activities, and playgroups, guides and youth clubs organised by the families themselves in the Station. There were two garrison primary schools and a large secondary school. The Higher Education Centre provided the German language courses for BAOR's unit instructors, through whom it was hoped to teach the soldier and his wife enough German, at various levels of competence, to mix with the local community.

HONG KONG

The lease for this Crown Colony expires in 1997. Meanwhile, it houses 8000 soldiers, mostly Gurkhas, with one British regiment at Stanley Fort. Its families, scattered round the colony in high rise flats, enjoy life amid its teeming Chinese population. There is something for everyone — festivals all the year round and food to suit every taste and pocket. There are cinemas, theatres and Chinese operas and a non-stop round of night life from disco and 'go-go' dancing to the topless bars and 'bottoms-up' clubs of this world of Suzie Wong, where white girls outstrip the Orientals. One climbs the Peak to see Hong Kong laid out in a glittering fairyland of lights or visits Happy Valley, once a malarial swamp, for one of the fortnightly race meetings, started by army officers in 1846. After occupying the Victoria Barracks for 135 years, the Army has moved its HQ into a modern 23 storey skyscraper block opened by Prince Charles in 1979 on the island's naval base. All that remains at Victoria is a new community centre, a NAAFI shopping complex and two high-rise blocks of officers' and NCOs' married quarters.

THE MEDITERRANEAN

Apart from the one battalion family station at Gibraltar, the only British garrison left in the Mediterranean today is Cyprus. Here the United Nations maintains a Peace Keeping Force in the north of the island consisting of a number of units from different member states of the Organisation and tasked with the maintenance of peaceful relations along the dividing line between the Greek and Turkish communities. In the south are the two British Sovereign Base Areas of Episkopi and Dekhelia where a substantial number of married soldiers and airmen have their families. The main family area is around Episkopi, where the British headquarters is located, but a number of families are housed in Berengaria Village some 15 miles away or in hirings in Limassol — the latter tending to be for the younger families with the least quartering points and, often, the greatest problems. Life centres round the extensive facilities at Episkopi which provide all the amenities that the soldiers have learned to expect in a modern garrison. There is a military hospital at the RAF airfield of Akrotiri nearby and this is linked by helicopter with a 'cottage hospital' on the other side of the island at Dekhelia. The Dekhelia Sovereign Base Area is very much an enclave outside which the families of its 3500 servicemen may not live, for security reasons. This small family garrison is almost a self-contained military town with its own schools, cinemas, banks, thrift shops, library and NAAFI shops and canteens. Here the wives take part in all sorts of activities that they would have never tried at home — gliding, go-karting, parascending, rifle shooting and even the assault course in addition to the more traditional sports of netball, tennis, squash, hockey and every form of water sport. They run Guides and Cubs and other Youth activities but miss their television and up-to-date newspapers. Their quarters are built on a hillside overlooking the Mediterranean with 500 families in Dekhelia, 125 at Pergamos, 165 at Ayios Nikolaos and others at Slim and Richmond villages.[12] Cyprus is a most beautiful place and steeped in antiquity. Here is probably one of the last places where the families of both the soldiers and their officers can enjoy a life-style quite unknown to the civilian equivalents in Britain — except on an expensive holiday!

NORTHERN IRELAND

The troubles in Northern Ireland which began in 1969, not only pose a military problem to the Army but social and welfare problems for the soldiers' families. The fortunate ones are those who live in Northern Ireland with their husbands on their 18 months to two year tours and share with them the dangers and tensions. Anne Armstrong told the story in *Soldier Magazine*[13]

'Seven years have passed since the troubles returned to Northern Ireland. We have seen ceasefires, battles, the peace movement, bombs, death and injury to British troops — and sometimes to their girlfriends. The wives are perhaps at times forgotten. Yet there is no word of complaint from them — just loyalty and devotion to duty. All the families I spoke to praised the excellent education their primary school children were receiving. I visited their homes, schools, community centres, playgroups, youth clubs and hospitals and found there was plenty for them to do.

In Londonderry, opposite the notorious Creggan, in a former naval station but now a military camp, were the 2nd Battalion The Coldstream Guards. Some 234 families with 200 children had opted to accompany their husbands during their 18 month tour. The families live in five separate groups of quarters. The furthest is 15 miles away, the nearest within walking distance of the camp. Despite the frequent absences of their husbands in these notorious trouble spots, the wives make the best of life. 'It makes a big difference to the men having their wives and children with them' said one senior wife.

Security checks, though necessary, were irksome. 'Some young wives feel nervous and frightened when they first arrive but, provided they take sensible precautions, they are advised to lead as normal a life as possible', said one officer'.[14]

Holywood Barracks Belfast was home to the Gordon Highlanders, despite the high wire fences and the searches. The NAAFI has the meeting place and its notice board the communication centre for Thrift Shop, Launderette times, crèche, kindergarten, keep-fit classes, badminton, swimming and hairdressing salon. There were notices too for the drama club, folk group, ballet, Guides, Cubs and Brownies, a youth club and the Boys Brigade. One wife was studying for an Open University degree, others were acting as foster mothers, official or voluntary, one was running a library, another decorating the church wall with a magnificent mural of Joseph, Mary and the infant Jesus. All were using old or discovering new talents as they pooled their resources for the communal good.

A MARRIAGE LINK WITH CHARLES II

In September 1981 Prince Charles married Lady Diana Spencer. The Prince invited a corporal or private and their wives from each of the regiments of which he was Colonel-in-Chief to be present at St Paul's Cathedral. His own connections with the Army, through his descent from almost every sovereign of England and Scotland, lacked one link — that link with which I began our story and which was supplied by his bride. Lady Diana Spencer belongs to the Spencer family, which divided into two branches when Charles Spencer, third Earl of Sunderland married Lady Anne Churchill, daughter of the Duke of Marlborough, son of the original Winston Churchill. The younger branch, created Earls Spencer in 1765, from which the Princess of Wales's father, the 8th Earl Spencer descends, proudly claims amongst their ancestors Field-Marshal the 4th Earl of Lucan, of the Charge of the Light Brigade fame; Field-Marshal the 1st Marquess of Anglesey, who as Earl of Uxbridge lost his leg commanding the Cavalry at Waterloo, and such famous military names as Admiral Howe, Sir Richard Grenville of The Revenge, the great soldiers, Marlborough and Peterborough and the gallant Sidneys. Lady Diana supplies that link with Charles II, through his mistress Barbara Villiers, Duchess of Cleveland, with whom the modern soldier and his wife claim military kinship, as our story has related.

THE FALKLANDS WAR

The Falklands campaign of April–May 1982 brought home to the public, thanks to the immediate and graphic television pictures, all the drama of soldiers at war and of womenfolk who must wait and hope at home for news of their loved ones. The tears of departure and separation, the days and weeks of anxiety and the final joyful reunion or tragedy were brought into the homes of a nation daily following the events with equal concern.

'Soldier' reported the scenes as the troop reinforcements boarded the 'Canberra' and the hastily converted luxury liner Queen Elizabeth II, whose predecessor had been known to many thousands of World War II American and British soldiers.

> 'The viewing platforms and docks at Southampton were packed with relatives and dependants, friends and well-wishers, bands played 'Don't cry for me, Argentina' and television cameras recorded the carnival atmosphere of cheers, wolf-whistles and farewell waves from ship and shore'. Singing telegram girl Linda from Aldershot turned up in scanties, opera stockings, suspenders and high heels to see her brother on his way. But hit of the day was a 22 year old Army wife, who found a place on the viewing platform exactly opposite her husband. She whipped off her blouse and bra to give him and his pals a real farewell treat. A helpful crane driver swung the bra over to her husband — all done with delicacy and the utmost aplomb'[15]

Once victory had been achieved, the Forces returned to even more rapturous and emotional scenes, and the Prime Minister, Mrs Margaret Thatcher, proudly announced in the House of Commons 'The Falklands campaign was boldly planned, bravely executed and brilliantly accomplished'.

When HMS Invincible docked at Portsmouth, the Queen with other members of the Royal Family welcomed home her son, Prince Andrew, joining other mothers, wives and sweethearts in tears of joy, mingled with sadness for those who would not return.

> 'It was essentially a family affair,' reported *The Times*,[16] despite the hosts of well-wishers and the inevitable topless girls.

In course of time, arrangements were made for the bereaved next-of-kin to visit the lonely graves of their loved ones in the Falklands. As Mrs Sara Jones, widow of Colonel H Jones VC, said: 'Time is a great healer: you don't forget, you just learn to live with it.'[17]

SSAFA, too, added its obituary — Long after the Falklands have faded from the headlines and in the years to come, SSAFA in the cities and the shires will still be quietly at the service of the families of those who served us so gallantly.[18]

DISSATISFACTION AMONGST ARMY WIVES

In 1985, the Army began a study into the causes of 'a worrying rise in the rate of Premature Voluntary Release (PVR) over the last few years'.

In its terms of reference to its Study on Army wives (Gaffney Report),[19] it noted that there was some evidence that distaff influences were behind much of the recent increase in such retirements, particularly amongst officers.[20] As Spencer had reported ten years earlier, Army families suffer from frequent postings and much enforced separation and the Army,

> 'much more than any ordinary employer needs to make sure that wives (and families) are properly cared for both within and by the Army system; particularly as, notwithstanding the disadvantages of Army life in family terms, we still look to our wives to play a major part in the many voluntary welfare activities that make such an important contribution towards high morale and efficiency.'[20]
>
> The Army must seek 'not just to minimise any discontent but actively to make married life with the Army as attractive an option as possible'.[20]

The Government and the Army had taken little notice of the first detailed Survey of the Army's married families (The Spencer Report 1975) and had certainly not implemented its main recommendation that the Army should establish a comprehensive civilian run Social Work Service to supplement the voluntary efforts of the regimental system, which the Army feared, with some justification, was under attack. The regiment had been, for many years, the well-tried unit for leading men into battle, the envy of other armies, and was still the corner stone for operations and administration in peace and war. In BAOR, where the Army had to provide all the statutory welfare services, it preferred to employ SSAFA under contract to support its medical services and voluntary help, including unit wives to assist commanding officers take care of their families. At home, there were the facilities of the Welfare State, which Army families, as taxpayers, were entitled to share equally with civilians. But, to meet the additional problems caused by its own unique life-style, the Army had appointed Housing Commandants and Unit Families' Officers to work with the statutory and voluntary agencies.

But the Gaffney Report revealed that the Army was less stable in 1984 than it was in 1975 and that, in common with civilian experience, family problems were on the increase. Spencer had recommended lengthening tours to three years to reduce the number of postings and the creation of 'home' bases to give units more stability — but 10 years later, Gaffney found even shorter tours and more movement, as the reduced Army tried to meet increased commitments. But doubling the average tour from two to four years would increase family stability with other benefits to schooling, medical care and employment opportunities for wives: the resultant financial savings could be used to provide more generous baggage and travel allowances. Could not the Army also eliminate much of the loneliness experienced by families in small garrisons and isolated housing 'ghettoes' (like Tidworth), by building 'Garrison Towns' with the concomitant amenities and welfare facilities enjoyed by the Royal Engineers in the larger towns of Maidstone and Ripon? Should the Army encourage more home-ownership by assisted house-purchase schemes as the Navy does (RN 65.5%; RAF 42.9%, Army 24%) with an eye on inflation and eventual resettlement, despite its own married quarters standing empty and an increase in voluntary unaccompanied tours? Is the answer to the perennial complaints of its families against the poor design, fixture and fittings, maintenance and furnishing of its married quarters to involve to a greater extent the wives of all ranks in formulating and carrying out the Army's housing policies?

These and other questions occupied the Army Wives Study, but Gaffney also made a plea for a greater personal and group identity for its wives, especially other ranks' wives. No longer is Judy O'Grady satisfied with the half-rations of yesteryear, a corner in the barrack-room, the status and privileges bestowed by her husband's rank; no longer is she content with regimental 'hand-outs', doing the Company's washing and a place in the baggage train. She wants to be known as Mrs O'Grady (not as the wife of Corporal O'Grady) with an Identity Card of her own, valid world-wide for use of amenities and security purposes. She rejects regimental patronage and privileges, claims her 'rights' and is ready to voice them.[21] Often as well-educated and professionally qualified as the officer's wife and just as accustomed to decision-making, she seeks an equal and purposeful part in the management of her affairs and those of the wider community. She is ready to serve in a regimental Wives Club or to represent it in the Federation of Wives Clubs (formed 1982); to sit on a Housing Committee or to work in a Garrison Information and Advice Bureau. Qualified as secretary, midwife, nurse or teacher, she seeks employment, within or outside the Army. She feels entitled to her own career and to earn a second income for her family, even if such aspirations clash with her husband's army career and postings or with the expectations of his regiment. If Judy O'Grady has problems of her own she expects expert and professional help and advice in complete confidentiality, not the well-meaning but often ill-directed efforts of untrained, uniformed or voluntary staff in the Army's Command structure.

The Army's dilemma is that it remains, what it has always been, a hierarchical organisation, based firmly on its regimental system, trying to control and regulate marriage and its married personnel so that they do not interfere with its prime functions of war, military training and duty. Such female appendages as it has permitted through the ages, the Army has tried to integrate into the administration, ethos and discipline of its male-orientated units, which for many generations of regimental women were the only homes most would ever know. But the Army has usually been outside the mainstream of social change, especially in its attitudes to the status and roles of women and marriage. Now that its dependants outnumber the men and women are increasingly refusing to be regimented, can the regiment and its commanding officer continue to be responsible for the care and well-being of its wives, as they are for the men? Many of the officers' wives feel they no longer have the right nor the expertise to become involved in social work. On the other hand, many of the junior rank wives distrust the regimental hierarchy of voluntary support and believe it prevents problems being aired outside the unit to preserve its good name. Can the communication gap be bridged by selecting and training volunteers from all ranks with the neccessary talents to work in the field of preventive welfare under paid organisers, with 'neutral' advice bureaux working in support of the regimental system? Certainly the commmanding officers need to be reassured that they will be kept informed 'in confidence' of cases which are referred to outside agencies.

Recently, there have been encouraging attempts to address these problems by the wives themselves. Since adopting its Charter in 1983, the United Kingdom Land Forces Federation of Army Wives ('Clubs' was dropped in 1986) has gone from strength to strength in representing the views of army wives, both within and outside the Services, on committees concerned with their housing and welfare and in finding (and training) volunteers to help with youth, families' and children's activities in units and garrisons. 'The Federation is the most exciting thing that has happened to army wives for many years', commented Lady Kitson, wife of the then Commander-in-Chief United Kingdom Land Forces.[22] 'A real opportunity to work constructively to improve conditions in the Army and in the quality of its family life'. There has been a 'buzzing in the Hive' (Hohne Information and Volunteer Exchange) in BAOR as one garrison seeks to provide a wide range of information and volunteers for its family needs and communal activities. Munster Garrison has pioneered a voluntary home visiting scheme to provide friendship, caring and practical support, and links with SSAFA and garrison resources, for families in difficulties. The more army wives associate to help each other, supporting, but not run by, the Command structure, the better for themselves and for their families.

In April 1966 that archetype of the Regimental Commander, Field Marshal Montgomery put to the House of Lords his solution to these intractable problems — a Bachelor Army, that is to say

> 'armed forces composed solely of unmarried personnel or of married officers and men, whose wives and families would be unrecognised'.[23]

There would be considerable savings to the public purse, he argued, because there would be no need for married quarters, furniture, schools and teachers, family hospitals and doctors, nor the cost of transporting families to and from garrisons overseas. The savings could be given to soldiers in the form of very high rates of pay, 'which they richly deserved'.

Lord Shackleton, answering for the Government, had no doubt of the answer —

> 'Your idea would have a disastrous effect on recruiting and a catastrophic effect on the retention of officers and men in the Services. The key to recruitment is usually the recruit's mother and the key to the retention of a serviceman nowadays almost certainly lies with his wife. Whitehall is confronted with a problem it has never faced before, how to deploy all its regular forces to meet a military need, while at the same time having to pay the highest regard to the welfare of Service wives and families'.[24]

As this continuing story has amply demonstrated —

> '*Mars and Venus make uneasy bedfellows*'.

Appendix A to Chapter 17

SOME STATISTICS FROM THE SPENCER REPORT 1975
(The Tables shown below are taken from The Spencer Report 1975. Published by Her Majesty's Stationery Office).

TABLE 1   *Average age for Marriage of Infantry (other arms similar) (Page 19 Table 4)*

Rank	Husbands	Wives
Cpls and below (Junior Ranks)	21.5	20.1
Sgts and above (Senior Ranks)	23.2	21.6
Junior Officers		
(Captains and below)	24.3	23.0
Senior Officers		
(Majors and Lieut. Colonels)	28.2	24.3

TABLE 2   *Number and Percentage of Married Soldiers & Officers by Arm, Rank &*
                              Location (Dec 1973) (Page 177 Table 6)

	Infantry				RAC/RA				Other Arms			
	UK		BAOR		UK		BAOR		UK		BAOR	
	No.	%	No.	%	No.	%	No.	%	No.	%	No.	%
Junior Ranks	7,866	39	3,571	57	3,725	46	4,117	44	14,150	44	10,450	48
Senior Ranks	3,642	93	1,020	93	2,150	93	1,579	94	11,240	93	6,512	94
Junior Offrs	620	46	193	51	461	56	275	49	2,208	74	1,080	77
Senior Offrs	1,007	90	260	93	787	91	260	92	2,800	94	991	96

TABLE 3   *Age distribution by rank for the whole army (Dec 1973) (Page 178 Table 7)*

Age in Years	Junior Ranks %	Senior Ranks %	Junior Officers %	Senior Officers (All): Majors and above %
19 and under	22	—	2	—
20 under 25	42	1	22	—
25 under 30	26	23	31	1
30 under 35	7	30	16	11
35 under 40	2	30	7	24
40 and above	1	16	22	64
Total 100 equals	108,474	31,574	8,627	8,579
Average Age	24	34.5	31	42.8

TABLE 4   *Age distribution and average age at marriage of army wives by husband's rank*
                              in infantry in the United Kingdom (Page 179 Table 9)

Infantry	Junior Ranks	Senior Ranks	Junior Officers	Senior Ranks (All)
Age in Years	%	%	%	%
19 and under	12	—	—	—
20 under 25	40	9	14	2
25 under 30	33	30	37	17
30 under 35	10	31	21	33
35 under 40	4	21	8	18
40 and Over	1	9	20	30
Total 100 equals	248	280	73	99
Average Age at Marriage	20.2	21.2	22.9	24.1

NOTES

Introduction

1. Charles Oman. *Wellington's Army 1809–1814*. Arnold 1912.
2. Maud Diver. *Honoria Lawrence*. John Murray 1936.
3. V. Bamfield. *On the Strength*. Charles Knight 1974 p 9.
4. *Soldier Magazine*. 1980.

Chapter 1 – Husbands in the Days of Charles II and Marlborough

1. E.M.G. Routh. *Tangier 1661–1684*. Murray 1912.
2. J. Childs. *The Army of Charles II*. Routledge & Kegan Paul 1976 p 115 & 120.
3. Lieutenant Colonel J. Davis. *History of the Second Queen's Royal Regiment*. 1887 Vol I p 114.
4. Colonel L.I. Cooper. *The King's Own (4th Foot)*. Oxford 1939 Vol 1 p 24.
5. Colonel N.T. St. John Williams. *Tommy Atkins' Children*. HMSO 1970 p 7.
6. *PRO Calendar of State Papers: Domestic Series 1661–1678*. Entry Book 7 p 6.
7. Davis op cit. *Appendix C*.
8. E. Chappell. *The Tangier Papers of Samuel Pepys* (N.RS) 1935 Vol LXXIII p 89. A Commission was appointed to consider the Portuguese complaints.
9. Dartmouth to Jenkins 19 August 1683. *PRO Colonial Office Papers 279, 32*, f 87 and f 269.
10. Quoted Davis op cit pp 249–251.
11. Cowper op cit p 31 and Davis p 7.
12. Colonel D. MacKinnon. *The Origin and Services of the Coldstream Guards* 1833 Vol II p 261.
13. Childs op cit p 24.
14. Colburn's *United Services Magazine*. Aug 1867 Pt 2 p 506-9. Articles for His Majesty's Guards in 1663, 'made by H.M. Charles II on the advice of George, Duke of Albemarle.'
15. Dalton: *Army Lists VI* p 263.
16. Colonel C. Walton. History of the British Standing Army. London 1894 p 714. The Mutiny Act of 1692 forbade all ranks from lodging their wives, children and maidservants in their billets without the landlord's consent.
17. Ned Ward. *The London Spy* – quoted Godfrey Davies, Recruiting in the Reign of Queen Anne. J.S.A.H.R. Vol 28 1950 p 147.
18. *Dictionary of National Biography* 1888.
19. Ward op cit p 199 and J.S.A.H.R. 1951 Vol XXIX p 118. 1696 Act authorised Sheriffs 'to seize all idle, loose and vagabond persons and have not wife and children'.
20. See MacKinnon Vol I, p 427 for Regimental Numbers 1 Jan 1763.
21. Lieutenant General Sir Reginald Savory. *His Britannic Majesty's Army in Germany during The Seven Years War* O.U.P. 1966 p 447 and MacKinnon op cit Vol I p 427.
22. Major R.E. Scouller. *The Armies of Queen Anne* Oxford 1966 p 253.
23. Scouller op cit p 254.

Chapter 2 – Unhappy She Who Takes a Soldier

1. Farquhar. See Chapter 1.
2. Walton. *History of the British Standing Army 1660–1700*. Harrison 1894. p 491 and 493n. 'At the end of the year 1698 the British Army was composed wholly of bachelors'.
3. Colonel D. MacKinnon. *The Origin and Services of the Coldstream Guards*. 1833. Vol II p 261 and Walton p 840.

238

4. J.W. Fortescue: *A History of the British Army Vol II*. Macmillan 1910. p 32.
5. William Wycherley. The Plain Dealer Act II. 1676.
6. Antonia Fraser: *The Weaker Vessel:* Weidenfeld and Nicolson 1984 p 196.
7. *Dictionary of National Biography* 1891.
8. J.W. Fortescue: *Following the Drum*. Blackwood 1932. p 99. Hannah Snell served for four years in the 6th Foot (later, The Royal Warwickshire Regiment) and followed her sweetheart to India 'because he had been impressed'.
9. Daniel Defoe: The Life and Adventures of Mrs Christian Davies, Commonly called Mother Ross.
10. Standing Orders of the Duke of Cumberland 1755 'Soldiers' wives may suttle'. J.S.A.H.R. 1945 Vol 23 p 104 etc. and J.S.A.H.R. Vol 5 1926 p 194–6.
11. Robert Kirby: *The Life and Surprising Adventures of Mary Anne Talbot 1819*. History of the Army Vol II p 584 and DNB.
12. Colonel Cowper L.I. The King's Own (4th Foot). The Story of a Regiment. O.U.P. 1939. Vol I. p 57.
13. Thomas Lediard. The Life of the Duke of Marlborough (3 vols.) Wilcox 1736. Vol II. p xviii.
14. Cowper p 91.
15. Cowper p 96.
16. Quoted Lieutenant Colonel J. Davis. History of the Second Queen's Royal Regiment 1887 Vol 1, p 153.
17. Quoted Byron Farwell. For Queen & Country. Allen Lane 1981 p 229.
18. Colonel H.C. Wylly History of the Manchester Regiment 1923. p 8.
19. Quoted A.E. Sullivan: Married Quarters – A Retrospect. Army Quarterly 1951.
20. Standing Rules of the Fraser Fencibles 1798 quoted in Alexander Crawley Dow. Ministers to the Soldiers of Scotland: Oliver and Boyd 1962.
21. Laffin. Surgeons in the Field. Dent 1970 p 47.
22. Cowper p 145 and p 164.
23. J.F. Findlay: Wolfe in Scotland: Longman Green 1928 p 160.
24. Findlay p 230.
25. Findlay p 232.
26. Findlay p 297.
27. Lieutenant B. Smyth: History of the 20th Foot p 35.
28. Cowper p 145. Quoted Alexander Dow *Ministers to the Soldiers of Scotland*. Oliver & Boyd 1962 p 228.
29. Walton (p 573) quoting Grose: Military Antiquities 1786. 'Applicable to camp followers only'.
30. Walton p 560 and Article 37 p 813.
31. Sir William Blackstone: *Commentaries on the Laws of England (1753)*. 1793 Vol 1 p 65.
32. Anon. *The Laws respecting Women 1777*. p 55-6. See also Thomas Hardy's '*The Mayor of Casterbridge*.
33. Cowper p 327, p 180 and p 186.
34. E. Hopkins. *A Social History of the English Working Classes*. Arnold 1979 p 203.
35. Standing Orders to be observed by the whole Corps of Dragoons, by His Royal Highness the Duke of Cumberland's Order circa 1755. *Journal of the Society for Army Historical Research Vol 23 1945*. (Reverend P. Sumner) p 105.
36. H.M. Walker: *History of the Northumberland Fusiliers 1674–1902*. John Murray 1919 pp 113–4. See also Chap 1 p 6.
37. Daniell: *Cap of Honour. The Story of the Gloucestershire Regiment*. Harrap 1951. p 40.
38. *Barrack Regulations 1817*.
39. Collection of Regulations and Miscellaneous Orders 1760–1807. p 513.
40. *Directions to Paymasters No. 69*. Section III Part 2pp 187–189.
41. Ibid p 150.
42. *General Order 13 April 1800. Army Regulations 1760–1807*. Miscellaneous Order Section IX pp 517–8.
43. *General Order for Troops destined for Continental Service* dated 15 April 1807.

44. W.H. Fitchett: *Wellington's Men; Some Soldier Autobiographies 1900*. quoted p 243.
45. Major General J.F.C. Fuller: *Sir John Moore's System of Training 1924. The 95th Rifle Corps became The Rifle Brigade after the Battle of Waterloo. Company Commanders 'will chuse sober, industrious and cleanly women' to wash for the men of their barrack room.* Orders of 40th Foot. 1800.
46. Donaldson: *Recollections of the Eventful Life of a Soldier 1845*.
47. H. De Watteville. *The British Soldier*. Dent. 154. p 125. Fencible regiments were recruited for internal defence but during the Napoleonic Wars some regiments served in Europe & Gibraltar.
48. G.W. Oxley: *Poor Relief in England and Wales 1601–1834*. David and Charles 1974. Leicester Records p 29.
49. Scouller p 336.
50. M. Trustram: *Women of the Regiment: Marriage and the Victorian Army*. Cambridge University Press 1984. p 92.
51. *W.O. 40/13 Relief for Families of Soldiers 1800*. (quoted Trustram p 92).
52. Walton p 598–600. Site now occupied by the Eagle Star Insurance Co.
53. Walton p 605–606.
54. *London Gazette 1673–4*. (9/12 March).
55. MacKinnon Vol 11 p 373.
56. See Colonel N.T. St. John Williams: *Tommy Atkins' Children 1675–1970*.
57. Colonel Coote-Manningham's Article V dated 25 August 1800.
58. *Hansard*. 22 February 1812.
59. RAEC Museum, Beaconsfield.
60. Letter dated 1799 PRO WO40 12/9.
61. DNB and British Parl Papers. *The Conduct of the C in C 1809*. (20) Vol II. Military and Naval I. Irish University Press.
62. *Army Quarterly Vol IX. 1924*. p 284. He founded, for example, a lying-in-hospital for the wives of Foot Guardsmen.

Chapter 3 – Aristocratic Ladies

1. Fortescue J.W. *A History of the British Army*. MacMillan 1930 Vol 1 p 294.
2. *Dictionary of National Biography (DNB) 1899*. and Colonel MacKinnon. *History of the Coldstream Guards 1833*. Vol 1 pp 128–9.
3. Charles M. Clode. *The Military Forces of the Crown. Their Administration and Government*. 1869. Vol 2 p 62 and Vol 1 p 106. *Colburn's United Services Magazine Pt 3* Sept 1857 pp 122–8.
4. R.E. Scouller. *The Armies of Queen Anne*. Clarendon Press 1966 App IX (C) for Rates of Pay.
5. Fortescue I p 575 and II p 31.
6. *The Letters of King Charles II*. Ed. Arthur Bryant and *Memoirs of the Count de Grammont*. Allen and Unwin 1926, p 262 'as for husbands, the Court is not the place to find them, for unless money and caprice make up the match, there is but little hope of being married, virtue and beauty in this respect here are equally useless'.
7. E.N. Williams. *Life in Georgian England*. Batsford 1962 p 29.
8. Correlli Barnett. *Marlborough*. Eyre Methuen 1974 p 39.
9. Grammont p 262.
10. DNB, B.H. Forneron. *Louise de Kéroualle. Duchess of Portsmouth 1649–1734*. London 1887, p 166.
11. E. Burnet. *History of His Own Times 1900*. Vol 1 p 476.
12. Grammont p 262 'The Courtiers look upon maids of honour only as amusements, placed expressly at Court for their own entertainment'.
13. Sir Winston Churchill. *Marlborough. His Life and Times*. Harrap 1933 Vol 1 p 125.
14. DNB 1899 and Gibbs. *The Complete Peerage*. 1913.
15. 'In consideration', as the official declaration stated, tongue in cheek, 'of her noble descent', her father's death in the service of the crown and by reason of her own personal virtues'. John H. Jesse. *Memoirs of the Court of England during the Reign of the Stuarts 1857 Vol III*. p 182. Gibbs *'the wages of her prostitution'*.

16. DNB and Jesse p 196.
17. John Evelyn. *Diary 9 October 1671*. 'She was for the most part in her undress all day and there was a fondness and toying with that young wanton . . . . She was bedded one of these nights (at Euston Hall, near Newmarket) and the stocking flung after the manner of a married Bride'.
18. DNB (Lennox and Napier).
19. J.T. Findlay. *Wolfe in Scotland*. Longmans 1928 p 201.
20. Gibbs. *The Complete Peerage 1949*.
21. *The Reminiscences and Recollections of Captain Gronow 1810–1860*. Bodley Head 1964 p 167.
22. Created Earl of Middlesex in return, it is supposed, for yielding Nell to the King.
23. *The Works of Mr Thomas Brown 1719 Vol II*. p 303.
24. Gibbs and DNB (Notes and Queries 10 Aug 1935 pp 92–94). J.M. Bullock. *Peers who have married Players* and Cranstoun Metcalfe. *Peeresses of the Stage 1913*. Two of Mrs Jordan's children by the Duke of Clarence served as officers in the 10th Hussars.
25. Russell Braddon. *All the Queen's Men*, Hamish Hamilton p 151. Lord Alvanley died unmarried, aged 60.
26. Hubert Cole. *Beau Brummell*. Granada Publications 1977 p 43.
27. J.M. Brereton. *The 7th Queen's Own Hussars*. Leo Cooper 1975 p 112 and Gronow pp 261–2.
28. Lawrence Stone. *The Family, Sex and Marriage in England 1500–1800*. Penguin 1977 p 5 and p 212.
29. Scouller p 327 and p 337. Percy Kirke's son was made an ensign in his father's regiment at the age of 12 months on 3 May 1684 and was promoted captain on his sixth birthday.
30. C.U.S.M. Sept 1857 p 125.

Chapter 4 – Following the Drum

1. Ian Hay. *Argyll and Sutherland Highlanders. The King's Service 1938* p 74.
2. J.W. Fortescue. Following the Drum. Blackmore 1931 p 21. *History of the British Army Vol III 1911*.
3. Jack Russell. *Gibraltar Besieged*. Heinemann 1965 p 158.
4. *Journal of the Siege* by S.H. Gibraltar Museum.
5. Fortescue p 4.
6. Colonel T. James. *A History of the Herculean Straits 1771*.
7. *The Royal Engineers Journal. Vol XVI. 1912*. 'A Lady's Experiences in the Great Siege of Gibraltar.' 1779–1783.
8. Mrs Catherine Upton. *The Siege of Gibraltar* (No date).
9. Russell p 112 quoting S. Ancell. *A Journal of the Long and Tedious Siege* Pub 1784.
10. *Journal of the Society for Historical Research Vol II 1923*. p 181.
11. Allen Andrews. *Proud Fortress*. Evans 1958 p 155.
12. Lieutenant General H.J. Warre. *Historical Records of the 57th West Middlesex Regiment 1878*. p 74. R. Hughes. *The Fatal Shore*. Collins Harvill 1987 p 253.
13. Colonel L. Cowper. *The King's Own Vol II*. O.U.P. 1939. pp 56–68.
14. Captain C. Knight. *Historical Records of the Buffs (3rd Foot)*. Medici Society 1935 Vol II p 432, 436.
15. R. Hargreaves. *The Bloody Backs. The British Servicemen in N. America (1655–1783)* Hart Davies 1968 p 74.
16. Paul E. Kopperman. *The British High Command & Service Wives in America (1775–1783)*. J.S.A.H.R. Summer 1982 p 14.
17. *The Times. 26 April 1889*. p 5.
18. See Chapter 2 p 11 and Kopperman.
19. General Edward Braddock's Orderly Books 26 Feb–17 June 1755 Pub 1878. MOD Library. 17 May: 27 March: 11 June: 7 April respectively.
20. J.S.A.H.R. vol XXX No 121 (Spring) 1952 p 13 and Kopperman p 16.
21. Braddock. 10 May 1755: 21 May: 23 May: 6 June.
22. J.S.A.H.R. Vol 8 p 76.
23. Kopperman p 17.

24. Ward. *The Blessed Trade*. p 220.
25. Ward p 223.
26. *Journal of the Royal United Services Institute Vol CVI Feb 1961*. p 13 Article Lieutenant Colonel Laws. Welfare 1760.
27. H.H. Woollright: *History of the 57th Regiment of Foot*. 1893 p 46.
28. H.C. Wylly. *History of the Manchester Regiment (63 Foot) 1923 Vol I p 50. War Office Embarkation Return 17 March 1776.*
29. Colonel MacKinnon. *The Origin & Services of the Coldstream Guards 1833 Vol II*. p 435.
30. Wylly p 48 and Dictionary of National Biography.
31. Cowper. Vol I p 233.
32. Esmond Wright. *The Fire of Liberty*. Hamish Hamilton 1984 p 129.
33. Cowper pp 242, 248 (and Wylly p 50) and p 229 D.N.B. (Howe).
34. Kopperman p 32.
35. Kopperman p 33. 3 August 1776.
36. Ward p 291.
37. Lieutenant B Smyth. *History of the XX Regiment (1688–1888) The Lancashire Fusiliers 1889*. p 335.

Chapter 5 – Women Campaign with Wellington

1. See Chapter 2 p 15 and *General Regulations and Orders for the Army 12 August 1811 and Amendment 10 April 1813*. p 370.
2. *Records of The Devonshire Regiment.*
3. Charles Oman: *Wellington's Army 1809–1814*. Arnold 1912.
4. George Bell. *Soldier's Glory. Rough Notes of an Old Soldier*. Bell 1956 pp 61, 74, 75.
5. Godfrey Davies. *Wellington and His Army*. Blackwell 1954 pp 129–130.
6. 21 September 1850. *Letters of the Duke of Wellington to Mary, Marchioness of Salisbury 1850–2*. John Murray 1927. *J.S.A.H.R. Vol 7 1928*. pp 136–7.
7. *General Order 23 August 1809.*
8. *Orders 1 October 1809 and 25 June 1815.*
9. *Orders 14 September 1810.*
10. James Anton. *Retrospect of a Military Life 1841*. Quoted W.H. Fitchett (Ed) *Wellington's Men: Some Soldier Auto-biographies 1900*. p 237.
11. Fitchett (Republished 1976, E.P. Publishing Ltd) pp 242–3.
12. Fitchett p 244.
13. Fitchett p 249.
14. Lieutenant William Grattan. *Adventures with the Connaught Rangers 1809–1814*. Ed. Charles Oman 1902 p 276.
15. August Schaumann. *On the Road with Wellington. The Diary of a War Commissary in the Peninsular Campaigns*. Ed. A.M. Ludovic. Heinemann 1924 p 102.
16. Schaumann p 99 and Sergeant Joseph Donaldson: *Recollections of the Eventful life of a Soldier 1845*. p 219.
17. Fitchett p 255.
18. Edward Costello. Ed. A Brett-James. *Military Memoirs 1852* Longmans Green 1967. p 102–3, p 162.
19. Rifleman Harris. *Recollections* 1829. Quoted Fitchett p 201.
20. Bell p 130.
21. Davis p 123.
22. A. Brett-James. *Life in Wellington's Army*. Allen & Unwin 1972, p 286.
23. Lejeune *Memoirs Vol II* p 108. Oman believes the officer was Captain R. Currie (see Oman p 277 note).
24. William Tomkinson. *Diary of a Cavalry Officer in the Peninsular War 1809–1815*. Muller 1971, p 188.
25. William Napier. *History of the War in the Peninsula*. 1886 Vol 3 p 66.
26. Bell p 46.
27. Cecil Woodham–Smith. *The Reason Why*. Penguin Edition 1953, p 32.
28. *Reminiscences and Recollections of Captain Gronow*. Bodley Head 1964 p 32.

29. *Military Panorama Vol 2* p 167. Quoted Colonel H.C. Wylly. History of the King's Own Yorkshire Light Infantry Vol 1. p 253.
30. Earl Stanhope. *Conversations with the Duke of Wellington.* London 1888.
31. D.N.B.
32. Richard Blanco. *Wellington's Surgeon General, Sir James McGrigor.* 1974, p 254.
33. Brett-James p 264.
34. Bell p 100.
35. Fitchett p 162.
36. Bell p 48.
37. Brett-James p 171 and p 159.
38. Wylly Vol I p 248 p 254.
39. Oman p 276.
40. Schaumann p 386–8.
41. Notes on '*To Portugal For Love*'. Captain William Waldron Kelly's Escapes. Correspondence Wellington and General Sir Lowry Cole. Freneda 19 & 25 March 1813.
42. John Laffin. *Tommy Atkins.* Cassell 1966 p 92 and Costello (Brett-James) p 97.
43. Order dated 7 April 1812.
44. Bell p 75.
45. Sir John Kinkaid. *Random Shots from a Rifleman.* T.W. Boone 1835 p 167 and Colonel Willoughby Verner. *History and Campaigns of the Rifle Brigade.* London 1919 Pt 2 p 384.
46. G.C. Moore-Smith. *Autography of General Sir Harry Smith.* 1901.
47. Army Quarterly Vol 21. 1930–31. pp 68–69.
48. Army Quarterly Vol 15 1927–8. pp 359–360.
49. Ed. Captain B.H. Liddell Hart. *The Letters of Private Wheeler (1809–1828).* Michael Joseph 1951 p 162.
50. David Howarth. *A Near Run Thing.* Collins 1968 p 15.
51. Howarth p 221.
52. Gurwood. *Wellington's Despatches Vol XIV.* 1837. pp 455, 551, 554, and XXXII Murray 1838.

Chapter 6 – Matrimony by Regulation

1. J.W.Fortescue. *History of the British Army.* MacMillan 1923 Vol VI p 445.
2. *Standing Orders of the 73rd Foot 1858.* (Regimental Museum of The Black Watch).
3. L. Cowper. *The King's Own.* O.U.P. 1939 p 53.
4. *General Regulations and Orders for the Army 1822–39; General Order 415 dated 24 May 1824.* After 1881 kept by Command HQ's (The Registration of Births, Deaths & Marriages (Army) Act 1879.
5. Norman MacLeod D.D. *Good Words 1863. Soldiers' Wives.* p 258. *Queen's Regulations 1844* p 315.
6. *Army Medical Report 1860.* XXXIII p 21.
7. *Royal Commission on Recruiting 1861* (C2762) XV Q3752.
8. Ibid p 419.
9. *Queen's Regulations 1865.* para 1343.
10. 35 VIC 3559.
11. *Q.Rs 1844.* paras 6–10 p 316.
12. Quarterly Review Vol 77 1846 p 556.
13. *Household Words.* 6 Sep 1851. *Soldiers' Wives.* pp 561–2 and *The Times 22 Nov 1866.*
14. *United Services Gazette.* 1 April 1851 p 4.
15. *U.S.G.* 21 Oct 1854 p 4.
16. *The Herald of Peace 1 May 1859.* p 204 and *The Times 11 Feb 1858 p 10.*
17. *Household Words* 1855 Vol XI pp 278–9.
18. *Barrack Accommodation Committee 1854–5* and *Edinburgh Review: The Health of the Army* 1858 Pt 106 p 136–144.
19. B.A.C. Q1821 and *The Times 7 Aug 1855.* p 9.
20. Russell Braddon. *All the Queen's Men.* Hamish Hamilton p 84.

21. *Report of the Barracks & Hospital Improvement Commission 1861.* p 53 and Pall Mall Gazette 12 Nov 1867 p 4.
22. *Army Circulars 9 August 1867.* pp 1–3 and para 40.
23. *War Office Circular 849 of 30 Jan 1864.*
24. *Army Circular No 53 April 1871.*
25. Colonel H. De Watteville. *The British Soldier.* Dent 1954 p 187.
26. *USG* 31 December 1853. p 8.
27. Quoted V. Bamfield: *On the Strength: The Story of the British Army Wife.* Charles Knight 1974 p 24.
28. *Letters to Sidney Herbert.* H. Scott. Saunders & Otley 1854.
29. *Good Words.* Norman MacLeod. *Soldiers' Wives.* 1863 pp 259–261.
30. *Good Words. On Army Children.* 1871 p 219.
31. Mrs Young. *Aldershot and all about it with Gossip Literary and Military Pictorial.* Routledge 1858 p 44.
32. *Pall Mall Gazette.* 12 Nov 1867 p 4.
33. Juliet Piggott. *Queen Alexandra's Royal Army Nursing Corps.* Leo Cooper 1975 p 9.
34. A.L. Skelley: *The Victorian Army at Home.* Croom Helm 1977 pp 45–6.
35. *Royal Warrant for Pay 1884.* p 211.
36. Colonel N.T. St. John Williams. *Tommy Atkins' Children.* HMSO 1971 p 71.
37. Williams p 72 and p 73.
38. Williams p 79 and p 85.
39. *Quarterly Review Vol 77 1846.* p 556.
40. Good Words 1863 p 258–261 p 263.
41. Good Words *Married Soldiers 1875.* p 599.
42. *Wellington's Despatches 1838.* p 460.
43. *Pall Mall Gazette Vol 4 No 580 18 Dec 1866.* p 1881.
44. *Standing Orders Queen's Royal Regiment 1877.* p 52.
45. *St. Paul's Magazine VII Oct 1870–Mar 1871.* p 370.
46. *J.S.A.H.R. Vol 5 1926 p 112.* 'Martial Laws of Charles I' C.U.S.M. Pt 3 Sept 1867 p 73.
47. Hough's *Commentary on Courts – Martial 1825.* p 665.
48. *Census of England & Wales 1871. General Report Vol IV.* HMSO 1873.
49. *1901 Census.* App A Table 25.
50. *Myna Trustram. Women of the Regiment.* C.U.P. 1984 p 37.
51. E.M. Spiers. *The Army and Society.* p 50.
52. Report of the Commissions on Army Recruiting 1861 (2762) XV Q 2627.
53. *1871 Census of England & Wales Vol 4.* Tables 134 and 133.

Chapter 7 – Early Home-Making in India

1. T.A. Heathcote. *The Indian Army.* David and Charles 1974.
2. Brian Gardner. *The East India Company.* London 1971 and Theon Wilkinson. *Two Monsoons.* Duckworth 1976, p 99, 100 (Contains an excellent bibliography).
3. J. Ovington. *A Voyage to Surat in the Year 1689.* Ed H.G. Rowlinson O.U.P. 1929.
4. Wilkinson p 100.
5. Mark Bence-Jones. *Clive of India.* Constable 1974 p 167.
6. *List of Marriages in the Presidency of Fort St. George, Madras 1680–1800* (India Office).
7. Colonel H.C Wylly. *History of the Manchester Regiment 1923.* p 204 and Lieutenant Colonel L.B. Oatts. *Proud Heritage: The Story of the Highland Light Infantry.* Nelson 1959 Vol 2 p 125.
8. Sir William Hunter. *The Thackerays in India and Some Calcutta Graves* 1897 p 19.
9. Wilkinson p 101 and 118. *The Church was later consecrated as St Mary's. Masulipatam.*
10. Ed. John Howell. The Life of Alexander Alexander by Himself. Edinburgh 1830 and Dennis Kinkaid. British Social Life in India (1608–1937) 1938. Republished Routledge & Kegan Paul 1973, p 68.
11. George Bell. *Soldier's. Glory. The Rough Notes of an Old Soldier. 1867.* Repub. Bell 1956 p 198.
12. Mrs Henry Sherwood. *Autobiography, Journal and Letters.* London 1814.
13. Quoted Major General James Hunt. *Scarlet Lancer.* Hart-Davis 1964 pp 109 and 120.

14. Bishop Reginald Heber (1793–1826). *Narrative of a Journey through India 1824–26*. John Murray 1828 Vol 3 p 373.
15. William H. Russell. *My Diary in India 1858–9*. Pub 1860.
16. Lunt p 164.
17. Emma Roberts. *Scenes and Chracteristics of Hindostan and Sketches of Anglo Indian Society*. Allen 1835. Vol 2 p 42, 48, Vol 3 Chap 2 pp 47–49. India Office. Also DNB.
18. Philip Mason. *A Matter of Honour*. Cape 1974 p 176.
19. Emma Roberts p 175.
20. Emily Eden. *Up the Country. Letters from India. Gwalior 11 Jan 1840 and Simla 8, 10 Sept 1839*. 'Her mother, Mrs Craigie, . . . had remarried and was the wife of the Deputy Adjutant General.
21. *The Europa Biographical Dictionary of British Women 1983*. See also Chapter 12 p 168.
22. Staff Sergeant J. MacMullen. *Camp and Barrack Room 1846*. q. T.H. McGuffie *Rank and File* Hutchinson 1964, p 122.
23. Mrs Leopold Paget *Camp and Cantonment. A Journal of Life in India* 1857–59. London 1865 p 3.
24. J.W. Fortescue. *Following the Drum*. Memoirs of a Saddler Sergeant of the 13 Light Dragoons 1810–14.
25. Emma Roberts pp 42–3.
26. L/MIL/5/376/7. *Guide to the Records of the India Office (Military Dept)*. Anthony Farrington 1982, p 62. See also Brigadier VCP Hodson. *Officers of the Bengal Army*.
27. Emily Eden Delhi 20 February 1838 and DNB.
28. Emma Roberts pp 43–4.
29. Reverend W. Tennant. *Indian Recreations 1803 Vol 1*. p 69.
30. Ed. Major M.L. Fisher. *The Diary of Colour/Sergeant Calladine 1793–1837*. Published 1922 p 72 and *Historical Records of The Green Howards (19th Regiment)*. Major M.L. Ferrar 1911, p 174.
31. L/MIL/5/390/129A. India Office. *Grant of Allowances for the support of the British European Soldiers and The Nabobs*. Curzon Press 1932 p 64.
32. Calladine p 78.
33. John Laffin. *Surgeons in the Field*. Dent 1970 p 71, quoting Stocqueler.
34. John Lawrence and Audrey Woodwiss (Ed). *The Journals of Honoria Lawrence: India Observed*. (1837–54). Hodder & Stoughton 1980 and Maud Diver. *Honoria Lawrence. A Fragment of Indian History*. John Murray 1936.
35. Maud Diver. *The Englishwoman in India*. 1909.
36. *Letters from an Unknown Lady*. John Murray 1846. pp 82–3.
37. Ibid. Letter 1 November 1829. p 142.
38. Bishop Heber Vol 3 p 200.
39. Mrs Marianne Postans. *Western India in 1838*. Saunders & Otley 1839. Vol 1 p 161–2.
40. Sergeant R. Waterfield. *Memoirs (1946–57)*. London 1868. q. Pat Barr. *The Memsahibs. The Women of Victorian England*. Secker & Warburg 1976 p 96.
41. John Lawrence op. cit.
42. Postans Vol 2 p 217.
43. Ed. Patrick Macrory. Lady Sale. *Journal of the First Afghan War*. Longmans 1969 p 150.
44. *The Times 26 July 1844*. p 6.

Chapter 8 – The Camp Followers at Scutari

1. *Illustrated London News 18 Feb 1854*. p 145 and 22 Feb 1854 p 166. See also Lieutenant Colonel Ross of Bladensburg. *History of the Coldstream Guards p 139*.
2. *ILN 4 March 1854*. p 186.
3. *The Times 27 Feb 1854*. p 9 and ILN 25 Feb 1854 p 166.
4. *The Times 4 March 1854*. p 9.
5. *ILN 4 March 1854*. p 184 and *The Times 25 Feb 1854*. p 9.
6. *The Times 27 Feb 1854*. p 9 & 2 Mar 1854: Captain R.H Burgoyne. *Records of the 93 Regiment 1883 p 93*.
7. *The Times 25 Feb 1854*. p 12 & p 7.

8. *The Times 8 March 1854*. p 10.
9. *ILN 4 March 1854*. p 186. (1, 7, 19, 23, 88 & 95 Foot Regiments).
10. *Journals kept during the Russian War 1856 and Compaigning Experiences in Rajputana and Central India during the Suppression of the Mutiny 1859.*
11. Major E.S. Jackson. *The Inniskilling Dragoons 1909*. pp 158, 175: *The Times 17 June 1854*. p 9.
12. Charles Dickens. *Household Words*. 6 May 1854.
13. Colonel Cowper. *History of the King's Own Regiment*. OUP 1939 Vol II p 88.
14. Dictionary of National Biography: *The Times 24 June 1824 p 2 and 28 Feb 1844 p 7. New Weekly Despatch*. 2 February 1834.
15. *The Times 9 May 1854*. p 10 and *16 May 1854*. p 10.
16. Ross p 144. *Orders dated 31 Dec 1854*. 'Some women's clothing has arrived and will be issued to applicants who are certified as fit persons to receive it'.
17. *The Times 22 May 1854*. p 9 and Piers Compton. *Colonel's Lady and Camp Follower*. Hale 1970 p 45.
18. David Scott Daniell. *Cap of Honour. The Story of the Gloucestershire Regiment (1694–1975)*. 1951 p 175.
19. *The Times 23 & 25 May 1854* and *8 June 1854 p 8*.
20. George Bell. *Soldier's Glory. The Rough Notes of an Old Soldier 1867*. Republished Bell 1956 p 195.
21. *The Times 5 Oct 1854*. p 7. Burgoyne p 100.
22. E.E.P. Tisdale. *Mrs Duberly's Campaigns*. Jarrold 1963 p 125.
23. *The Times 23 Nov 1854* and *8 Jan 1855*.
24. Bell p 205, 256.
25. *The Times 19 May 1855*. p 11.
26. Elizabeth Grey. *The Noise of Drums and Trumpets*. Longmans 1971 p 92.
27. *The Times 4 Dec 1854*. p 7.
28. *The Times 3 & 15 Nov 1854*. and *12 & 13 October 1854*.
29. *The Times 12 Dec 1854*. p 10.
30. *The Times 12 Jan 1855*. p 7.
31. *Household Words 19 April 1856*. p 316.
32. *The Times 9 March 1855*. p 11.
33. *Compton*. p 119.
34. *The Times 1, 6, 13 Feb 1855: 12 April 1855* and *9 Jan 1855*. p 8.
35. Army Quarterly Vol XXIII 1931–2 p 70 *The Times 23 Aug 1855*. p 7.
36. *The Manchester Guardian 21 Aug 1865* p 3 and *D.N.B*. See also Isobel Rae. *The Strange Story of Dr. James Barry*. Longmans Green 1958 and June Rose *The Perfect Gentleman* Hutchinson 1977.
37. *The Times 29 June 1855*. p 6.
38. *The Times 29 May 1855. 11 July 1855* and *25 Dec 1855*.
39. *DNB* and Gibbs. *The Complete Peerage*.
40. Donald Thomas. *A Life of Cardigan of Balaclava*. Routledge & Kegan Paul 1974. Skittles (Catherine Walters) see Chapter 12 p 166.
41. *The Times 27 May 1915*. p 11 (Obituary Notice). *DNB* and Gibbs. *The Complete Peerage*.
42. Grey p 24.
43. *The Times 9 Nov 1855*. p 6.
44. *The Times 25 April 1856*. p 9. Today The Royal Soldiers Daughters' School in Hampstead High Street. (See Soldier 5 Sep 83 for story and photos).
45. *The Times 22 Jan 1856*. p 8.
46. *The Times 26 Jan 1856*. p 10 and 10 April p 9.
47. *Garrison, Ten British Military Towns (Ed. Peter Dietz)*. Brassey's Defence Pub. Ltd 1986, p 14.

Chapter 9 – Women Face the Indian Mutineers

1. The Marquess of Anglesey. *Sergeant Pearman's Memoirs*. Cape 1968 p 25 p 27.
2. Marie Rye to the London Female Middle Class Emigration Society 1862.
3. Colonel N.T. St. John Williams. *Tommy Atkins' Children*. HMSO 1970 p 41.

246

4. Lewis and Foy. *The British in Africa*. Weidenfeld & Nicolson.
5. Anglesey. p 60.
6. Anglesey. p 108 & 110.
7. Mrs Marianne Postans. *Western India in 1838*. Saunders & Otley 1839. Vol 1 p 164.
8. General Sir Neville Lyttleton. *80 Years Soldiering*. 1927 p 79.
9. Smyth. *In this Sign Conquer*. Mowbray 1968 p 96.
10. Ed. Jane Vansittart. *From Minnie, with Love*. Peter Davis 1974 pp 11–15.
11. Fd. Marshal Earl Roberts. *Letters Written during the Indian Mutiny*. MacMillan 1924 p 6.
12. *The Times 24 Aug 1857*.
13. Philip Mason. *A Matter of Honour*. Jonathan Cape 1974 p 296.
14. *The Times 4 July 1857*. p 6 and *29 June 1857* p 2 (First detailed accounts from Meerut and Delhi) and Pat Barr. *The Memsahibs*. Secker & Warburg 1976 p 6.
15. Alexander Llewellyn. *The Siege of Delhi*. MacDonald and Jane's 1977 p 33.
16. Christopher Hibbert. *The Great Mutiny India* 1857. Allen Lane 1978 p 96 and Harriet C. Tytler. *Through the Sepoy Mutiny & Siege of Delhi*. Chambers Journal Vol 21 1931 p 187 et seq.
17. Richard Collier. *The Indian Mutiny*. Fontana Books 1966 p 47.
18. *The Times 17 July 1857* p 12 and *24 August 1857*. p 5.
19. Veronica Bamfield. *On the Strength*. Charles Knight 1974 p 97.
20. Vansittart p 83 and *The Times 17 July 1857*. p 12.
21. Roberts p 16.
22. Dennis KinKaid. *British Social Life in India*. Routledge 1938 Repub. Routledge & Kegan Paul 1973 p 200 & Hibbert p 192.
23. Hibbert p 207 and W.H. Fitchett. *The Tale of the Great Mutiny*. London 1907 p 140.
24. Philip Mason. *The Men Who Ruled India*. Cape 2 Vols 1954. The Guardians Vol 2.
25. *The Times 22 August 1857*. p 9.
26. Hibbert & Fitchett.
27. Barr. p 118.
28. Hibbert. p 195.
29. Hon Lady Inglis. *The Siege of Lucknow*. Osgood 1892. Quoted J.K. Stanford. *Ladies in the Sun* (1790–1860) Galley Press 1962 p 113.
30. Mrs Katherine Mary Bartrum. *A Widow's Reminiscences of Lucknow*. London 1858 pp 1, 10, 11.
31. Bartrum. p 101.
32. Stanford. p 113.
33. Hibbert. p 385.
34. Reverend A. Fuhrer. *List of Christian Tombs and Monuments*. 1896 (India Office).
35. Vansittart. p 93.
36. E.E.P. Tisdale. *Mrs Duberly's Campaigns*. Jarrolds 1963 pp 176–7.
37. *Queen's Army Schoolmistress*. December 1938 p 24.
38. Angelesey p 115 and p 123.

Chapter 10 – Aldershot and Degradation

1. *Household Words*. 19 April 1856 p 316–8.
2. John Walters. *Aldershot Review*. Jarrolds 1970 p 39.
3. *United Services Journal March 1879*. Vol I pp 324–5.
4. Fraser Harrison. *The Dark Angel*. Sheldon Press 1977 p 222.
5. *United Services Journal March 1879*. Vol I p 323.
6. Walters op cit p 50.
7. Anon. *Experiences of a Soldier enlisted in the 2nd Battalion Royal East Kent Regiment in 1891*. National Army Museum MS Account No 7008-13.
8. *Report of the Commissioners inquiring into the Regulations affecting the Sanitary Condition of the Army, the Organisation of Military Hospitals etc*. Sessional Papers (House of Commons) XLIII (1857–8).

9. *Military Dictionary* by Major Charles James of the Royal Artillery Drivers 1816 (4th Edition).
10. *The Times 24 Feb 1857.* p 11.
11. Cecil Woodham Smith. *The Reason Why.* New York 1955 p 400.
12. *The National Review.* XVII 1863 p 336.
13. *Report of the Committee upon Venereal Disease in the Army and Navy 1863.* WO33.12. Also Henry J. Wood. *Rough Record of the Events connected with the Repeal of the CD Acts, 1864, 1866 and 1869 in UK etc.* Sheffield 1906.
14. *The Broad Arrow.* 29 May 1878 p 677.
15. *Army Medical Department Report 1866.* p 29.
16. *Report of the Royal Commission on the Administration and Operation of the Contagious Diseases Acts 1866–1869.* (1871) Parl. Papers 1871 (c 408) XIX p 17.
17. *The Methodist Protest. January 1877.* pp 6–7.
18. *The Lancet II 1863.* p 517.
19. *Report from the Select Committee on the Contagious Diseases Act.* P.P. 1868–9 (306) VII.
20. *The Broad Arrow.* 12 Dec 1874 p 750.
21. *All The Year Round.* 16 July 1864 p 545.
22. *The Times 3 July 1855.* p 10.
23. *The Times 26 July 1855 p 9.*
24. An argument used by recruiting officers (see Hansard 11 March 1864 CLXXIII Col 1823).
25. 7 WILL IV and I VIC C7 S3.
26. *The Herald of Peace 1 October 1872.* p 128.
27. *The Shield No 210 May 1874.* p 116. Evidence to Royal Commission 1874 Q 4090.
28. *The Times 1 April 1873.* p 12 (4 children in 500 Unions out of 632). *The Times 3 May 1883.* p 5.
29. *Hansard 5 April 1883.* Col 1601.
30. *Brigade of Guards' Standing Orders 1922.* Appendix 11.
31. *Brigade of Guards' Standing Orders 1899.* p 125.
32. *The Times 28 November 1864.* p 10.
33. *The Times 10 March 1881.* p 6.
34. *United Services Gazette 30 March 1867.* p 4 and *The Broad Arrow 25 Dec 1875.* p 802.
35. *First & Second Reports of the Royal Commissioners of the Patriotic Fund.* P.P. 1857–8 (163) XIX p 4 & p 33.
36. *Reports of the Royal Commissioners of the Patriotic Fund.* P.P. 1863–79 (1871 Report p 11).
37. *Reports of the Royal Commissioners of the Patriotic Fund.* P.P. 1863–79 (1874 Report).
38. E. Hodges: *The Soldiers Dream. Quoted in Historical Record of the Soldiers Sailors and Air Force Association.* (SSAFA) 1885–1916. Col. Sir James Gildea 1916 pp 274–5.
39. *O'Byrne's Collection of The Army Circulars (including Royal Warrants) and The General Orders from 1867 to 1876.* Published 1877. April 1871 Cl. 53 paras 1, 5 and 6.
40. Ibid Cl. 165 paras 1 & 1c.
41. *The Broad Arrow.* 21 March 1874 p 371.
42. Good Words. 1875. '*Married Soldiers*' by a Field Officer pp 596–600.
43. Juliet Piggott. *Queen Alexandra's Royal Army Nursing Corps.* Leo Cooper 1975.
44. *The Army Barrack and Hospital Improvement Commission Parl Paper 1861 (2839). Vol XVI State of Accommodation for Sick Wives and Children of Soldiers.* p 10.
45. London Guards (544 Wives & 495 children): Woolwich (894 : 1330): Chatham (456 : 662) Dover (241 : 318) Portsmouth (390 : 487) Gosport (200 : 301) Plymouth (433 : 577): Aldershot (1053 : 1397) Dublin (697 : 875): Fermoy (187 : 311). Ibid p 144.
46. Ibid pp 144–6.
47. General Sir Neil Cantlie. *History of the Army Medical Department Vol 2.* pp 207–8.
48. Juliet Piggott. p 19.
49. *O'Byrne's Collection of Army Circulars. Op Cit April 1871.* Cl. 53 paras 63, 64, 66, 68 & 71.
50. *Army Orders 1878 Hospitals for Women and Children.* (See also Royal Warrant for Pay 1884 para 779).

51. Pigott p 21 and Ian Hay: *One Hundred Years of Army Nursing:* Cassell 1953 p 356.
52. Skelley: *The Victorian Army at Home.* Croom Helm 1977, p 52.

Bibliography

Myna Trustram: *Women of the Regiment.* Cambridge University Press 1984 (A most authoritative account of the conditions of the soldier's women during the Victorian period, with an excellent bibliography).

Chapter 11 – The Memsahibs

1. Correlli Barnett. *Britain and Her Army.* Allen Lane 1970 p 278.
2. Maud Diver. *The Englishwoman in India.* Blackwood 1909 p 5.
3. Pat Barr. *The Memsahibs: The Women of Victorian India.* Secker and Warburg 1976 p 1.
4. Dr Gilbert Hadow. *Letters* (Worcester College, Oxford) quoted Christopher Hibbert. *The Great Mutiny: India 1857.* Allen Lane 1978, p 36.
5. A.A. Ewen. *Letters.* (National Army Museum) quoted Hibbert p 36.
6. Dennis Kinkaid: *British Social Life in India 1608–1937.* Kegan Paul 1938 p 163.
7. Honourable Emily Eden: *Up the Country 1837–1840.* Bentley 1866. Letter dated Meerut. Tuesday 6 February 1838.
8. *Report of the Commission on the Sanitary State of the Army in India (SSI) 1863.* p XXIV.
9. SS1 1863 p XXV and p LV. In 1864 the Government of India's scale of accommodation for married soldiers was — 2 rooms, one 16ft x 14ft, the other 14ft x 10ft with bathroom attached. The floor to be at least 1 foot above the ground. *(Broad Arrow: 18 Dec 1875).*
10. *Report of 1871 Commission to enquire into the Constitution and State of the Several Lawrence Asylums in India.* (Sunawar, Murree and Calcutta).
11. SSI 1863 p LXX and p XXIV.
12. Theon Wilkinson: *Two Monsoons.* Duckworth 1976 Chapter 5 p 149, p 109, p 107, p 151.
13. J.W. Kaye: *Peregrine Pultuney or Life in India.* London 1844, Vol I p 133.
14. Mrs Colonel Elwood: *Narrative of a Journey Overland from England to India. Colborn and Bentley 1830.*
15. SSI 1863 p XLI.
16. Frank Richards. *Old Soldier Sahib.* Faber 1936 p 159.
17. SSI 1863 p LXII and p 143.
18. *The Times 20 August 1890 p 7.* 'The average age of Hindu child brides among higher castes is now 7. She is handed over body and soul into a sensual slavery'.
19. Emily Eden op cit. Letters Dinapore 10 Nov 1837 and Simla 9 May 1838.
20. Bishop Heber: *Narrative of a Journey through India from Calcutta to Bombay 1824–1826.* John Murray. 3 Vols. 1828. Vol I p 42.
21. Kenneth Ballhatchet: *Race, Sex and Class Under the Raj.* Weidenfeld and Nicolson *1980 p 10.*
22. SSI 1863.
23. L/MIL/7/13809–13902. Farrington's *India Office Catalogue.* p 115.
24. Major-General E.B. Johnson, QMG. India 2 Jan 1874. India Office Collection 315 (as 23) C.D. Acts 1873–1927.
25. *Sentinel 12 Feb 1888* p 52.
26. *Memorandum issued by Major-General E.F. Chapman, QMG in India, to General Officers Commanding Divisions and Districts 17 June 1886.* Army HQ Simla.
27. 8 May 1888. *Hansard Vol 325. 5.6.1888.* Cols 1617–8.
28. *The Times 15 May 1897* p 10: *18 May 1897* p 8: *25 May 1897* p 12.
29. Frank Richards op cit pp 117–8.
30. SSI 1863 p 209 & p 199.
31. L/MIL/5/390/129A *Grant of Allowances to support the Families of European soldiers 1821–5.* Farrington *Guide to India Office Records* p 69.
32. C.U.S.M. June 1867 p 175 and *The Broad Arrow 4 April 1874.* p 433.
33. SSI 1863 p. LXXV.
34. J.H. Stocqueler. *The British Officer 1851.* pp 217–8.

35. *Governor General Order 1315 dated 28 December 1872.*
36. Gillian Tindall. *City of Gold.* Temple Smith *1982 p 179 and Illustrated Weekly of India. Dec 1936.* Quoted Kinkaid p 165.
37. Maud Diver: *The Englishwoman in India 1909.* p 24.
38. *The Garden of Fidelity, being the Autobiography of Flora Annie Steel.* (1847–1927). MacMillan 1930.
39. Charles Dickens. *Household Words.* 20 March 1858 p 318.
40. Maud Diver op cit p 21 et seq.
41. Heathcote: *The Indian Army 1822–1922.* David and Charles p 149.
42. Richards op cit pp 160–1.
43. K. Ballhatchet. *Race, Sex and Class under the Raj.* Weidenfeld and Nicolson 1980 p 149.
44. David Dilks: *Curzon in India.* Hart-Davis 1969 Vol I p 212 and Leonard Mosley. *Curzon.* Longmans Green 1960 p 81 and p 100.
45. Richards op cit p 232.
46. M. Diver op cit pp 11–12.

Chapter 12 – Regimental Ladies

1. W.E. Cairns. *The Army from Within.* Sands 1901 p 43.
2. Wolseley G.J. *Story of a Soldier's Life.* 1903.
3. Colburn's *United Service Magazine Vol I IV 1889–1890.* p 214.
4. C.B. Otley. *The Social Origins of the British Army Officers. The Sociological Review. New Series Vol 18 No 1 March 1970.* p 215–9 and David Thomas. *Population Studies March 1972 (Table 10).*
5. *The United Service Magazine Vol 9 May 1894.* p 290. et seq.
6. Frances 'Daisy' Countess of Warwick. *Life's Ebb and Flow.* Hutchinson 1929 p 42 and p 171.
7. *The Times 3 July 1861.* The Daily Telegraph 4 July 1861.
8. Anita Leslie. *Edwardians in Love.* Hutchinson 1972 p 15.
9. Mrs Gerald Paget. *Going Through the Mill.* p 69. One of her lovers was Douglas Haig, a Captain with the 7th Hussars, later C in C of the B.E.F. 1915–1919.
10. Anita Leslie p 40 and p 230 and Giles St. Aubyn. *Edward VII.* Collins 1979.
11. D.N.B.
12. Cranstoun Metcalfe. *Peeresses of the Stage.* 1913.
13. Ruth Bradon. *The Dollar Princesses.* Weidenfeld & Nicolson 1980.
14. *The Times. 10 August 1849.* p 4.
15. D.N.B. and *The Europa Biographical Dictionary of British Women.* (See also Chapter 7 p 92).
16. *Household Words. Marriage Gaolers. 5 July 1856.* pp 583–4. Charles Booth. Life and Labour of the People in London. 1892.
17. Henry Mayhew. *London Labour and London Poor.* 1861 p 234.
18. E. Mole. *A King's Hussar: Being the Military Memoirs of 25 years of a Troop Sergeant-Major of the 14th (Kings) Hussars.* Collected by Herbert Compton 1893.
19. *Allowance Regulations 1890.* paras 76–81 and para 74. As late as 1902, the S.O's of the 21st Lancers were warning Other Ranks against marriage as 'an act of folly, an inconvenience to the service and the cause of poverty and hardship to the soldier'.
20. *King's Regulations 1912–14.* paras 1051, 1067, 1081 etc.
21. Horace Wyndham. *Following the Drum 1912.* p 51.
22. Colonel Sir James Gildea: *Historical Record of the Work of the Soldiers' and Sailors' Families Association 1885–1916.* Eyre & Spotteswoode.
23. See studies by Razzell, Spiers, Skelley & Otley.

Chapter 13 – War and Stagnation

1. Mrs C.S. Peel. *A Hundred Wonderful Years 1820–1920.* John Lane 1926 p 42.
2. Lyn MacDonald. *The Roses of No Man's Land.* Michael Joseph 1980 p 11.
3. *The Times 19 April 1915.* p 5.
4. Helena Swanick. *I Have Been Young.* Gollancz 1935.
5. *Army Order 27/10/14 XVII Sec 5.*

6. *Parliamentary Debates. House of Commons 1914–15.* Hansard LXX Col 268. (Mr Baker) 24 Feb 1915.
7. A.C.I. February 1916.
8. Mrs Alec-Tweedie. *Women and Soldiers.* Lane 1918 Chapter V.
9. George Brenan. *A Life of One's Own.* Cape 1962 p 190.
10. General E. Riddell and Colonel M.C. Clayton. *The Cambridgeshires 1914–1919.* Bowes & Bowes 1934 p 26 & 39.
11. A.C.I. April 1915.
12. A.C.I. 1069 of 1917.
13. Mrs C.S. Peel. *Howe We Lived Then 1914–1918.* Bodley Head 1929 p 126.
14. Arthur Marwick. *Women at War 1914–1918.* Fontana Paperbacks. 1977 p 94 & p 101.
15. Lady Angela Forbes. *Memories and Base Details.* Hutchinson 1922 p 264.
16. Marwick p 127.
17. Quoted M. Brown. *The Boys Come Home.* p 99.
18. *The Times 12 August 1920.*
19. Brown. *The Boys Come Home.* p 99.
20. Corelli Barnett. *Britain and Her Army.* Allen Lane 1970 p 410.
21. Brigadier Gordon Blight. *The History of the Royal Berkshire Regiment.* Staples Press 1953 Chapter 2.
22. Secretary of State for War 27 March 1928.
23. *King's Regulations 1923.* Paras 294 & 295.
24. Idem para 297.
25. Idem para 299 and 325.
26. *King's Regulations 1935.* Paras 319, 323 & 325.
27. A. Dixon. *Tinned Soldiers.* Cape 1941.
28. Major D.D. Maitland. *The Care of the Soldier's Family.* RAMC Journal 1950 p 120.
29. *The Army Schoolmistress, Oct 1919.* (Journal of the Queen's Army Schoolmistresses).
30. *The Army Schoolmistress 1927.*
31. *Journal of the Army Educational Corps* quoted Colonel N.T. St. John Williams. *Tommy Aikins' Children* HMSO 1971 p 129. (Army & Civilian Schools were 'reorganised' under The Hadow Report 1926).
32. *Army Quarterly 1939* p 107 & *King's Regulations 1935.* para 1354.

Chapter 14 – The Second World War

1. *Queen's Army Schoolmistress.* December 1944.
2. Colonel N.T. St. John Williams. *Tommy Atkins' Children.* HMSO 1971 pp 145–6.
3. *RAEC Journal. June 1946* and *The Link, October 1982.*
4. Brigadier Gordon Blight. *The History of the Royal Berkshire Regiment 1920–1947.* Staples Press p 221.
5. *Notes for the Guidance of Commanding Officers (1943)* and *This India (1945).* Published by Directorate of Army Education, India.
6. Charles Graves. *Women in Green. The Story of the WVS.* Heinemann 1948 p 228.
7. Brigadier Sir John Smyth VC. *Percival and The Tragedy of Singapore.* MacDonald 1971 p 161.
8. *Queen's Army Schoolmistress.* December 1944.
9. Kenneth Attwell. *The Singapore Story.* Muller 1959 p 214.
10. Mr F.C. Gimson, Senior Government Official in Hong Kong. *Colonial Office 980 59 HN 00495 p 13.*
11. The Japanese made use of their own front line girls — geishas for the officers and 'comfort girls' (mostly Koreans) for the enlisted men.
12. Helen Long. *Change into Uniform.* Dalton 1978 p 101, p 104 and Barbara Cartland. *The Years of Opportunity.* 1939–45 Hutchinson 1948 p 165.
13. Ed. John North. *Memoirs of Field Marshal Earl Alexander of Tunis 1940–5.* Cassell *1962, p 13.*
14. Norman Longmate. *The Home Front 1939–45.* Chatto & Windus 1981 p 172 and John Costello. *Love, Sex and War 1939–45.* Collins 1985 p 319.

15. Barbara Cartland pp 149–150.
16. Angus Calder. *The People's War. Britain 1939–45*. Cape 1969 p 313.
17. *The Times 27 March 1946*. 8a and 5c.
18. *About NAAFI*. January 1981.
19. Arthur Marwick. *The Home Front During the Second World War*. Thames and Hudson 1976 p 94.
20. Walter B. Maass. *The Netherlands at War 1940–45*. Abelard Schuman 1970 p 249.
21. *The Times. 11 June 1945*. 4c.
22. *The Times. 19 June 1945*. 4d.
23. *The Times 19 April 1945*.
24. In Sourabaya, for example, 6000 women and children were escorted from their inland camps past Indonesian mobs threatening mutilation, rape and murder.
25. Daphne Jackson. *Java Nightmare*. Tabb House 1979 p 144, p 146.
26. Sir W. Churchill. *The Second World War*. Cassell 1954. Vol VI p 653.

Chapter 15 – Post War: The Families Return Overseas

1. *The Times. 17 October 1946*.
2. Colonel N.T. St. John Williams. Tommy Atkins' Children. HMSO. 1971 p 159.
3. Spencer Chapman. *The Jungle is Neutral*. Chatto & Windus 1949.
4. *The Times 6 Feb 1947*. p 8.
5. *The Times 14 Feb 1948: 23 Jan 1948: 6 Feb 1947*.
6. Douglas Botting. *In the Ruins of the Reich*. Allen and Unwin 1985 p 192 and 190.
7. Tim Carew. *The Glorious Glosters*. Cooper 170 p 28.
8. Williams op cit pp 152–3.
9. William Smith. *A Voyage to Guinea*. London 1846.
10. Francis Moore. *Travels in Gambia*. 1838.
11. Harold Bindloss. *In the Niger Country*. Edinburgh 1898.
12. *Soldier Magazine. August 1951*.
13. W.C. Lindsell. *Military Organisation and Administration*. Gale & Polden 1953.
14. Queen's Regulations 1955 paras 1240 and 1241.
15. *AG Statistics 1950*.
16. *Soldier Magazine April 1953*.
17. P.E. Razzell. *Social origins of officers of the Indian and British Home Army (1758–1962)*. British Journal of Sociology XIV 1963.
18. Williams op cit p 156.
19. *About NAAFI*. Published NAAFI p 14.
20. *Soldier Magazine. February 1969*.
21. *Soldier Magazine July 1955*.
22. *Soldier Magazine 1957*.

Chapter 16 – The Swinging Sixties

1. *Report of the Advisory Committee on Recruiting 1958*. Chairman Sir James Grigg.
2. 1959 SSAFA Annual General Meeting.
3. *The Times 10 December 1962*. p 8.
4. *The Times 14 December 1962*. p 8.
5. *The Times 7 June 1962*. p 6.
6. *3rd Report of The National Prices and Incomes*. HMSO.
7. Colonel N.T. St. John Williams. Tommy Atkins' Children. HMSO 1971 p 214–5.
8. *Soldier Magazine. October 1955*.
9. Williams p 168.
10. *Soldier Magazine. 31 October 1983*.
11. Army publication: *Family Guide to Singapore*. 1970.
12. *Soldier Magazine. 31 October 1983*.

Chapter 17 – Judy Comes of Age

1. *Soldier Magazine. 21 October 1985.* p 37.
2. *Army Welfare Inquiry Committee (Spencer Report).* HMSO 1975.
3. Spencer. para 9.
4. Spencer. paras 41-2.
5. Spencer. paras 21–24.
6. Spencer. Tables 10 (p 41) and 11 (p 42).
7. Spencer. paras 142 and 168.
8. Spencer. paras 431, 445 and 450.
9. *Soldier Magazine. Nov 1977.*
10. Spencer. para 274.
11. Henry Stanhope. *The Soldiers.* Hamish Hamilton 1979 p 124.
12. *Soldier Magazine.* April 1982.
13. *Soldier Magazine. June 1977.*
14. *Soldier Magazine. 4 April 1982.*
15. *Soldier Magazine. 31 May 1982.*
16. *The Times. 18 September 1982.*
17. Soldier Magazine. 19 May 1986.
18. Soldier Magazine. 20 Sept 1982.
19. Colonel & Mrs M. Gaffney. *The Army Wives Study.* MOD June 1986.
20. Gaffney Part I. Annex A paras 1–3.
21. In 1977, the Army wives, together with their sisters in the other two Services, took the unprecedented step of marching to the House of Commons to protest about their husbands' pay and conditions of service.
22. *Soldier Magazine. 10 Jan 1983.*
23. *The Times. 23 April 1966.* p 10.
24. *The Times. 26 May 1966.* p 12.

Index